Varina Howell
Wife of Jefferson Davis

MRS. JEFFERSON DAVIS—
THE FIRST LADY OF THE SOUTHERN CONFEDERACY.

Varina Howell
Wife of Jefferson Davis

BY
Eron Rowland—
Mrs. Dunbar Rowland

VOLUME II

A FIREBIRD PRESS BOOK

PELICAN PUBLISHING COMPANY
Gretna 1998

Manufactured in the United States of America

Published by Pelican Publishing Company, Inc.
1000 Burmaster Street, Gretna, Louisiana 70053
ISBN   1-56554-570-2

iv

CONTENTS

ILLUSTRATIONS

PREFACE

HISTORICAL accuracy has been sought throughout in the preparation of this second volume of the biography of "Varina Howell, Wife of Jefferson Davis." It was written not alone for readers of an extensive cultural acquaintance with all historical sources dealing with the subject who are not dependent upon a historical background for interpretation, but for the more general reader who must get in closely connected narrative form a full comprehension of the biographical study from a social, civil and military standpoint. In the study made of William H. Seward, I have sought for motives rather than indulging myself in a quibbling discussion of certain phrases and methods to which he resorted in his effort to attain his object. In the preparation of this volume, I have had the use of an extensive library containing the principal works of distinguished American and English authorities and historians among which are numerous writings of contemporary eye-witness historians. Among the last mentioned, I am especially indebted to Sir William Howard Russell, war correspondent of the London *Times,* whose thorough understanding of the American trouble and keen analytical observations have been too little used in the earlier pages of books about the Southern Confederacy. Other eye-witness sources include the conscientious study of social conditions in the South by Catherine Hopley (S. L. J.)—"Life in the South During the War." I can scarcely estimate how much the interest shown in both volumes by Mr. Gamaliel Bradford, Mr. Claude Bowers and Dr. William E. Dodd has meant to me. To Mr. Bowers I am further indebted for numerous photostat copies of articles from old files of the New York *World*. I am also indebted to the New York *Times* for the use of contributions by Frank G. Carpenter. I wish to acknowledge my obligation to the following for assistance of a varied nature: To the Library of Congress, and the Confederate Museum of Richmond for permission to use their files; to Miss M. Alston Buckley of New York City for painstaking research; to Mrs. Phelan Beale for the use of valuable papers; to Miss Page Williams for faithful services in making copies from the records of the Museum; to Professor Albert G. Sanders for helpful suggestions; and to my husband, without whose historical aid and sympathetic assistance this volume could never have been written.

E. R.

Varina Howell
Wife of Jefferson Davis

VARINA HOWELL, WIFE OF JEFFERSON DAVIS

CHAPTER I

THE SOUTHERN CONFEDERACY'S FIRST LADY

"Varina Davis is a lady in any event," Southern women of the aristocratic circles of Washington told the war correspondent of the London *Times* who had been sent to the National Capital to report all the news he could gather concerning the secession of the Southern States from the great American Union.[1] There was a finality in their tones and manner as if that fact settled the whole question and right of secession. And being such perfect ladies themselves, who could be a better judge of what it took to be one? The Englishman was amused but intensely interested. With pricked ears, he lingered near them in the parlors of the rich Banker Riggs' fine old mansion, which still stands in stolid indifference to its surroundings. It was where secessionist ladies and gentlemen of the Capital gathered in brilliantly lighted drawing-rooms to air their grievances against the Black Republicans.[2] They further informed him that Varina was popular and had friends and social influence in Washington, adding with pursed lips that she belonged to the set they called 'nice people'; not like 'such people' as he had seen in the White House. Thus Mrs. Jefferson Davis was described to one who, with piqued curiosity, was soon to meet her as the First Lady of the

[1] William Howard Russell, who was Knighted by Queen Victoria for his brilliant war correspondence.
[2] "Diary" of Gideon Welles, vol. 1.

I

Southern Confederacy. But critics coming under the spell of Pollard have overlooked the verdict of the Southern gentry in Washington.[1] These infer that Varina was assuming, overtopping, mannish. However, the London *Times* correspondent would see for himself. He was not a poor judge in such matters and had seen many women of high station in his travels from place to place. His interest grew. He had seen it stated in the New York papers that Southern society led in the social life of Washington, and certainly Southern society must know its own.

But Varina Howell Davis came proudly to her high station. She was not without a due understanding of its significance, nor was she without the feeling that she, in some degree, deserved the distinction. The rose slips cut from the Glory of France that grew by her front gate, which she had helped Jefferson Davis pare for grafting, lay neglected on the garden walk where they had been cast on the day that it was announced to them that he had been elected President of the Confederate States of America. Like Jefferson Davis she loved roses, but there was no time for roses now. Nothing mattered but the tumult and clamor following the separation of the Southern States from the American Union. It was called secession since, they said, it was the withdrawing from a compact that had been violated by those who were parties to it. To an Englishman in the country it bore a striking resemblance to the Great Revolution in which Washington had wrested the Colonies from British Dominion. Although it rocked the Federal Union to its foundations and was as calamitous as any in history, it had been more dignified and orderly than the revolutions that usually occur with nations.

[1] Edward A. Pollard, associate Editor of the *Richmond Examiner.*

It has always been something to marvel at that if it were regarded as treason and conspiracy, why some attempt was not made to deter its leaders in its incipiency.[1] But the truth is, the right of a state to secede from the Federal Union had lingered in the minds of the people everywhere in the country.[2] The indissolubleness of the Federation was not as clearly defined in the compact as wedlock, if the comparison will hold. There had always been threats of dissolving it heard both in the North and in the South, and when the break did come it did not have the shock of a revolution beginning with a sudden bloody uprising in the streets. It had in it something of an inalienable right.

The most interpretative explanation perhaps of the separation in a broad way is Gardiner's, "that it was the inadequacy of the intellectual methods of the day to effect a reconciliation between opposing forces that had interpreted differently the organic law." Another Englishman said humorously that they should make the constitution over to suit both sides. But the failure of conciliation cannot be equally shared. The failure is clearly attributable to an alliance of the Puritanical element of the new Republican party with its political element to satisfy the demands and interests of each. It has been said that the Puritan and the Cavalier were again to the fore in a last conflict; but while there was a distinct social credo to differentiate them, politically they seemed to have changed bases.

In its first steps there was no restraint laid upon disunion, and the separation took place much in an open

---

[1] There was some hint that Jefferson Davis and his *confreres* should be treated as traitors, but the attitude of Washington and New York silenced the suggestion.

[2] Since 1798-99 and on, the doctrine can be traced in the records of Virginia, Kentucky and Massachusetts.

court fashion. At first it seemed rather to interest than irritate public thought. People flocked to the National Capital to see a state leave the Union. William H. Seward, later the half-willing Secretary of State in Lincoln's Cabinet, said flippantly that withdrawing from the Union got to be something of a fashion of the day. He himself likened it to a flurry of snow in April. The "irrepressible conflict," for which he had become so famous, had died completely out of his speeches.[1]

The deep-seated, what might be termed legal, cause of secession was, the Southerners believed, a total disregard on the part of Northern leaders of the Sovereignty of the States. It is certain that, let their differences have touched slavery or what they may, if the South had not had this to point to, it would have never left the Union. Any infringement of Constitutional rights always drew its threat.[2] State Sovereignty had become for them as sacred as their religious faiths. It was easy for South Carolina, the home of the great nullifiers, to fan its recent flames.

After the dramatic withdrawal of six of the Southern States—South Carolina, Mississippi, Alabama, Georgia, Louisiana and Florida—numerous brilliant leaders and their following throughout the seceded section gathered in Montgomery, Alabama, on the fourth of February to organize a Confederate States of America. It was the name that they selected for the New Republic. It was rarely used except officially and became generally known as the Southern Confederacy, which accounts for its constant use in these pages. The political situation of the country is neces-

[1] The phrase has also been claimed by Roger Pryor and the editors of the Richmond *Examiner*.

[2] See the decisions of the Virginia Court of Appeals, the Kentucky States Rights Resolutions, and authors like John C. Calhoun.

sary to the story which deals largely with the social life of the period.

The secessionists, for several reasons, pitched their tent in the very heart of the seceded region, the most important of which was the solidarity of its territory. During the Convention, the little city was selected for the first capital. Next to South Carolina, it was one of, if not the most affluent cotton markets of what is poetically called the "deep South." Situated in a beautiful, undulating, well-wooded park—of oak, gum and other queens of the forest, and rising away from the banks of the Alabama, provincial, and careless of its prospects, and heedless of its lavish beauty, it had by a tragic twist of fate become one of the most historic spots in America by the middle of the nineteenth century. The whole semitropical region lying inland above the Gulf of Mexico has certain spots that show the same lavish growth of trees and flowering shrubs. None is more pleasing to the eye than the environs of Montgomery. Many have described it as a beautiful town with rows of tall white mansions bowered in roses and magnolia. There was about it an air that family tradition, wealth and provincialism create. Jefferson Davis himself had said that it was a handsome town. It took its place in history in the vernal season; but while Venus protected its gardens, Mars erected signs in its streets. More has been written about its flowers than those of any other city of the Confederacy. The deep recesses along river and brook, the open uplands and the winding valleys lying between baroque-shaped red and orange hills were now beginning to show a light sprinkle of snowdrop, wild violet and windflower, among the first woodland heralds of spring in the far South. From lawns and along sunny garden walks of white, many-columned

houses, the fragrance of jonquils, violets, hyacinths and narcissus scented the air.   The city, however, was more straggling than visitors who had come down to take a look at the
Confederacy expected.   Signs of wealth and poverty mingled
in vivid contrast.   And where in any place or in any period
of history, have they not done so?   The inevitable slave
block, too, that had so much to do with the people's prosperity, stood in its midst, and W. H. Russell paints a
hideous picture of "Auction Day."   But the white Alabama
moonlight, lying like a silver film over the little town standing amid its wealth of trees, swathed even this telltale object in softer outline.   The gibbering savage, wearing clothes
it might be for the first time, auctioned off today, would
by a few tomorrows be learning speech and worshiping God.
In the matter merely of happiness, some might claim that
he had better have been left in his own habitat in blissful
ignorance of Christianity or any civilization of the day.
But the missionary does not look at it in this light; nor did
the Cotton King who, though some insisted that he was
bungling it, contributed his part in the matter of both the
catechism and lawful food.   It is a long way from a naked
savage with cannibalistic propensities to setting down one's
age in the Bible.[1]   But of late strange things had happened
in the country, and the Squirearchy had ridden to town to
mend matters.

The pretty little riverside city, set in its grove of quiet
trees, hardly seemed the place for staging a revolution,
though some historians have thought that the Confederacy,
with its deep, underlying insistence on the principle of civil
liberty, had its birth in this strong Anglo-Saxon region, so
conducive to such a sentiment and theory.   But it was a scion

[1] "Domestic Slave Trade in the Old South," by Frederic Bancroft.

of the Palmetto, and though a transplanted stock, it became every whit as strong as the parent tree. Some even to this day might well marvel why it was not established in Charleston since the earliest and most vivid pages of the history of the revolution are those of the secession of South Carolina. All others pale into insignificance beside it.[1] Yancey, of Alabama, may have lost influence by too much secession agitation in the far South, but that of the two Rhetts of South Carolina grew stronger with every edition of the Charleston *Mercury*. And South Carolina was not all. That the revolt was flaming along the northern borders of the South is clearly seen in the columns of the Richmond *Examiner*, whose influence, with that of Roger Pryor, had stirred the rural mind of Virginia with the spirit of secession as strong as that in Alabama. In truth the spirit of revolt was flaring up everywhere in the South and the leaders were denounced for their tardiness.

It was sound sense, however, on the part of the people of South Carolina to place the revolution, in its incipiency, far in the South. It should not be localized in one stronghold. Besides, the selection of its standard bearer from another state would come with more grace and prove more effective. Still, many strong secession leaders of South Carolina were anxious that their own brilliant son, Robert Barnwell Rhett, should be the choice for President of the New Republic. But for Jefferson Davis' outstanding figure in the National Government, one that for leadership, dignity and moderation had attracted the attention of the entire congressional body, and of that of the South as well, these would have urged more strenuously the claims of the influential, fiery and forceful

[1] Rhodes, vol. III.

editor of the Charleston *Mercury,* contemner and denouncer
of all things republican.   Both Howell Cobb and Robert
Toombs, Southern leaders of much repute and influence, but
of a totally different type, had their following; but there
was little real contention among the factions.   Every finger
of fate pointed to Jefferson Davis.   The name so long and
favorably connected with democratic victories stirred them
as no other in the South.   His constitutional interpretations
and the fact that it was said that he wore the cloak of Calhoun made the choice desirable and gave the cause prestige.
He was one of the few public men of his day who was then
known in Europe.   He had been Minister of War for the
whole country and had in the senate for decades made the
Republicans wince under his biting logic.   Besides, people
still called him "Colonel" in much of the South and the
title was no disadvantage to a revolution.

The Convention had attracted prominent leaders from all
the Southern States.   There were daily gathering in the
Southern capital such ardent spirits as Mason, Pryor, Rives
and Hunter of Virginia; Chesnut and the two Rhetts of
South Carolina; Bartow of Georgia and Preston of Kentucky.   These and many more of national reputation came
to confer with Toombs, Yancey and other stout-hearted
leaders of the revolution.   Jefferson Davis, grafting his
favorite roses in the gardens at Briarfield on the Mississippi, was later to add his magnetic, but more restrained,
and intense presence to the throng.   The town swarmed
with men of every class, of every profession and vocation,
begging for commissions, or else clamoring to be among
the first to serve their country in some capacity.   The
thought seared itself in their brains.   To them the Federal
Union today held no such meaning.   Those whose fervor and

enthusiasm rendered them hysterical, denounced any falling off from the first outbursts of passionate resentment.

But with all this one gathers from the records made at the time and from Varina herself, that here and there in these first days a sigh could be heard at the thought of the breaking up of the old Union. Such expressions as "Secession was the last resort—would to God it could have been averted," were sometimes heard in undertones. Although historical accuracy demands that some notice should be taken of this regret on the part of some at leaving the Union, there were few who did not agree that with the attitude of the Republican party, its uncompromising, tyrannical methods, and more than all else, what was believed to be an utter disregard of the Constitution, there was no other choice for the Southern States. It was revolt or political domination, in view of the fact that Northern politicians were preparing to republicanize through settlement and population the whole Western territory, a territory that they had done so little to acquire. That party, through the merging of Whig, Free Soiler, Abolitionist and what not, had now become powerful and menaced Democratic supremacy. Wherever it pioneered, it carried its political banner and the South, with its scantier population, unless it could take its slaves, could get nowhere in numbers sufficient to dispute it.

As yet Virginia had not left the Union. That the majority of her people, however, was looking to it if certain guaranties were not forthcoming, is clearly shown in the original records of that day. Her sympathizers with the revolution were already at the Confederate Capital, urging the election of Jefferson Davis whom they had so often seen put to rout Republican coteries and cliques in Washington.

For all the quiet efforts on the part of the followers of

the several aspirants for the highest office in the provisional government of the new Confederacy, the majority was soon proclaiming that Jefferson Davis would be the choice of the Convention. His following from the first was strong and in the final vote there was no other name proposed. "Everybody," a shrewd and close observer recorded at the time, "wants Jefferson Davis to be General-in-Chief or President. Keitt and Boyce and a party prefer Howell Cobb for President and the fire eaters *per se* want Barnwell Rhett." [1] But the controlling spirits of the Convention had determined that men of moderation should be selected to head the new government. They resented the ridicule of their Northern critics that "the volcanic South was in eruption." Consequently, neither Rhett nor Yancey, the acclaimed "fire eaters," was seriously considered.

Notwithstanding largely suppressed ambitions, as the work of the Convention progressed, Jefferson Davis became the outspoken choice for President, and Alexander H. Stephens of Georgia for Vice-President. The latter had written the new constitution in the manner of a scholar and jurist, but with an inelastic vision had largely forgot that the revolution must first win its independence before it could set up a permanent government. Still enough of the old crept into the new document for defense in times of war if the ignorant had known how to interpret it. But States' Rights was the note that blared from its pages, and there were many minds as dense as Governor Brown's of Georgia. The Convention was orderly. There was little boasting.

The proceedings passed off with a flourish; all differences were smoothed out and every one seemingly satisfied. Yancey congratulated Francis M. Gilmer and

[1] "A Diary from Dixie," by Mary Boykin Chesnut.

introduced the President in apt phrase, "the man and the hour have met," and the newly-established government, to the utter surprise of England and all other foreign nations, proceeded to arrange and regulate its affairs without a hitch. One shrewd observer, however, who was present, recorded that the intrigue going on was very much like that left behind at Washington.[1] Still, every one, expressing it in different phrasing, was shouting that the newly-elected President "would make short shrift of the Yankees." This and numerous other expressions of confidence greeted Jefferson Davis on his arrival in Montgomery. He had been greatly perturbed at the thought of separation, and an able historian agrees that he came to it as a last resort.[2] Still he had warned the Republicans a hundred times that it was coming if some timely cure for it was not provided. The great Webster, in the past, had not more clearly pointed out the danger.

Jefferson Davis now realized that the Southern Republic was an actuality, not a "temporary delusion," as William H. Seward was still declaring. If he suspected any serious opposition to himself, or was annoyed by it at this period, he gave no sign. He had throughout life exhibited more than ordinary self-control. His past had been unusually free of the wrangling common to public men. Still he was forceful, and in the performance of duty, sometimes drastic.

There was now, in the main, harmony in the official circles of the new government. But some soon caught a dissonance that grew more pronounced with time when the combative, brilliant editor of the Charleston *Mercury* be-

[1] Chesnut.
[2] "Jefferson Davis," by William E. Dodd.

gan a decided opposition to the head of the Confederacy.
Our shrewd diarist, with eyes and ears always on the alert,
again records, "Honorable Robert Barnwell says that the
Mercury began this opposition to Jefferson Davis before he
had time to do wrong. They were offended not with him
so much as with the man who was put into what they considered Barnwell Rhett's rightful place. The latter had
howled nullification and secession so long that when he
found his ideas taken up by all the Confederate world, he
felt that he had a vested right to leadership." [1]   A coterie
was inevitable and so sure were certain leaders of the
permanency of their government that the question of future
high positions called for some preliminary maneuvers and
plans on their part.   It would not be the truth of history to
say that there were not numerous eyes in all that assembly of
aspiring, ambitious souls cast towards self-aggrandizement
in the New Republic.   But the people as a whole were proud
of the grave, quiet man, who, long a leader in national
affairs, they said, looked every inch a President.   With his
coming the tumult began, and Jefferson Davis rode to his
inaugural behind four splendid white horses amid plaudits
and flowers.   Both aristocrat and poor white mingled together for the first time with a common purpose.   Men
cheered themselves hoarse, and women, whose overflowing
emotions filled their eyes with tears, threw armfuls of
flowers at the brilliant cortège as it passed.   Jefferson Davis
must have been gratified, but he missed Varina and his children, and was a little pathetic, a little whimsical, about it
in his letters telling her of the cheers that greeted him.   In
times of danger to the country, he was stern and unyielding

[1] Chesnut.

in his request for her to keep their children out of his way, sometimes offending her with his insistence; but in the hours of triumph and ovation, he wanted them with him.

Notwithstanding the floating cloud of opposition, the political sky was now clear; much clearer than that at Washington, where the grotesqueries and general unfitness of Abraham Lincoln were the main topics of conversation in every group that gathered in parlors, offices or upon the street and that among people of his own party. Still he had the advantage of Jefferson Davis in that new adventures in government cannot stand what old established governments can successfully cope with. The South possessed one conspicuous advantage—that of a common aspiration for civil liberty as embodied in constitutional government. The contest bore a resemblance to Runnymede. The poorer classes, largely ignorant, were not as well acquainted with States' Rights, the South's political fetish, as the haughty aristocracy; but there was a similarity of temperament throughout and they became apt pupils. These followed with much of the old clan spirit of original stock, and no Macgregor was ever more loyal to his chief. The haughty chieftains, however, found it hard to follow any one; still they strove together surprisingly well considering their temperaments. But united as they were against the North, Jefferson Davis in administering the public affairs of the Confederacy was confronted with difficulties before which the stoutest heart might have grown faint. Not only would he suffer from the standpoint of isolation among the nations and from the unsystematic, one-sided economic conditions that existed in the South, but from much arising out of the individualistic and self-centered nature of the people.

This condition is early noted that all angles may be viewed from which the wife, from the very nature of circumstances, was to be affected. No woman of the Confederacy had as difficult rôle, and of no other woman connected with it was there as much expected. She had endurance, if not the pliancy attributed to her sex at that day. This is discovered in the story of her young womanhood; still her life, in the main, had been one of comfort and ease and she had experienced little else but success. This new position would be only the next of the many high distinctions that had been conferred upon her husband; distinctions that had in a way brought her *éclat* as well, and never undervalued by women. All Washington knew of her many accomplishments, *esprit,* and love of gayety; few knew of her but vaguely throughout this far-flung Confederacy with which she was to have so much to do. Even distinguished historians of today have been confused in the matter of her early surroundings.[1] It was left to the accomplished and widely traveled war correspondent of the London *Times* to inform his readers that Natchez, Mississippi, her birthplace, possessed as "charming villas and gardens," and the "most beautiful lawns," he had "found anywhere in America—greatly resembling Sussex." [2]

But Varina did not come as a novice to her new position. Socially it was only a transference, and the thing that particularly appealed to her vanity was that she was the wife of Jefferson Davis. If she was somewhat curious about the new life she was to lead with him, it was natural. Besides, there were her children whose lives in

[1] "Wives," by Gamaliel Bradford.
[2] W. H. Russell.

after years were to be colored by all that affected and happened to their parents in the present. She was more practical than her husband, and a degree more selfish. She had always turned things over in her mind from a shrewder point of self-interest. After all, had Jefferson Davis accepted the best for his own flesh and blood? A revolution is not a coronation, and failure with its aftermath has to be reckoned with by the one who heads it. But Varina herself had come of the best American fighting stock and inheritance means much in the texture of character. She knew how to make sacrifices, and at such times her personality was strong and compelling. She had never been exacting of Jefferson Davis in any personal service to his country. She saw him leave her, not once but twice, when she was scarcely more than a child, to defend the country's western frontiers, the region about which it now had its misunderstanding. In the same spirit, she stood by him in this, his reddest flower of adventure. "Buckling down" is the way she expressed it for that which, as William H. Seward had admitted, he was better fitted than any of his compeers.

Varina was too good a student of public responsibility not to appreciate her husband's sense of difficulty in the added confidence in his letters telling her that in the public demonstration he saw "innumerable thorns" amid the roses and plaudits. If the Southern Confederacy, he wrote her from Montgomery, were permitted to establish itself without war, he felt confident of success; with war he feared a struggle that might become catastrophic before the revolt was completed and independence established. Historians agree that she had always shared his public thought. Not only did Pollard clothe her with aspirations of this nature, but a more authentic historian has observed that she always assisted Jefferson Davis in the discharge of his public affairs.[1] Far better than any of the vast concourse of flaming spirits, clamoring for independence of a government they no longer trusted, no longer loved, Jefferson Davis knew the utter unpreparedness for a revolution that carried war in its provisions; and the wife had a grasp of the situation hardly less strong than that of the husband. It was not the position in the new government, she tells us, she preferred that he should hold. As a soldier, if war came, she believed that he would be less exposed to the whims of others. She remembered the old Washington days that had seethed with fierce political conflict. She would protect him from future strife and hardship; her disposition for mothering him was already perceptible.

Still it was a high place to which he had been elevated, both officially and socially. Both realized it, and the woman, coming then to join him in Montgomery, took more pride in the fact than the man. She had her aspirations, but she was to appear in the new capital of the young Republic as one to whom presidents and their wives had been neighbors and familiars. A long and intimate acquaintance with national affairs on a large scale had given her a trained mind, and a stronger taste for weightier matters than were possessed by the women of her period. Still she was not without her small vanities. She had not been careless in the matter of her dress nor that of her children, or even that of her maid when she left the Briarfield plantation for Montgomery. With a keen sense of the fitness of things she valued outward appearance for the advantage it might have to the more important aims and purposes of

[1] "Jefferson Davis," by William E. Dodd.

life. Her silks had all been pressed under her eye and her jewelry was carefully selected. Though always well dressed, she had never been frivolous in the matter of personal adornment. Of what some would call the peacock type, she often told friends that with her size and height she could not bear many decorations; but she wore her clothes well and her bearing was unusually good.[1] In her pictures, which reveal perfect taste in dress, she arranges her hair in the same way that Kate Chase Sprague does hers, and certainly *à la mode.* Her pictures show that she wore the same jewelry throughout the Confederacy, which is a strong proof of her moderation.

At this time she was about thirty-five years of age, active, graceful and in good health and possessed a vividness of personality that slightly endangered its charm. This, however, asserted itself with a lighter mood, and at such times her personality was appealing. In any mood she was convincing. Historians have rarely failed to remark in a critical manner upon the full lips; but it is a contradiction of the cruelty they hint at as suggested by her mouth, since students of such matters ascribe this quality to thin lips. As she grew older her complexion at times had a swarthy tinge that Pollard spitefully described as mulattoish. Every one has agreed that her eyes were wondrously beautiful and earnest. When not animated, they suggested a reflective mind, which newspaper reporters took for sadness. There was an air in her bearing at this period of her life that for a more definite term one may call queenliness. It was an air that some took for arrogance, and there may have been some seeming justification for the impression. At least many people suspected

[1] Conversation.

it.   Celebrated students of the famous women of the world, however, have observed that such an air is more often the sign of strength.   That Varina was born to be a great lady was a midwife prophecy that came true.   The proof of it, partial contemporaries have said, "was stamped upon her from head to toe."   Though what they of the South termed "a womanly woman," it was a worldly-wise and thoughtful one, with a strength of purpose and insight far deeper than were generally possessed by her sex of that day, who was to occupy the highest position accorded women in the newly-formed Southern Republic.   Besides her own personal attractions, and those of her husband, all records agree that her children were unusually beautiful, intelligent and high-spirited.   One may easily believe that the family group that headed the Southern revolution would have attracted the favorable attention of any court in Europe.

CHAPTER II

ON her way to Montgomery, Varina stopped in New Orleans for a visit of several days with her parents. The family had removed from Natchez to that place, where her father was engaged in a somewhat unremunerative business. His inability to get on in the world had for some years placed heavy family responsibilities upon the daughter. There were four children younger than herself, none of whom was settled in life. Even now, when there was so much else to think about, she was giving some thought to the future place and position of her young brothers, Jefferson and Beckett. It is to be hoped that she was not the cause of Jefferson Davis' being accused of nepotism. But she may have been; her family's welfare had always been on her mind. Her brothers, however, were placed in minor positions during the war and none served the Confederacy more gallantly and faithfully.

Her husband's letters, among other things, continued to tell her of his splendid inaugural, the approbation and enthusiasm expressed in the firing of guns throughout the day and in lighting bonfires at night. With the whole South she had given way to an intense emotion. The scene swam before her vision like a brilliant pageant. How often in reality would she behold it! They had been used to a great deal of public attention in Washington and it is doubtful whether this brought for herself the thrill a novice would have experienced. Still she liked any situation of high place and power and this was a new form of it. She does not admit it in her "Memoir," but one can see that she was elated when on her arrival at her father's house in New Orleans, Captain Dreux, a young French officer, came with his battalion to serenade her. Public demonstration had always stirred her. This today had a personal note. The woman in her was strong, and she does not forget to tell us that the young Captain brought her large clusters of early violets. It was the same Captain Dreux, she records, who was the first to fall near Yorktown in the Peninsular Campaign. His body was sent to Richmond and she was to look on the "fresh young face in death." He confided to her that he felt a premonition of his fate, but gayly assured her that he "would not shrink from the task" before him. It was this spirit glowing in the eyes of men everywhere that moved her to tears.

The influence, too, of her husband's confidences that he "saw troubles and thorns innumerable," affected her. She knew that he was fully aware of the hardships that confronted him. Why had she ever agreed for him to undergo them? But was he not always sacrificing himself for the public good? Womanlike she counted the times. For the moment, the high distinction had no appeal. Everything about it depressed her. She could not be buoyed up, she says.[1] It seems something to be regretted that she felt such deep depression at the outset of the distinguished position she was to fill; but her "Memoir" reveals it and it must be believed that she was not writing for effect. Besides, Varina, as well as Jefferson Davis, had felt the sting of their last weeks in the National Capi-

[1] "A Memoir," vol. II.

tal. The fierce wrangling still sounded in her ears and it is small wonder that she did not want her husband to head the revolution. The old men here who spoke of "the soldiering as an expected circumstance" seemed to depress her even more for the fact of their simple faith in their ability to win. They did not mind Jefferson Davis' being a "little slow," but each thought "they had a right to secede." Still again, they told her, "We see that he at last thinks we ought to assert our rights; but we began to fear that he stayed too long up thar with the Yankees."

She noticed that in the matter of secession they kept calling him "slow," [1] but thinking that it would confuse them should she go into an elaborate explanation, she let them babble on. They represented a middle-class society that received its views and impressions from those higher up, from those who in '59 had said "Jefferson Davis is at sea." Evidently he had not quite lived down his good-will tour through the New England States.

In the meantime, South Carolina through the Charleston *Mercury* had spread the doctrine of secession broadest throughout the lower Southern States. The Richmond *Examiner,* too, as has been said, had scattered its seeds plentifully, and it is admitted by all that these high oracles colored the thought of the more primitive Southern press. But now while the North was laying secession at his door, and denouncing him as the arch conspirator, the South thought Jefferson Davis too conservative. However, one should not judge from his serious views of the situation, nor his real pain at the necessity for separation, that Jefferson Davis was not prepared to give himself to the task before him. He had been bred and educated in the theory of Consti-

[1] Memoir, vol. II.

tutional liberty, and his present task was to become to him much in the nature of a quest for Jefferson and Calhoun's ideal of government. However secession may have been furthered by many of its adherents, the exalted aspiration for Constitutional liberty embedded in the Southern cause was planted there by his hand. It was known to the Republicans that he not only possessed a strong and cultivated intellect but magnetic power and an iron will as well. They had heard him too many times plead with them to do no violence to the Constitutional bond that united them. He would be a hard adversary to deal with.

The keen-sighted Seward, who was looking on in alarm at the turn affairs had taken in his "glorious Union," would rather have seen any other Southern leader in his place. He had told Russell of the London *Times* that Jefferson Davis was the only man in the South who had brains enough to carry the revolution through. One cannot believe that with its limited resources and beleaguered ports and in the clutches of a powerful foe the Confederacy would have lasted four years under the leadership of any other. One has only to study the story closely to know that its most ardent and impetuous advocates gave way before his strong spirit was extinguished. Like a solitary flag upon its battered ramparts he seemed, when all others had been torn down. It was his iron will that compelled a reratification of the thing that was done in the meadow called Runnymede near Windsor and Staines on the Thames.

But many of both the husband and wife's present apprehensions were the result of the fierce and unrestrained debate that had gone on for months, even years, in the political circles of Washington. There was cause and a meaning for their depression. As hard and implacable spirit as the country has ever witnessed dominated the Federal Government at this period, and there was no longer a Clay nor a Webster to counsel and warn. Such ardent and vindictive spirits as Stevens and Sumner, Chase and Wade were acknowledged stars in the political firmament; and the Blairs, with the zeal that marks new converts, were vying with Seward for control of the administration. To supplement the bad politics, the fires of abolition were burning as fiercely as ever the fagots around Mary's heretics. The country was passing through the last of a series of changes that occur in the elemental period of all governments and had reached a crisis.

Varina did not have a weak sense of her husband's responsibility. Her journey up the historic Alabama to join him in Montgomery, after leaving her parents in New Orleans, she says, continued to be a "sad one." He had still further written her in his last letter, "We are without machinery, without means and threatened by a powerful opposition." There was nothing that Jefferson Davis, from a practical standpoint as well as considerations of humanity, dreaded more than war; and she, perhaps more than any other, shared this dread with him. He knew that the outstanding advantage in the establishment of the new government lay in a peaceful adjustment of all differences between the North and the South. Still, knowing the bitter spirit of the controversy, he believed that if the North was determined to hold the South, there would be war, and war of a stubborn nature. With that in mind, he wrote her that he had immediately begun "to prepare for the worst." But no intimation of his anxiety ever appeared in his public utterances. With the keen intuition of the leader, he gave to his speeches a confident, even defiant, ring that cleared him of all the lukewarmness of which he had been accused. They had made him their standard bearer; their faiths were his own; the foe would quail before him many, many times.

And now both the official and social circles of the New Republic, that had been so feverishly excited over public affairs, were anxious to get a glimpse of Mrs. Jefferson Davis. Perhaps there never was a political revolution in which the social element on the seceding side entered more largely. This was natural since its social fabric was woven largely of Cavalier colors. The city papers had announced that the wife of the President would arrive on a certain day and the prominent ladies of Montgomery, much in a flutter, looked forward to her coming. The President's suite at the hotel had been converted into a bower of early spring bloom. Even the beating of drums and the fierce roar of cannon in the street could not check her delight in it. A "flowery kingdom," she says, greeted her eyes and helped to relieve her depression. There must have been a lavish display since she measures them by "hampers." [1]

She found the Alabama Capital in a state of wild excitement. Men and women were riding about in handsome carriages or hurrying on foot through the city in every direction. Everywhere they were hysterically discussing the future of their Confederacy. The picture was a gorgeous one that stirred and fascinated her. The city had already begun to take on a martial air. The new flag selected by the Provisional Congress waved from a monster pole in an open space on one of the principal streets. It had been

---

[1] A name for the larger size cotton baskets used on the cotton plantations along the Mississippi.

raised by the hand of a Montgomery girl—the daughter of Colonel Robert Tyler and granddaughter of ex-President Tyler. As yet they viewed it more with a feeling of pride and haughty defiance, but this was soon to burn itself through the heart and brain—the real *sentiment du drapeau* that strangers among them believed once lighted in the breast would be hard to quench. "It was not as gaudy," one wrote of it, "as the splendid Stars and Stripes, but it held a magical power for those who had raised it." [1] Again he mused, in half Biblical phraseology, as he watched it waving from dome and steeple and tree top, from public building and wayside church, "In this Confederate flag there is a meaning. It marks the birthplace of a nationality and its place must know it forever." Varina herself wrote tenderly of it in after years, "Under it we won our victories and the meaning of its glory will never fade. It is enshrined with the existence of the Confederation in our hearts forever." More each day as she viewed the scene about her, she felt assured that all would be well and easily experienced a return of her naturally gay and spirited mood. At this period of life she still possessed a youthful air and manner and was readily diverted.

As the days passed, bevies of public officials gathered around her; and a fanciful illustration of the day shows her greeting them with a girlish grace hardly possible to her at that time. But as yet she was cautious, carefully taking stock of each one's talents and merits. She would have much to tell Jefferson Davis from time to time. She may have told him too much. Women have keener insight and are more given to discover flaws and defects

[1] W. H. Russell.

than men.   The new government, she tells us, "labored day
and night."   The "scratching of pens" was sometimes heard
at the "breaking of day."   It was a Herculean undertaking.   There were both a civil and a military government
to be set on foot at the same time.   Some have said that
Jefferson Davis did not stress preparation as vigorously at
first as he should have done; but at the very outset he warned
the governor of Mississippi to buy guns to the limit of his
ability to pay—to purchase them anywhere and everywhere
they could be found in the North or in foreign markets.   Besides, he had, as War Minister in the old government, shown
his preference for a regular army.   It is not logical to think
that he would have regarded the matter indifferently at the
present crisis.[1]

The masses, less thoughtful, swarming upon the streets
of the new capital and rejoicing over the separation, believed that if it would be a test of physical prowess, if there
must be war and fighting were necessary, they could do as
much of it as any people in the world.   "All creation could
not whip the South," was a favorite boast of both old and
young.   Their war spirit at present was all that Jefferson
Davis could ask for.   None among them, they cried, must
hang back.   If any now so much as appeared to do so,
they were to be summarily dealt with, which meant any one
of the primitive punishments kept in store for the guilty,
such as tarring and feathering and ordering out of the country.[2]   The fires of Etna never burned fiercer than their
new-found patriotism.

[1] The South generally believed in the English theory of a citizen
soldiery, and this in time was to face Jefferson Davis.

[2] Tarring and feathering was a punishment sometimes meted out to
offenders by the lower element of the South, but Whittier's poem, "The
Women of Marblehead," shows that it was a New England custom.

The boasting and swaggering continued to be received in some places in the North with ridicule. The madcap South would soon tire of its new-found freedom, Seward was saying. He felt certain that the storm would pass. But beneath the vaunting, as time proved, burned as true spirit of selfless dedication to a cause as the world had ever witnessed. One who came among them with the eye of a hawk—one not entirely pleased with their prating and bluster, their pride and *hauteur,* and bitterly opposed to their institution of slavery—wrote of their leaders, "I could fancy that in all but the garments they wore they were like the men who first conceived the great rebellion which led to the independence of this wonderful country—so earnest, so grave, so vindictive—at least so embittered against the power they consider tyrannical and insulting." "Here," he also says, "were Balfours and Burleighs with the word of liberty flaming on their lips along with the prayers that God might exterminate their enemies." [1] Like all Christian nations engaged in war, they believed that they were a chosen people and objects of divine favor. Hebraic theology was never more fully accepted than at their day, although their interpretation of it was joyous and rarely accompanied by severity. That they impressed foreigners in their midst with their earnestness, dignity and orderliness is full worthy to be recorded in their history. Their revolution may have seemed the unexpected, but one has only to study closely the past history of the country to know that it had been moving to that end before the white Alabama moonlight had ever cast a ray upon a slave and cotton plantation.

It had reached the Southern Capital that Seward in his correspondence with Lord John Russell had laid all the

[1] W. H. Russell.

blame on the South, and had called the revolution a movement to protect the institution of slavery. Varina was filled
with anger. She always knew, she exclaimed, that he was
unscrupulous. Had he not told her that he cared nothing
whatever for the "slavery question" only as it served his
purpose to stir the minds of others? It was years and years
before she could record gratefully that he had come through
the heaviest snowstorm that had ever visited Washington to
inquire about her when she lay at the point of death.

With the women around her, she was eagerly discussing
all unfavorable criticism in the papers about the South;
was reading every letter sent overseas by W. H. Russell,
who was still at the National Capital engaged in open discussions with Seward and, perhaps having private ones, with
Lord Lyons. And indeed, both governments were watching
him.

CHAPTER III

THE Provisional Congress in session at Montgomery, before Jefferson Davis' arrival, had already taken steps to provide for a conference with the Northern States. He was entirely pleased with the plan. It was arranged for the Confederate Government to send a Commission to Washington to treat with the authorities upon a basis that insured peace and friendly relations between the two nations.[1] The Confederacy was now proclaiming itself *The Confederate States of America,* a designation that sounded well to the ears of all Europe. It is thought by some that Jefferson Davis might have, even at that stage of the revolution, considered a reconciliation between the states had the authorities at Washington cooperated with the Southern Commissioners in the spirit of William H. Seward; that some form of reconstruction was still in his thought, based, it is true, on the inviolability of Constitutional liberty, when he sent his Commissioners to Washington. The sentiment for reunion, however, was now weak everywhere in the seceded states. The Rhetts of South Carolina would have been the last to have considered a restoration on any grounds. Seward, now Secretary of State, and the glittering, peculiar star of Republicanism, was using all his power to arouse Union sentiment in the seceded section. It is easy to think that he wanted

[1] A. B. Roman of Louisiana, Martin J. Crawford of Georgia, John Forsythe of Alabama.

Jefferson Davis to know of his conciliatory attitude; but they never came together after the latter left Washington, and as a harsh fatality, nothing ever passed between them on the subject.

It is certain, however, that any compromise would have had to assure the Southern States of all the rights and privileges guaranteed by the Constitution before Jefferson Davis would have favored it. Wendell Phillips might regard it as an instrument in league with the devil, and other abolitionists might cast it in the street and burn it; but in the eyes of the Southerners it was the organic law that bound the states together, any infringement of which dissolved the compact. Washington and the great rebellion had left it to them and nothing pertaining to the Union was as sacred in their eyes. In the proposed conference Jefferson Davis was so sure that the South would demand every right and privilege that it guaranteed before it would become reconciled that he could afford to be generous in the matter of entrusting the Commissioners with large powers. Mrs. Davis specifically records that he appointed as members of the Commission, "men who had represented entirely different views of secession." "Determined that there should be no cut-and-dried procedure on their part, these were given no secret instructions." "Their own convictions and an honest and peaceful purpose were to be their guide." Still it was to be understood that they represented an established government and would enter negotiations in that position. All of any nature that might grow out of the conference would be submitted to the Confederate Government at Montgomery.

President Buchanan had given assurance that the Commissioners would be received and the moment seemed ripe for something better than what lay between the people of the great Union. He soon found however that a great storm was brewing in Republican quarters and assumed a vacillatory, rather a hedging, rôle, methods and tactics that have been derided by numerous historians, bent largely on upholding the policy of the next administration. Left entirely in the hands of Buchanan and Seward reconciliation might have followed before the former left office. He had sympathized with the Southern situation in nearly every particular except in the matter of secession, and had been harried day and night by both sides. Worn out with the turmoil and confusion, he was glad to quit and hurry to the seclusion of Wheatland, "shutting his eyes at every promising clearing along the route for fear of seeing himself blazing in effigy." The "great Buck," as some had named him, the cynosure of all eyes, had been relieved of all further responsibility of keeping Seward's "glorious Union out of war." One sometimes can but think that he was one of the first converts of Seward's prophecy of "sixty more of suns" to get nothing out of a worthy purpose than jeers and scorn. In addition to other indignities he was soundly berated by no less a personage than General Scott—fond of, in pompous inflated phrases, berating those about him. It was the President's duty, he had thundered, to garrison the now discussed forts at Charleston and Pensacola. It was nonsense to acknowledge South Carolina and Florida's claim to them. But the forts were neglected, and they were now Abraham Lincoln's problem, if Seward's distress. The wily Secretary of State was to later witness, to his entire satisfaction, a decided change in the gouty old hero of Churubusco and Lundy's Lane. As yet, with Virginia opposed to secession, the latter could with safety bluster about the duty of the government to protect its property. To his great relief, Virginia still remained in the Federal Union. She had herself arranged a peace commission upon a large scale, to be attended by delegates from every state, both North and South. She had believed, even at a late day, that there could be compromise of a nature that would insure peace and harmony between the states. Should these reach a satisfactory compromise, this would be sent to each of the states for ratification. But while this movement proved abortive, Seward and his following, which does not seem to have been very large, still held that the South might be induced to reconsider its position. Horace Greeley, more or less shiftily it is true, had at first advised that it would be the right and sensible thing to let the "wayward sisters" go in peace. But Seward held to his dream—"negotiations, entreaty, sisterly kindness"—a tender dream for one who could take the law in his own hands and browbeat the Cabinet at will. All that could now be done, he reiterated, was to hold one's tongue and wait until the storm had spent itself.

Scott was later to take this position, and it is clear that he got this viewpoint from Seward. They were now constantly conferring with each other, talking about what no one else knew, and Seward was in high feather as to what he was going to do with the new administration. But leading Republicans thought that they saw in the efforts of the Confederate Commissioners a purpose to be recognized as representatives of a permanent Southern Republic, and were daily advising Lincoln to that effect. The Secretary of State really preferred to ignore the whole matter of

¹ Speech of March, 1861.

secession and give them a hearing, and in a hundred boasts to every one who would listen, at dinner parties, state functions, rubbers of whist in his own parlor, continued to maintain that "Give the South a little time and it would cool off." It was "just a short madness that could be cured by a mild application of philosophical essays."[1] But when New York ceased to be as a "company of *savants* wonderingly watching an electrical storm," and decided that the northern half of the country could not do without the southern half, which under the tariff laws was daily enriching it, the Secretary began to take the matter more seriously. He now busied himself with the one thought of reuniting the fragments of the *ci-devant* Union before there had been a break too great to be mended. It cannot be doubted but that his heart was also engaged since he had no antipathies, nor it seemed scruples, that could not be easily got rid of in any matter he regarded as one touching the public good. He was modeling after the form of his great predecessor, Webster; but despite evidence to the contrary it is not often the case that the pupil goes farther than the teacher. His command of public opinion was not as strong as that of the great New Englander's. In the President, he at first believed he had an ally, and if not an ally, one who could be made to become so. The records here may seem to be evasive, but it cannot be doubted that Lincoln at first was given to Seward's general policy.

Silently and without Seward's knowledge, though he jauntily claimed that he knew everything going on in the administration, certainly in the Cabinet, other heads were daily influencing President Lincoln. There would be no conference in the matter; no recognition of the new Con-

[1] W. H. Russell.

federacy whatever, which official conference with its Commissioners would seem to imply, in fact there would be no conciliation. This was now their attitude. And, too, something would have to be done about the forts, especially the one in the Charleston harbor, the fountainhead of secession. Still, none in the Cabinet but Blair, as yet, was in favor of using force.[1] Seward was ardent, more so than any other, in the matter of restoring the Union before the wound had become too deep. He had spent much of his public service declaring to all foreign powers that nowhere on the globe was there another such perfect government to be found as that of the American Republic. He still reiterated that there should be no movement of a provoking nature to stir the Southern States to any act of defiance. He had striven to make the President's inaugural address as noncommittal as possible in the matter of war; nor is it seen that Lincoln himself desired that it should be otherwise. The office and its intricate duties and responsibilities were new to him, and he, to a great extent, was feeling his way in the dark. He was at first in as conciliatory mood as Seward, and it is clear that he regarded the brilliant Secretary of State as the brightest luminary in the Republican party. Seward had won the championship of a higher law; to take license and make concessions was the air he breathed. That Lincoln, to a great extent, adopted his methods throughout the war is readily seen, and the disposition to take the law in his own hands was so clearly Seward's method that one can but acknowledge its influence. But Seward had not yet gained the supremacy. Lincoln was now coming under the influence of those who were of the opinion that the Peace

[1] "A Diary," by Gideon Welles.

Commissioners were in Washington not to arrange the matter of secession and return to the Union, but merely to arrange for peaceful relations between the two governments. That put a new aspect upon the situation. And the radicals determined that Lincoln should present an uncompromising front in the matter. With full and hearty cooperation with the Confederate Government through its Commissioners, what might have been accomplished towards reuniting the states is a mere conjecture, but it was well worth the trial. A wholly uninterested statesmanship in all probability would have accomplished it, but no such thing existed at that time in American Government. The utter failure of this last effort on the part of the South to establish any sort of friendly relations with the Federal Government destroyed all possibility of its ever being peacefully restored to the Union. The hope of reconciliation henceforth will have to be set down as "Seward's dream."

It was a one-time justice of the peace from Illinois, "a novice," they said, and much worse, who must now steer the good Ship of State that was careening and sinking before their very eyes. To the brilliant and sardonic Seward who, though totally unlike in physical appearance, possessed much of the manner and temperament of the famous Lord Melbourne of the English Court, the President was as yet not much more than a pawn on a chessboard. Thousands of members of his own party thought so to the end, though historians have sought to deny it while making much of the opposition of certain Southern leaders to Jefferson Davis as an evidence of his failure.

But Seward, in the scheme that he preened himself he was working out in the interest of good government, though he refused to admit it, had soon to face the fact that he was being reduced to second rank; pressure stronger than the Secretary's was now being brought to bear upon the President. The fact that solves much of the contradictory appearance surrounding those days during which the South resented and misunderstood Seward's methods while he, at the same time, was under the suspicion of the Republican party was that both he and Lincoln, though acting from a different standpoint, were alike anxious to preserve the Union. Their difference was that the Secretary of State sincerely believed that the breach could be healed without force, and Lincoln in the matter was being lectured and persuaded by injudicious advisers. "Give them more time, more time," the domineering Secretary kept insisting in endless repetition. War between the states of the great American Union would be the most shameful and humiliating thing that could be conceived of; and how could he longer boast of its power and glory to Lord Russell and the Emperor Napoleon. Admitting his high-handed near Machiavellian intrigues and schemes, the justice of his seeking to prevent its dissolution will have to be accorded him in history. Much was permissible in the face of theory, he decided with few qualms of conscience, for the sake of good government. In the matter of reenforcing the Carolina fort, he announced in the Cabinet in a more manly, open fashion than he usually conveyed his sentiments: "If it were possible to peacefully provision Fort Sumter, of course I should answer that it would be both unwise and inhuman not to attempt it. But the facts of the case are known to be that the attempt must be made with the employment of a *military and marine force*[1] which would provoke combat and probably initiate a civil war, which the government of the

[1] The italics are the author's.

United States would be committed to maintain through all changes to some definite conclusion."

One of his wiles, especially one that the shrewd London *Times* reporter discovered, was that while he coaxed and wheedled the Cabinet and the Republican party with the assurance, "We will concede no more than we have promised," he was constantly deprecating the use of any force whatever in coercing the states. With such natures as those of Stevens, Wilson, Morton, Sumner, Wade, Schurz and the Blairs to deal with, his position was a trying one. Still he stoutly continued to maintain that any course was better than pressing matters in the instance of Fort Sumter around which the storm was gathering. Try it on Fort Pickens, where it would not be noticed so much, try it anywhere, but for heaven's sake not on the Charleston fort— the powderhorn of the Southern Revolution, was his continual argument in Cabinet meetings and in private conferences with its members. He had lived in Georgia and knew something of the hot, inflammable temperament of the Southern people; and he was not alone in his position. Strong men in New York were proclaiming that any reenforcement of Fort Sumter would be the overt act in the matter of war.

But the Secretary of State's schemes were getting tangled, and his policy of delay and noncoercion was being questioned and ridiculed. The Commissioners who had arrived in Washington on March 5th were still without official recognition from the President. They were claiming that they were not properly received. The time had come, after the great inaugural stir was over, for the President to give attention to important business. They could not understand it. It was not courteous, a manner that the Southerners regarded as necessary to a gentleman as the air he breathed. But the thing kept looming up before the Republican President that to treat with the Commissioners officially meant recognition of the Southern Confederacy. Seward would have autocratically put by the fear and held the Conference had he been in Lincoln's place; but Lincoln was now hampered by a score of unwise counselors who cajoled and hectored him as it suited their purpose.

But aside from the ineradicable animosities like those of Thaddeus Stevens' that darkened all counsels, how to secure a delay that would give an opportunity for reconciliation between the States was too fine a piece of diplomacy for the crude American statesmanship of that day. Seward saw the necessity of some delicate but shrewd maneuver on the part of the government; but, like Lord Melbourne, he was facing a turn of fortune. There were sinister forces at work of which he knew nothing.

But he was not through. He still believed that it was nothing more than Scott's "hasty plate of soup," although he made fun of the conceit, so the pompous old hero grumbled to a dinner guest. Seward did not hear him; could hear nothing but his own voice. "When the Southern States see that we mean them no wrong," he cried hysterically to the London *Times'* war correspondent, "they will return to the greatest and most glorious Union in all the world!" But the Peace Commissioners—how were they to be put off from day to day? Could the wily Secretary invent excuses enough to satisfy them? Why did they not receive official recognition? The slight was rasping their nerves, and they had Southern nerves. The Secretary of State must have seen that the truth had to come sooner or later. But he continued to dally with the situation, carrying on "backdoor negotiations" through others with them, Gideon Welles tells us, and dealing in all sorts of intrigues and subterfuges to gain delay. This rôle he continued to play for many days, sincerely believing that the end in view justified his actions. He feared to confer with them officially since they were likely to discover his ulterior purpose of reuniting the states, and he had no authority, as much as he would have liked to do so, to open up a conference for the discussion of the whole matter of secession, its rights and its present status. There has been some slight repetition in order to make his position—so often questioned—more clearly understood.

The Peace Commissioners, too, had their dreams, but not of reunion, unless some generous concessions on the part of the North were forthcoming. They were clothed with discretionary powers.[1] They were beginning to doubt the numberless promises of the Secretary. There was entirely too much talk about supplying Fort Sumter—reenforcing it was what they secretly meant. Judge J. A. Campbell, a member of the Supreme Court, had gone out of his way to assist them, but to no avail. Seward himself was at times losing patience with the Cabinet and breaking out in denunciations of the various members, to draw from the Secretary of the Navy the peevish comment, "That was like Seward." [2]

Weary of urging a conference with the President and disappointed with the results, the Commissioners had begun bitterly to resent the fact that he would not receive them; would not confer with them except through intermediaries, and that not officially. The situation was intolerable. They little dreamed that the hard-pressed Secretary of State was scheming for more time for the whole disturbance to blow

[1] A "Memoir," by Mrs. Davis. Vol. II.
[2] A diary by Gideon Welles.

over. They began to show their irritation to outsiders, to talk to any one who would listen in reference to the evacuation of the Southern forts, and soon gave out an ultimatum themselves. Strange and dark rumors reached them through sympathizers with the South, and "all who claimed to be respectable in Washington," Russell says, were said to be on its side. Daily they were told of "great activity in military circles"; "Preparation going on in the navy yards of Boston and elsewhere"; The North preparing for "an invasion of the South"; "An expedition was at that very moment headed for South Carolina to put down the rebellion." It began to be whispered that the test of secession would be made by reenforcing Sumter. The rumors thickened.

Although Seward was still seeking by fair means or foul, as it best served his purpose, to balk the attempt, the Confederate Commissioners could not understand him. In hot indignation they wrote back that everybody was cordial—more than cordial—sympathetic—both men and women; everybody except certain high officials of the government. Since many in Washington and all leaders in the city of New York believed that the reenforcement of Sumter would precipitate war, they were not slow to give out that it would. In that event, the Southern element of Washington believed that the city would be taken over by the Confederacy. Society women, disgusted with the present administration, were telling the London *Times* reporter when he left for the South, "When you come back here you will see *nice* people in charge of the government—ladies and gentlemen." They continued to praise Varina.

CHAPTER IV

THE WITHERED DREAM

AFTER the failure of the Commission that he had sent to Washington, with the hope of establishing peaceful relations between the two sections, Jefferson Davis busied himself at Montgomery with the defenses of the country. He saw what really lay behind the wavering, equivocating methods of the Federal Cabinet with which he unfortunately believed Seward was acting and whose deliberations he was in all probability guiding. He as much as Seward favored delay, but he would not remain inactive. The South must be prepared for any contingency. He had claimed as a War Minister that all nations should have a reliable defense; and though the country was not yet at war, he acted from that standpoint. In the disposition of the military forces he had, as early as March 2d, appointed Major P. G. T. Beauregard of Louisiana, a graduate of West Point and a brilliant young officer, in command of Charleston, her forts and the territory lying around it. Jefferson Davis knew that if hostilities actually took place, they would begin here.

The beautiful old colonial city, spreading out on an elevated spur of the mainland, between the Ashley and Cooper Rivers (What staunch Cavalier had named the three?), with its wharves, warehouses and imposing public buildings bowered in gardens and groves of evergreen shrubberies and trees, was considered by both natives and foreigners the most beautiful in America. By the latter it was said to be

41

more like a European city. English travelers in the South proclaimed it the most cultured and delightful city in the Confederacy. Its stately, white-columned mansions, churches and luxurious gardens and celebrated Battery or Esplanade facing the sea, all produced an old-world air that charmed the traveler. It gave, one said, the impression of a pleasing combination of London and an old Venetian city.[1] Its churches and more imposing public buildings were English, while the piazzas and Venetian blinds of some of the larger mansions suggested Mediterranean influences, a suggestion that the water doubtlessly emphasized.

The Union Government was more sensitive about the Charleston forts than any other in the South, for here the revolution had had its birth, and constituted the dead line over which the proud young nation dared any foe to pass. The very inhibition, with its usual subtle power to offend, piqued and irritated the authorities at Washington. But South Carolina had proclaimed that she would resist any Federal reenforcement of her forts and had asked for its evacuation. Still she had not pressed it with any act of violence. The state was one of the most celebrated in the American Union; its very name suggested all that the Southerner most longed for—wealth, culture and proud family traditions. It was opulent and ease-loving and had begun a literary and artistic culture that luxury and ease in time foster. But the world was pretty well acquainted with the temperament of its people. Many prominent citizens of New York had told Russell, on his arrival in the country to report the revolution for the London *Times,* that the Union would be irreparably destroyed the moment the authorities at Wash-

[1] "Life in the South," by a blockaded British subject. Catherine Hopley (S.L.J.).

ington reenforced the Carolina fort, and "in the split" they "would go with the South." Seward still boasted that the Union was safe; but things in the Charleston harbor looked threatening. From steeple and dome and the low white parapets of Beauregard's sand-bank earthworks, the new Confederate flag floated by the side of the sacred Palmetto. Everywhere the eye turned, on Morris Island at Cummings Point, on Moultrie, and farther away on Castle Pinckney and Fort Johnson, on all except the famous Fort Sumter where the Stars and Stripes still waved, the colors of the young Republic flew. Far out through the salt-water marshes, upon the distant sand hills, and amid the vari-colored scrub undergrowth it could be seen waving above the army tents about which swarmed thousands of tall, slim, fine-faced young South Carolinians. Both gentry and piny-wood whites, no matter what their station in life, were mingling together, filled with one burning passion.

European travelers in the South, who witnessed the fierce outburst of patriotism that united all classes, were amazed as they beheld the scene. Nor were the demonstrations confined to the men. Delicately bred mothers and their *svelte* young daughters, and women of all walks of life, were coming together in close proximity, making uniforms, embroidering and presenting flags, and urging their men to resist what they believed to be the tyranny of the North. "Women spend their time here making flags," was an item constantly sent to the English papers. Try as one might to find the real motive for the burst of emotion moving and stirring the people with a fervor little short of frenzy, one must believe that it was the desire for separation from the North. Slavery among them, the main thing about which some Northern historians have claimed they disagreed, had been

offered them in the proposed Thirteenth Amendment, and
this had been approved of in Lincoln's inaugural message,
doubtless as an attempt of Seward's to reconcile them,
which takes the ethics, that William Lloyd Garrison contended for, out of the Emancipation Proclamation.

However they might have felt towards the Union in the
past, nothing now appealed to the Southerners but an independent nationality. They had determined upon more commercial freedom. Beauregard's fortifications scowling with
guns was their reply to Lincoln's jesture in reference to
slavery. Some solitary soul like Pettigrew might still de-
plore the step that had been taken; a few might sigh for
reunion; but not the brilliant, fiery Rhetts, the Hamptons,
the Chesnuts, the Lees and Mannings, nor the countless tall
young Carolinians, parading and drilling companies throughout the day and far into the night. Something had snapped
in the bitter controversy difficult to mend.

Seward was alarmed. Throughout the South, poet, publisher, cotton king and cracker-folk were united in a common
cause. There was but one thing these now asked of the
North, that, total separation. They had begun to suspect as
much in Washington. A test must be made; and seek as
Seward might to delay the whole movement, President Lincoln was daily yielding to the influence of certain leaders of
his party who favored force in the matter of the Carolina
fort. Many who had nodded acquiescence as the various
states left the Union, were now proclaiming that "it was the
duty of the Union to reenforce Sumter."

The wild talk and still wilder rumors regarding the reenforcement of the fort that had been heard in Washington
and all the way down to Montgomery continued. "It was
enough," wrote the London *Times* correspondent, "to make

one tired of all this jabber about reenforcing Fort Sumter."
But the determination on the part of certain Federal authorities to strengthen the garrison was destined to become a
realization before the roses of Washington came to bud
and bloom. Whatever was in the communication sent from
the White House to General Scott at a notable dinner he was
giving, which was hastily read by Seward, and immediately
pitched into the fire by the former, will never be a matter
of record; but one can safely believe that it had much to
do with a movement on the part of the President to reenforce Sumter. An influence stronger, more dominant and
insidious than that of the impatient, erratic, dictatorial
Seward was now shaping the course of the administration.
While it is not set down in many histories as one would an
example in arithmetic, Gideon Welles, in his faithfully-kept
diary, discloses the fact that the Blairs, the elder Blair especially, more than Seward and Scott and their following,
were now steering the Ship of State, and in the direction
that Stevens, Sumner, Chandler and Wade intended it to go.

The historian Rhodes expresses the opinion that much was
being done in the work of Congress along conciliatory lines
to induce the states to return to the Union. But much of this
seemed to hold a sinister purpose to the Southerners, who
for all their naïveté were shrewd politicians. To their minds,
President Lincoln's inaugural address, written in some part
by Seward, while it was couched in fair enough phrases, was
unconstitutional and unethical. Its attitude was meant to
satisfy the South by a promise of non-interference
with slavery in its midst, but at the same time to prevent it
from enjoying equal political advantages in Congress in the
future control of the new territory in the West. It was
hardly an ethical interpretation of what later was shrewdly

made a war measure, nor was it at all in accord with Jefferson Davis' sense of political justice as provided for by the Constitution of which he, like Calhoun, had made a rite.   Seward, shocked and exasperated at the thought of war between the two sections, had attempted the rôle of Webster.   But unable to fight the radicals of his party in the open, he was vain enough to believe that the inaugural address would satisfy the South.   He himself had never really held any ethical opinions about slavery that he could not dispense with in his efforts to preserve the Union.   Shrewd eyes, however, did not see in the address equal rights and privileges for the South in the Union, but future political domination in Congress.   The address, to Lincoln's and Seward's dismay, was regarded throughout the South as a signal for war; while some in the North, including Douglas, now an abandoned ship beached on alien shores, were proclaiming that it was an overture of peace.   It was the great Douglas who now decided that it was best for him to hold Lincoln's hat at the speech-makings.   Seward might have suggested more specific terms of reconciliation in the address, but, as well as Lincoln, he knew that he had to satisfy the Republican leaders who were already ridiculing his rosy dream of reconciliation.   Despite his warnings, every gesture of the Republican party acted like a firebrand in numerous places even in Virginia, the very state it was most anxious to conciliate, and where many leading public men were striving to catch any true light of pacification that flickered in the stormy skies.   The sullen spirit of secession continued to burn like a slow fire from community to community throughout the state, especially in the eastern portion.   It burst into higher flame with every awkward movement of the government at Washington. In time there was as much clamor for separation from the Union in Virginia as anywhere else in the South. When the hour arrived that conservative leaders themselves were forced by the harsh terms of the North to declare for independence, these had no difficulty in summoning to the defense of the state both the poorest and the wealthiest of its population. Republican diplomacy was never more crude than in the instance of Virginia. Having no such military advantage there as was possessed in retaining Maryland, certain generous compromises would be necessary to keep it in the Union.

In his policy in the matter of the Carolina fort, Lincoln was equally unhappy, and it was not difficult to see what would follow. South Carolina had already claimed the chain of forts in the Charleston harbor as her own property; and since other forts in the Confederacy were being taken over with flags torn down and trampled underfoot, why, Seward persistently asked, press the matter so openly at its most dangerous point? The scholarly and keen-sighted historian, Channing, though writing largely in the sense of *we* and *they,* admits that the Federal Government could have presented Sumter to the State of South Carolina without any serious loss to the Union. Besides, there was no real necessity at this time for supplying the fort to which Major Anderson, its commander, had recently removed from Fort Moultrie even if the Federal authorities had determined to do so in future. The lull, if not truce, was of more value to the interests of good government than anything else at the acute stage of the situation. There was not a compelling plea of any nature in Anderson's official communications that showed the necessity for supplying it. He did say, in substance, that in view of the short rations it would be best to evacuate the fort. Every communication from him suggested more discretion on the part of the Federal Government. "Any interference will be sure to bring on war," was the spirit and often the words of every letter he addressed to the authorities at Washington.

In the face of Anderson's plea that no action of a belligerent nature should be taken in respect to Sumter, it is astonishing how the historian can seek to make it appear that he was in sympathy with the Federal Government in relieving it. Anderson's men had had access to every grocery store in Charleston, and this would have continued for some time had the situation been ignored. Because of his better judgment, he was unjustly suspected by some in his own Government of being disloyal. He knew that strict non-interference on the part of the authorities at Washington would bring him all the food he needed from Charleston. He was at all times on friendly terms with the people in the city. In the kind of truce that existed between the two governments the reenforcement seemed to Governor Pickens and the Carolinians to be an open act of aggression and defiance on the part of the Federal Government, and a determined effort to test secession, let it cost what it may. The spirit of compromise and true statesmanship and diplomacy would have favored indifference to the whole Southern situation as long as possible.

There is no disposition to attribute to President Lincoln any rash desire to go to war. It is certain that he did not want war, but it must be conceded that not Seward nor Scott nor Adams and other conservative leaders were in the ascendancy at this juncture. It is perfectly clear that radical political influences, united with that of both Blairs, were at work to clear the path for the President, who,

it is claimed, said, in various phrasings, that he was there
to carry out the wishes of his party. That the Blairs, especially, brought such influence to bear upon him as to "elec-
trify" him as to his duty in regard to the fort, is clearly
shown in the Diary of Gideon Welles, a member of his
Cabinet; although he, Welles, was relieved that some influence stronger than Seward's, of which he greatly disap-
proved, had finally been brought to bear on the head of the
administration. Welles records that after certain interviews
with the Blairs, especially the elder, the President found his
mind clear of all doubts as to his duty in the matter of reenforcing the fort.

Intimation now hourly grew into a confirmed public statement, secretly as it was being kept, that the President had
determined to reenforce—supply they liked best to call it—
the South Carolina fort. The Secretary of State was not
at all satisfied. It was spoiling his rosy dream of reconciliation. He had permitted Justice J. A. Campbell to believe that
all would yet work out well. He still believed that given
time he could effect a reunion of the States. His self-sufficiency was abnormal—but the radicals were proving too
much for him. He was at times in a state of nervous ex-
haustion, but outwardly self-sufficient and confident; he
attended innumerable dinners, and in fierce, ejaculatory sentences sought to quell the storms. He would not readily
relinquish his dream. While the dogwood and wild plum
whitened the Virginia and Maryland roads leading down to
the newly-formed Confederacy, he would keep trying to
evoke some magical power to perform the miracle. Although
the situation had been taken out of his hands and he had
to acknowledge that he was beaten, he was not to be totally
effaced. He determined to keep the promise he had made

to Campbell as an expediency that if the fort were reenforced, authorities there should be notified. What supremacy!

A strong fleet that had been prepared with the utmost
secrecy for the expedition had put to sea, when a strange
telegram that nobody knew anything about, flew softly and
secretly over the wires to inform Governor Pickens that the
authorities at Washington had determined to reenforce the
now famous Sumter.[1] It was a name on every tongue in
America, and one that was to become familiar to every
nation of the earth. Balked in his efforts and plans to
reconcile the two sections, the audacious Secretary had
failed to "keep faith" as he had thought to do with the
government at Montgomery. Believing that he was acting in close concurrence and agreement with the administration, it held him responsible for all action taken to
reenforce the Carolina fort. His name was henceforth
prominent in all the denunciation reserved for the Washington authorities. Earlier, he had stood up before the scowling faces of Stevens, Sumner, Hale and Wade and cried,
"If we keep entirely cool, entirely calm, entirely kind, a
debate will ensue which will be kindly in itself and prove
very soon either that we are wrong and we shall concede to
our offended brethren, or else that we are right and they will
acquiesce and come back into fraternal relations with us."
He was now to see his dream wither with the early April
bloom along the Potomac.

Let his conduct, pointed out as a gross usurpation of
power by some historians seeking to sustain the Republican
administration, be as artful and dominating as any that
has been recorded in history, it must be acknowledged that

[1] It was sent by Harvey, a newspaper man, who was afterwards recommended by Seward for Ambassador to Portugal.

he was acting in the interest of a peaceful restoration of the estranged sections. One, at least, may cherish the thought that had he received the full and sympathetic cooperation of his party, there would have been reconciliation between the States. It is clear that party leaders were now marking out the President's course, while the dictatorial Secretary of State was being condemned for trying to do so in a much better cause. In the instance of Dix, Black and Holt, the historian Rhodes seems to think well of them for taking things in their own hands in the attempt to stiffen the spine of the wavering, irresolute Buchanan. But what condemnation for Seward who, after surveying the Cabinet, decided that it was some one's duty to try to save the country from disunion and war.

But there is a further story connected with the bombardment of Sumter that amuses in spite of the gravity of the situation. Having failed in a series of efforts to prevent the reenforcement of the fort, one can without effort imagine the irrepressible advocate of "Higher Law," seeking Scott— who can say—in an attempt to wreck the expedition to the Charleston Harbor. State affairs were getting to be very mysterious and exciting. A contretemps is nearly always humorous and one stands by half suppressing a laugh at the consternation of good old Welles as the audacious Seward detaches the flagship *Powhatan* with the main reenforcements from the fleet destined for Sumter and sends it over other seas, leaving it to the *Lady Harriette Lane* to do the honors in the Charleston Harbor. This done, Seward perhaps took a pinch of snuff; his scraggy, eagle-like physiognomy, that smoothed down by a curled wig would have greatly resembled Chatham's, contracted into a contemptuous smile as he told Scott in some such words, "Not one of them

is civilized." He would for all the wide gulf that yawned
between them soothe Jefferson Davis, with whom he
had had many a hard tilt in the halls of Congress. They
had known each other outside of its halls; had visited each
other in sickness; he liked Varina; he and Jefferson Davis
pronounced the word Europe alike, and there had been much
in common between them. They were now to become bitter
foes, for unfortunately both Jefferson Davis and Varina attributed what they termed "political crookedness" to him
as much so as to any other connected with the reenforcement
of the fort.[1] The story should be rewritten.

The self-centered, sardonic and seemingly *sang-froid*
Secretary of State, a scholar and statesman and a connois-
seur even in the matter of words, was too nicely loyal to
his government to expose its hand. There is no word
left to show that he publicly denounced the Cabinet,
though he bitterly opposed its course. If he could prevent
it from wrecking the chances for reunion, that was his own
affair. Scheming now to prevent war, he was to spend four
years in prosecuting it; but at the same time, seeking more
than once by some intrigue or other to bring the states back
into the Union. Stabbed about the face and neck three
times because of the thought that he had helped to bring on
the war, he spent the remainder of his public life upholding
and sustaining President Johnson in his efforts to protect
the devastated South. It is certain that he had much to do
with shaping Lincoln's attitude in the end towards it and
that he wielded a strong influence in the instance of Johnson. The South held a fascination for him. He was unwilling to see it separate itself from the Union; but after

[1] It seems that late in life Jefferson Davis understood Seward better.
See Mrs. Davis, "Memoir," vol. II.

it had been conquered he was equally unwilling to see the North scourge it. There was a better way, he ejaculated at whist and dinner parties, and sometimes in heated argument in Cabinet meetings; but discovering that he could not make others agree with him as to the "better way," he resorted to numerous daring schemes and measures to secure ends that he believed justified his course. That Lincoln, who was never a willing follower of the "slay the traitors" element of his party, was tremendously influenced in his outlook by this dominating, persistent, subtle, highly-polished, educated and humanized being, whose mental angularities scarcely exceeded his physical ones, can but be believed. It is claimed by Welles that Seward was buoyant and optimistic to the last; but it is believed that it was an inflated ego rather than lightness of spirit that kept him up those last strange and trying days which hourly became more mystifying to the Cabinet. They all looked at Seward, Welles says, when things went wrong or seemed to bear a hidden hand.

When the secret telegram, that the Cabinet suspected was Seward's work, was received at Charleston, Governor Pickens immediately informed General Beauregard. That done, he touched off seven rounds of cannon to arouse the people and bring the Seventh Regiment to Charleston. They were preparing before Lincoln's message arrived. Charleston was now in a state of wild commotion. Telegrams flew thick and fast between Beauregard and Jefferson Davis. The ultimatum, after a council had been held in the Confederate Cabinet, was to request Commander Anderson to surrender the fort, and if it was refused, since Federal forces were expected, to reduce it. Later, a telegram went from the Confederate President to Beauregard to act with

discretion in the matter but to resist any invasion as an act of
war.   General Beauregard and Governor Pickens immediately held a council of war.   James Chesnut, an eager and
ardent secessionist, with two other aides, were appointed
to negotiate the terms of the surrender.   His equally
eager and ardent wife wrote in substance that, rigged up
in the bravest of aide-de-camp toggery, "sword and red
sash," he went over at two o'clock P. M. of April 11, in
a gay little boat to demand the surrender of the fort from
Major Anderson.

All the commendable efforts of Major Anderson to warn
the Federal authorities against the disastrous step, and any
one who studies them will agree that they were full of wise
discretion, were of no avail.   Chesnut, the principal nego-
tiator for surrender, reported that his interview with him
had been "deeply interesting" but to no purpose, adding that
he "felt for Anderson."   Beauregard again sent his aides
to the fort after midnight to demand its surrender.   Both
sides were beginning to realize that it was war, and "with
no concessions" was the dark little Creole's order if the
fort was not surrendered.   Excitement was at its highest
pitch.   Chesnut and Lee [1] were boasting that "the Federals
would have to give up that fort, or be burned alive in it."
Seward's dream of reunion had withered.

[1] Stephen D. Lee of the Lees of South Carolina.

CHAPTER V

PRESIDENT LINCOLN, urged by the Blairs and others of his party, had decided to test secession at the Charleston harbor where Federal authority was disputed.[1] The Confederacy, no longer a party of scattered, insurrectionary spirits, but an imposing Federation of States, had determined to resist the invasion. Beauregard, from the moment that the strange telegram had been received at Charleston, had kept his eyes fixed on Sumter, the only fortress in the harbor the Federals now possessed. But though ready, not yet would he strike. Chesnut, who had been sent again to ask the surrender of the fort, stayed and stayed. Charleston was out of bed. The bells of St. Michael were pealing far out across the waters. Did it bring assurance of peace to the tense people, or a warning of coming calamity? Women rushed in and out of their houses and mingled with the men on the streets with a freedom they had never before felt. So long restrained beneath tight stays and billowing hoops, it was amazing how nimbly they got about. Some were praying, but others were proudly boasting that every man in her family was on the Island with Beauregard's army. The hour for Anderson's reply drew near. He pleaded his sense of honor. He too must defend his flag. He had received instructions from his government and reenforcements were hourly expected. Confusion reigned and dazed the

[1] "A Diary," Gideon Welles, vol. I.

mind. The April night was ebbing when, to end the suspense and send a shock through the city at four-thirty on the morning of the 12th, the first roar of cannon was heard. It was the signal gun from Fort Johnson, said to have been touched off by the aides on their way from Fort Sumter. Hostilities between the invading North and the resisting South had begun, whatever one might later get out of the constant twaddle as to who "struck the first blow." Cannon immediately began to roar from Morris Island at Cummings Point and Fort Moultrie, the principal batteries now engaged. Soon the skies became lurid as solid sheets of flame lit the waters of the bay. As unrestrained as Southern enthusiasm had become, hundreds of hearts in the city felt for the brave defender of his fort, who, as yet, had replied with but a single shot. War news flew farther than the roar of guns. South Carolina to her farthest borders had heard. "Eteocles and Polynices had met," they were shortly saying in London. "Give the Tyrians equal chance with the Trojans." But Victoria was more partial than Dido. "The Southerners are like the British," was whispered at the Court of St. James. "There really is a war; let them have it if nothing else will satisfy them," the pompous lords in Parliament were observing. In South Carolina one could read it in every eye. Outside the Charleston bar, the newly-arrived Federal fleet was lying in grim silence. If it could have approached, despite the loss of the flagship *Powhatan,* the city would have been reduced to a shapeless mass. Lucky for the old colonial city that it had its "much regretted bar" over which it had fretted and fumed in the past. No moat had ever better protected a feudal castle. It is certain, however, even if the fleet could have taken part, that Beauregard would not have surrendered to the invasion without exhausting his batteries. "Independence or death" was stamped upon every face, searing the heart and brain. It has ever been the way of revolutions and will be until in the justice of things men will find no need for them.

All through the night the heavy firing kept up. Women, old and young, had sought the high balconies and rooftops of stately mansions, or any perch that could be had to witness the scene. The Battery, where long rows of stately old houses overlooked the bay, was so crowded with them that it attracted the attention of the news reporters; they had never seen so many women out of doors before. Though they at first cheered wildly and frantically their boasting soon took the form of prayers and tears for the safety of the men swarming about the guns. Monster shells were bursting among them, for the doomed fort was now returning the Confederate fire. But its chance was small. Beauregard's guns continued to roar and flame against its dull, red walls. At every discharge the Confederates cheered, and hooted the Federal fleet lying powerless to render aid. With some assistance Anderson could have swept away the loose earthworks gleaming white across the bay. They were in truth mere sand-banks in the history of fortifications. But never were guns more eagerly served.

With a short cessation, the Confederate batteries resumed fire early the next morning and continued until three o'clock in the afternoon, when the Federal garrison failed to reply. Flames were now bursting from the sides of the fort and its silence was an intimation that it had ceased to resist. Still the Confederate batteries sent occasional shells in its direction, during which one of those strange feats that singular people are given to perform astonished the Federal garrison. A small boat secretly put off from Morris Island

and rowed through the bursting shells straight for the burning fort. Besides the dusky oarsman, it contained a solitary figure who held aloft on the point of his saber a white handkerchief fluttering in the breeze. Landing on the quay, the unauthorized ambassador clambered through an embrasure and presented himself before the astonished garrison with a summons to surrender. The circumstance, it is said, led to the capitulation of the fortress.[1] The feat of the self-appointed ambassador was not the only unusual one performed that day. Everywhere men were taking the initiative. Roger Pryor had taken it upon himself to speak for Virginia, setting the time by Shrewsbury clock when she would join the Confederate States. From the balcony of a Charleston hotel, his fierce, defiant words and pale passionate face continued to stir the crowd in the street below as he exultingly promised Virginia to the Confederacy. Lesser spirits were as rampant. In excuse for some lack of obedience, commanders were saying of their roistering young troops, "Remember they are all volunteers and do just as they please." Amid their swaggering, smoking and drinking, had they set fire to the Island, it would scarcely have surprised European visitors.

The city which for days had been overflowing with civilian and military organizations had now become a seething mass of humanity. Every open highway, every footpath, every train, brought them in until it was said by an eyewitness that you could look nowhere that you did not see all of South Carolina in Charleston. Long-haired and unshaved, tall, lank, back-country whites and well-groomed

---

[1] Louis T. Wigfall, former United States Senator from Texas. The correspondent of the London *Times* tells the story for a true one, describing it as a remarkable feat of a "remarkable man."

sons of the cotton kings were now smoking and drinking together as if there had never been a dusky hand to divide them. The high contemptuous airs and manner with which the young lords at first had regarded their back-countrymen passed with the sound of Beauregard's guns. They had suddenly become brothers. One rose upon a thorny, thorny bush.

And now the thing had happened that all the country, both North and South, had warned the authorities at Washington would happen if an attempt to reenforce the Carolina fort was made. Seward was telling Scott, "I told them so." But as uproariously as the cannon had sounded it was still a bloodless victory, a fact that Jefferson Davis noted with relief. Women laughed and cried. Rejoicings were heard everywhere that the garrison had surrendered without the loss of a life, and not a gun of Beauregard's silenced. Later they were distressed to find that several of the Federal garrison had been mortally wounded by its own men, when Anderson was giving the parting salute to his flag, a high courtesy that had been gladly extended him by Beauregard. The young troops were as generous. "Yes, let him salute his flag fifty times, or as many times as he wishes, the Carolinians would salute theirs—let everybody salute his own flag." "Will you take a drink with me sir, for the victory?" they were asking every stranger who appeared.

But what wonder that the city was filled with excitement! News flew that Virginia was as wild with enthusiasm over the capture of the fort as any in South Carolina. Down at Montgomery, the Confederate Capital, they were firing cannon every minute in a perfect frenzy of delight over the news. Jefferson Davis sat in his office grave and pale, but callers noted the determined look on his thin, quiet face.

The iron in his soul was beginning to show upon his countenance, and his manner was becoming more drastic with each telegram from Beauregard. Varina was receiving the women of the city at the new White House. All were talking and gesticulating at once and wondering how Mrs. James Chesnut and others of their friends in Charleston had stood it.

Charleston continued to be the news center of the Confederacy. As the days passed, joined by regiments from Alabama and other states, Beauregard's men were improvising what was soon to be known as the "Confederate yell." It awoke the delicate, sensitive Charleston women sometimes at night with a shock that left them cold and trembling. Where had it originated? Who had composed it? "A note higher than a cheer, and indescribable," wrote the London *Times* correspondent to his paper. It is certain that it was none of that class to which the debonair ex-Governor Manning belonged, reciting classical lore and but moderately acquainted with brandy and tobacco. Still, the young aristocrats who proffered champagne and other commodities of high living seemed to get it off as musically as the poor whites—the poor whites who usually went barefooted, chewed tobacco incessantly and were dexterous enough in spitting to hit a spot fifteen feet away. What superb nerves! What quantities of tobacco! If it gave out on the dreadful marches they would miss it more than they would bread.

And the proud, exclusive, colonial dames of the city, a city that had overnight become famous throughout the world—what of these? Shut off in a realm of their own, where the Gadsdens, Rhetts, Sumters, Pinckneys, Pringles, Hugers, Rutledges, Ravenels, and their kind, had by sheer force of example brought an exclusive class up to the rank of Cavalier, how had these so soon been able to discard their pretty, graceful manners, their numerous petticoats and great hoops and mount the walls to watch the blaze of cannon and rejoice when Beauregard's batteries set the fort on fire? But in justice to them it should be recorded that they constantly paused in their rejoicings to ask, with tears in their eyes, if Anderson and his men were safe. There would come a day when they would not feel that way about any Yankee, but not yet. The thicker-fibered, hardy, piny-woods woman, with her sons already enlisted, might tell Russell how disappointed she was that Beauregard had not killed every Yankee within the walls of Sumter, but not Mrs. Chesnut, Mrs. Preston, Mrs. Means and their kind who had spent the night upon the housetops, their nerves singing like delicate wires in the wind as they prayed that no life should be sacrificed. War would go hard with these soft, gentle beings, the white flower of a highly emotional and sensitive race. But the women of such races have great powers of endurance. As yet these were tender. Still, what exhilaration this early for their dormant energies! And indeed patriotism, which is one of the strongest stimulants, was stirring the hearts of both men and women as it had never stirred a generation since the great Washington's day. All classes were beginning to understand the issue that had divided the country, but the most dominant one that State Sovereignty had bred was *hate*. A statement was flaunted in the Northern newspapers, a source which in both sections of the country had done much to bring on the war, that "the Federal Government was only attempting to relieve a starving garrison." It drew from the Carolinians, good friends of Anderson, a burst of derisive laughter. There was another shrill jeer at General Scott and Seward's boast that it was only a cloudburst. None dreamed how much the gouty old Virginian and the baffled would-be-mediator wished it had been.

Leaders among the Republicans in the North were now exclaiming, with frantic efforts to arouse the people, that the country was threatened with destruction. In Wall Street stocks had a downward movement, and depression was felt throughout the business world. The North could not do without the South—oligarchy, autocracy, slaveocracy or whatever it might be in its eyes, it was necessary to the whole. Independence for the South and free trade with England would in time destroy Northern prosperity in trade and commerce. When the vanquished Secretary of State went to New York, there was an understanding that the North would prevent by armed force the secession of her most prosperous and remunerative section. Through the operation of the tariff laws, which were sapping the South's prosperity like the fatal tillandsia upon tropical trees, millions upon millions yearly flowed into her coffers. This must continue or the North would in time find itself impoverished. Seward had made his last effort to quell the storm at home and had been made the butt for the ridicule, even the suspicions of the Republican party, to later become one for the Northern historians in explanation and defense of the reenforcement of the Southern fortress.

But though his supremacy had been threatened, the autocratic Secretary of State was not ready to quit in the face of defeat. Henceforth, he would lay schemes that involved outside powers. Domestic solidarity had often been maintained in this way. These, however, were only other Sewardian dreams for the Republican party and the war correspondent of the London *Times* to deride, each from a different standpoint. The famous English reporter was now frequently entertained by Lord Lyons, and what was said between them will never be a matter of history. Seward was talking recklessly, and both ambassador and reporter agreed that he would bear watching. The roar of Beauregard's guns, however, had for the moment dazed the Secretary of State. In the Cabinet, henceforth, he would make no more pleas for "good government," and like the President, would drift with the tide. But there would be further differences of opinion. The Republicans were now for a "little blood-letting," and though set on saving the Union, Seward was bitterly opposed to the method. A war with England or any other country, he decided, would be better than what he termed Civil War in the American Union. His jingoism had a purpose in it. With Scott and Adams and others he continued to listen aghast at the news that South Carolina had resisted the Federal invasion with cannon, a thing that in his heart he believed had been forced upon it, though he later told England point-blank that the South started the war. But his party had acted and it must be sustained. Lord John Russell must not be left to infer that he, a recognized leader, was out of harmony with it. His vanity was consuming. His supremacy must seem to be secure even though it was inadequate for his purposes. However, his doctrine of "higher law" and expediency was beginning to be accepted by every member of the Federal Government. Washington was in greater confusion than Charleston and swarming with unwise counselors.

While the *Harriette Lane* was turning her prows homeward without honors, fashionable society was gathering at the handsome Riggs mansion to exchange congratulations. Seward was angry, half-distraught, but strove to get new

bearings. Lincoln, wondering, disturbed, moved in and out
of the Cabinet meetings bent on doing his duty of which
others had convinced him.[1] The crisis, too, was beginning
to hasten his own pulse. The first move after Sumter was
his call for 75,000 troops with which to "put down the
rebellion." But he little dreamed how soon he was to lose
Virginia by the act, and Virginia's was the voice that might
have quelled the storm. The Blairs, especially the elder,
and the powerful coterie in Congress that formed what the
Democrats termed the "black wing" of the Republican party,
were heaping blame upon the South, upon Jefferson Davis,
upon everything below the Mason and Dixon line. Fully
half, if not more, of Washington was in sympathy with
the Southern Confederacy; thousands after the bombardment of Sumter were resigning and hurrying southward.
Editors, newspaper men, both seasoned and fledgling reporters, of every shade of thought and opinion, were packing
their bags and hurrying to get as near as possible to the
scene of action. Among them was the famous war correspondent of the London *Times.* He came with a passport
that the South accepted—the Anglo-Saxon South which he
was to see so much of for days and days. With all its
shortcomings, it was the side of the revolution, he infers,
that treated him as a gentleman to the end, though he was as
critical of one as of the other. He had studied the secession
movement from the Northern point of view. He was now
to do so from a Southern angle. How little, he kept telling
himself, did Seward know a gust from a hurricane. The
more he saw each day of the spirit of the South the more
he was convinced that it would not now return to the
Union without a death struggle.

[1] Welles, vol. I.

Of all the Federal leaders at Washington, he found Seward's name, more often than any other, connected in condemnation with that of President Lincoln's. The former had never got clear of his scheming with the Confederate Commissioners who had never understood him. "And who could?" Welles was daily asking himself in his famous Diary. The "ablest but most unscrupulous among them," the commissioners had said of him to their people at home. These were both perceiving and unperceiving in the matter. Seward was being denounced for that which he had not done while Lincoln was meekly taking all responsibility for that which others had thrust upon him.[1]

Still, Lincoln felt the shock, but was relieved as the radical wing of his party began to commend his actions, and to thrust him more in the center of things. He had been fearfully ridiculed and denounced by the Republican intelligentsia, and would be again and again, but this slight consideration aroused in him some of the assurance of the old court days in Illinois. He was beginning to feel that, after all, he was the President. They had taught him how to break Seward's chains—he would in time test theirs. He found it difficult to throw them off, if he ever did, but earnestly and uncomplainingly kept on with his task, to finally find them out in those last days when the task was finished and Seward began to whisper in his ear to "let the dead past bury its dead."

For days following the bombardment of Sumter, Charleston was filled with the noise of drums, cheering and the clatter of spurs and sabers. The hotels were crammed with mixed crowds of both civilians and soldiers. The streets, said the correspondent of the London *Times,* presented some

[1] Welles, vol. I.

such aspect as those of Paris in the last revolution. Bands
of armed men were marching and singing—"the battle
blood seething in their veins—the hot oxygen which is called
the flush of victory on the cheek." The conviviality and
wilder demonstrations, however, were confined to the
Island, where Beauregard's troops indulged in every form of
jubilation. In the city they took their victory more in the
spirit of awe and thankfulness. Still the people made much
of taking the fort in the face of the Federal fleet. Although
an easy victory, it was to prove fatal to any reconciliation of
the sundered Union. State Sovereignty had been converted
into the easier term of States' Rights. The young blood
of the South was boiling for a fight to maintain what they
termed the "principles of their fathers," a phrase they had
caught from the fervid oratory of the day. They were of
the breed of the old Nullifiers of whom Washington Irving
had said, "they are all perfect gentlemen but political Hot-
spurs."

In the volunteer army, the days were spent in boasting,
drilling, parading, feasting and drinking, and consuming
large quantities of tobacco. The latter habit was universal
with the masses at that period. The better class generally
smoked; still many of these used the weed both in the shape
of snuff and quid. They were also "Americanizing Bacchus
to Bourbon," if eyewitnesses are to be credited.[1] Neither
did they mind letting those who came among them know
their commercial rating. It was highly necessary, they had
gathered from their elders, at this juncture that they should
do a little boasting. They particularly let it be known to the
London *Times* reporter that there were whole companies
made up of exclusive Southern gentry, whose wealth some-

[1] W. H. Russell.

times reached the million-dollar mark. Although he found the well-bred Carolinians as prostrate before the "almighty dollar" as their Northern brethren, he was struck by a certain careless and graceful indifference to it. The avarice was not as harsh and apparent as that displayed by the Northerner. The Carolinian had the look and manner of the aristocrat, though he tauntingly observed that not all were Cavaliers who possessed the air. Nor were they; yet so strong had been its influence upon all that it gave uniformity to the upper class. Not only the leaders of the Southern Colonial group, but those farther South had established a landed gentry that carried as high a head as any who had ridden with Charles. As they grew older, their manner became pompous and authoritative. They were not only masterful, but their bearing and manner told one so. Russell wrote back to his paper that in the manner of the great lords of England there was no such assumption of authority as that which marked some of the great Carolinians.

Among other glimpses that reflect the social status of the people, especially those of the city, one gets frequent snapshots of a certain type of Charlestonian that fascinated the English war correspondent no little. After having seen men of many kinds from all over the world falling under the spell of ex-Governor Manning, he found himself wondering who could fail to do so. Charming glimpses, too, one gets through the seeing eyes of Mrs. Chesnut, who recreates the atmosphere in colors, such as, "Colonel Manning came in red sash and sword. He had been under fire and did not mind it at all; not near as much as he had thought he would." Again Russell, very critical of much he saw, wrote in amused admiration, that "with all his faults and provincialisms, your true Carolinian is as charming and fascinating a being as one ever encountered."

However, this type is not the only kind that looks out of the historical pages of that day. "Then came Senator Wigfall, the hero of the surrender of the fort, boasting of his feat with a light in his eye like that of a surly lion's." The gallant Colonel Chesnut, too, was there; not so graceful perhaps as the debonair ex-governor, not so martial as the Texan, but telling the story of Sumter with such accuracy that every one was convinced. "I did not know one could live in such days of excitement," his approving wife recorded. And now she herself "must take that ride around the Battery."

The celebrated esplanade for days swarmed with women with all glasses turned on the battered fortress where the colors of the young Confederacy and the Palmetto were now flying together. "And where throughout the South," Russell asked, "were they not flying?" Seward had not counted on what a piece of bunting would mean once it was "twined in the heart and brain" of a people. Willie Preston, they were saying, had the honor of cutting Sumter's flagstaff in two with his rifle. Heavens! If the spirit of Washington should appear! But the old grandmother was not at all afraid of the shade of Washington and telegraphed to congratulate her grandson, "Well done, Willie." What a change had taken place in the placid, well-ordered city! "The largest crowd I ever saw and everybody talking at once." "And such feasting, such dinners, such suppers!"

The English reporter remained in the city several days and although he moved about with a seeming nonchalance he was shrewdly taking stock of the young Confederacy.

Many eyes watched him narrowly, none more so than those of Mary Boykin Chesnut, who resented his smiles as he listened to their boasting, his sneer at their institution of slavery which she was sure he did not understand. But the thing before his eyes interested him tremendously. Nascent as an April leaf and bud, it was beginning to bloom with colors that took on the hues of Crimea. He marveled a hundred times that Seward could have been so deluded. He would have good stories and to spare to send home to his paper. Seward and Scott and Lincoln, with long heads, had courted him in Washington, but without making as satisfactory impression as they had desired. The South Carolinians were just as thoughtful. The more sedate among them made many opportunities to talk with him on the subject of cotton, the tariff, the general commercial freedom they sought and England's interest in those subjects. Would they finish the white marble Custom House now in a state of incompletion? Certainly not. The Custom House was the one building not suited to their future use. But it was the tall, slim, good-looking young men, flaunting slightly their foreign education, with lanky stride and clattering saber, and boasting that England could not do without them, that more than their elders amused and fascinated the Englishman. Such exuding ego! Such charm!

"So we took Fort Sumter," was the one important information they gave him, with a gleam in their fine young eyes.

CHAPTER VI

VIRGINIA

VIRGINIA had been watching in painful anxiety and perplexity the course affairs were taking both in the North and in the South. "Good, slow, old Virginia," as an English woman long a resident of the state observed, "who never lost her head nor took sides in any question until she had a full understanding of the right and wrong of it." Every straw that blew as a sign that she might not join the Southern Confederacy was watched by President Lincoln and the Republican party with open anxiety—every word of indifference on her part, every note of warning, of deprecation, or of censure was hailed with delight and boasted of by the government at Washington. Shrewd Republicans, not especially drawn to Virginia, and often deriding what they called her "effete, decadent First Families," still boasted that she, having done so much to create the Union, would never leave it. Seward kept praying, if that attitude could be ascribed to his self-sufficient majesty, that she would lead the others back into the fold. Give it a little time and Southern rage would cool down. It should be "left to time, to negotiation, to entreaty, to sisterly kindness," were phrases that should have charmed the most obdurate ear. He was not as proud as he once was of his coined phrases of the past. There was no such thing, he kept repeating, as an "irrepressible conflict." It was only a temporary aberration and delusion that had, for the moment, run away with the South.

But the South would not cool down and secession flamed in the eyes of more of Virginia's people than she liked to believe. It would take a generous compromise, and if that could not be had, a rare diplomacy, to even keep them neutral. But there was no diplomacy. While the South burned, cold materialistic forces were at work in the North, and Wall Street was beginning to exclaim, "without the South we are ruined." Industrialism, that fierce rival and competitor of the humanities and the gentle art of living, had begun to beat its drums throughout the North, to find that war actually made them sound louder. It was the beginning of its mad race for industrial supremacy among the nations of the world. Its energy, however, was now to be expended in the preparation of materials and commodities that perish with war. The lesson should sink in.

Amidst all the fierce, public clamor that agitated the people, one incident that occurred earlier, too beautiful to be lost to so dark a page of history, is further preserved in this chapter since it relates to Virginia. The following interesting letter sent by L. H. S., a poet of Hartford, Connecticut, and member of the Ladies' Mount Vernon Memorial Association, to a prominent Richmond woman whose name is not given, reveals, despite all action to the contrary, a growing spirit of social unity between the sections.[1]

"My Dear Mrs.——

"Has not the great Mount Vernon cause, and purchase, made sisters of us all? It ought so to be. Yet I have known you before, through that intellectual intercourse, which is sometimes better than the sight of the countenance or sound of the voice.

[1] "Life in the South during the War," by a blockaded British subject.

"I have been sending Thanksgiving presents this morning, for this is an old New England Puritan festival, and though you have no such observance in the Ancient Dominion, take upon me to speed the gift of a book to you, upon the wings of the Express. You will perceive that such of its poems as bear upon the interests of our country, though written before our recent discords, breathe a spirit of harmony.

"I am so grieved at our increasing disturbances and dangers. I love Washington and his birthplace, and all his children, and was early taught by my father, who shared in the wars of the Revolution, to hold our union a sacred thing, like the Ark of the Israelites.

"I pray you, is there nothing to be done? Nothing that we women can do, without departing from our proper sphere? Can we not throw filaments of love, like the spider's filmy thread, which the God of peace may bless?

"I enclose a little extemporaneous poem, warm from the heart, which I trust to your judgment. Please make the best use of it you can, for the sake of one who loves her *whole country,* and is

"Your admiring friend,   L. H. S."

The pathetic stanzas referred to in the letter are also given here as a proof of the sacred manner in which the Union was held by many before the war:

STARS OF MY COUNTRY'S SKY

Are ye all there? Are ye all there?
Stars of my country's sky;
Are ye all there? Are ye all there,
In your shining homes on high?
"Count us!" "Count us!" was their answer,

As they dazzled in my view,
In glorious perihelion,
    Amid their fields of blue.

I cannot count ye rightly,
    There's a cloud with sable rim;
I cannot make your number out,
    For my eyes with tears are dim.
O bright and blessed Angel,
    On white wing floating by,
Help me to count and not to miss
    One star in my country's sky.

But a crisis had arisen in which Virginia was not to
be turned from her course, as sentimental and emotionally
patriotic as she herself was known to be. She had known
travail in the past. As a Colonial Province, proud of the
manner in which she had been planted and fostered by the
Mother Country, it had been bitter to her to sever her
connection with it; but she had not been deceived as to
her inalienable rights. Nor was she now, with all her
national pride and forbearance, to be deceived by overtures in which she discovered no real guarantees of equal
privileges under the compact between the states of the
Federal Union. The proposed Thirteenth Amendment
favored in President Lincoln's inaugural address assured
her of future favorable legislation in the matter of her
slave property if that was what she wanted. But she
was asking for far different rights and privileges, and taking a humorous view of the matter, she was not asking for
what she already possessed. Her clear-cut ultimatum as
far back as the Charleston Democratic Convention was still
in her thought. Her accumulating "ifs," she informed the

Republican President, were all well taken. Throughout the
Peace Convention she had striven in vain to bring her
position to the thought and mind of the North, but to no
avail. She was now having serious objections on her own
account to the course pursued by the Republican party.
She herself had grievances that disturbed her peace of
mind. Still her more conservative leaders had waited, hoping against hope for a peaceful adjustment of the controversy. If the reconstruction she had outlined in her
Peace Convention failed, her honor and interests would
force her to cast her destiny with the South.

Furthermore, she was on record and had plainly given
it out that she was opposed to any coercion of the seceded
states. As matters stood they must be brought back by
peaceful measures. She was also opposed to the reten-
tion of Southern ports and the collection of duties. A
thorough readjustment of all difficulties to conform to the
Constitution, she felt, was the only sure ground upon
which she and the other Southern States could hope to
build their future. She had not been overcaptious; her
strongest voices had reproved her fiery young newspaper
men; but she could see that her population was growing
more rebellious each day. A spirit was now in her midst
that such powerful voices as Letcher, Baldwin, Stewart,
Randolph and Preston could not pacify. Other voices, like
those of Roger Pryor, Edward Pollard of the Richmond
Examiner, and the younger Wise of the Richmond *Enquirer,* no longer echoed the moderation and discretion of
the Old Dominion, but were bringing her people employed
in official positions in Washington and throughout the
North home in vast numbers to defend her rights.

In spite of the desire among her leaders for a peaceful

adjustment of all differences, impatient men and women were bitterly denouncing the delegates to her state convention as submissionists, unmindful of the people's rights. Ministers of the Gospel known for their "dignity and simple piety," who prayed in a theoretical manner for peace in the pulpit, out of it were denouncing the "dilatory action" of the state convention. An irate minister, representing a class much higher than the unlettered masses, had been heard to say of the reenforcement of Sumter, that "scalding and skinning is the least mark of distinction we can bestow upon these invading swine." Gentle, soft-voiced women wanted peace, *"but not at any price."* Everywhere, whether in Tidewater or Piedmont, they were breathing naïve prayers, "Oh, that there might be no bloodshed," to be immediately followed by, "But we must have our rights. We will *never* submit." [1]

Still, Virginia waited. The news of Texas joining the Confederacy while it increased the anxiety of her leaders stirred her people with an enthusiasm that could not be mistaken. But it was to the Old Elizabethan Dominion, the pride of Raleigh, the land of Washington, the Mother of all, that the young Republic was now looking. The leading Southern papers were printing such dicta as, "When Old Virginia utters the decisive word, the Republicans at Washington will have to look about for their safety." "Virginia made the Union; her fiat can unmake it."

Virginia was facing her crisis, was daily feeling the trembling of the earthquake, was having to admit that her population was becoming a part of it, when the news burst upon her that an expedition from New York had been sent to relieve Fort Sumter; that Beauregard had

[1] "Life in the South during the War," Catherine Hopley (S.L.J.).

been ordered to resist the invasion; had demanded the fort
as the property of South Carolina, and in the face of the
Federal government's effort to hold it, had bombarded and
reduced it. Virginia was in a fever of unrest. One by
one her ablest leaders were taking sides with the South.
Her people everywhere were clamoring for separation. Before the walls of Sumter had cooled the North had followed up its first action with a declaration of war, and
President Lincoln's call for 75,000 troops decided the
Old Dominion. She would never consent for the South
to be invaded by hostile troops. Although she had not
been a party to its action, she now felt that her destiny lay
with it. Besides, her leaders declared that it was an unauthorized declaration of war, a power only possessed by
Congress. Resistance was stamped upon every face
and written in lurid headlines in every newspaper within
her borders. It was no longer called a civil war; but
"The War." Sober, earnest men and leaders who had
counseled restraint had no further word with the people.
"There are no more Union men in Virginia," they proclaimed to the North. On April 17th, after a long and
trying convention, the state passed an Ordinance of Secession in which they acknowledged the Southern Confederacy and allegiance to its cause. Its action cast a gloom
over the Republican administration but Seward's dander
rose and he, as usual, sought first position in the Cabinet.
Welles says he rarely ever consulted Lincoln in the transac-
tion of foreign affairs. Taking a confident position about
the situation, or rather assuming one, as early as May 4th,
he sent Faulkner, then on the high seas, these cocky instructions for the Quai D'Orsay. "You cannot be too decided or too explicit in making known to the French gov-

ernment that there is not now, nor has there been, nor will there be, the least idea existing in this government of suffering a dissolution of this Union to take place in any way whatever. . . . Tell Mr. Thouvenel, then, with the highest consideration and good feeling, that the thought of a dissolution of this Union peaceably or by force, has never entered into the mind of any candid statesman here, and it is high time that it be dismissed by statesmen in Europe."

Stocks rose two per cent when Seward instructed Dayton that there would be no disruption of the American Union. Down in Montgomery bells were merrily pealing and cannon roared one hundred times to announce the great news that Virginia had joined the Confederacy. If its strength lay in the Mississippi Valley, its prestige was drawn from that state, and one sometimes counts as much as the other in the eyes of the world. Seward was aware of all that he had lost, but the darker the situation the bolder front he assumed. If the storm could not be quelled, the Union must be saved. He would make up his mind to war, bitter as the thought was to him.

President Lincoln's call for troops had included all states that had not seceded. Tennessee, though slow in the matter of secession, was now, in the most fervid and feeling oratory of the day, denouncing the Federal call for troops as wicked and unconstitutional. She had already announced that Northern troops should not pass through her territory in any attack upon the South. Missouri, North Carolina and Arkansas were all showing a marked revolutionary spirit and daily threatening to leave the Union. With the withdrawal of Virginia, to be soon followed by North Carolina, Tennessee and Arkansas, Southern pa-

triotism ran riot. At the theaters in Montgomery, Mobile
and New Orleans they were hissing "Yankee Doodle,"
and promising the North mortar, musket and Beauregard,
in verses that were printed in the various newspapers of
the country and sung throughout the South. The gallant
little Creole's name was on every tongue.

Lincoln and his counselors shrewdly continued to use
every effort to check the secession of other states. Maryland, one of the most celebrated of the Union, began to
be the topic of discussion. Although wedged in between
the two sections, and soon occupied by those she regarded
as her foes, her people, to a great extent, continued firm
in their allegiance to the Southern cause. The correspondent of the London *Times* could not but be aware
of it on his way southward, especially as he crossed the
thresholds of the stately old baronial manors. That the
masters of these would have peremptorily demanded an
Ordinance of Secession but for the position they occupied,
with Federal troops massed in their midst, is seen in their
every movement. Sympathizers with the Confederacy instantly began to wreck the railroads and burn the bridges
within the state in order to render the territory useless in
an attack upon the South. Bitter editorials of Northern
papers also indicated the true position of Maryland. The
New York *Tribune* carried the following diatribe which,
with its astounding threats, grows ludicrous when read
today:

"We hold traitors responsible for the work upon which
they have precipitated us, and we warn them that they
must abide the full penalty. Especially let Maryland and
Virginia look to it, for as they are the greater sinners, so
their punishment will be heavier than that of others. Vir-

ginia is a rich and a beautiful State, the very garden of the Confederacy. But it is a garden that is doomed to be a good deal trampled, and its paths, its boundaries, are likely to be pretty completely obliterated before we have done with it. It has property in houses, in lands, in mines, in forests, in country and in towns, which will need to be taken possession of and equitably cared for. The rebels of that state and of Maryland may not flatter themselves that they can enter upon a war against the Government, and afterward return to quiet and peaceful homes. They choose to play the part of traitors, and they must suffer the penalty. The worn-out race of emasculated First Families must give place to a sturdier people, whose pioneers are now on their way to Washington at this moment in regiments. An allotment of land in Virginia will be a fitting reward to the brave fellows who have gone to fight their country's battles, and Maryland and Virginia, free states, inspired with Northern vigor, may start anew in the race for prosperity and power."

The South was not guilty of all the intemperate speech of the day. People coming from the North had many stories to tell of the war spirit existing in some places there. In New York, though its leaders now favored the preservation of the Union, it seemed slow in getting started, but in abolition centers the spirit had grown as rampant as in the South. "It is impossible," one brought the news to Richmond, "to believe the fury and excitement that reigns in the North." To exterminate the "F. F. V." and lay the South in ashes was the constant threat. Every cargo destined for the South was seized with quantities of arms that Jefferson Davis had already paid for. Provisions for Kentucky coming through Cincinnati were stopped; no more

papers were to be had from the North in the future and all
communication would be entirely suspended. But with all
the sudden upheaval the last would be difficult in a land
that had been bound together by both social and commercial ties. Despite the difference that Russell saw between the people at Cairo, Illinois, and those down below,
despite Abraham Lincoln and Jefferson Davis, there would
be affairs of the heart, and both Jew and Gentile would
trade across the Mason and Dixon line. Since the North's
anvils rang loudly during the war, it would have been
better for the South whose anvils grew cold to have encouraged the last. But spying kept it fearful. The man
who sold it a gun might at the same time be finding out
how few it had. It was stealthy espionage that hurt the
Confederacy more than will ever be known to history.
Throughout, all its unpreparedness and lack of men and
munitions was constantly laid bare to the enemy. Besides
those who made it their regular profession, there were
thousands of Northern men in their midst ostensibly engaged in some occupation. Telegraph and railroad employees were in the majority of instances from the North.
The South's isolation and economic disintegration from the
first began to slowly take place.

The next maneuvers that passed between the two governments in the month of April continued to be outstanding
ones. One came on the eighteenth when the President of
the Confederacy issued a proclamation inviting application for letters of Marque and Reprisal and recommending
the Confederate Congress to grant them. The North was
not referring anything as yet to Congress and took it for
granted that the offer on Jefferson Davis' part had meant
to clear the naval operations of the Confederacy—the little

there was—of the charge of piracy. Suddenly President Lincoln, on the advice of Seward,[1] countered with the proclamation to blockade the Southern ports. With these two resounding war declarations, things narrowed down to a definite understanding, and each side began to boast. They had many qualities in common and one in his own way boasted as much as the other. *"They are all Americans,"* Russell wrote home to his paper. But the feeling with which the average Southerner viewed the ability of the North to compete with the South in any particular, was one of contempt. The "slick little clerks" and "greasy mechanics" would never stand the shock of battle. The Northerner, however, had determination if not so much air and arrogance. They were soon to get better acquainted with each other than they had ever been.

But now war was all that engaged their minds. The blockade furnished a topic for unending discussion and denunciation. Jefferson Davis was well enough aware of its terrible handicap; knew how difficult it would be to arm his troops with the purchasing agents compelled to send their purchases overseas like a fish darting away from the hook. But it was his unvarying method to put the best face on any untoward circumstances in order to give the people stamina. He knew that a leader could sap the spirit of his people by faint-hearted admissions. His speeches often contain an amount of optimism that he himself did not feel; although he was never given to any form of despair. Certain historians have failed to see that he, more than any other connected with the government, kept up the war spirit throughout the Confederacy. If the people scouted the paper blockade and wanted to believe that

[1] Bancroft, vol. II.

England was their friend, it was better than depression. He, too, valued England's good will but never to any blind extent. He knew that all depended upon the spirit of the people. If the women wanted to collect pennies and jewelry and say many prayers for the Confederacy, he knew its worth. To his sympathetic encouragement is due much of the intensity and duration of the war spirit among the women, which, let any deride who may, did as much as anything else to animate the armies of the Confederacy. Pollard, and a small coterie of historians who have never been able to get away from him, failed to perceive that the Confederate President was utilizing every available source of strength in a struggle that he knew was an all unequal one. In the World War, all such methods were encouraged as an incentive to the purchasing of Liberty Bonds and "carrying on." Vast sums were expended merely to keep up the war spirit. Had Jefferson Davis neglected this feature—the persistent inspiriting of his people—no such front would have been put up as suggested recognition to foreign powers. It was this that won their admiration.

The blockade at first furnished a topic of amusement for the people, much of which, no doubt, was feigned by the stout-hearted revolutionists to hide the fear of it. When news of it reached the dinner table of a certain Virginian, the following conversation took place:

"Whom the gods wish to destroy, they first make mad," exclaimed the host, a pompous minister of the Gospel, looking up from his carving.

"Another proof of their increasing insanity," replied one of the guests.

"Are there not brains enough in the Northern cabinet to

know that paper blockades are scouted by the naval powers of the world? Do they not know that France and England will be brought down upon their vessels of war if they attempt to shut those nations out from Southern ports?" said the senator.

"As if England will submit to be shut out from our ports!" the minister's wife exclaimed.

"Cotton is king, Madam; cotton rules the world," said the doctor.

"Besides," said the senator, "it is a contradiction of terms. Lincoln claims possession of the Southern ports as still a part of the United States; and it is unconstitutional to blockade his own ports."

"Pshaw! Europe will never consent to that!" returned the colonel. "There is every reason to believe that the Confederacy will be immediately recognized by the great foreign powers. When we shall command the entire trade of America, our produce will be exchanged for their manufactured articles. We can supply England with all she requires; and it is the most natural thing in the world for her to trade with us. Indeed, it is probable that we may form an alliance with England; we are more closely related to her than to those canting Puritans."

"I would rather have one of the English princes for a king, than be under the Lincoln government," said Mrs. ——.

Some joking about an alliance of the Prince of Wales with a young lady from South Carolina, who was said to have created a rather tender sentiment, ensued, and one gentlemen added, quite patronizingly, "That young Prince who was here was a very modest, intelligent young man. I was quite pleased with his manners and appearance at Richmond." [1]

"Yes," rejoined another of the sovereigns of the New Republic, "I rode fourteen miles to the railway the day he passed by here. I have a great respect for his mother, and on her account I thought I would take a peep at him."

At a later dinner in the minister's home, in reply to a threat on the part of the North to dethrone the effete Squirarchy, the colonel said, "Yes, and if these are the benign results of cultivated intellect, barbarism may blush upon the detection of its unsophisticated innocence and simplicity."

"When Lincoln sees the determination of the South, surely it will soften him in his blind perversity," said the doctor.

"Union!" cried the minister, "Preserve the UNION! Will he even preserve the Union of the *North,* to say nothing about the South? Has not the Union been irremediably destroyed already?"

"It is reported at Richmond that a train of gunpowder is laid under the Capitol at Washington and the White House in order to blow them up, should the Unionists be obliged to vacate the city," said a guest.

"If I could only apply a match to the train of gunpowder," returned Mr. ———, "that vilest of offscouring of creation, Lincoln, would soon be nearer heaven than he would have a chance to be again."

"I wish some one *would* put an end to him," said Mrs. ———, "it would be a benefaction to the country."

"I feel like taking up arms myself, and joining the troops," said the minister.

[1] Edward VII, who visited the country in 1860 as the Prince of Wales.

"Oh, if I could only transform myself into 100,000 men!" exclaimed his wife.[1]

It was thus that rural Virginia made ready for war. With the state's withdrawal from the Union Lincoln and Seward, at the latter's insistence, began more earnestly to stress the preservation of the Union as the cause of the war, and in this they became as one. Slavery, however, as the cause, was daily being brought into prominence by numerous abolition leaders in much of the discussion of Congress. Russell, traveling all through the South, had pronounced it decidedly a constitutional argument with the Southern people. States' Rights was the battle cry and old men caressed their blue cockade, a States' Rights badge, when talking. The shrewd correspondent of the London *Times* had more than once sent word to England that he found a people bent on independence who had never owned a slave. Its political doctrine cemented the South. It would now have been a task for Sisyphus to win it back. But along with other burdens, it had to bear the one of favoring slavery. Sensitive and vexed over the world's condemnation of their domestic institution, and knowing that it was being misrepresented, it began early to devise means to put a stop to the impressions daily created throughout Europe by the North. The *Index* was regarded as its mouthpiece, but Bright and Cobden had means of their own in controverting its influence. Both sections soon began to flood England and France with private representatives and stacks of what is today called propaganda.

Jefferson Davis, however, knew that William Lloyd Garrison, abolitionist of abolitionists, but no advocate of war,

[1] Taken from "Life in the South During the War," by a blockaded British subject.

was a more insidious and reliable force than the Republican party in shaping foreign opinion in this particular. Seward had disclaimed the question altogether. Europe should understand that it was for the Union that this war was on. Sumner was rabid, but his grievance at South Carolina in the Preston Brooks affair had weakened his influence in the matter. His anxiety to see the slaves elevated to the same scale as their masters, and the uncouth, bitter mouthings of Thaddeus Stevens were regarded by foreigners more as an exhibition of hate than a mark of wisdom. That the institution was being misrepresented and misunderstood in Europe gave Jefferson Davis many anxious moments, although the powerful Palmerston had treated it lightly to the disgust of all abolitionists. Certain forms of emancipation as recommended in his speeches before the war were taking definite shape in Jefferson Davis' mind at the present; but not yet, not at the present crisis, could a complete reversal of a social system be undertaken. Nations could commit suicide as well as individuals. But discovering the Pharisaical use the Republicans were now making of the question, he was anxious to eliminate it entirely from the struggle. The Confederate Congress later perfected a bill providing that if the slaves would assist in the defense of their homes and firesides against invasion, they should be given their freedom. There was no other requirement of them. Thus slavery and everything was cast into the scale for independence. This had become the *sine qua non* with the South.

CHAPTER VII

MONTGOMERY

THE SOUTH and Jefferson Davis were now bearing the sole blame of having, in the favorite phrase of the day, "struck the first blow" that started the war between the states. It was, in truth, the act of resisting the first blow and could not logically be regarded as the initiatory step. Seward, after countless, and, those about him sneered, foolish and incoherent, efforts to delay action between the sections, had lost his game. He now had to face the fact of what the world called "a Civil War" in the American Union, a Union that he had boasted was indissoluble; one which, with all its popular government, Edward Everett had contended was the most successful in the world. How humiliating to see it go to pieces before all Europe, especially before England, who derided its lax restrictions in the matter of its franchise, and held its nose at its raw democracies.

In the cabinet it was now accepted that President Lincoln was under the influence of a number of strong leaders in his party, and Seward suspected as much.[1] But though the radicals were putting the officious, self-assertive Secretary down, he haughtily refused to desist from forcing his ideas upon the administration. His struggle for supremacy was to last to the end, with victories and losses of divers variety. The majority of the cabinet resented him, and sought to discredit him; but one can read between

[1] Welles, "Diary."

87

the lines, especially of Welles' Diary, but not intended for
praise, that he was still looked up to. Though several
sought to estrange them, Lincoln was fascinated by his
larger vision and unique personality. Others might at times
come closer to him, but he never quite got over the frank
and naïve inquiry, that if he could not trust his Secretary of State, whom could he trust? Though physically
one was huge and the other diminutive, the large man always looked to the small one in something of the light
that a boy does to an elder brother upon whom he still
relies, even though he must take his perpetual scolding.
There were only instances that he seemed unable to avoid—
and more the pity—in which his party outclassed his Secretary of State. But it was not so difficult for them to keep
together now, since after Sumter Seward himself set his
face towards war. The American Union was the altar at
which he worshiped morn, noon and evening. He would let
Lord Palmerston and his great Queen know that it was as
indissoluble as the universe.

Although war seemed to have started in the Charleston
harbor, Jefferson Davis was greatly relieved that there
were no casualties, and this is in line with his caution
to Beauregard. He believed that war had been forced upon
the South, although in the North it was denied and admitted in the same breath. But war was now the inevitable.
Henceforth, he would resist invasion wherever it appeared.
There were several things he did not want to do in establishing the new government.[1] He did not want the adoption of a new flag, but wanted to keep the old one in the
name of Washington. But when they gave him the new
banner as their chosen colors, he pledged himself in its

[1] "Memoir," vol. II.

defense. To him it became the symbol of Constitutional Liberty. It would pass, but the principle would henceforth prevail in American Government, sealed with the blood of the nation. Wherever reverence for its Constitution is lauded or else demanded, his name must be heard. He did not want to move the capital out of the Mississippi Valley; but though accused of being arbitrary and despotic he yielded to the wishes of the people. After they removed it to Virginia, to become the objective of the enemy, no soul in the Confederacy was more ardently devoted to it and none suffered more in its defense.

Life for him had undergone a complete and harsh reversal, and in all the peril and uncertainty of revolution and war, Varina and her children, more than any others, were to feel the effects of the battered walls of Sumter. She was later to be accused of seeking joint control with him in public affairs by one of the most prejudiced, embittered and brilliant minds of the Confederacy.[1] But at this time he hardly could have said as much. Life was too full of present honors suited to her sex. Still no woman in the provisional capital joined in the public rejoicings and demonstrations with quite as much flair and enthusiasm, and none knew as well what the South was really facing. Not even did the intellectual, alert, and shrewd Mrs. Chesnut, keeping a diary this early, have the political acumen and knowledge possessed by the lady from Briarfield. The former had returned to Montgomery, after the bombardment of the Charleston fortress, full of its details, not one of which was drab or tedious. There were

---

[1] Edward A. Pollard, the brilliant and erratic associate editor of the Richmond *Examiner,* whose accusations against the womanhood of Richmond during the war place him beyond the pale of accepted authority in the instance both of Jefferson Davis and Mrs. Davis.

constant discussions by the two over public matters. On
Varina's arrival in Montgomery they had renewed their
Washington acquaintance, and while still there became intimate friends, to remain so to the end. Victorians, mate-
rialists, religionists—they were as good examples of what
all these in their best sense meant as any of their day.

Montgomery was now the heart of the Confederacy and
with Charleston was the news center of the South. News
reporters from everywhere oscillated between the two
places. After viewing the famous Sumter and acquaint-
ing himself with the details of its capture, the war correspondent of the London *Times* continued his journey to
Montgomery. He had planned an extended tour and in-
spection of the Southern States. As he traveled, he was
amazed at the intensity of the war spirit. He found not
only the leaders but the masses filled with the desire for
independence and determined upon a separate nationality.
"So far, I had certainly no reason to agree with Mr.
Seward that the South would rally around the Stars and
Stripes the instant they were displayed in their sight. To
a man, the people went with their states and had but one
battle cry—States' Rights." And one finds one's self thinking that the famous war correspondent himself, with all
his determination to play fair with both sides, would have
given much to raise his voice at least once for Jefferson
Davis and the Southern Confederacy. It was a shout that
was marshaling vast armies, and possessed a charm that
clings to it today.

Along with the political news, the Englishman had gathered social items as well, and was now pretty well acquainted
with the social status of the two irate nations. Like other
English travelers, he was astonished, after hearing that

everything about the South was bad, to see all the "pale, pretty, svelte" women and tall, fine-faced men of the Carolinas. He was about to commit himself to the "pale, pretty" type, but soon discovered that the much-talked-of land had its Junos as well. Often such types as Varina Howell Davis appeared in its population. The "pale, pretty," a standard type, best describes Varina's sister Maggie, whose manner was the acme of the refined and studied grace of the women of what has been romantically called the Southern Squirarchy. Maggie nibbled her sweets in privacy with the same delicate precision that she did in company. Varina ate hers more greedily, especially if she were hurrying to write a note for Jefferson Davis who did not like to write notes. The young sister at times might have suggested for Varina a slightly less convincing personality. But who, in or out of the Howell household, could take liberties with Mrs. Jefferson Davis? The London *Times* reporter was now to pass upon her. What would he say of her at so critical a juncture?

He was in Montgomery, eager to report the young revolution for all the world's reading and amazement. "A storm bird of battles," Varina names him in her "Memoir," to whom the names of Sebastopol, Crimea and Lucknow were familiar words. It was a novel sight to him to witness a revolution taking place in such an orderly, dignified and socially brilliant manner. The whole movement fascinated him. Nothing like it had ever occurred in history. Jefferson Davis, too, stirred his fancy. What kind of man was he that people cheered at the mention of his name? And what kind of people were these Southerners, who had been regarded as behind in world progress, that a revolution could occur in such a decent and lofty manner? The joyous-

ness and earnestness with which they set about to establish
their new government was a thing to marvel at.   It was
decidedly the best story of the middle nineteenth century,
and would make numberless choice and racy chapters for the
world's entertainment.   And finally his own country, he half-
suspected, was in sympathy with the young republic. Besides
having cotton, and favoring free trade, or at least satisfactory free trade, if any portion of America was English,
he felt that it was here.   Secretly sympathizing, one can but
suspect, with the new government, he guarded the fact and it
is generally an unbiased story that he endeavored to send to
the outside world.

It was known that Seward had early kept his eye on the
shrewd, discerning representative of the great London
paper—a paper that had much to do with making premiers
and ministers. No one knew its influence better than Seward,
and on occasions he could be a rare diplomat.   The Southerners had heard of much "wining and dining" of Russell
on the part of the arch and resourceful Republican autocrat.
If the war correspondent of the London *Times* liked cards,
every one played whist.   If he liked dinners, these were frequent.   "Seward is fêting the outsiders—the cousin of Napoleon and Russell, the famous reporter of the London
Times," had reached Southern ears more than once, one
gathers from records of the day.[1]   In Montgomery the
English reporter was soon discovered and pointed out to be
watched and often taken to task, but if possible to be won
over to the Southern point of view.   One thing was apparent, he notes with a mixture of humor and irritation,
they would not stoop to conquer, as tight box as
they were in.   Still he found the haughty Southerner the

1 Chesnut.

soul of graciousness, even if he did lack tact. It was this naïve and tactless sincerity, mixed with suavity and good breeding, that he found so beguiling. In time, tossed between the Scylla and Charybdis of the Southerner's appealing personality and the "Sewardian" wile that, too, had its subtle charm, the lynx-eyed near-satirist resorted to some taunt and ridicule of everything and everybody concerned, causing both sides to flare up at his deft but deadly touches. These hid a deeper meaning than their manner inferred and were resented by more than one whom he thought too dense to understand. It is evident, however, that he felt the charm of the young Southern Republic. He noted with amazement the easy self-confidence of both the official and unofficial classes. In conversation with more than one young enthusiast, he was found asking how a people could be so light-hearted when the Northern press was predicting dire failure for the new government.

But not every paper in the North was so optimistic about the outcome. The influential Greeley was saying in editorial comment that the young Southern men were better bred and better educated than those of the North and would make better fighting men. They had not boxed and fenced and ridden to hounds all their lives not to know what a blow on the body meant. And as for spirit, Russell reported that in comparison with the Northern temperament they were as "fire to ice." The comparison was nowhere more pronounced than in the Alabama Capital among both men and women. Of the latter, there was none that he was more anxious to meet than the wife of Jefferson Davis. On arriving, he seized the first opportunity to see her. Contrary to what others of the North had told him of the South, the aristocratic circles of Washington had informed

him that he would meet lovely women when he came South.
Fashionable society there had taken special pains to describe
Varina. He was to see her now for himself at one of
her afternoon receptions. The President's family had removed from the Exchange Hotel to the house the citizens of Montgomery had set apart for the White House,
and Varina was once more in the midst of entertaining.
It was with an extra smoothing of his cravat and a last
glance in his mirror that the Englishman got himself ready
for her reception. He had seen many types of men and
women in his wanderings in the train of war. He instantly saw a difference between Jefferson Davis and the
more boastful spirits, both at Washington and Montgomery. It was his business to scrutinize certain men and
women closely, and it was of Varina Howell Davis that
he wrote for all the world to read that she "was a comely,
sprightly woman, verging on matronhood, of good figure
and manners, well dressed, ladylike and clever"; that she
"exercised considerable influence in Washington," where he
had met "many of her friends"; that she remembered to
"invite him to come back in the evening when he would find
the President at home." Few women of history have won
from a critic as many fair-meaning adjectives as he employed
in describing her, and he was not lavish with his compliments, either of men or women. He was describing her
for the world's reading and if there had been an especially
hard expression about the mouth or any other detracting
feature he would have been certain to see it. What he did
see was that she was "well mannered, ladylike and clever."
He did not seem to hold it against her, as Pollard would
vehemently have done, that "she was inclined to be angry
over a report that the Republican government had offered

a reward for the head of that arch-rebel, Jefferson Davis."
Perhaps he thought she had the right. "They are quite
capable of such acts," he quotes her saying with significant
emphasis.

He had now talked face to face with the Confederacy's
first lady and in these light strokes of his hurried pen is
sketched the attractive, well-bred, and high-spirited woman
that leaders of society at the National Capital had prepared him to see. With eyes and ears open for the slightest
sign in taking the measure of the people he says, "They were
now calling her 'Queen Varina.'" It sounded nearly as
well to the ears as Queen Victoria. He, furthermore, sets
down that the purely aristocratic element of the Provisional
Capital, especially the feminine portion, was monarchically
inclined. They preferred an English Prince any time to
reunion with the "Lincolnites" he more than once infers in
his correspondence. Allowing much for diplomacy, which he
suspected, he believed them serious. He had heard the
matter discussed, and in no jest, by the landed gentry of
South Carolina where the glamor of it was undeniable.
Here in the deeper South, women at least were fascinated
with the thought. It amused him, but it is evident that he
liked it since he frequently left off telling his story to make
note of their many allusions to it. It evidently appealed to
his vanity that the Southerners wished to be like the English and wanted to be told that they were.

He lost nothing of the stirring pageant about him, and
not only made it his duty to study Varina, but it was his
opportunity to observe the Southern women en masse.
He had never seen quite the type of woman that he had met
in Southern circles at Washington, and thus far throughout
the Confederacy. It could not be so easily interpreted but

he soon suspected that underneath all the soft, clinging appeal and coy reserve there was a sharp self-assertiveness and a something that showed its teeth between set lips. He was satisfied that from Varina down, the women of the newly-formed Republic would stand the shock of war as well as their men. More than once on his Southern tour with an odd little smile he thought of Seward and his "glorious Union."

With a nose for all varieties of news he was more intent for the present upon social matters than political theories. He noted that Varina "seemed to be a great favorite with those around her." He did, however, hear one say in a tone in which he evidently thought he discovered a tinge of jealousy, "It must be nice to be the President's wife, and the first lady of the Confederacy." One cannot say, even after studying her, whether or not it pleased her when they called her "Queen Varina." It pleased her, however, that they were willing to do so. But since she knew that Jefferson Davis objected to all such talk as fanciful and was annoyed by it, it is very probable that she put her finger warningly on her lips whenever they gave her that title. As strange as it may sound to some ears, Varina was afraid of her husband. It was not fear of him as one with whom she would never assert herself, and whimsically enough at times, but she did not like to appear at a disadvantage in his eyes and throughout life dreaded for him to discover that she had made a mistake. Her "Memoir" reveals many such instances.

Although she now treated the idea of a Southern monarchy humorously, there is the story, told in all seriousness, by Rear Admiral D. D. Porter to Gideon Welles, Secretary of the Navy in Lincoln's Cabinet. Welles, sometimes given

to a little passing gossip, tells us that on the evening after
the reception of the news that South Carolina had passed
an Ordinance of Secession, Porter, a friend and frequent
visitor, was at Senator Jefferson Davis' home in Washington where a number of Southern leaders had gathered to
discuss the startling news. The weather was inclement, and
"Mrs. Davis came downstairs all wrapped up and bonneted
to go out." Seeing him in the company, she gayly accosted
him relative to the "glorious news." South Carolina had
done the great thing, and she was "going to see President
Buchanan and congratulate him." The weather was bad
and young Porter secured a hack and went with her. On
the way he inquired of her why she was "so elated over the
news," when Varina told him that she "wanted to get out
of the old government; that they would have a monarchy in
the South and gentlemen to fill official positions." Varina
was hearing similar remarks today, but she must not herself
indulge in such chimeras if she ever meant more than indulging in a little gay banter with the future Rear Admiral
of the Federal Fleet. For her sex at that period, she was a
good politician, and was now making every effort to hearten
the new government and to popularize it with her Northern
friends in Washington. "Should young Major Emory come
South," Mrs. Chesnut tells us, "he would have a good time."
"Mrs. Davis adores Mrs. Emory." The remark implies that
Varina was not only fond of her friends in Washington, but
had an eye to winning them for the Southern cause. If
young Emory were coming to join the Confederacy, one suspects that she would have done her best, unless she believed
him wholly unfitted for high position, to see that he got a
good place in the army. Women of every rank in history
have been known to do as much for their friends.

That she was not to have some part and influence in matters pertaining to the future of the new government with which she was so closely and intimately associated, is an unnatural exaction, one that no fair-minded historian wishes to make. However, she did not this early openly stress her opinions and preferences. How much she did secretly will never quite be known, since she knew that in her world it injured women socially to take any open part in public affairs. If in time she went beyond this, her attitude was always more or less affected by this restriction. How much the war would do for women was another matter, but at present they were a hothouse variety that came high. Martha Washington was the accepted model, though one suspects that Varina, subconsciously at least, thought of woman as exemplified in Queen Victoria's privileges. For the present she was engaged largely with social affairs. At a certain reception, while in Montgomery, a gay participant [1] records her "in fine spirits," and again, "I drove out with Mrs. Davis. She finds playing Mrs. President of this small Confederacy slow work after leaving such friends as Mrs. Emory and Mrs. Joe Johnston in Washington. I do not blame her. The wrench has been awful with us all, but we don't mean to be turned into pillars of salt." It was proof that the old life at Washington had been very pleasant for this particular group of brilliant Southern women. But Varina early accepted the responsibilities of her position. Accustomed to a great deal of personal entertainment in the past, she was now using it more in the interests of the Confederacy. She knew what it meant in public life and one of her keen regrets was that

[1] Chesnut.

circumstances prevented it at times during the war.[1] At present there was a lavish hospitality, not only for the town people, but for the many strangers flocking to the Alabama Capital. Every celebrity in the South at times was there. To these, when not giving receptions, she constantly gave luncheons and dinners. Although it was not her first aspiration, she had at times a woman's ambition to excel in purely social matters. On May 20th, in Montgomery, we find her giving a luncheon that for elegance attracted the attention of her Charleston friends. "Nothing in their city had ever surpassed it," and Varina was "as nice as her luncheon." "She is always clever" and in some moods "I do not know so pleasant a person." [2]

For Varina, the thorns had not begun to grow. She took part in all the gayety of the city, and since war, even with the outburst at Charleston, was not considered a certainty, this idle and lavish society was at times full of fun and frolic. Jefferson Davis took his place in it in a quiet, somewhat absent-minded way. Varina knew his indifference to it in Washington. Still he was not without social charm and women treasured the smallest attention from him.

Of the social life of the first Capital of the Confederacy, Mrs. Wigfall, wife of Senator Wigfall, a member of the Provisional Government, wrote to her daughter Louise in Texas, "Such dinners at the Bibbs', such balls at the Pollards', and such receptions at Governor Moore's mansion." Mrs. Chesnut, too, at the time recorded that the Confederate Capital was gay and confident. It was not many months old, but participants said that for political spirit and noise

[1] "Memoir," vol. II.
[2] Chesnut.

it was a small edition of Washington.[1]   The old families
at times were appalled at the sight of their placid little
city filled with clamor and confusion.   Russell, who had
seen many foreign cities in a state of distraction, admits
that it at times got on his own war-hardened nerves.

Judging from Varina's eager participation in it, one
might get the impression that she was looking alone to
the social side of her high position; but the impression
fades when we are told that she took the trip, full of hardships and dangers, to Pensacola and other points with her
husband to examine the coast defenses of the Confederacy.
It was an undertaking that taxed the energies of the highly
energetic London *Times* reporter, who was taking the same
trip.   All up and down the labyrinthine forest filled with
poisonous insects of many varieties, over sloughs and lakes
and in range of the Union guns from Fort Pickens, she
went with Jefferson Davis in the very first days of the
Confederacy to inspect General Bragg's army.   Again we
hear her making to her friend, Mrs. Chesnut, one of the
sagest and most incisive observations recorded of that day.
With a deeper insight into the situation than was common
to the women about her, and evidently in rebuke of some
exacting demand of an epicure, a growing tribe among the
Southern aristocrats, she observed with a contemptuous
purse of the lips, "I fancy these dainty folk will live to regret losing even the fare of the Montgomery hotels."   Could
Lee, could Jefferson Davis himself, have said better?   And
yet one suspects that she had heard some such comment
fall from the latter's lips.   He had a more thorough knowledge of the situation than any about him, and it was like him

[1] "Four Years in Rebel Capitals," by De Leon.

to expect men to forget self in the discharge of duty. There was always a close exchange of confidences between husband and wife and many of Varina's more virile ideas and expressions show his influence.

For all the strangeness and distractions of their new position, they were happy. Varina's finest art lay in her ability to create an atmosphere of ease and comfort. People liked to be in her company, and for a husband with nerves like Jefferson Davis' this was good fortune indeed. The modest, two-story mansion that had been set apart for them and proudly called the White House of the Confederacy, soon became known to the people of the city as a place where one could find hospitable entertainment any day of the week. The house still stands and is one of Montgomery's shrines where they will show you, among other mementos, a high-back chair that Jefferson Davis sat in. Much imitation of the old government at Washington went on in the proceedings of the new government, both officially and socially, and certainly they declared their new capital must have a "White House." It was here that Jefferson Davis, after the day's strenuous labor, played with his children, Margaret, Jefferson and baby Joe, all born in Washington. He took great pleasure in them and they were at perfect ease in his company. Many pretty stories are preserved of them, and it was humorously declared that, barring the military demonstrations, their voices were the most incessant sounds in the city. Of the part that Varina took in the social life of the Confederacy's first capital, and in the stirring scenes daily enacted around her, she writes with delicacy and restraint. One finds nowhere any great claim that she made either to superiority or social prestige, nor any bid for popularity. But it had always been hard for her to resist opportunities of being diverted. Her liberal disposition in this respect was one of the things for which she later was criticized.

CHAPTER VIII

THE STREETS OF BALTIMORE

APRIL was passing, and, as yet, there had been no blood shed in the strife that had dismembered the nation. In the North, however, the word Sumter was like a hot coal on the tongue. It was the first definite note of the coming strife that had reached its people, and there had been a speedy response from Pennsylvania and Massachusetts to President Lincoln's call for troops. The city of New York at first was slow to respond, but finally the recruiting there got under way. But the State had not fully made up its mind as to war. The Massachusetts and Pennsylvania regiments, coming more under the spell of the reformers and radicals, were already on their way South. On April 19th they had passed the Mason and Dixon Line and a skirmish, more of the nature of a street fight than an encounter, took place in Baltimore between a mixed crowd and the troops of the 6th Massachusetts Regiment. The latter were passing through on their way to Washington, and had been told that they were sent South to put down the rebellion. They did not know what it all was about, but the flag had been fired on "down in Sou' Kerlina," and the rebels under Jefferson Davis were about to capture Washington.

In the face of Governor Hicks' protest that the soil of Maryland should not be used by the Federal government in hostilities against the South, the presence of the troops had greatly incensed the people of Baltimore. The state in official circles in some instances had assumed a neutral position. It was known that any armed resistance, exposed as it was to the Federal army, would result in immediate ruin to the whole state. The neutrals, however, were bitterly criticized and condemned by the staunch Southerners, who invariably belonged to the upper class. These had a strong following among the poor whites of the city and the riot was begun principally by the "Plug Uglies," a name given to the rowdy element, though a number of young sons of the city's best families joined the fight before it was over. During the collision, the people were further outraged when R. W. Davis, a prominent citizen, not in any way connected with it, was mortally wounded by a fusillade of revengeful shots from a squad of Federal troops. The people resented what they termed the willful murder of one of their best citizens and instantly demanded of Governor Hicks to call the Legislature in session and pass on an Ordinance of Secession. The affair aroused so much indignation that one could not long be in doubt as to the nature of public sentiment. The war correspondent of the London *Times,* who visited the city both before and after the collision, found it intensely Southern, especially in aristocratic circles. Old Marylanders held parleys of their own; their young sons formed the Maryland Guards. Little, in all the military array of the Southern Confederacy, outshone the Maryland Zouaves when they appeared in the camps at Richmond. A corps *d'élite,* the flashing blue and orange of their uniforms and gallant, confident air, charmed every eye.

The news that the streets of Baltimore had been wet with the first blood of the war stirred the country, both in the North and South, as even the resistance in the

Charleston Harbor had not done. The first clash of arms did much to inspire the ringing Southern song, "My Maryland," which became one of the stirring marching songs of the Confederacy. Retain the state as the North might, its fervor and romance belonged to the South. Many English writers who were in the country at the time noted the dark mood of the people at the predicament they found themselves in, and Lord John Russell, British Minister of Foreign Affairs, doubtless had unofficial communications in his morning's mail from across the seas. Somewhere in a long closed secret draw of Whitehall a batch of yellowed papers may yet be found that would prove for all time that but for the presence of the Federal army, Maryland would have accomplished secession. In spirit she did. She might long since have come to regard her failure to do so as a blessing in disguise, but her historical truths should be sacred to the whole country. No exploit of Bruce nor of Cromwell is resented by England.

Baltimore could not forget her dead, and Governor Hicks, urged by the citizens, demanded of President Lincoln a second time not to send troops through the state. The spirit of the people greatly incensed the Federal authorities, who undiplomatically assumed power to punish any who opposed them. It was not diplomacy but force that the Republicans were using in subduing Maryland. It took no seer to prophesy what the spirit of Reconstruction would be in the South after the war. The tree was now blooming for the bitter fruit to come; and one sometimes doubts if Lincoln, though urged and abetted by Seward, could have rooted it up.

The Federals now had Maryland intimidated. Northern troops also held Fortress Monroe, which had been indis-

creetly reenforced before Virginia had withdrawn from the
Union. Troops also were in Missouri and other places along
the border states. Maryland had no military connection with
the states below her, and some of her middle class population were averse to secession, and more in sympathy with
the working classes of the North. The position of the state
became one of anxiety to both North and South. The
North, however, had the advantage, and the state's investment by Northern troops, which closed around it like a
vise, was soon complete. The city of Baltimore writhed
under the bayoneted hand that held them in submission.
Old citizens, the reporter for the London *Times* wrote
home, compared its subjugation to anything that had
ever occurred in Venice, Warsaw or Rome. Armed
forces began to curtail the state's activities in behalf of
the Confederacy. Still, much has been and still could be
written of its daring and untiring efforts to aid the Southern
Confederacy with which it was so closely allied in blood and
tradition. There is little more romantic in history than
the stealthy midnight burning of its bridges and the secret
destruction of its railroads, in the face of armed forces, to
prevent the invasion of the South. Old residents still tell
us of the spirit, "make the enemy fear you," that existed
among the women as they waved their new-made flags in
the face of the foe. These, in defiance of every threat,
which was sometimes accompanied with arrest, made uniforms for the Southern army and, walked through the lines
with their bodies weighted down, under their great hoops,
with powder, caps and even side arms. Often a full Confederate suit that had been made the day before was worn
under their wide skirts and conveyed to some Southern
soldier across the lines. Children dressed their dolls in the

colors of the Confederacy: and women wore the colors on their breasts and in their hair. "See those Baltimore boys," a Georgia soldier exclaimed. "They have given up home, friends and wealth to fight for the South. If my Colonel didn't insist that I was useful where I am, I'd take a musket among them. I like that sort of stock." The correspondent of the London *Times* wrote to his paper, "I was visited by some gentlemen of Baltimore who were highly delighted at the news of the bombardment of Sumter." "De gen'lemen of Baltimore will be quite glad of it," the barber confided to him. Later, when passing through Annapolis, he wrote that the people "came down to the tea table and talked secession," but "their spirit has been broken by the Federal occupation."

The Federals now boasted that they would "give the rebels a hot time of it." Still, with all the bluster and swagger that the country belonged to them—there was a conspicuous absence of United States flags on the private buildings of Baltimore, and the front doors of the handsome homes were kept closed. But Federal occupation wrought havoc with the peace of the city. The streets were filled with sullen faces, and people were daily thrown in jail for displaying the Confederate colors, or for any act that indicated their sympathy with the Southern cause. Women, however, continued to flaunt the significant white and red and took the consequences. Maryland's famous heroine, the beautiful Hetty Cary, whose daring won from one Federal officer the keys of the city, was arrested and imprisoned by another for persisting in wearing the Confederate colors. Her portrait should hang in Maryland's Hall of Fame. There were others who suffered every indignity. Noncombatants, when suspected of loyalty to the

Confederacy, were convicted without a hearing. "Remember the cells of Fort McHenry," became a war cry.

"See how we treat the Plug Uglies," a Federal conductor on the train said, as he showed the correspondent of the London *Times* windows along the route battered by Federal shot. Seward was boasting that he could touch a button and imprison every rebel sympathizer in the country, but in the instance of women he refused to take any part in their punishment.

The same opposition to troops entering the state arose in Kentucky and in Missouri, although the authorities at Washington had learned to be more diplomatic in such matter. Little, however, in all the hot indignation and wordy defiance of the day has a more decisive ring than one catches in the reply of the Governor of Missouri to President Lincoln's call for troops: "Your requisition, in my judgment, is illegal, unconstitutional and revolutionary in its object, inhuman and diabolical. Not one man will the State of Missouri furnish to carry on any such unholy crusade." But by degrees Federal authorities pushed their troops forward all along the border states and soon had them largely in their power. Still a majority of the people sympathized with the Confederacy, and no more intense loyalty to it was found anywhere in its armies than in the stanch border regiments that marched to its defense.

After Maryland was invested with Northern troops, its young men continued to make their way down to join Johnston and Beauregard; and women continued to secretly spend their time scraping lint and making bandages for the wounded of the Southern army. This they kept up throughout the war. The nature of the people, both in the North and South, puzzled English subjects in the country. These people in many respects had been one. What lack of genius and statesmanship, if not of amity, had brought war between them? Seward, it is clear, felt humiliated that all Europe was witnessing the utter failure and dissolution of the great experiment in democratic government, but if any other connected with the Federal Union felt the mortification, it is not recorded. A would-be premier and dictator, as some ridiculed, he would have liked better than all else to show Europe that a national spirit could yet be aroused in the American Union, even if it had to be accomplished by the means of a divided household uniting in the face of an outside foe. But while he juggled with the situation, and was being laughed at for his pains, blood had been spilt and war in his boasted Union had been set on foot by rash intemperate counselors.

The riot at Baltimore aroused as much feeling in the North as in the South. The papers there used it as a torch to fire the passions of the people and increase enlistment. The South has always been accused of furnishing the fire, but there were threats in the leading Northern papers which "sound, one wrote, like the implacable malevolence of the lower regions." [1] Besides the bitter unstatesmanlike utterances with which the speeches abound, there are newspaper threats that for downright cruelty surpass any utterances heard in the South, where the "fire eaters" were said to dwell. The historian has failed to sound the note of persecution towards the Southern section of the country, and in fact, towards everything Democratic, either North or South. Among Northern Democrats free speech was always met with severe rebuke and imprisonment if it in any way sought justice for the South.

[1] "Life in the South," by a blockaded British subject.

Heretical fires may have been, in moments of fanatical passion, suggested by the reformers; but political hands had applied the torch.

One cannot believe that calamities that occur in governmental affairs are ever the so-called blessings in disguise. There is always, as Seward unsuccessfully claimed to the radicals of his time, a better way. True statesmanship finds ways and means to prevent evil. Certainly the Federal government displayed as little of this in dealing with the present crisis as did George III in the instance of the American Colonies. The visionary, idealistic but erratic and overbearing Secretary of State caught the light, but was not strong enough, or else was too dogmatic, to make others see it. With the best brains and spirit of compromise in his party his failure to bring others to his view embittered him. Historians have described his methods but have been silent about his motives. It is to Lincoln's credit, though at times unable to resist the demands of the radicals of his party, that in his heart he preferred Seward, and in the end preferred his views as to the restoration of the South.

After hostilities had broken out in the streets of Baltimore, Jefferson Davis accepted the situation with a hard compression of the lips. He had been from the first aghast at the thought of war, had hoped much from the Peace Commission he had sent to Washington, but war had come as he feared, and he would wage it to the bitter end. And like the true and artful leader, he told his people in every utterance that they could win. He counted heavily on the spirit of the people, upon that miraculous something that the spirit sometimes accomplishes. His hope was that their stubborn resistance might in time tire out the North, the North that had so many times admitted the right of secession.

With the reenforcement of Sumter, the sudden Federal call for 75,000 troops, blood on the streets of Baltimore, and statesmanship fled the Union, there was no longer a possibility of any amicable relations being established between the two sections. More troops for Johnston and Beauregard were rushed to Virginia, weaken as it might the lower areas for the future, and more enthusiasm throughout the South, the cheering, marching, singing South that had only a thimbleful of powder in its horn. But sing it would, and the stirring strains of "Dixie," and of the "Bonnie Blue Flag," were in a few days to be followed by the heartbreaking new song "My Maryland." There was now as much music on the air as there had been secession oratory. The Confederacy was moving in one vast volume, and Russell, after his tour of the South, came back to Washington and reported to the London *Times* that the people there were vowing eternal separation from the North. Lord Lyons, M. Mercier and the famous London *Times* reporter were now having little private dinners of their own to which Seward was not invited.

CHAPTER IX

WAR SETTLES UPON THE COUNTRY

THE National Capital was the lode that drew all Northern feet, and once under way the Federal army continued to gather in vast numbers. Washington was safe, though nobody in the city believed it. Troops could not arrive fast enough to allay their fears. The Federal authorities had worried over the seemingly slow response of the 7th New York; but with its arrival "the glorious uprising," as Northern journals called it, began. Since it must take war to preserve the Union, Seward had now become as active as any Republican who had denounced the South in reckless speech in the halls of Congress. In fact, with all their dictation, the heavy task of carrying on the war was laid upon Seward and Lincoln. Their animosity was of a different nature from that of the radicals who seemed to revel in the thought of war. Seward would have resorted to any measure to prevent the dissolution of the Union. A foreign war was a small price to pay for such an end. In his own state the war spirit had not flared up, as it were, in a night, and it is certain that he had, at first, approved of its slow appearance. As a fact the people of New York were never in the war in any spirit to punish the South. Industrialism had set in in the North and greed and avarice had made it eager to hold the cotton lands. Factories did not mean much to the North without the South. To keep this hold upon its prosperity, the South must be retained, and for political reasons the West must be republicanized, even if it took war between the states to accomplish it. This was the harsh and deeplaid policy of the Republican party under whose control all forces had now united to whip the South back into the Union.

So the troops continued to gather, since the people generally furnish the emotional fervor for the powers above them. Still Russell saw women in New York throwing stones at the recruiters, and at times there was open rebellion against enlistment in the city. He had, furthermore, peeped into the Federal military rolls and found that only two out of every twelve were native-born Americans. Many who talked to him at Manassas could scarcely speak enough English to be understood. "That our young Southern gentlemen would be called on to fight such creatures!" the wife of a Virginia minister exclaimed. But May was not fully in bloom along the Potomac before Washington began filling up with fine American troops. The beautiful environs of the city, where Rock Creek wound its woodland course, were a mass of fragrant bloom; but its streets were littered and dusty and filled with the noise of the fife and drum. The city's danger all along had been overestimated, and gossip had it that the Federal government and the Lincoln household were ready to fly from the Capital at every alarming report from the South. The Confederates believed, and in this the Charleston *Mercury* agreed, that it was unwise to lead an attack on the Union capital. Its editor hoped that President Davis would not attempt it. Nor was it his policy. As far in the present matter as Jefferson Davis wished to go was to protect the Confederacy's interest in Maryland.[1] He had sent word to that effect after the riot at Baltimore. The fact should not be overlooked that the Confederacy had,

[1] "Jefferson Davis, Constitutionalist."

at the outset, disclaimed a war of invasion, and it is evident
that there was no desire to attack and capture Washington at
that time.   Circumstances that later might make invasion
desirable were not then foreseen.   The Southern policy was
not now one of aggression, but of resistance.   All the South
now desired, as Jefferson Davis had said, and as Buchanan
had previously pointed out, was to be let alone to achieve its
destiny in its own way.

While Washington was in a state of hysteria, exciting incidents occurred here and there in Virginia.   No sooner than
the state had seceded than local hostilities began.   On April
24th, Richmond, before it had become the Capital, was
thrown into a panic by the news that the *Pawnee* was steam-
ing up the James to attack the city.   The great bell at the
State House suddenly began to toll, causing both men and
women to rush from the churches during morning services.
The few troops in the city hastily assembled.   Other young
men armed themselves with any weapons they could procure, and the old men carried little baskets full of stones to
throw at the invaders.   Women, alarmed and trembling,
gathered in knots upon the streets; but did not neglect to denounce the impudent Yankee for daring to pollute the sacred
waters of the James with his presence.   The excitement
soon subsided to leave among them a half humorous story
dubbed, *"Pawnee Sunday."*   This and similar rumors that
the Federal gunboats were attempting to land troops and
attack the towns at various points on the James and the
Rappahannock served to hasten preparations for war.   At
the Virginia fort, volunteer militia were gathering to resist
any demonstration on the part of the reenforced garrison.

The state described by the New York *Tribune* as "the
gardenspot of the Confederacy," became quite early in the

conflict the battle-ground of the Southern Republic. During the early hostilities, the capture and occupation of Harper's Ferry, the scene of the famous John Brown invasion, occurred on the 18th of April. Virginia troops made the attack, and its abandonment by the Federals elated the people throughout the state. The destruction of the arms and munitions, however, by the Federal garrison before it gave up the fort, robbed the gallant Turner Ashby and his men of some of the sweets of victory. As out of date as the guns were, they were better than none in a blockaded country.

For much of the time during the spring, hostilities in the state were confined to slight collisions between the gunboats and the Confederates on shore. These, in many instances, amounted to no more than the throwing of stones and the firing of cannon between the boats and the land batteries. However, the powder and rock battles were occasions of great excitement in the neighborhoods where they occurred and served greatly to arouse the war spirit of the people.

"Who will protect you when the men are away?" a young Virginia country girl was asked. "We will protect ourselves," she replied, coolly displaying a pistol that was given her by her brother. "As long as our men can pull the trigger of a gun we will resist." Thus numerous, piquant stories that interpret the people's attitude and spirit multiplied to be recorded by the hundreds in such publications as "Campfire and Battle-field" and the various memoirs and reminiscences of the war. In a skirmish at Aquia Creek between the people and the boats *Pawnee* and *Freeborn* on the river, father, son and grandson were found fighting side by side. Hearing that her husband was in town and not knowing that he had been sent there on duty, a woman cried, "If they are fighting on the Creek, what is my husband doing here?" It was during this skirmish that a company of young Tennesseeans, suddenly arriving, attracted the attention of a Virginia bystander. Their grandfathers, they told him, had been with Andrew Jackson at New Orleans. The Virginian's admiration grew when one of them, tall, and as lithe as a young sapling, settled his knapsack more comfortably at his side and asked, "How far is it to Mr. Lincoln?" On being told that it was seventy-five miles, he replied, "Well, boys, we will be there tomorrow." Another good story selected from many of its kind runs that on seeing them detailing picket guards for duty near Harper's Ferry, a tall, lank, young soldier, known in the army as "Po' white," exclaimed in utter disgust, "What's the use of gwine out thar to keep everybody off? We all kem here to have a fight with them Yankees an' if you send fellers out thar to skeer 'em off, how in thunder air we ever gwine to hev a scrimmage with 'em?"

But with all the varied preparation and boasting on both sides, not a single collision had so far occurred that was of sufficient importance to be listed as a battle. Not before the roar of Big Bethel that came over the James and Appomattox on June 10th, where the North Carolinians led the fray, could it be said that there had been any real fighting. Still every fatal clash between the people, such as Jackson defending with his life the Confederate flag waving over his hotel at Alexandria, and the various sharp conflicts with an occasional loss of life along the Rappahannock and other places, served to increase the volunteer army of Virginia. Its women, too, knew the part they were to play. These lost no time in seeking out Jackson's widow and orphans whom they took under their care and protection.

CHAPTER X

THE war correspondent of the London *Times* had presented both Jefferson Davis and Varina in a favorable light to England and the other European nations. In the former's dull, slate-colored suit he did not see the carefully dressed United States Senator that Seward had prepared him to meet; but he immediately saw enough to place him in the most exclusive class of Americans. So had M. Mercier to M. Thouvenel, French Minister of Foreign Affairs, so had many others. Varina was elated and fluttered a little over the good inpression they were making on other nations, especially on England. She was shrewd enough to know its value to the Confederacy. Social affairs, however, in the Confederate Capital were taking up much of her time. They had named a boat up at Charleston for her and there was much to make her happy.[1] But while adjusting herself to her new rôle, holding state levees and giving numerous luncheons and dinners, she was still deeply interested in public affairs. With the dinner guests she constantly discussed them. Nothing interested the Southerners more than the foreign attitude towards the South. Dreams of a western empire were then slowly taking shape at the Court of Napoleon, some of which in time slightly affected the Confederacy. England's interest in the American quarrel was to a large extent of a social nature. Still both England and

[1] *The Lady Davis.*

117

France, from standpoints of their material welfare, were interested. The latter generally echoed the former's policy in the matter, but lure of empire made it more eager at times for some participation.[1] The Quai D'Orsay was just across the channel from Whitehall and a mutual understanding had shortened the distance. Both the Queen and Palmerston were known for their sympathy with weaker nations, and some communication had passed between them relative to the American situation. Then suddenly without the least warning came the great sensation that stirred and nonplussed the administration at Washington for days.

Jefferson Davis was still in Montgomery perfecting the military organization of the Confederacy, when news was received that Queen Victoria, in a Royal Proclamation issued on May 13th, had recognized the war between the American States and had declared the Southern Confederacy a belligerent power. Though not the hoped-for recognition, for England was more guarded in her declaration than the North gave her credit for, it held out hopes to the Southerners of her future favor. Jefferson Davis was disappointed but not surprised. He had shared the hope of his people in the matter of recognition; but as well or better perhaps than any man in America, he knew England. Knew her to be one of the most cautious and far-seeing nations upon the globe. Still he valued the many advantages of the Proclamation, and some, at least, were of a vital nature. On the whole it seemed to be a victory. Southern patriotism in fervid speech and varied demonstration broke out afresh. Bonfires lit the skies at night, and cannon were fired for days to announce the great news. The Federal government

[1] Napoleon III during the last year of the Confederacy, placed Maximilian and Carlotta on the throne in Mexico.

at Washington, with Seward for its most rampant mouthpiece, was bitterly incensed with her Majesty, Palmerston and all England as well. The outburst of anger in Washington made the Southerners feel that in the matter they had been greatly preferred by the foreign powers. Seward continued to rave. Lincoln, with no such ability to relieve himself, was gloomy, all unable to get off his customary joke, and reported drunk. This is not regarded as true of President Lincoln. Historians, however, who take such keen delight in citing the harsh criticism of Jefferson Davis by his own people seem to forget that Lincoln was constantly an object of misrepresentation and ridicule by his own party. Only the victory of the Federal armies saved him from obloquy and oblivion by a world that looks askance at failure, since he did not hold the affection of his people in life that the Southern people gave Jefferson Davis. Leaders and politicians, towards the end, made the Confederate President the excuse for all their failures; but the historian mistakes when he says the great body of the people withheld their love and allegiance. It was the magnetism of his name that in '64 made Lee's last great army, and in the winter of the same year they were still shouting his name in the streets. Truth compels one to say that had it not been for Jefferson Davis' hold upon the people, there would have been no such victories as Cold Harbor and the Wilderness and the later glory of Robert E. Lee to point to in Confederate history.

The Republicans continued to bitterly denounce England for the Proclamation. They did not at first seem to see that it was largely a declaration of her neutrality. There was something high-handed about it that inferred a rebuke. No longer did the North have the right to call the South traitors. And more, Jefferson Davis and Robert E. Lee's heads were safe. Seward contemptuously disclaimed any necessity for any interference in the matter. The American Union was a civilized nation. He began even to make threats. The whole affair was getting into an irremediable mess, try as he may to see a way out. Deep in his heart he loved the South—subconscious memories were sometimes stirred of the pay-school offered him when he lived in Georgia a lonely youth—but now that it had gone off after strange gods, he hated it for the time being as much as he did its supposed defender across the seas. He was now criticizing everything about it. It was an old fogy, and behind the times generally and needed for its own good to be kept in the Union. He would send Whitehall word that the United States could attend to its own business and was not afraid of all creation, and something about its "wrapping the world in flames."

The consternation that had taken hold of everybody in the North clutched the Abolitionists. The Proclamation had come after the able war corespondent of the London *Times* had been sent to make a tour of the South and among other things report on the condition of slavery. His attitude towards the institution was well known, and the reformers fondly hoped that any report of it printed in the London papers would turn England against the Southern cause. His report from Charleston and Montgomery relative to the institution had been damaging to the South, overdrawn and "cursory," he admitted; but the Proclamation followed swiftly on its heels.[1] England, after all, was not proving so

[1] Historians do not seem to know that Russell's letters relative to slavery were written to the London *Times* before the Queen's Proclamation was issued.

"coy" in the matter. The delightfully facetious Benjamin had a ready-made smile to back up his prophecy made to the Confederate Cabinet. But henceforth, the Abolitionists would taunt the proud Mistress of the Seas—she had nearly countenanced slavery while she was claiming to be the most civilized nation in the world. Was free trade her reply to "Uncle Tom's Cabin" and "John Brown's Body"? Had she really exchanged the wool sack for a cotton bale?

Jefferson Davis has been accused by historians of making cotton the working-beam by which to gain recognition. But allowing for his interest in the matter, it was rather the pet device of the cotton barons of South Carolina and the lower Mississippi valley country, aided by the Charleston *Mercury's* loud declaration of the freest of free trade. These and not Jefferson Davis had blatantly proposed and urged it more than once to W. H. Russell. Jefferson Davis' manner in the matter of enlisting England's assistance struck him as one to commend. "We do not seek the sympathy of England by any unworthy means, we respect ourselves and invite the scrutiny of all men into our acts." Russell took down his words *verbatim* as he sometimes did those of the great editor of the Charleston *Mercury*. Philip Day and other foreign war correspondents might come to take note of the Confederacy, but it was the ubiquitous correspondent of the London *Times* who knew everything going on in America these first years of the revolution.

Jefferson Davis' instructions to William L. Yancey, Pierre Roast and Dudley Mann, the three Commissioners sent to England and France, were to first stress the justice of the cause, then free trade and cotton. He could not have put in their mouths a better and more practical argument, and besides it was that of the people he represented. It is unthinkable that he would have immediately delegated to commercial agents such powers as would have required in the handling the most astute brains of the new-born nation. Besides, it is assuming a great deal to say that England could have been summarily brought to recognize the Confederacy had Jefferson Davis given his commercial agents free powers. England knew that recognition would be certain to involve her in war with the Federal States. This she did not want and did not intend to have unless her own rights should become involved, her own flag on the high seas disputed. But allowing for the self-interest of which she has been accused, it was neither cotton nor free trade, as much as she valued both, that drew her sudden Proclamation. She knew that, like slavery, they could be overstressed, and suspected the latter had been. An impulsive sympathy that had much in it of dominant pride and self-glory had instigated Victoria's declaration. England would lead the world in civilized methods of warfare. It is true, too, that the sting of the past still faintly lingered. She had never been interested in raw Democracy and expected it to go to pieces. Of the two sections she preferred the South, that had modeled its social structure something like her own.

CHAPTER XI

JEFFERSON DAVIS got out of the Proclamation all that was in it, although he, and not the cotton kings, knew just how far England had gone. Even with the Royal paper staring Lincoln and Seward in the face like a thing of doom,—a fact he noted with pleasure, Jefferson Davis knew that he had a war facing him that none but the South would have to wage. He looked for and sought encouragement from outside sources, but he did not expect them to do his fighting, and he made up his regiments of native-born Southerners. From the first hours of taking hold of the government, he had foreseen many difficulties and labored unceasingly to overcome them. The organization of a great revolutionary government in all its branches while at the same time engrossed in preparation for war, was one of the most stupendous tasks that history has recorded. The miracle stands irrespective of failure. Jefferson Davis was both practical and systematic or he could never have straightened out the tangles that confronted him. Newspaper correspondents noted that "fifty men a day came to him with infallible plans to save the country." It was enough to rasp his nerves, but he had sought no bed of roses and those about him said that his patience was remarkable. The correspondent of the London *Times* noted that his fine, lean face looked careworn. He also noted that his manner was drastic, effective, a good manner for a leader; but there was no mention, by the hawk-eyed critic, of arrogance, for there was none.

Some paint him as a doctrinaire, a lover of books and an idealist; others paradoxically as tyrannical, arrogant and self-willed and of the soldier type; but his whole past career was marked by success, and his intercourse with the public men of Washington was one of good will. Even if his four years as President of the Confederacy were not without some drastic self-assertion, his life before and after the war shows no despotic tendencies. Every effort of his past life had borne fruit and the same vigorous mind and determined will were now at work. At an early date, just three days after his election, he had set about securing arms and equipment from England, the North and every possible source of supply. Since secession was permitted without any restraint whatever, it was not certain that the North would resort to arms; but he did not wait to urge defenses. His orders to Captain Raphael Semmes on February 21st, long before Sumter was bombarded, were to immediately find vessels that could be used for naval purposes. But few effectives were to be found, and for his own purpose of destroying any of the enemy's strength, Semmes had to wait until the *Alabama* was constructed. Neither could arms and equipment come freely overseas through a blockade which Welles and other historians boast had "so soon been made effective," by the Federal wise men. The South was unprepared for war, was strong only in spirit, and Jefferson Davis was more aware of this than any other; but he concealed the fact in every public utterance.[1] He was now taking every precaution. He lengthened the service of volunteers from months to years. He displayed genius also in raising

[1] "Jefferson Davis, Constitutionalist."

armies. In planning his military defense on May 14th, he appointed Samuel Cooper Adjutant General, Albert Sydney Johnston General and Robert E. Lee and Joseph E. Johnston Brigadier Generals in the army of the Confederate States. Of his labors in the first hours of shaping the Provisional Government, Varina tells us in her "Memoir," and other records bear out her statement, that everything moved forward with precision and order. The members of his cabinet were not chosen from his intimates. It was formed of men preferred and insisted upon by the States they represented. There was scarcely one but was *un veritable homme d'état*.

In the matter of securing England's further favor, one changed in the official roster, if one may suggest diplomacy at this late day, would at least have been prospective. Benjamin, the suave and erudite attorney-general, might have been made ambassador to England. Basking in the famous smile that played about a cupid-bow mouth, Victoria might have yielded to his ardent entreaties. But others, too, of the Confederate government had the looks on that of Lincoln's. Foreign visitors in Montgomery pronounced it the finest looking body of men they had ever beheld. Many, too, as well favored could be found throughout the South—plantation lords in areas about Charleston, and along the Mississippi, not so pompous and self-assertive, perhaps, as some long in public position; but all noticeably pompous and self-assertive. They boasted incessantly of certain things, but the major theme of all their conversation was States' Rights. Russell on his tour also heard a frequent denunciation of the tariff and much talk around Charleston of what the South could do with its cotton if it had commercial freedom.

The proud aristocracy, as aggressive and determined as it

had become, was not more in earnest than the class termed the "mean" or "poor" nonslaveholding whites. The latter, if anything, were more boastful and far noisier in their declarations of independence. These throughout the South ranged from the shiftless, the slightly thrifty, up to the owner of one or two slaves. The latter formed the connecting link with the upper and lower ranks and did much to weld them into one social order during the Confederacy. One slave, even two, while it did not insure the owner a carriage or a satin waistcoat, helped him in the eyes of the men of his community. At the same time, it did not separate him from his neighbors who had none. The women with many airs still held aloof. The one and two slaveowners were often men of influence in their communities, had their small holdings; were recognized in the pay schools [1] and churches; and sometimes, with the acquisition of other slaves, took a somewhat questionable position in the "charmed circle." This did not apply to young married couples just starting in life whose families were known to be great slaveholders; the fact of a limited number, in their instance, did not affect their social position. The poorer classes were thickly settled on the thin uplands, sometimes forming a settlement that covered a dozen miles or more. Deeply attached to the particular section known to them as the *South,* they moved about in it a great deal, seeking better ground to work, but they rarely ventured beyond its borders. While some of them became slaveholders of a second rate social standing, the majority stayed as they were. Professional and educated newcomers

[1] What were called pay schools were in vogue to some extent before the free system came in, and these were often taught by Northern teachers.

—and these were invariably men—did not need this backing to enter society. A young lawyer or a young doctor from a distant state could locate in a community with good chances of being received. These were usually waited on by hired servants, and their professions placed them in the eyes of the community. There were some professions, however, that were regarded with contempt. The dancing master was tolerated merely for his service. He danced with the Master's daughter just as the butler removed her cloak and the memory of him is bitter in the thought of his descendants today. In temperament all were much alike. Southern suns for generations had made them warm blooded, and when stirred, fiery. Far western territory meant nothing to the poorer classes since they never expected to get any farther than Texas. Let the question of economics, of political advantages or of constitutional rights have what weight it might with Southern leaders in the quarrel between the states, with the poor whites of the South it was an inborn love of their particular section that for them decided all issues. They had been made to believe by the lordly class that theirs was the greatest and most powerful portion of the Union. The Federal Government was, in comparison, but a shadowy outline, barely an illusion. But this land was as real to them as the faces of their children. They would defend it as fiercely as they would their own lives. Seward might say there would be no war; that secession was a mere abstraction and would wither when exposed to sunshine. He still might hope against hope that the South would abandon it, and after the excitement was over, one by one, the seceding States would come trooping home. But could he, Russell, who traveled everywhere, tells us, have witnessed the many mani-

festations of revolt throughout large areas of the South settled almost exclusively by the poor white class he would have
been less sanguine. After one has studied carefully not only
Russell's reports but all original sources, it is easy to see
how he could write back to England that the "bucolic South
would stand the shock of battle." The spirit of its women,
too, of both high and low degree, he felt, would stand every
test of war. Many times he paused in his story to marvel at
their passionate outbursts and eternal sewings of flags and
uniforms in Montgomery, in Mobile, in New Orleans. Were
there ever such women since the days of the Romans?

No woman in the Confederacy, people wrote from Montgomery, was more zealous and active than the wife of its
President. Varina might hold her levees, outshine any
woman in the drawing-room and do most of the talking—
as one of her sex has accused her of doing—might laugh
with the lively Mrs. Chesnut over the proud swashbuckling
air and swagger of certain new generals; but her thought
was constantly on the affairs of the government. There
was little that escaped her and it was thought that she at
times carried things to her husband. At least when people
were found gossiping about official affairs, they invariably
inquired if Mrs. Davis was around.[1] People soon discovered
that she was always on the *qui vive* to put her husband in a
favorable light in the eyes of others. Did any one suggest
that his temper might be improved upon—might be in his
way—she was ready to prove that he was patient with every
one, often emphasizing the fact by quoting some confirmation of it by others.[2]

There is no disposition on our part to prove that Jefferson

[1] Chesnut.
[2] "Memoir," vol. II.

Davis was not a man of heat and temper; but no one can study his letters and all papers and not see that he, in the main, had great patience and self-control under the most trying circumstances.[1] There was much to irritate a nature like his, bent upon the single task of winning the war, and believing that it should be that of every soul about him. Had the Confederacy been as stable as the Union, it is certain that his task would have been less difficult. As matters stood, he was performing the marvelous feat of creating a nation in the midst of revolution and war and in the face of the organized opposition of a powerful government. He, furthermore, was accomplishing this within a haughty aristocracy given to democratic assertiveness. A condition that was pointed out by more than one English statesman.

In the stir and excitement of the present, neither Varina nor her husband was affected by the disappointments and hostilities that were cropping out here and there. Jefferson Davis was laboring over a thousand important details that nothing but the most painstaking efforts could straighten out. He went to his office before nine o'clock, and it was often six when he returned. His task was fast becoming for him a quest. Varina wrote that "he derived great comfort from the certainty that the Provisional Congress would heartily cooperate with the Executive in all essentials."[2] With but a few exceptions it did, and it was this that enabled him to set up as formidable a government in the beginning as he did. The later duly elected one, in all probability, in power at the present, would have wrecked it years earlier than it was dissolved.

[1] "Jefferson Davis, Constitutionalist."
[2] "Memoir."

The Confederate Government was now fully established with all branches functioning in an orderly manner. Early in May there was a proposition before Congress to remove the Capital from Alabama to Virginia. Delegations from that state had been in Montgomery urging it for many days. Jefferson Davis did not think that it was a wise thing to do, and there was a rumor that he would veto the measure. Still, he did not undervalue the advantage of having the Capital in Virginia, the land of Washington and other great revolutionary leaders. But massing the troops and war activities so far on the border left a large unprotected area in the rear. Varina, more tempted by the influence of Virginia's standing among the states of the Union, was for Richmond; and in discussing the removal with Mrs. Chesnut exclaimed, "I hope they will!" But she shrewdly added, "Wherever we go the Yankees are going to give us a hot time if the war comes." Mrs. Chesnut infers that she herself made some objections to the idea of any people giving the South a "hot time"; but Varina knew as much about the Northern temperament as her husband. In the removal of the Capital, she might not have recognized any disadvantage to the rest of the country, but she felt that Virginia would give the new government more prestige in the eyes of the world. She was not as yet taking any outward part in public matters; but women everywhere were expressing their opinions more freely each day. Women who would not be seen lobbying at the Capitol building for any purpose, who wore heavy veils when they were forced to go into the private offices on business, were glib enough within the walls of their own homes, at dinner parties and other social functions where women gathered.

Montgomery made no decided objection to the removal

of the Capital, and no sooner was Richmond selected than a fresh outburst of patriotism swept over the seceded states. In Texas and across the coastal plains to Florida, thousands of volunteers were daily mustered in. If Jefferson Davis only had had arms to supply them! It is a weak argument, however, to say that he could have easily got them when the North was using every means within its power to prevent him. Neither Lincoln nor his advisers had been sluggards.

But the young Confederacy led bravely on. A highly romantic phase of the revolution is the manner in which the young sons of the Old Dominion scattered throughout the South in pursuit of their professions, rushed back to join her armies. It was, they boasted in the florid speech of the day, as if Washington himself were calling them back to resist the yoke of the tyrant. And were not Washington, Jefferson and Patrick Henry, those greatest of revolutionaries, bone of their bone? It was to be expected that they should burn incense to their patron saints.

The government remained in Montgomery until the latter part of May. The magnolia and Cape jasmine with banks of roses filled the place with a fragrance and color intensified by the heat of coming summer. The weather was getting warm, even hot, but Montgomery, throughout the month of May, continued to be a gathering place for all the South. So excited had the town become over the preparation for war, with the streets and byways filled with volunteers drilling and bands blaring, that the newspaper reporters found it a relief to escape to the shady parks. But even there amid the flower beds and sparkling fountains young children were found playing at war, setting up rows of red-painted soldiers or else blowing miniature bugles.

Patriotism took the place of every other emotion. Women gathered in churches or any vacant building, and made uniforms out of heavy, unwieldy cloth. Their delicate fingers, unused to coarse sewing, bled as they stitched the stiff rough garments far into the night. Then beneath the white Alabama moonlight, amid roses and jasmine, no lovelier than their own faces, they took their way home to pray and weep and write letters to their men to "never submit to Northern tyranny." Their earnestness stirred foreigners in their midst, as nothing they had ever before witnessed in warfare.[1]

The country, both North and South, had now begun definite preparations for war; if in earnest by the former, more so by the latter. But it was the South's first realization of how much stronger the North was in all the materials necessary for war. Conceal it as it strove to do, it could be detected by sharp eyes. Stragglers of every class and sentiment from the North were roving the country and congregating about the Provisional Capital to report the meager military resources of the country. Spies were lurking around the very house in which Jefferson Davis lived. He constantly received letters that contained curious warnings, some, open threats, and on one occasion a man was driven from the window of his bedroom.[2] Descriptions of unknown men and women who did not look or talk like Southerners were daily brought to the occupants of the White House. The reported warnings of assassination distressed Varina, treat them lightly as Jefferson Davis was disposed to do. She began to be alarmed, and was glad, she says, that her husband was soon to leave for Richmond, forgetting, in her

[1] Russell.
[2] "Memoir," vol. II.

anxiety, how many spies and would-be assassins would flock to the new Capital.[1] It distressed her that Jefferson Davis was still sick when he left Montgomery. With a mind filled with anxiety and a body that, she said, "ached day and night," she waited for news of him. The black cloud of war that hung over the land at times filled her with fears and foreboding. What did the future hold for the country and for her husband? But Varina could easily rid herself of depression. Her laughter came readily, and she was not lacking in a reasonable egotism. She was Mrs. Jefferson Davis and had learned to speak of her husband as the President. She had become a favorite with the people of the city; and many stories still survive of her airs and manners and gorgeous white silk dresses.

[1] "Memoir," vol. II.

CHAPTER XII

JEFFERSON DAVIS reached Richmond the last of May to establish his government. The sound of hammers was heard in the city far into the night. Large public buildings were speedily cut up into offices for the numerous government officials, and the Custom House, with a satirical boast, was taken over for Jefferson Davis and his Cabinet. The city extended him a gracious welcome. The Virginians would have their President something more than a modest democrat. As much as they admired the beloved Jefferson, they were more after the fashion of Washington although the former was himself of their kind. Flags, cannon, music, flowers and hoarse cheering greeted Jefferson Davis as he rode to the Spotswood Hotel behind four mettlesome white horses strapped in glittering harness. He continued to put the Confederacy on as solid war footing in Virginia and elsewhere as materials and resources enabled him. The historian who follows Pollard in the supposition that he could have in these first days equipped his army better has lost sight of conditions in the South. The scarcity of all resources and equipment necessary for carrying on war daily faced him. The Confederacy had few ships, rather none, with which to communicate with the outside world. Those it had helped to build had all become the property of the United States.[1] The blockade, as some

[1] All United States vessels were returned to the government when their commanders joined the Confederacy. These retained nothing but their sword.

Northern historians boast, had soon put a cordon of high speeding craft around the ports of the Confederacy.[1] Even if cotton could have been converted into a treasury for the South, there were no ships to carry it to Liverpool. Besides England had a good supply of cotton and could afford to take her time. And, as much of the staple as the South had on hand, the future supply was still in the weed, and cut down to half a crop; nor is a cotton boll converted into a cannon at a moment's notice. Besides England was not given to dealing in uncertainties. It is said by some historians that Jefferson Davis depended too much on recognition from England, but all his movements plainly show that he did not hang his hopes upon foreign recognition. The cotton barons of the South were more wedded to the delusion. It is true, as was eminently proper, that he made advances to England in the matter of recognition, but in none of these did he forfeit his self-respect.

Another matter early in his administration has been attributed solely to Jefferson Davis by some historians, and in a manner almost as if it were a blunder. Virginia had placed Colonel Robert E. Lee in command of the Army of Virginia, thereby informing the world that she regarded him as her first choice in the Confederate Army. No other construction could be put upon her act but that it was Lee whom she wished to have first rank in any army that concerned Virginia. Joseph E. Johnston, another of her distinguished sons, had not liked it when Virginia reduced the number of her generals to one, and placed Lee in command of her army; nor had he liked it when Jefferson Davis, knowing his ability, continued to place Lee above him

[1] Welles, vol. I.

in the Confederate Army. It was the beginning of a knotty
tangle that ran through the skein of things, but it had less
influence upon the success of the Confederacy than has
been claimed, since both President Davis and General Johnston gave the cause whole-hearted service. No matter who
commanded, Atlanta belonged to the surrendering days of
the Confederacy, although Jefferson Davis would not admit
it, nor would he have his people think so. His great genius
lay in his power to make them believe they could win, and
this belief kept ragged and hungry armies in the field for
four years.

In the arrangement of the Confederate forces now in
Virginia, Lee was this early displaying a masterly strategy that won the warmest praise from the President. The
disposition of the troops calls to mind the same necessity
that Andrew Jackson faced in the defense of New Orleans
and the same care that he took in meeting that situation.
The more important approaches to Richmond from Washington where Northern troops were assembling in great
numbers were to be defended by the three armies. Harper's
Ferry—the route of John Brown's insurrection—was, with
the entire Shenandoah Valley, covered by General Joseph E.
Johnston. General G. T. Beauregard was to hold Manassas
and guard the direct approach from Washington to Richmond. The approach from the seaboard was covered by
Generals Huger and Magruder with headquarters at Norfolk and in the Peninsula between the James and York
rivers. The armies were daily strengthened by new troops
from the states below. As in the case of Andrew Jackson's
situation at New Orleans, it could not be determined as a
certainty by what route the enemy would approach the city.
However, Johnston could cross the Blue Ridge without

much loss of time and unite with Beauregard should the enemy approach in that direction. It was known that the Federals had a powerful army in preparation, and all three approaches would be menaced by a superior force. Every eye was now turned to Jefferson Davis. Despite the lack of a regular army, the scarcity of war material and the stupendous undertaking of setting up a new government in the face of war, he had wrought order out of chaos, and had won the respect of all foreign powers. At that time the new Confederacy stood nearly as well in the eye of Europe as the Federal government.

Impatient, however, as both armies were to come together, only fragmentary warfare continued. The first two weeks in June, with the exception of Big Bethel, light mock battles which have already been referred to, occurred continually along the rivers, growing more severe in the rugged hill country of West Virginia, where two-thirds of the people were assisting the Federals. Still the people as yet were not war-hardened. As wide as they were apart, and as vindictive as they appeared to be, wherever prisoners were taken in these first collisions, they became, in a manner, friendly with their captors. Many pathetic stories have been told of the discovery of kin in their midst. For all the glory that valiancy might win for both sides, there would be pain and tragedy to match it. That war between kindred people had to be to cement them in a closer constitutional bond is the only possible vindication that can be claimed for it.

The Confederate Capital now felt secure. With cannon planted along the James, Beauregard guarding the approach to Manassas, Joseph E. Johnston holding Patterson, who was hovering about the valley approach to Richmond, and the Queen's Proclamation regarded by Lincoln and Seward as the last word in intermeddling, the outlook was vastly assuring. It is true that West Virginia had formed itself into a separate state and was giving the parent state much concern. General Lee was sent into that region to use his influence with the Unionist in behalf of the Confederacy. Though he went as their own fellow countryman and was one that they might well have been glad to follow, he could not bring them to the aid of the South. It was not a region where the F. F. V. were to be found in any great number and its interests seemed to lie with the Union. It was rich in war materials and great influence was brought to bear by the Republicans to annex it to the North. Branding the inhabitants as "traitors," Lee turned his attention elsewhere. Skirmishes continued to occur in this region from time to time with results much in favor of the Federals; but the first real success of the Federals was at Philippi where a detachment of Ohio and Indiana troops aided by local troops had been successful. The engagement was all in favor of the Union forces and with this assurance a bigger and more decisive battle became a fixed idea with the Northern leaders.

Still with all their success in West Virginia the "Lincoln-ites," the people jeered, "notwithstanding their boasting had accomplished little." "They had done nothing more to help their cause," an angry minister of the gospel ridiculed, "but give up their fort and war materials." At that rate "the South would capture all the arms and ammunition it needed." With the usual ignorance of the people and of some historians, these materials were made much of in the equipment of the Confederate armies, when in fact, as

Pollard admits, to taunt Jefferson Davis for ordering them saved, nearly all the firearms were out of date. Still this was better than none at all and Jefferson Davis encouraged the taking over of all stores and materials found in the arsenals throughout the South. The shops were immediately set to repairing and bringing the old guns up to date.

As yet the war had not caused any real depression and gloom. Much light badinage and raillery were indulged in by the still care-free people during the months of May and June throughout the South. But while they made light of every difficult situation they did not cease to make flags and fashion homemade uniforms. In New Orleans it was reported that women were giving their whole thought to the soldiers.[1] A Maryland heroine confided that she spent Sunday cutting up Union flags and converting them into Confederate banners and felt that God under the circumstances would forgive her for "breaking the holy Sabbath." Cutting up the flags did not matter.

With the removal of the Confederate government to Richmond, the great crowds that had lined the streets of Montgomery vanished, though the place continued to be a strong recruiting station. The "first families" opened their front doors again, glad to be relieved of the office-seeking political horde against which they had begun to rebel. Of the soldiers, however, they never tired. If the king can do no harm in the eyes of a subject, neither can the soldier in the eyes of those whom he defends.

Varina did not join Jefferson Davis immediately in Richmond, but remained with her children in Montgomery until July.

[1] Russell.

She was now making preparations to join him. Her stay in the city had been pleasant. In after years she recorded that her "memory of Montgomery was one of affectionate welcome." "There were many charming people there."

On her way to Richmond, she found the country filled with soldiers. Companies at every town and small village were either drilling or waiting for transportation. They were the volunteer troops en route to Virginia, tall, straight and clear-eyed, and "larger," the correspondent of the London *Times* wrote, "than their Northern brothers." Their uniforms in many instances, of gray homespun with epaulets and facings of yellow cotton, while not the best fit and make, were worn with a free and easy grace that blended well with their care-free, self-confident manner. Each company carried its own flag emblazoned with the emblems of the state it represented. Mississippi flaunted the magnolia, Texas the lone star and Louisiana the pelican. At every place where the cars stopped, on finding that the wife of the President was on the train, the crowd broke out into loud and long hurrahs for Jefferson Davis and the Southern Confederacy. At every station, volunteer troops stood around the car doors to be taken to Richmond. At various places in Tennessee, companies serenaded and cheered—Tennessee that had offered Jefferson Davis a place in its borders for the capital of the Confederacy. Varina often came out with her children and greeted the throngs around the stations. She felt that these should have this opportunity of seeing the President's family. She had not entered into the war with any squeamishness as to woman's place in the struggle, and in truth felt that she would like to cheer as loudly as any lusty voice among them.

On her arrival in Richmond, she was met by President Davis and a large reception committee. People flocked to the streets as curious to see her here as they had been in Montgomery. For the present, she was to stay at the Spotswood Hotel as a guest of the city until the house selected for the President's family was ready to be occupied. She was a little agitated at the tremendous ovation that greeted them, but soon regained her poise. The Richmond papers contained a vivid and graceful account of their passage through the streets on their way to the hotel. Every small incident was noted. A large bouquet of flowers, thrown to Varina by a little girl, fell just outside the carriage and Jefferson Davis got out and picked it up. The incident touched every heart as a beautiful courtesy to a young child. The Virginians applauded. They had determined to make grandees of the heads of their government. However, Varina eyed with some embarrassment the glittering carriage drawn by four white horses that was sent down for their use by the citizens of the town. She had not forgotten that there had been some very critical comment among the middle classes of the four horses that the President was pressed to use in Montgomery. She knew that, while the Randolphs and their social circle accustomed to wealth and its display, would approve of even six horses, Richmond had a number of the same sort of people in its population that Montgomery had. These, too, would be likely to object to "trappings more suited to royalty." She was a shrewd interpreter of public sentiment. That she and her husband were embarrassed to even grow sensitive about the imposing manner in which they appeared on the streets is shown in her remark that "This equipage was a sore trial to us and as soon as possible we reduced our establishment to a carriage and pair." It was not that Varina especially objected to a certain amount of distinction being accorded them in their new rôle; this she believed was due the position they occupied and in this she was exacting enough; but she had always claimed that in good taste there was a certain simplicity, and shrank from an over-amount of display and ostentation.[1] One gets this impression as a fine and distinguishable quality of her "Memoir." Besides, she had much of the thrift and sturdy practicality of the Prince William County Grahams, a strong Scot family that had removed to America. It was said of her that she often remarked among her neighbors that "one's dress and general expenditures should never exceed one's ability to pay." She had always been accustomed to some display, and a handsome carriage and a pair of splendid horses was all that her critical tastes now called for. She was fond of horses. The Briarfield stables always had them and the pair she used in Richmond must always be the pink of perfection. These, from all accounts, with the advice and assistance of friends, she stubbornly continued to keep throughout the war, notwithstanding the vitriolic comments of the editor of the Richmond *Examiner*.

Varina's horses were in time to become a subject of anxiety to herself and friends. She, however, attracted a great deal of favorable attention as she drove about the city in the flush days of the Confederacy, and one fine old Virginian was determined that, come what may, she should always ride in state. Numerous memoirists have recorded that Mrs. Jefferson Davis was often seen in her carriage drawn by a "pair of spanking bays," at the parades,

[1] "Conversations."

drillings and flag raisings which now claimed Richmond's daily attention.[1]

Of the appearance of the city, Varina wrote that "Richmond was one great camp; men hurried to and fro with and without uniforms and arms, and with that fixed look upon their faces that they acquire when confronted with danger and the necessity for supreme effort." More arrived daily, company after company from the larger cities of the South, well equipped and already possessing a soldierly bearing. Others came, made up almost entirely of lank, long-haired and loose-jointed back-countrymen; but all were animated with the same spirit. With due respect to certain historians, the word "saturnine" does not describe the temperament of the poor white Southerners. Though possessing a crude immobility and fixedness of purpose, they were neither gloomy nor morose. To Richmond's utter embarrassment they were oversanguine, fiery and horribly "touchy." Notwithstanding this, Virginia welcomed them to her bosom. They were her children, bone of her bone, come to defend the civilization that sprang from the Colony of Jamestown, the beginning of all things American. It played upon the imagination. Virginia! The gorgeous dream of Elizabeth and Raleigh—the magnificent head of the American Revolution, and now synonymous with the slightest mention of the Southern Confederacy. It sounds something of envy and covetousness for current Northern newspapers to have at that day prophesied that the proud "F. F. V." would yet bite the dust, would yet be effaced by the superior race of the North. But it must be remembered that the South was calling the North the "scum of the earth." Virginia, with all the South at its back, was

[1] Chesnut.

confident that no such calamity would ever befall its civilization. Both men and women were in a state of emotional fervor that patriotism generates with such violent force and intensity as to resemble madness.

Still, it was an undisciplined, riotous and motley crew that she was now receiving at her very hearthstones, and but for the love she bore them, she would have been helpless before their ebullitions either of joy or anger. But as naïve, unrestrained and unkempt as they were, she recognized in them the clean Anglo-Saxon feature and limb, and held them as close to her heart as she did the best the South sent her. With what pride Jefferson Davis and Robert E. Lee were to see them molded into one of the greatest armies the world had ever beheld!

The army and the people throughout the South became intensely proud of the Capital of the Confederacy. They had every right to be. No city in America has a more beautiful and inspiring situation than Richmond. To describe it as it is at present would not be true of the day of which we write when it saw its first street cars; though in every age, seated on its clustered hills above the James, the first historic river of America, it bursts on the eye with the same flashing beauty that it held for Jefferson Davis in the bloody 60's.

One describing it at that day wrote that "the city was jammed; its ordinary population swelled to many times its number by the sudden pressure." With the coming of the government, "all the loose population along the railroad over which it had passed seemed to have clung to and been rolled into Richmond with it." Mingling with the "wealthier and well-to-do classes," were men who in the "queerest costumes of the inland corners of Georgia and Tennessee disported themselves with perfect composure at hotels and on the streets." This is not strange when it is remembered how London was turned into a great democratic community during the World War. It cannot be denied but that calamity makes the world more given to democracy.

Richmond was now the general rendezvous for thousands of troops before assignment to the armies commanding Norfolk, the Peninsula and the Potomac lines. Among the famous regiments and companies were the Hampton Legion, the Virginia Howitzers, the Jefferson Davis Volunteers, the Washington Artillery and the Montgomery Grays, many in gold-trimmed uniforms and white shakos. The camps were some distance out of town, but both officers and men thronged the streets from daylight to dark carrying their company flags, and singing and cheering. The sight was pleasing to the eyes of the Virginians. If in time it oppressed them, they gave little outward sign.

CHAPTER XIII

LIFE AT THE SPOTSWOOD

With Jefferson Davis and his Cabinet for the present located at the Spotswood, Varina was now surrounded by "her ladies," as they were called with more earnestness at times than merely in pleasant jest. The desire for their government to be something like England's, fanciful as it was, lurked in the thoughts of women. At this time Varina's relations with the wives of the various government officials were cordial. She knew that her husband had had some slight differences with Robert Toombs, the fiery and arrogant Secretary of State, who, they said, imagined himself a military genius and was already longing for a sash and sword. He was no stranger to her, and his French phrases and oaths and handsome grandiose air and manner stayed in her memory with Washington days. This early, too, some said the disappointment that General Joseph E. Johnston felt at not having ranked Lee in the army, had been shared by his wife.[1] The seed for the thorns were already in the sowing. However, Spotswood receptions, where society gathered, were brilliant and pleasant affairs for all. Mrs. Chesnut, popular and observant, and fully able to hold up South Carolina's end of the social program, records harmony everywhere—Mrs. Davis' calling Mrs. Johnston "My dear," and as yet no uncomplimentary comment about anything or anybody. Memoirs and reminis-

[1] "Reminiscences of Peace and War," by Mrs. Roger A. Pryor.

146

cences of the time are flatly contradictory. It is gained from various sources, however, that Varina at this time had all of the wives of the Cabinet members with her except Mrs. Toombs. The latter soon adopted her husband's attitude to make, Mrs. Chesnut infers, a social matter of it, a tendency of a people who looked at nearly everything from that standpoint. Senator Wigfall had not this early had any marked difference with the President. Varina was not as yet suffering from that now dormant, but vital enough personality. She still rode out with Mrs. Toombs and at times both ladies seemed to be doing their best to heal the breach. However, the Secretary of State's constant swearing held little prospect of permanent harmony. Varina could easily command a certain amount of conventional affability, but it was galling to her nature to be forever trying to keep difficult people in a good humor. How was she to shape this new life? Diplomatic as she knew how to be on occasions, she had never fawned nor flattered in any obsequious manner. But there was the Confederacy! It must be served, Jefferson Davis insisted, suffer who may. But Varina as yet had no such endurance as her husband who made everything subservient to the welfare of the country. She was not as yet as much absorbed in it as Jefferson Davis was, and to be always engaged in pacifying some dissatisfied soul who appeared in the name of the Confederacy was more than she, with all her diplomacy and good intentions, was willing to do. At times she gave way to an outburst with the famous Southern protest that she "would rather die" than do this or that. Jefferson Davis had often to advise and caution her and she sometimes drew him into vexatious little defenses of herself. But she possessed his confidence throughout, and it was his good opinion that she valued more than that of any other who ever touched her life. Life, at the Spotswood, where women were doing nearly as much talking as the men, was full of excitement and interest. They gathered in its parlors and bedrooms, not even averse to stopping, with a somewhat shy and mincing manner it is true, in the corridors or the lobby, to discuss the latest war news. There were among them such famous women as Mary Boykin Chesnut, Mrs. S. B. Preston, Mrs. S. R. Mallory, Mrs. Robert Toombs, Mrs. Joseph E. Johnston, Mrs. L. P. Wigfall and many others, wives and daughters of the leaders of the nascent young Confederacy.

In addition to the long list that Constance Cary, with such meticulous care, made of the four hundred of the Richmond Confederacy, others from time to time joined it, stellar lights, not only here, but of first magnitude in the social skies of other Southern cities. A number were to become intimate friends of the family at the White House. Some in time were to become alienated, with hints that Varina might have been the cause. To several of her own ladies Varina was very close. The Montgomery days had strengthened their friendship. Mrs. Chesnut and Mrs. Preston, both of South Carolina and of Charles-Cooper-Ashley tradition, became her intimate friends. These continued to be a comfort and solace to her throughout the tragic experiences of her life. Few women of her day were more brilliant, witty and possessed of a shrewder insight into character than Mary Boykin Chesnut. Admire it as one may, one sometimes gasps at the frankness of her characterizations. The President, General Lee, General Johnston and even Varina herself came in for a shrewd little clip of her chisel when she thought the immortal marble needed it.

But it was never a deep thrust that she gave the occupants of the White House. These she had sworn to stand by; had given them her heart and had looked deep into theirs.

Social life in the city, notwithstanding the war, continued the same; war in fact, as is so often the case, seemed to have given it sudden animation. In the brilliant company of women, famous as representatives of the social life of the Confederacy, none attracted quite as much attention, both favorable and unfavorable, as the mistress of the White House. But it was not entirely on account of her position that Varina drew attention, but to an extent from the fact of her superior mentality, strong and unusual personality and ability and inclination to still be *the woman*. It was a combination of gifts and graces that, unless there is diplomacy savoring of dissimulation and feigning, the less favored of the sex resent. Varina's resentment of criticism at times got the better of her diplomacy, and hypocrisy she did not possess. Mrs. Chesnut sees her in many moods, but rarely if ever displaying the overtopping manner ascribed to her by several of her critics. From the first she finds her concerned about public affairs, but at the same time seeking to entertain and make those about her comfortable. She, herself, arriving at the Spotswood under unsatisfactory circumstances and finding the room she was to occupy already taken, meets Varina accidentally in the corridor. She is at once reassured and is cordially invited to take her meals at "the President's table." The mistress of Mulberry Place, South Carolina, is delighted and loses no time to record in her "diary" that "It is always pleasant at the President's table." One often finds her there full of quip and shrewd observation, demurring, but secretly pleased when young Colonel Davis, the President's Aide,

implies in a gay challenge that she is "young" and of course
pretty.   James Chesnut is to be kept aware of this.   There
were subtle ways, even at that Victorian day, of knowing
how to keep a husband.

Many others found it "pleasant at the President's table," and no one who sat there was more given to sparkling
repartee and laughter than Varina.   Some, even this early,
were setting her down as a pleasure-loving if not frivolous
woman and with an appearance of condescending to those
about her.   Some thought they could detect a slight sneer
about her mouth, an intimation that historians have since
made much of.   But Mrs. Chesnut, though quick to detect
any flaw, strangely sees nothing of this, and they get along
famously.   They would have a long journey to make together and would find each other out thoroughly, before
they came to the end.

Among other friends that Varina found in the city were
the Ritchies, Masons, and Harrisons of Brandon left over
from old Washington days.   It was not until the fortunes
of the Confederacy had commenced to wane that she found
herself at differences with people.   But it was of her husband's critics that she was now thinking.   She was not blind
to the fact that he already had such bitter ones as Keitt and
the Rhetts, both senior and junior, of South Carolina.   To
her dismay, not only the caustic Daniel, editor-in-chief of
the Richmond *Examiner,* but the brilliant young associate
editor, Edward Pollard, a devoted admirer of General
Joseph E. Johnston, had joined them.   But Jefferson Davis
was still popular, and regarded everywhere as the strongest
leader and statesman within the Confederacy.   The path was
so smooth at present that Varina at times felt that there
might never be any thorns.   Besides, there was entertainment

enough to divert one's mind from the disagreeable. People often found her in the merriest mood. At other times those closest to her said that she was concerned alone about the things that affected her husband and the country. In the hotel, Mrs. Chesnut discovers her on one occasion helping to locate persons needed at council meetings. Varina in evening gown acting as a page for the administration, looking for General Chesnut, and telling him to go to the President's room where General Lee and General Cooper were already conferring with him about McDowell's army, then getting ready to advance southward. Again Mrs. Chesnut notes Mrs. Davis' warm reception of young Emory who came to the Southern capital for a few days' visit. She felt sure that she was seeking to enlist him in the Southern army. And yet again, her shrewd eye sees Varina refusing to let anything mar her friendship for Mrs. Joseph E. Johnston caused by small talk and gossip. Both were often seen together at public functions and "in fine spirits" over the bright outlook of the Confederacy. It is particularly this last that our lynx-eyed diarist sees, and if other records are true, despite gossip, the two ladies involved suppressed their differences sufficiently to remain friendly in public.

With all her quick retort, Varina knew how to ignore the disagreeable, especially when there was a definite purpose to serve. She would do her best to keep peace among all these haughty, thin-skinned aristocrats. To keep them from harrying Jefferson Davis was her main purpose. At the Spotswood, she continued to keep up an entertainment of a varied nature. Everybody belonging to or claiming to belong to the gentry was there for some purpose, or staying for the next session of Congress. Receptions were constantly held in the large parlors to newly-

arriving celebrities. Gifted orators of Virginia and of the
other Confederate states, from the President down to gallant young colonels of even more gallant regiments, made
open-air speeches in front of the hotel to the fine old "first
families" during the evening hours. The Virginians had
laid aside their reserve. But there still was a dignity and
earnestness in the manner in which they gave assurances of
the right of their cause that in contemplation today possesses
both pathos and beauty. They were a people any land might
be proud to claim, and in a sense were erudite, and certainly
well-bred. They thought of themselves as an exclusive,
almost peculiar people, wholly unlike the North and not altogether like the rest of the South. Their excessive pride
made them, even among themselves, bitter in their rivalries
and jealousies. The other states more than once claimed
that Virginia wanted everything, and even South Carolina's
grand dames found her claim of superiority at times grat-
ing on their nerves. But their Confederacy was at stake
and society fraternized as best it could and was full of gossip
and small talk. Besides their whispered confidences relative to each other's shortcomings, tidbits of gossip from the
National Capital were constantly reaching Richmond to
divert them. Lincoln had never quit saying "interruptious,"
and Mrs. Lincoln was eternally scolding him, and—whisper
it, Victorian ladies—on one occasion she had in a fit of
anger snatched his trousers away from him when he was
dressing to attend a Cabinet meeting. The Chesnut Diary
reflects the usual taste for light gossip among women and
none at times more than Varina liked it better. But nothing
interested and excited them like that which related to the
army. The Wade Hampton Legion, the Washington Artillery of New Orleans and many more of as martial bearing,

passing in review, to march out next day and join the commands guarding the approaches to Richmond, set their patriotic emotions on fire. Among the young officers none was more admired than the eloquent young Lucius Lamar of Mississippi,[1] indignantly scorning the New England implication that slavery was the cause of this widespread revolt on the part of the South for independence. While waiting for orders, to charm the ladies, he is sometimes found citing Homer's heroes as examples in battle. It is vastly inspiring, and his listeners know, or think they know their Iliad by heart. In more earnest mood, for boasting was not his forte, he brought tears to their eyes as he told them that, "to fight long and well and risk the loss of everything that made life dear to them, were the sworn resolves of his brave regiment." And everywhere in camp and on the street, young soldiers with their hands upon their sword, or caressing their banners, were pledging themselves to what they had begun to call their *Cause.* Strangers among them felt their eyes grow moist as they realized what a bit of sewed bunting had become in their sight. Not a steeple, tower nor perch in the city nor a niche about the Spotswood that did not flame with the magic colors.

If war creates great armies, it also brings women into view. The capital of the Confederacy teemed with them. Bevies of Southern women of a varied social position swarmed in the hotels and boarding houses. Here and there an Englishwoman, more often a teacher or a governess in some wealthy family, was caught in the blockade. Among them, circulating so quietly that none felt their pres-

---

[1] L. Q. C. Lamar, Justice of United States Supreme Court after the war.

ence, were still-faced women spies and their male conspirators who had followed from Montgomery to instantly gather recruits. Every hotel, the American and others of less note, and even the boarding houses had them.[1]

The Spotswood was headquarters only for the *élite;* none but the favored of whom every one knew could get a foothold there. But there was gayety everywhere and so far the scene was more like a brilliant carnival than war. Women frankly admitted that they enjoyed it. Cooped up for generations, the present experience was an outlet. Even more than their drawing-room with its petty rivalries and feats, they enjoyed their visits to the camps where drillings, parades and presentations of flags were the brilliant spectacle of each day. In the last exercises, they took a distinctly personal part, presenting, with many mincings and airs, their embroidered banners to favorite commanders. Constance Cary sent hers to the debonair Van Dorn to wave in Grant's face at Holly Springs. In many instances these special flags were made of last year's gorgeous silks that had been evening gowns at White Sulphur and other famous resorts. How little does one know to what purpose the dress one purchases will be put—whether it had better be a black than a blue one. But nothing, they cried, with tears in their eyes, was too beautiful nor too costly for their Confederacy.

And at first, how it shone and glittered! The President was riding past. They rushed to the doors and windows to see him, with handkerchiefs fluttering in the air. And none in the army, they said, could ride as well. And the grand reviews! Varina coming on in her landau behind spirited bays, her ladies in handsome open car-

[1] "Life in the South," by a blockaded British subject.

riages, officers on mettlesome steeds, and hundreds of fine equipages filled with beautiful Richmond women. It seems much to regret that the London *Times* correspondent could not have been present to preserve it in his brilliant incisive style flavored with such rare humor. One feels that it would have been greatly to his liking. What a loss to history! Tennyson, too, could have made another "Round Table" of it.

But did Jefferson Davis and Varina enjoy the display and pageantry? It was quite enough to fill them with a sense of their own importance since much of it was centered around themselves. But admitting that the woman did, and at times keenly, it is not believed of the man. But if it suited the Virginians to establish something like a royal court, he would not oppose them, although he took little part in it. Even Varina had warned them down at Montgomery that such food as they objected to in the hostelries there might some day be regarded a feast. Still she was fond of diversion and the brilliancy of the scene about her surpassed anything she had ever witnessed in Washington. Too, she could not forget that she was one of its central figures. Neither did Jefferson Davis feel that it dampened the war spirit. And it was war spirit, let it manifest itself in any form it may, that he always asked for. If that burned their breasts, he could condone much else.

Varina was now getting much out of her distinction as the first lady of the new Republic. Pollard, except in the instance of a humorous reference to a war precipitated by several noted ladies at the Spotswood, had so far confined his attacks to the President, although the latter with his armies daily growing stronger was hardly a subject for attack of any nature. Besides, the Richmond *Enquirer,* known as the President's paper, kept its eye on the *Examiner* to offset any criticism. The newspapers, too, were complimentary of Varina. Throughout the South she was described as a "handsome, charming woman of an engaging personality, and equal in every way to sustain her high position." And admitting a slight disposition on her part to, at times, give herself airs, it is doubted that any with a reasonably clear insight into character will agree after reading the Chesnut Diary that if snobbish she was ever so in the common sense of the word. With all her assumption she was never given to the vulgar practice of patronizing the socially prominent. Nor was there any disposition on her part to snub those in the humbler walks of life. To the contrary she manifested an interest almost amounting to curiosity in people of an humble station in society. About her influence upon public affairs, we are more curious. Was she this soon ˙exercising it? It did seem, when she gayly told Roger Pryor to come out from behind the palms and take his honors, that she had earlier known that they were coming. To trace through the labyrinth of four distracting years the slender story of a woman of whom Pollard has said, that she to a large extent directed the Confederacy from behind the throne, and had much to do with its fate, is at times baffling. Few have thought of her as wishing to assume joint control with her husband in the affairs of the Confederacy, but one must take seriously the arraignment of an eyewitness who was himself intensely interested in public affairs. Never in her most ambitious moments did Varina think that such distinction would attach itself to her name. In all that array of headlong, impetuous, autocratic spirits, possessing natures and characteristics that many historians have agreed did as much as anything to prevent the success of the Confederacy, was she one of the most salient and potent influences in its history? To have wielded, if she did, a sufficiently strong joint-influence with her husband to keep it going for four years until every shred of resistance was exhausted, would entitle her to high distinction among women. It was an honor that Pollard unwittingly paid her. And since, though a rabid and injudicious partisan, he invests her with this power and influence, it makes one curious to know if she possessed greater ability than has ever been accorded her. Could Varina have administered the affairs of the Confederate government herself? Historians generally have thought that though she came in much contact with it, she was inclined, except in a few instances, never quite explained, to leave things to her husband's judgment. These instances, however, have significance.

But Varina had social and family interests as well. All Richmond soon discovered that she was a "devoted wife and loving mother." Her children were constantly claiming her attention. Kept in, much of the time, they clamored for drives to the river and walks in the parks. High-spirited, humored and petted by all with whom they came in contact, they were at times a great care to her. She was now counting the days when she could have them in the privacy of the home the city was getting ready for them, where there was a garden with grassy nooks and corners sheltered from the midsummer suns by the pear and peach. They had already named it the White House, and there was much talk among the visiting ladies about the elegance of its interiors.[1] The Virginians were lavish in their arrangements for the heads of the government. The best

[1] "A Belle of the Sixties," by Mrs. C. C. Clay.

the city had was placed at their service. No such negligence and scrimping as was reported at Washington were tolerated by the "first families," given themselves to much wanton waste. Besides, all Richmond felt that the Confederacy was securely established. The outlook was bright enough to assure them. No more confident note was sounded during the war than the one that came to the Spotswood in the summer of '61 from the Valley approach where Joseph E. Johnston was holding Patterson. "We are strongly posted," it said, "and have now at our command the finest troops in the world. Our outposts have felt the enemy several times, and in every instance they recoil. The enemy, although always superior in numbers, is invariably driven back."

CHAPTER XIV

PRESIDENT LINCOLN, on account of his position, had come squarely into view in the South. The intellectuals of his party merely tolerated him. Still, bolstered up and sometimes commended by the radicals who must use him, he was beginning to feel and take responsibility. Gideon Welles in his Diary makes him out a ball tossed between the radicals and Seward, the outcome generally depending on which at the time was the stronger. Seward, he claims, in many things got his way, but the radicals were equally as persistent. Lincoln knew what they wanted and put an extra touch of Stevens, Stanton, Sumner, Wade and Chandler in his messages to Congress. If they had been disappointed in him at first, they now found him willing to serve them. He was there, he claimed, to serve the party. But it is clear that in many matters he still looked to Seward, who was determined to keep as much control of affairs as possible. However, after Sumter, there was less friction between them. Seward, though his views were different, was now more in line with the Republican policy to coerce and subjugate the South. The conceit and vanity of the Secretary of State under all circumstances was amazing and he never ceased to believe that he could control public affairs. But Lincoln soon discovered that his Secretary was half the time at cross purposes with the radicals and fearing the array of flashy intellect around him, he realized that to a great extent he would have to obey their mandates or be cast out of the scheme of things. His greatest genius lay in his complacency. His ability to conform to and carry out the policies of his party was marked, although he was never as bitter and vindictive as its leaders. Personally he had little ill will towards the South.

The Secretary of State had no such subserviency in handling the radicals of his party, and with his many angularities and haughty disdain had to move among them as best he could, inconsistently at times favoring their harsh policies in prosecuting the war and at other times rebelling against them as uncivilized. This attitude in Seward toward the South, harsh and inconsistent as it makes him appear to the casual reader, is explainable in the fact that he was so violently opposed to disunion, and regarded secession as the greatest calamity that could befall the American nation. He would never be willing to the separation. The American Union was perfect. In his efforts to prevent disunion he was at least consistent with his theory. But what can one say in defense of men like Wendell Phillips, Greeley, Sumner and Beecher, who had favored secession in a hundred utterances as a deliverance to the North, to soon become the most rabid denouncers and persecutors of the South for leaving the Union. These and numerous others of the party had totally reversed themselves and were now gathered in Washington to assist in setting the war spirit on fire. The Federal Congress was at that moment in session, as a "Ways and Means Committee for carrying on the war" (a waggery of the day), but furthermore to approve the unconstitutional and Tudor-like action in declaring it. The cold, bitter note of persecution heard in its proceedings was totally unlike the hot, indignant speech of the South, whose every tone was one of self-defense. W. H. Russell, on his return to the city, was astonished at the threats of the radicals whose acquiescence had so soon changed to the cry of "slay the traitors." Seward's haughty attitude toward England also struck him as undiplomatic in the extreme. But the irate Secretary of State would not this soon forgive England for conferring belligerent powers and rights upon the Southern Confederacy. There also had been bad feelings earlier; he had publicly insulted the Prince of Wales to please the Irish. By this time he was forgetting that he had spoken in such high terms of Jefferson Davis to Russell. He was also realizing that Lincoln was more successful in getting on with the radicals than he had at first thought he would be. After all was it not the safest to row with the tide? Did it not at least get one somewhere? "I've learned a lesson," he said, and one suspects in disgust, "that it is best to mind one's own business." "He is the wisest of us all," he was one day saying at some new discovery of Lincoln's shrewdness that he claimed was a cunning that amounted to genius, to ridicule him on the next as a "Simple Susan." Lincoln's jokes, too, with which partial historians strew their pages all unaware that these make him appear buffoonish, were the despair of his Secretary. Seward, himself, made many, but he prided himself upon the well-bred manner in which they were expressed. Others, also, while using Lincoln for far worse purposes than his Secretary did, were sneering at him in the most contemptuous manner and jocularly referring to him as "His Accidency." Little pleased the pretentious Salmon P. Chase more than to hear him thus derided, since he believed that he himself should have been "His Excellency." The Republican President was not afflicted with any of the cultivated sensibilities and his boorish laughter and good nature more often than otherwise disconcerted and disarmed his critics. They, at least, were not jealous of him, and to use a quirk savoring of his own, he had time to grow.

This was the color, personally and politically, of the government at Washington on the eve of Manassas. The Southern political and social attitude has already been noted. There were only a few as yet who were giving Jefferson Davis trouble; but these were his equals, and jealousy easily crops out among equals. Jefferson Davis might have fared better with the contempt of the lordly Rhett or the fiery, undisciplined Toombs, or the choleric Yancey, than to have been the object of their rivalry and jealousy. In the latter case, opposition is fiercer, since envy, as Bacon has said in some such words, is a sunbeam that beats hotter upon an eminence than upon a plain.

But the war had come, brought on in an hour that was unpropitious for peace, and Abraham Lincoln was blamed by the South for having initiated it, while Jefferson Davis was charged with it by the North. Both sections had decided to test their strength in a decisive battle. They had been skirmishing around to little purpose. Despite the fact that President Lincoln had for months been gathering a great army in Washington, there was still much uneasiness that the Southern army under Beauregard might surprise the city. Russell, who among more cryptic observations, was spying about for any humorous contretemps that might amuse him, early gained the impression that from the first it had been the belief that the South-

erners might come at any moment and take possession of
the city. The middle class especially believed it. "There's
a powerful lot of them Seceshers in this country. Folks
have taken a fancy to it like a woman with a new bonnet," a lank Virginia countryman had confided to him
before he went South.

But Washington, if alarmed, was active. Stories today
are told of the construction of subterranean exits from
the city for any emergency. In the meantime, a vast army
had gathered to protect the city. General Irwin McDowell,
a young West Pointer with service in Mexico to his credit,
had been placed in command, and was in close communication with the authorities at Washington in all matters
relating to the city's defense. This was nervously carried
on, even while plans for an attack on the Confederates below the Potomac were going forward. On the main roads
from Havre-de-Grace, Baltimore and other points, all
bridges, and forest paths that joined an approach to the
National Capital were guarded by detachments of soldiers,
living in tents, ready at any moment to give the alarm.
From these, sentinels radiated like spokes in a wheel, with
every face on the lookout for some sudden foray or ava-
lanche from Beauregard's army stationed across the Bull
Run. This occupied a position on Young's Branch, near
Manassas Plains. It numbered about 21,000 partially-
trained but high-grade troops, an early volunteer of the
first families of the South.

Baltimore was now occupied by the Federals, and the
road from that place to Washington was lined with Union
soldiers. A riotous lower element was everywhere on the
rampage, and local citizens told Russell that many crimes
had been committed in and around Washington and Balti-

more that barbaric warfare, for sheer cruelty, little surpassed.

The higher-grade regiments guarding Washington and
swelling McDowell's army were composed of splendid, well-
behaved American troops.   Not so tall and pleasing in appearance, Russell says, as the young Carolinians, but well
built and steady of purpose.   Jefferson Davis, a good judge
of a soldier, had told his people more than once that these
would stand the shock of battle.   Still there were swagger,
swashbuckling and braggadocio to spare.   Such traits were
not alone characteristic of the Southerner; the manner,
however, was different.   The Southerner was more haughty
in his claims, but not any more self-confident nor purpose-
ful.   The two from special but different standpoints were
well matched, and had there been an equality in numbers
Jefferson Davis might have won his independence.

The disposition of the Confederate army throughout Virginia had been carefully planned.   Still its strength was
much inferior to that of the Federals.   But what it lacked
in numbers, it made up in spirit.   While its lines extended
from the Peninsula above Fortress Monroe on the east and
ran south of the Potomac through a portion of the state to
Harper's Ferry, they were not solid.   There were great
gaps wholly unprotected by troops.   McDowell in case of
a battle would contend alone with Beauregard's army if
Joseph E. Johnston could not reach him in time from across
the Blue Ridge.

McDowell's plan was that while he was engaging Beauregard across the Bull Run, Patterson should hold Johnston
in the Shenandoah Valley.   The outlook for the Federals
was good.   McClellan was driving forward inch by inch
with success in West Virginia.   The possession of that ter-

ritory cut an artery in the Mother State that bled throughout the war. Federal forces there were full of fight and indulging in as many boasts as were heard in Tidewater regiments. Rich Mountain, Beverly and Carrick's Ford were still in their talk.

It was now a little past the middle of July. The weather was sultry. Washington was in a turmoil. The spring bloom that had made the straggling, tree-shaded little city at least pretty, was gone. Few flowers bloomed anywhere and what remained in the yards were neglected. Litter was strewn everywhere. The summer rains puddled the streets and swelled Rock Creek where a tangled undergrowth matted the hollows and ravines which in places ran close up to the city. Still the sight of military preparations was inspiring, and continued so for many miles out from the city where McDowell was preparing to advance and attack the Confederates under Beauregard. The Federal army had taken on great shape, but when Russell rode out with others to inspect it, he found its commander much at sea as to how or when to advance. That he even feared so much as a reconnaissance was admitted. Still the army made a splendid show. State officials and their wives flocked daily from Washington to admire it. The old Southern families stubbornly held aloof. They even kept their front doors closed when the Union regiments passed in the street. Mrs. Taylor had crêpe on her door and chandeliers. Lincoln and Seward were often seen at Headquarters, the former seated with long legs crossed, tilted back against a wall in a chair that was too small for him. There was comradery between the two, though the Secretary of State threw out his hand in a gesture of impatience at times at Lincoln's untimely jokes;

still he had more faith in the man in the chair than he did in any other connected with the administration.

On the 17th of July, a rumor reached the Confederates that McDowell had ordered a reconnaissance and would advance on the 18th from Fairfax Court House, according to a plan in which he would attempt to turn the left wing of Beauregard's army. He had already moved down for a better position. On the 18th, he did advance, but with indifferent success owing to several awkward movements. He had to face, also, the Confederate batteries commanding the several crossings on the Bull Run. On his march so far, from Fairfax Court House through Centerville in Prince William County, he had accomplished but little, and had the misfortune to see General Tyler in an ill-conducted reconnaissance throw a considerable force at Blackburn's Ford across the Bull Run to receive a heavy fire of artillery and musketry from the Confederate lines. Though the Federals at this juncture were slightly worsted, Northern papers reported the skirmish on the river bank as a brilliant success; the Congressmen shook hands and vociferously declared, "We'll be in Richmond in twenty-four hours." For several days, short skirmishes frequently occurred between the armies with a slight loss on both sides. The dead, wounded and prisoners of Beauregard's forces were daily being sent to Richmond and other points. The Federals sent their captured wounded and dead to Washington.

Reports of the first skirmishes varied according to the location of the papers, North or South. Eyewitnesses wrote that the streets of Washington were crowded with ladies whose faces were wreathed in smiles, significant glances passing between them whenever the reports were in favor of the Southern Army. However, the new official circles now at Washington were strong in their allegiance to the Union, and the Southern troops below Bull Run were not any more impatient for the decisive battle than those who were daily clamoring for the army to advance and take Richmond. "On to Richmond!" was heard in singsong rhythm among all classes.

The great battle, however, had still to be fought. South of Bull Run, Beauregard's army was strongly entrenched. It had not moved about much, only enough to meet any demonstration of the enemy. So far the Confederates seemed to understand their position better than the Federals, to whom the rugged country was new and covered in places with trees and a heavy coppice that in places obstructed the view. While severe skirmishing had marked McDowell's advance, all so far had been in favor of the Confederates. But Beauregard soon realized that he would need reenforcement to cope with the large army advancing upon him, superior to his in numbers, training and equipment. A telegram was sent to President Davis at Richmond, asking for reenforcements which Jefferson Davis granted with an imperative order to General Johnston. With General Robert E. Lee now his military adviser, the President had planned the defense of Manassas and their policy was to await action until McDowell should advance too far inland to withdraw. By July 20th, 6000 troops from Johnston's army were arriving in contingents at Manassas Plains without Patterson's knowledge that Johnston had left the Shenandoah Valley, much to the dismay of the authorities at Washington. Patterson's blunder brought the sharpest reproof from the aged Scott. As much as he at first had been disinclined to see the war begin on Virginia soil, he felt the battle spirit stir his blood when it came to a clash of arms; at least he pretended to do so. Seward, perhaps, better than any other, knew his real state of mind.

It had been McDowell's first intention to attack on the 20th, but he had been worried for days over the topography of the country. The picturesque landscape enchanted the eye in times of peace but was puzzling and misleading to an invading army. He now concluded to make the attack the following day, which was Sunday. But when the command was given before daylight to move forward, Tyler's Division again seemed unwieldy. It was not in readiness for some time, which delayed the plan intended of making the long detour to the right. Finally by six-thirty it had marched over the Warrenton turnpike, reached the Stone Bridge across Bull Run and had there taken position. A gun was fired to announce its readiness. Hunter's Division also seemed to have delayed matters for the Federals. On leaving the turnpike it marched through the heavily wooded broken country to finally reach Sudley's Springs Ford where it crossed the Bull Run. Here it was in a short time confronted by the Confederates about ten o'clock upon a hill west and north of Young's Branch and below Bull Run. In a brisk engagement, in which the Federals far outnumbered the Confederates, the latter drew off where Beauregard's principal army was in position on Young's Branch. In the skirmishes covering a number of miles the Federals gained possession of the pike and the Stone Bridge where, just across the river, McDowell had his headquarters. Rhodes and other historians have the Confederates in full retreat only to be rallied by Jackson who guarded the plateau, for which both armies were contending as a vantageground. It was here, it is said, that the famous Confederate General won the name of "Stonewall," a designation said to have been conferred by Beauregard. It was a name that was to become an incentive to victory on every battlefield of the South. Channing does not go into detail but numerous historians agree that the Federals at this point were successful. Their position was now a favorable one. McDowell, pleased with his first attack, dispatched two more divisions across Bull Run to the army now making a furious advance with twenty-four pieces of artillery. Everything pointed to another Federal victory and telegrams flew thick and fast to Washington, announcing it as a certainty. Government officials publicly congratulated Lincoln and there was a continual hand-shaking among the Congressmen, many of whom had gone out to watch the battle. "Bravo! Bully for us! Did I not tell you!" the keen ears of the London *Times* reporter caught more than once.

With the arrival of Johnston's army, which came in detachments through the day, Beauregard feared that no sooner than Patterson discovered his absence he, too, would follow. He decided that he would not wait for all reenforcements, and with Johnston as ranking officer, immediately took the offensive. With a swift advance and onslaught they checked the enemy, now pressing them heavily. While they did not cross the Bull Run and attack McDowell as they had planned, they were now contending with the Federals with equal success. The fighting continued furiously along Young's Branch. McDowell still held to his original plan of a strong flank attack and continued to push a tremendous force across Sudley's Springs Ford four miles below, with the intention of moving around and up on the Confederates. The Confederate cannon there gave his plans away and Generals Johnston and Beauregard, both of whom were on the field, hurriedly concentrated a large force and bore down upon the Federals. It was a severe shock in the face of a well concerted plan, and at first the deadly set-to seemed to shock the Southerners. But with Johnston and Beauregard both leading, the Confederates gained confidence and for three hours the battle raged, the whole Southern army moving forward on the line of colors, with its commanders in the thick of the fighting. After a fierce struggle, in which an old, bed-ridden woman was shot to pieces in the lone house that stood upon it, the Henry Plateau was seized by the Federals. A number of their guns were soon brought and planted on the hill. At the sight of Sherman's batteries the Confederates rallied and ran forward with an angry cry, determined to capture them; but after a fierce struggle were repulsed. At two o'clock, the plateau was still in possession of the Federals, but Beauregard determined to take it in the face of the batteries. It was then that Jackson rushed the Union center with a bayonet charge and once more the broken Federal lines fell back and downhill in confusion. The plateau had become the coveted prize, and when the Federals rallied again and wrested it from the enemy, and without great effort they boasted, McDowell believed the repulse was final; that Johnston and Beauregard would make no further attack and the battle was won.

Why the Federals rested on their oars at so favorable a moment cannot be explained. Up to this point they were in the main victorious. But now in full possession of the plateau which had been the principal battleground, they seemed to have contented themselves with the day's work. They lolled about and began making themselves comfortable. Did a wraith in the old Henry House stick out its tongue at the intruders? But who cared? More good news, telegrams went to Lincoln at Washington. The Congressmen, watching the battle, renewed the hand-shaking, much to the amusement of the London *Times* reporter whose keen sense of humor always gained the ascendancy, no matter how tragic the circumstances. Rhodes makes out a good case for the Federals, but one must see that a good chance was lost.

During the fatal respite, Johnston and Beauregard rallied their forces again, disposed them squarely to the victors and rushed them uphill, determined to take the plateau and capture the batteries; or, as the Southerners shouted, "die in the attempt." It was in the midst of this last furious onslaught that General Kirby Smith with 2,300 fresh troops from Johnston's army arrived. Much has been made of the value of this small reenforcement and it came in the very nick of time. But what, perhaps, was of equal importance was that, although he had used his brigades sparingly, they were everywhere shouting that Johnston's whole army was marching up the plateau. This was more than the exhausted Federals had bargained for, and in utter confusion they fled from the field.

The report of the battle was variously given in the Northern and Southern papers, but it soon developed that it was a Confederate victory. In the dense crowd, made up of high government officials, newspaper reporters and civilians who had rushed out from Washington to witness it, not one in a way was more observant and interested than W. H. Russell, who was on hand to report on it for his paper. The "Thunderer" would carry a spicy story in its foreign news columns to entertain the Piccadilly wits at breakfast. But had the author known the dire consequence that would follow its publication, he probably would not have embellished his story with so much humor.[1] The following excerpts, which are no longer accessible to the general public, are given for the entertainment of the reader.[2] After describing with light humorous touches the civilian company near the battleground of which he made a part, in utter surprise at what had taken place, he continued in a somewhat nonchalant, half-humorous vein to picture the débâcle that had met his eyes:

"I had ridden between three and a half and four miles," he wrote, "as well as I could judge, when I perceived several wagons coming from the direction of the battlefield, the drivers of which were endeavoring to force their horses past the ammunition carts going in a contrary direction near the bridge. A thick cloud of dust rose behind them, and running by the side of the wagons were a number of men in uniform whom I supposed to be the guard returning for fresh supplies of ammunition. Both drivers and men cried out with the most vehement gestures, 'Turn back! Turn back! We are whipped!' They seized the heads of the horses and swore at the opposing drivers. Emerging from the crowd, a breathless man in the uniform of an officer with an empty scabbard dangling by his side, was cut off by getting between my horse and a cart. 'What is the matter, sir?' I asked. 'What is this all about?' 'Why, it means we are pretty badly whipped.' . . . By this time the confusion had been communicating itself through the line of

[1] When the Federal army under McClellan began to march in the spring of '62, there were orders from Stanton, Secretary of War, that Mr. Russell, correspondent of the London *Times,* was not expected to accompany the army.

[2] The excerpts have been slightly edited to condense the story.

wagons towards the rear, and the drivers endeavored to turn their vehicles around in the narrow road, which caused the usual amount of imprecations from the men and plunging and kicking from the horses. The crowd from the front continually increased; the heat, the uproar and the dust were beyond description; and these were augmented when some cavalry soldiers, flourishing their sabres and preceded by an officer who cried out, 'Make way there—make way there for the General!' . . .

". . . . The scene on the road had now assumed an aspect which has not a parallel in any description I have ever read. Infantry soldiers on mules and draught horses, with the harness clinging to their heels, as much frightened as their riders; negro servants on their masters' chargers; ambulances crowded with unwounded soldiers; wagons swarming with men who threw out the contents in the road to make room, grinding through a shouting, screaming mass of men on foot, who were literally yelling with rage at every halt, and shrieking out, 'Here are the cavalry! Will you get on?' . . . .

"There was nothing left for me but to go with the current one could not stem. I turned round my horse from the deserted guns, and endeavored to find out what had occurred as I rode quietly back on the skirts of the crowd. I talked with those on all sides of me. Some uttered prodigious nonsense, describing batteries, tier over tier, and ambuscades, and blood running knee-deep. Others described how their boys had carried whole lines of intrenchments, but were beaten back for want of reenforcements. Cavalry and bayonet charges and masked batteries played prominent parts in all the narrations. . . . Some of the officers seemed to feel the disgrace of defeat. . . . ". . . . The ground over which I had passed going out was now covered with arms, clothing of all kinds, accoutrements thrown off and left to be trampled in the dust under the feet of men and horses. The runaways ran alongside the wagons, striving to force themselves in among the occupants, who resisted tooth and nail. The drivers spurred and whipped and urged their horses to the utmost bent. I felt an inclination to laugh, which was overcome by disgust, and by that vague sense of something extraordinary taking place which is experienced when one sees a number of people as if driven by some unknown terror. As I rode in the crowd with men clinging to my stirrup-leathers, or holding on by anything they could lay hands on, so that I had some apprehension of being pulled off, I spoke to the men, and asked them over and over not to be in such a hurry. 'There's no enemy to pursue you. All the cavalry in the world could not get at you.' But I might as well have talked to the stones.

"It never occurred to me that this was a grand débâcle. All along I believed the mass of the army was not broken, and that all I saw around me was the result of confusion created in a crude organization by a forced retreat. I indulged myself a chuckle at the thought of certain boastful officials finding themselves enveloped in the flight. . . .

"Nothing was left for me but to brace up the girths for a ride to the Capital, when suddenly the guns from a battery very near opened fire, and a fresh outburst of artillery sounded through the woods. In an instant the mass of vehicles and retreating soldiers, teamsters and civilians, as if agonized by an electric shock, quivered throughout the tortuous line. With dreadful shouts and cursings, the drivers lashed their maddened horses, and leaping from the carts, left them to their fate, and ran on foot. Artillerymen and foot soldiers, and negroes mounted on gun horses, with the chain traces and loose trappings trailing in the dust, spurred and flogged their steeds down the road or by the side paths. The firing continued and seemed to approach the hill, and at every report the agitated body of horsemen and wagons was seized, as it were, with a fresh convulsion. Once more the dreaded cry, 'The cavalry! The cavalry are coming!' rang through the crowd.

". . . . I galloped on for a short distance to head the ruck, for I could not tell whether this body of infantry intended moving back towards Centerville or were coming down the road; but the mounted men, galloping furiously past me, with a cry of 'Cavalry! Cavalry!' swept on faster than I did, augmenting the alarm and excitement. I came up with two officers who were riding more leisurely, and touching my hat, said, 'I venture to suggest that these men should be stopped, sir. If not, they will alarm the whole of the post and pickets on to Washington. They will fly next, and the consequences will be most disastrous.' One of the two, looking at me for a moment, nodded his head without saying a word, spurred his horse to full speed, and dashed on in front along the road. As I turned my horse into the wood by the roadside to get on so as to prevent the chance of another block-up, I passed several private vehicles, in one of which Mr. Raymond, of the New York *Times,* was seated with some friends, looking by no means happy. He says in his report to his paper, 'About a mile this side of Centerville a stampede took place amongst the teamsters and others, which threw everything into the utmost confusion, and inflicted very serious injuries.' "

The next morning Russell continued his report:

"*July* 22d.—I awoke from a deep sleep this morning, about six o'clock. The rain was falling in torrents and beat with a dull, thudding sound on the leads outside my window; but louder than all, came a strange sound, as if of the tread of men, a confused tramp and splashing, and a murmuring of voices. I got up and ran to the front room, the windows of which looked on the street, and there, to my intense surprise, I saw a steady stream of men covered with mud, soaked through with rain, who were pouring irregularly, without any semblance of order, up Pennsylvania Avenue towards the Capitol. . . . Many of them were without knapsacks, crossbelts and firelocks. Some had neither coats nor shoes, others were covered with blankets. Hastily putting on my clothes, I ran downstairs and asked an 'officer,' who was passing by, a pale young man, who looked exhausted to death, and who had lost his sword, for the empty sheath dangled at his side, where the men were coming from. Well, I guess we're coming out of Verginny as fast as we can, and pretty well whipped too.' 'What! The whole army, sir?' 'That's more than I know. They may stay that like. I'm going home. I've had enough of fighting to last my lifetime.'

"The news seemed incredible. But there, before my eyes, were the jaded, dispirited, broken remnants of regiments passing onwards where and for what I knew not; and it was evident enough that the mass of the grand army of the Potomac was placing the river between it and the enemy as rapidly as possible. 'Is there any pursuit?' I asked of several men. Some were too surly to reply; others said, 'They're coming after us as fast as they can.'

"More bedraggled, more muddy, more downhearted, more foot weary and vapid the great army of the Potomac still straggled by. While the rain fell, the tramp of feet went steadily on. As I lifted my eyes now and then from the paper, I saw the beaten, footsore, spongy-looking soldiers, officers and men and all the *débris* of the army filing through mud and rain. . . . When the lad came in with my breakfast he seemed a degree or two lighter in color than usual. 'What's the matter with you?' I asked. 'I 'spects, Massa, the Seceshers 'll soon be in here.' "

As a somewhat humorous contretemps, in the last sudden repulse of the Federals from the battlefield, the Confederates, or at least the greater part of the army, did not know that the victory was theirs. Many expressed the belief that they themselves had been whipped—"cut all to pieces." Jefferson Davis, who at this time had reached the battlefield, rode among them and quieted their alarm. But who was sure about what had taken place in the deadly encounter between two raw, untrained armies, in what had become more of a personal combat to possess a contested field? This, too, had taken place in a thickly wooded, hilly country, threaded with creeks and small branches and ravines of the Bull Run. Still, it had not been without military skill on both sides. Since McDowell had failed in his original plan it was greatly to Beauregard's and Johnston's credit that they also shifted their battlefront from their first design. Jefferson Davis wrote in generous praise, "The promptitude with which the troops moved and the readiness with which our Generals modified their preconceived plans to meet the necessities as they were developed, entitle them to the commendation so liberally bestowed upon them by their countrymen."

With the general engagement at Manassas Generals Johnston and Beauregard became the first heroes of the Confederacy, the latter having already enjoyed that distinction because of Fort Sumter. Jackson, too, had won the first of the many laurels that were to bind his brow so thickly in coming days.

While the Southern leaders were holding war councils and all the South was rejoicing over what it contended was a great victory at Manassas, a place that seemed to become the "lucky ground of the Confederacy," authorities at Washington were filled with dismay and alarm. Seward was desperate; drank and talked incessantly. Lincoln's thoughts floundered. Besides the heavy loss of men in dead and wounded, the loss of all the army equipment so lavishly supplied was hard for the Federal authorities at Washington to realize. It would have proved a rich and timely acquisition to any army in a blockaded territory, especially an army that was, in comparison with the one it encountered, so scantily supplied. It had reaped a rich harvest at Manassas, but, as it turned out, was destined to lose it. Was it the first frown of the cold-hearted Necessitas that puts to flight all the "ifs" of the historians?

CHAPTER XV

NEWS OF THE BATTLE

RICHMOND was wildly excited over the battle being fought on the Bull Run near Manassas Gap. People lined the streets, talking, gesticulating and begging for the latest news. The Spotswood Hotel was like a disturbed beehive. It was filled with distinguished men and women from all sections of the South, and numerous English visitors who could not conceal their sympathy for the young Confederacy mingled with the crowd. Both men and women were streaming in and out of the building, oblivious of everything but the one subject—Manassas. President Davis had left for the battlefield, taking with him his young secretary, Burton N. Harrison. The people had cheered him through the streets while the bands threw high, raucous tunes on the air. Varina thrilled at the sight. Any demonstration of affection for him on the part of the people always gave her the keenest pleasure, and any neglect or indifference stung her to the quick. Today there were no thorns that she could feel. Life to her was beginning to seem as it did when they were the central figures of the Pierce Administration, and during those rosy years when Jefferson Davis was conceded to be the most distinguished Southern statesman of the United States Senate. The memory of these and the old Pierce-Davis-Marcy days always puffed her up with pride. Today, at the Spotswood, with life completely changed, she

waited for some communication from him that she knew
would come. He always treated her with the consideration
of an equal, and Victorian wife though she was, she expected it and probably would have made a scene had it
been withheld. There may have been times when she
thought him exacting of her. But there was always a
perfect understanding between them. At the Spotswood,
women gathered around her to discuss the battle which they
knew had been raging for several days. Their soft, languid
voices at times broke into shrill soprano notes that pierced
the doors to distant corridors. All were eagerly waiting
for news from Manassas Junction. They knew the two
armies had come together. It seemed significant that the
battle was fought near the place where Varina's ancestors
had settled on coming to America; where the bones of
her kindred were mouldering in forgotten, at any rate
neglected, graveyards, and where her mother was born.[1]
What occult power is it that lies behind some circumstances that make them sometimes appear as if a hand
that we know nothing of were shaping a pattern in all
human affairs? Prince William County—Varina—the
Confederacy—Manassas—what intent Clotho had worked
out the design? Somewhere near the famous battleground,
the graves of her ancestors might still be found. No in-
vestigations have been made, but one does know that all
over the South there are spots in the woods and in open
meadows that have rarely been planted, where one occasionally comes across old stumps of orchard trees or a
buried brick walk, or an old open well, half filled with
the cavings. In spring, too, one may find here and there
a bunch of daffodils or narcissus or hyacinths or clusters

[1] "A Casket of Reminiscences," by H. S. Foote.

of blue and white iris, known at that day as flags, that tell one that a garden had once been there. Instinctively one knows that it was near these old overgrown gardens, filled with bulbous bloom, that the landed gentry had their "big houses." [1] The more historic still stand as lonely survivals and testimonials of a gentle art of living that flowered from roots long planted in the soil. Gnarled and decaying china trees, too, the favorite shade around the old "homes" of the deep South, may still be seen on lonely roadsides, or along some narrow out-of-the-way street of growing towns. Somewhere, then, in Prince William County, Virginia, the Graham home may still be discovered. You are not sure, but you do know that near the famous Manassas Gap Mrs. Jefferson Davis' ancestors helped to build the great Virginia Commonwealth. [2] It is pleasant, too, to think that it became a favored ground of the Confederacy where its armies never failed, as if the dead still held some bond with the living.

That Varina then thought or knew much about where her ancestors were buried is doubtful; but no woman in Virginia felt more anxiety as to the result of that first passage at arms. Rumors of the advance of McDowell's forces, and of the fierce skirmishing between the two armies, had been received from day to day. Much of this, however, had been in favor of the Federals, and fear and anxiety at times shadowed every face. At any favorable news young women shrieked and clapped their hands in an utter abandonment of joy, and old women broke into a gentle burst of religious, emotional ecstasy called the "holy

[1] Fires have destroyed great numbers of these houses. Some were divided after the war to make tenant houses. Many were lived in by negro tenants after the owners moved to town.

[2] For ancestry see vol. I.

laugh." There were no hurt feelings today—Mrs. Jefferson Davis, Mrs. Robert Toombs, Mrs. Joe Johnston, all in perfect harmony with each other. "The effect upon *nous autres* was evident." As the telegrams began to announce severe fighting with a marked loss of life, with blanched faces they were everywhere kneeling at unexpected moments in prayer, or jumping out of bed, at some dreadful rumor, to pray. No woman could be loyal to the Confederacy, to God or anything who prayed on the flat of her back in 1861-65. And they prayed much, so confidently did they believe that it turned God's ear in time of battle. They were innocent of any unfairness in the matter; had never reasoned that God might not take delight in raising his hand against those to whom he had also promised to be a God. In this they were not unlike other Christian nations.

Rumors of the fighting followed by telegrams continued to flow into Richmond. Excitement grew with every report. South Carolina was sending word that Bonham's Brigade led in a severe repulse of the enemy. It was South Carolina who had begged to be the first to go into battle. Many had heard some fragment of news which they strove to piece together. They finally made out that General Johnston had reached Beauregard and together they had fought and won the great battle. General Cooper received the official notices at the Richmond office, but Varina felt a sense of growing importance when the prominent men at the hotel gathered around her for information. Still her manner was one that they, at that day, with a decided air of approbation, termed "womanly." Mrs. Chesnut says, "Mrs. Davis came in so softly that I did not know she was here until she leaned over me and said, 'A great battle has been fought; Joe Johnston led the right wing, and Beauregard the left wing of the army. Your husband is all right. Wade Hampton is wounded. Colonel Johnston of the Legion is killed. So are Colonel Bee and Colonel Bartow. Kirby Smith is wounded or killed.' She went on in that desperate, calm way to which people betake themselves under great excitement. 'Bartow, rallying his men and leading them into the hottest of the fight, died gallantly at the head of his regiment. The President telegraphs me only that it is a great victory. General Cooper has all the other telegrams.' " Again we find, "Mrs. Davis continued in the same concentrated voice to read from a paper she held in her hand, 'Dead and dying cover the field. Sherman's battery is taken. Lynchburg regiment cut to pieces. Three hundred of the Legion wounded.' "

That Varina would stand the strain of war was noted by all about her. Her composure, however, nearly deserted her when the ladies in the hotel selected her to take the sad news of Colonel Bartow's death to his wife. It was the first notable, tragic scene with which the women of the official circles had been brought face to face. "A woman from Colonel Bartow's county was in a fury because she was stopped as she rushed to be the first to tell the sad news to the young wife." But the Cabinet ladies held fast to their decision that none but the President's wife should perform this sad mission.[1] They had studied her during these last days and felt that no one could inform the bereft wife of her loss as calmly and gently as she. It was a painful duty, but such tasks would fall to her many times in the future, making, she said, "my very name sound like a heritage of woe."

The gallant Bartow was Georgia's first distinguished sac-

[1] Chesnut.

rifice to the war. His state was in mourning and the people of Richmond were deeply affected. The body, amid tears, was brought to the city and covered with a blanket of flowers. Then came the military funeral,—the empty saddle, the Dead March,—to come again and again through the streets of Richmond before the end.

The city in both private and official circles accepted the victory with little of the boasting of which they have been accused by some historians. The first shedding of blood brought the people a bitter realization of the price they were paying for the independence they had set their hearts upon. Horrible reports of the battle filled the papers, and ghastly tales were on every tongue. At the little church at Sudley the pews and communion table were said to be piled with arms and legs. As the days passed Richmond began to take on the appearance of a great hospital. Daily the wounded of both armies were brought in and the prisoners also had to be cared for. The city everywhere was filled with slightly wounded soldiers, limping through the streets. At St. Paul's the Sunday after the battle, for all their victory, the service was one shadowed with gloom, and "half the congregation," they said in sympathetic exaggeration, "had bandaged heads, and arms in slings." Crowded in among the civilian audience, the presence of the wounded brought tears to the eyes of women. Congress had appointed the day as one of general thanksgiving for the success at arms and gratitude was swelling every heart; but here in their sanctuary there was little outward rejoicing. Though proud and often haughty in speech and bearing, their quiet devotional manner of worship was characteristic. Today it was accentuated because of what they took to be Heaven's special favor. And it was a striking congregation that filled the pews of old St. Paul's on this day. English parishes could show no audiences with more dignity, more *savoir vivre*. English spectators among them noted that their manner was much like that of the churches at home.[1] Still they had their small vanities. Not one among them but could point out the pew at St. Paul's where the Prince of Wales had sat on his visit to the city, name the people who had met him and the great houses where he had dined; and one young lady had in her possession a small trinket that he left in his room.

But it was of other things they were thinking on this special Thanksgiving Sunday. The President with his family occupied the pew that had been set apart for them and it soon became a focus for quiet glances. Of Jefferson Davis, a British subject who attended the service at St. Paul's wrote, "For the first time I had an opportunity, irresistible in spite of time and place, of seeing and observing the new President of the Southern Confederacy. Character is stamped upon every feature. A broad, full, prominent forehead, nose somewhat aquiline, lips thin, firm and delicate. There is an expression of gentleness, kindness and benevolence, but withal a touch of sadness with the least shadow of bitterness melting into sorrow. But there is plenty of resolution and dignity combined with conscientiousness and you feel that words from those lips would not fall light and powerless." [1]

The correspondent of the London *Times* had said something the same of Jefferson Davis on his visit to Montgomery. And this was the manner of man and people who

---

[1] "Life in the South During the War," Catherine Hopley.

had won their first victory in a cause for the age-old aspiration for Constitutional liberties.

The devotional days soon passed, and there were other days when the "Great Victory," as they called it, was on every tongue.   Varina's drawing-room is again brilliantly lighted and she herself is in "great force."   Outside, the crowd was continually calling for the President.   After him came the heroes of the battle.   But to insure Varina perfect happiness, Jefferson Davis must be regarded as the greatest of all.   This consuming desire to see him the acknowledged superior of every one about him was a weak spot in her otherwise strong character.   At times it laid her open to the charge of selfishness, even jealousy of others; but the latter trait she did not possess, nor was there any cause for it since she believed that none excelled Jefferson Davis.   As the summer passed, some of the "innumerable thorns" were already pricking beneath her wealth of roses.   What disturbed her most was the thought that Jefferson Davis was feeling them.

Even this early in its establishment, critical eyes were narrowly watching the heads of the new Confederacy.   Disappointed politicians as well as jealous aspirants disputing over military rank were lying in wait, and chronic fault-finders were on the *qui vive* to discover a flaw.[1]   In the face of it, Jefferson Davis' strong will and singleness of purpose became an armor, and he wore it well. Varina had no such command of herself and possibly at first, not as single purpose.   In the privacy of her bedroom it is certain that she at times scathed his critics, to instantly refrain, for we hear her later saying with moist eyes that all were "working for the same glorious cause."

[1] Chesnut.

With all her quick resentments, she was more of a diplomat than her husband, but she lacked his self-control and patience, and to an extent, his persistency, although she herself possessed the last to an unusual degree.

She was not in the habit of taking her troubles to others; was rather reserved about them. It was ill breeding, she said, but knowing Mrs. Chesnut's friendship for the President, one finds her, in the beginning of the war, indignantly reading to her a criticism of him which had been reproduced in the New York *Tribune* from an Augusta, Georgia, paper: "Cobb is our man, Davis at heart is a reconstructionist," and other unfavorable comment. Mrs. Chesnut bridled. Varina had evidence of her loyalty daily, even if she did not see what the indignant lady straightway recorded in her Diary. "Mrs. Preston and I have entered into an agreement; our oath is recorded on high. We mean to stand by our President and to stop all fault-finding wherever we can, be the faultfinders Generals or Cabinet Ministers."

After the battle of Manassas, the women of Richmond were constantly engaged in war work of a varied nature. In addition to their own sick, there were the sick among the Federal prisoners. In the last analysis they were one people. With all the hate lying between them, Mrs. Randolph was insisting with much emphasis that both medicine and flowers should be equally divided between the sick of both armies in Richmond.[1] And Federal prisoners were declaring that if they had known how good the Southern people were, nothing could have induced them to enlist in a war against them.[2]

[1] Chesnut.
[2] "Life in the South During the War," Catherine Hopley.

That the recent victory had heartened the whole Confederacy was evident. More than ever they were convinced of its permanency. Prominent citizens from every Southern state gathered in the Capital. All that they now needed, they told themselves, was recognition from England and other European powers. While Jefferson Davis was as eager for this as any in the Confederacy, he never gave it the thought that some historians have inferred. He knew that a great army was what the Confederacy now needed more than anything else and wrestled with that subject until he finally raised a powerful one for service in '62.[1] This can never be disregarded by the historian. War was now his daily concern, and while there were gala days in the Confederate Capital in which society heartily joined, the hilariousness in reality was a manifestation more of the war spirit than anything else. Bright glimpses of the martial spirit exhibited in Richmond during the summer following Manassas abound in the memoirs of that period. "We drove to the Fair Grounds. Mrs. Davis' landau with her spanking bays rolled along in front of us." "The Fair Grounds are covered with tents and soldiers. As fast as one regiment moves off to the army, a fresh one is received and mustered in to take its place. Army flags are to be presented to the officers." "The President and his aides dashed by." "The President was riding his white Arabian steed." "Everybody cheered and the bands played 'Dixie.'" "My husband was riding with the President. . . . The President presented a flag to the Texans." "Such music, mustering, and marching, cheering, and flying of flags, and firing of guns, a gala day it was with a double-distilled

[1] "Jefferson Davis, Constitutionalist." His Letters and Speeches.

fourth-of-July feeling." [1]   The grave humility with which they had expressed their gratitude for their victory on that special Sunday in old St. Paul's had been reverently put away.   Today they were worshiping other gods.

[1] Chesnut.

CHAPTER XVI

MRS. DAVIS' LADIES RIDICULED

LIFE at the Spotswood Hotel continued to be the center of the official social activities of the city. In spite of war in their midst, women laughed, dined and discussed literature and the gossip of the day with innumerable distinguished Southerners passing in and out of the Confederate Capital. "We ought to be miserable creatures, and yet these are pleasant days," one gay participant recorded in her diary. Then apologetically for having thought them so, "perhaps we are unnaturally exhilarated and excited." [1]

Midsummer had come and Richmond was intensely hot. The glare upon roof and wall scintillated, and the heat settled about the still, green trees that lined the streets in films of heavy, tremulous air. But all through the day, unmindful of it, women dashed about in their handsome landaus and carriages—to the river on excursions, to the camps to see the new arrivals and to beg every soldier from the General down to the shy young private to come to church with them. It was a place now next in importance to the army. Religious zeal, always fervid with the women of the South, had increased tenfold. The churches were filled with women and women brought men. "It was their duty not only to God, but to *their country*," they said. The President's family was always at church, and its Rector, the cultured and benign Mr. Minnegerode, in

[1] Chesnut.

time became one of Jefferson Davis' most intimate friends. Pollard claimed that what one knew the other knew. The friendship must have meant much to the Confederate President.

Varina not only attended church regularly, but with her children was often seen driving amid the throngs that filled the streets. They made an attractive picture in the brilliant scene daily enacted. She was still at the Spotswood, and today there was cause only for pride and elation. None about her was in gayer mood nor more ready for diversion. "The President does not forbid our going," one as eager for pleasure as Varina said, "but he is very much averse to it. We are consequently frightened by our own audacity, but we are willful women and so we go." [1]

"I do not think I have ever known such pleasant days as these at Charleston," she had recorded just after the bombardment of Sumter. Richmond days were just as pleasant for her when the unexpected happened. Society at the Southern Capital, especially at the Spotswood, was in its gayest mood when suddenly amid the stir of dinners, receptions and balls, the chatter about what was going on in administrative circles, the noise of drums, tramp of marching regiments and blare of bands, came a story that, however humorously it may strike one today, rocked it to its foundations. Gasp at it! Mrs. Jefferson Davis' ladies had been ridiculed, pointed out in the dining room of the Spotswood as the veriest "back country" whose red frocks made one titter wherever they appeared. Varina may not have restrained her laughter. She was sometimes accused of levity in more serious matters. But criticism, wholly unexpected and undeserved, always struck her rather

[1] Chesnut.

as a humorous than a serious matter. The idea of the mistress of Mulberry Place, South Carolina, being ridiculed for anything she did, said or wore! Was it not the very acme of absurdity? What could one do but laugh at a thing so contrary to the truth, so preposterous! At any "take off," even about herself, she was disposed to grow humorous over it. She often told her dinner guests with much merriment that a servant who was about to leave her and go with the Federal army confided to her, "Naw, Miss Vrena, I laks youall, an' I ain't nebber gwine to tell dem Yankees how mean you is!"

But after all, these were *her ladies,* and it is more than probable that in time she advised them with a curl of her lips to ignore the whole matter—*"to consider the source,"* the last an emphatically impressed Southern injunction. But some of her ladies were not to be soothed by any of the calm processes of reasoning. One proud member of the established court at Spotswood—wholly "republican," they were now stoutly contending to please their President—was only biding her time. It was the first time that gossip had descended to such a level. It needed the severest rebuke, and the gallant lady herself was something of an adept at criticism. Between snapshots at every celebrity who entered her presence, and her close reading of the reports of the war correspondent of the London *Times* for fear he would do some harm to her precious "Secessia," between such interesting diversion, she lost no opportunity to ferret out and punish her traducer. Any one who dared to poke fun at this particular member of the Confederate Court—Mary Boykin Chesnut of South Carolina—whom all, including the President, not especially given to singling out the ladies, sought a seat beside on the sofas at the Spotswood, would not easily escape punishment. But after hearing the whole story could any one, historian or otherwise, say that Mrs. Jefferson Davis held first title as mistress of sarcasm, or of a hot and hasty revenge? "I heard people in the drawing-room say," the injured one resented, "Mrs. Jefferson Davis' ladies are not young, are not pretty, and I am one of them." "The truthfulness of the remark did not tend to alleviate the bitterness." Again, later, after having been inspected at the table at the Spotswood, "We heard Mrs. Davis' ladies described; they were said to wear 'red frocks and flats on their heads.' We sat as mute as mice." But later, to stir the city's social life with a buzz that for the moment rose above Johnston's cannon, came the culmination of the whole matter. The traducer had been discovered. "The woman who slandered Mrs. Davis' ladies and the ancient Republican Court of which we are honorable members by saying they were not young; that they wore gaudy colors and flats on their heads, well—I took an inventory as to her charms. She is darkly, deeply, beautifully freckled; she wears a wig which is kept in place by a tiara of mock jewels; she has the fattest of arms and wears black bracelets." What social harm after the lady from South Carolina had retorted, could any do Varina's court? But, this was not the first time in American history where the right was claimed to affront high station. They began it rather early in the history of the Democracy, for did not the first ladies of Philadelphia snub the great Lady Washington when she visited the city as the wife of the savior of his country? The story is hidden away somewhere in the minor chronicles of the Republic.

Varina's ladies, however, soon got back their poise. She had taken her revenge, and it was only an occasional saber thrust that the sprightly Mary Boykin indulged herself in. Several thrusts, however, she carefully reserved, to drive to the hilt. One that went to the bone and has served to embellish the pages of America's most engaging author was, that down in South Carolina people were so sure of their own social position that they did not think they would lose it by being seen with people of a humbler station in life.[1] One more thrust of the rapier, and she was through—the illustrious Mrs. Stanard had admitted that she "had never read a book." The Carolina dame gasped. How was she to get on in the company of the erudite Benjamin? Her dinners were famous social events and he was a rare conversationalist. There must have been some moments when one might like to talk about something else besides the contents of a sauce, or one's next-door neighbors, or even the quarrel between Beauregard and Johnston. Long afterwards, when the famous lady had laid by her sword, one finds her trying to analyze the different social customs in the Southern cities. However, it was not long before velvet, diamonds and point lace, much of that from Paris and worn with the inimitable Southern grace, took easy precedence. The mistress of Mulberry plantation, whether in her red frock and flat or a Parisian gown, had won. Surrounded by both young and old, she lived in a whirl of social diversion, vying with the famously beautiful Mrs. Randolph one suspects from her Diary. And since her charms had been questioned, she, perhaps, was more determined to leave behind a witness to her triumphs. So expertly, however, do the diaries and memoirs of a brilliant group of Confederate women portray their social triumphs of this period

[1] "Wives," by Gamaliel Bradford.

that one sometimes wishes that Mrs. Jefferson Davis might have left something of this kind to posterity. But so exclusively is her "Memoir" devoted to her husband that one has to examine other records and writings of the day to trace her. One sometimes feels that she was not as generous as she might have been with her own story. Thousands of pretty compliments paid her are lost for this failure.

Aside from an occasional titter at the recollection, the incident concerning the "red frocks and flats" of the Cabinet ladies passed out of the gossip of the city. There was much else to divert the feminine mind, with regiment after regiment arriving to be welcomed, mustered in and sent forward; others to be bade Godspeed, and banners upon top of banners to be made and presented. The hospitals, too, though the work there was daily growing lighter, drew them. There was little going on that escaped them. The correspondent of the London *Times,* now returned to Washington, they complained bitterly, was "writing outrageous things to England, of all places, about their institution of slavery," and offsetting the many handsome compliments he sometimes paid them. They felt that he did not understand the tie of affection that existed between master and slave. They, themselves, were growing sensitive about the institution, yet they must be diplomatic. Had Russell appeared in Richmond, every parlor would have been open to him. Aside from enlisting his interest, with all their pretty denial of it, the English tradition still survived from that far day when the old Southern cities and their streets were named. It has been seen what a strong appeal it made to the women of Montgomery, the deep Anglo-Saxon South, where, but for Jefferson Davis, they would have given more expression to it.   The historian would be careless not to take some notice of it here in Virginia.   It has also been said that Jefferson Davis was enamored of the thought, but it is not the only manifestation among the people that the historian has unjustly ascribed to him.   It was a popular sentiment that was not only embedded in the social fabric but was strengthened by the belief that the North had destroyed the Constitutional pact that bound them in the Union.   The South was free to choose for itself.

Monarchy with them was a passing fancy, a social aspiration; but it is a fact that the South as a whole sought close commercial and economic relations with England, and when their backs were to the wall, it cannot be doubted that *to win their independence,* so set were their hearts upon achieving it, they would have hotly pressed Jefferson Davis to form even a closer alliance with her than the American colonies did with France.   But notwithstanding their confidences given in emotional moments to Russell during his visit to the ruins of Sumter, they were in political theory a democracy, and no portion of the country clung to constitutional government as tenaciously.   However, their political doctrine was one thing and their social structure another.   Landed proprietorship of long standing, with innumerable poor whites as well as the slaves under their biddance, had created something of an English mode of life among them, not exactly a titled class, but somewhat resembling it.   Their women, who had little to do with the political, and all to do with the social, fitted nicely into the scheme of things.

CHAPTER XVII

THE WHITE HOUSE OF THE CONFEDERACY

DURING the last days of July the President's family removed from the Spotswood Hotel to the Brockenbrough House, which soon became known in Richmond as the White House of the Confederacy. Though not as large as some of the great houses in the city, the reception rooms were spacious and ample for all entertainment. It was one of the architectural boasts of Richmond, and had been in the possession of several wealthy Virginia families for near a century, all of whom made expensive changes and additions. For the present purpose, it had been recently purchased and refurnished.[1] Standing on an eminence with picturesque map-like views of the James Valley near it, and surrounded by trees and shrubberies, it was one of the most desirable and attractive situations in the city. Its stately walls, where Varina lived and assisted Jefferson Davis in his hopeless quest, still stand, a fitting repository for the records and memorials of the Southern Confederacy.[2] The lovely country lying far out around it, with its mass of blue and purple hills rising like fortifications about the high-pitched city, offered to the eye, and still does today, one of the most delightful prospects in America. Industrialism has erected its own gilded monuments and conferred its own insignia, but heroic struggles for liberty and justice have invested the country with

[1] Publications of the Southern Historical Society.
[2] Richmond Confederate Museum.

a beauty that mere gold cannot purchase for any laud. It was here that Chivalry with visor down once more rushed to do brave deeds.

It was a spacious and well-appointed home that the people had selected for their ruler. Responding to a deep but unacknowledged desire to be like the old Union, is more than probably the reason why they had named it the "White House." It was the second building in the Confederacy that had been given the name. Letters from Montgomery had told Jefferson Davis and Varina that the furnishings of the house that was known there as the White House of the Confederacy had all been sold at an enormous price for use in equipping the army. Every one wanted something that had belonged to the President's family; and it had greatly pleased them when told that friends in Montgomery were now in possession of their household furnishings. Though both buildings are entitled to the name and possess a like sentiment, the one in Richmond became the most noted in history. A committee of ladies, self-appointed or otherwise, one does not know, inspected the house from time to time to see if all the plans had been carefully carried out. The colors must harmonize, and the furnishings throughout must be in the splendid style to which the wealthy Virginia families were accustomed. The President's private reception room had a gorgeous carpet of cream—some called it white—that even General Lee did not like to walk on with his muddy boots. The Virginians never did things without emotion. They liked its sensations. All peoples live on either one set of emotions or another; and the patriotic are the most consuming. Romanticists, and sentimentalists, and not overpractical, they were by nature or rather circumstance and habit given to lavish expenditure. Besides, they felt that they should lose no time in placing their new Confederacy in a class with the other nations in such matters. "Kaint any of 'em beat ole Virginny when it comes to showin' off," was the interpretative remark of a bystander on one occasion when watching the various states parading in a notable pageant through the streets of Washington. It might have been considered a weakness in the eyes of the wealthy factory owners and tradesmen of the North, but the apparel of the butler and coachman of a Virginia family was a matter of serious discussion, sometimes for a period that extended into weeks.

That the state would one day become a source-mine for genealogical research that had to do with family crests and coats of arms and other heraldic signs, could have been a prophecy of that day. Sooner than any other American Colony, its people had come to esteem and reflect the social life of England. This had not been entirely effaced under a democracy. The appurtenances and uses of wealth were no small matter with a people who had built up a social order dependent upon wealth for its maintenance. But this also had its roots in old social forms, revered in spite of democracy. Neither men nor women of the ruling class performed any kind of physical labor. If idle tongues had ever hinted that they did, it was hard to refute it. It was not sudden nor fictitious wealth that raised them; but as landowners and slaveholders, their wealth, while enormous but in a few instances, was stable from generation to generation. It had produced an Old-World type, that prided itself as Cavalierian. Even the democratic masses, belonging to the democratic churches and other societies in out-of-the-way districts, had caught the spirit. Piedmont no less

than Tidewater reflected the Fairfax Light Horse Harry
tradition.   It is small wonder that cavalry, with its
gay feather and clanking spur, was a toast of the Southern
armies.   The hour could but give birth to a J. E. B. Stuart.
It was this Old-World social development that attracted the
favorable attention of Europe; and had it been able to establish its independence, the Southern Confederacy would have,
as a Union of States, occupied a high place among the
nations of the earth.   In that event, had the Napoleonic
dream lasted in the Western Continent, France would have
made many obeisances to her fair neighbor.

It was to no undistinguished position that Varina had
come. Each day she was more sensible of it. After the stir
and bustle of moving into the Executive Mansion, she made
some slight rearrangement in the furnishings to suit the
needs of her family.   A playroom was provided for her
children, the bedrooms selected and, to some extent, there
was a rearrangement of the drawing-rooms and the dining
room where she placed a number of tropical plants such as
she had been fond of using in Washington.[1]   She was always
opposed to excessive decorations of any nature.   She was
delighted, she says, with the house and its surroundings, and
some were whispering, "too much elated with the thought of
her high station."   Mrs. Chesnut, to the contrary, gives one
to understand in every reference she makes to her in her
famous Diary, that Mrs. Jefferson Davis had been used to
high position all her life.

There was much about the Confederate White House
and its surroundings from an artistic standpoint that interested Varina.   The Carrara marble mantels in classical
design, the large airy rooms and the graceful stairways, all

[1] "Memoir."   "Conversations."

are noted in her "Memoir." Her intense pleasure on finding the full relief figures of Hebe and Diana in the sculpture of the mantels instead of caryatids may indicate some sub-conscious rebellion at the general restrictions thrown around women at that period. Her powers of description were unusually good but never more pleasing than in the following lines: "The Mansion stands on the brow of a steep hill sharply defined against the plain at its foot, through which the Danville railway leads to the heart of Virginia."

While Varina's insight into human nature was keen, its revelations served more for a play of wit and humor than for censure. Scarcely anything is found in the literature about the State even after one searches Glasgow, Page, Johnston and others that is more interpretative, though delicately expressed, of the Virginia attitude than the following bit of characterization from her description of the Confederate White House. With a wit as kind as it is incisive, she tells us that, "Every old Virginia gentleman of good social position who came to see us, looked pensively out on the grounds and said, with a tone of tender regret, something like this: 'This house was perfect when lovely Mary Brockenbrough used to walk there singing among the flowers.' [1] Then came a description of her light step, her dignified mien, her sweet voice and the other graces that take hold of the heart. At first it seemed odd and we regretted our visitors' disappointment, but after a while Mary came to us, too, and remained the titular goddess of the garden." Whenever they thought they had done their best, she says, they wondered if Mary would approve. But

[1] Dr. John Brockenbrough, long president of the Bank of Virginia, in the city of Richmond, had the mansion erected.

Varina's presence, too, in the house was to be preserved
to history. When the Federals took possession of it in the
spring of '65, one of the officers was so much struck with
the refined taste of its mistress in the arrangement of its
furnishings that he made a permanent record of it.

The new White House of the Confederacy was the talk
of the city. It stirred the imagination. It meant that
the Confederacy was as a nation securely established.
The White House at Washington may have been a room
or two larger, but they preened themselves that there was
no such good taste in the arrangement of either the house
or the grounds as was displayed in that of the White House
at Richmond.   The fame of it reached England and
France, a fact in which the Southerners took great pride.
They continued to hear many ridiculous stories, some coming straight from Republican sources, of how crudely and
comically social functions were conducted at the President's home in Washington. Welles gives a highly humorous account of how Seward, on one occasion, took possession of a huge diplomatic reception, to, for all his
wiles to get rid of the other members of the Cabinet, find
himself at the tail end of the line. It was evident that
Varina had expected to conduct a different sort of public
entertainment than that instituted at the Federal Capital.
She was fond of entertaining at times, and had many
schemes in which the Executive Mansion was to be made
not only a social center, but helpful to the government in
many ways. There must be some formality, also, in public
entertainment, and in this she early showed an inclination to make hard and fast rules. It was a course that in
time brought upon her the harshest criticism. In the matter, however, of informal entertainment, she kept open

house for all who sought the President's home, either for pleasure or public business. There was rarely a meal without a guest or an evening without callers, and the numerous small parties in time were largely made up of the charming Cary cousins and their special friends. The everyday life at the executive Mansion was informal. Varina herself was informal, and with the exception of a desire to establish some fixed rule for state occasions, there was little effort at display. "It was," wrote Mrs. Clement C. Clay, "a commodious and stately structure in which our President lived with an admirable disdain of display." "Statesmen passing through the halls on their way to the discussion of weighty matters were likely to hear the ringing laughter of the carefree, happy Davis children issuing from somewhere above stairs, or the garden." From numerous accounts these were as strenuous as the Roosevelt children, and at will made the grand reception rooms their playground.

Varina generously leads one to believe that her children were fonder of their father than of herself; but one suspects that the passionate idealism of their love for him was much like that she herself felt. The perfect understanding between his children and himself has been noted so frequently in the memoirs and reminiscences of the period that one cannot dismiss it with a single reference. One, too, is led to believe that there was far more sweetness, adaptability and responsiveness in his nature than has been admitted by some of his biographers. He was always close to his children, sang for them and played with them. All his family relations were kindly and beautiful. It is admitted that he was to an extent of a doctrinaire trend of mind, but he was not given alone to intellectual sym-

pathies. His adaptiveness in the instance of the weak was
noticeable throughout life. He mingled freely with his
own slaves and encouraged them in self-expression and
often went out during the winter months and invited the
guard at the Executive Mansion to come in to the fire. As
War Minister, before secession had sundered the nation,
his sympathy for the very poorest and most unfortunate
of Washington was marked. The old woman sitting outside his office door knew when the grand man came out he
would always smile and drop a coin in her hand. His austerity, if there were any, did not offend her class.

Jefferson Davis was never neglectful of his family.
When in Washington during the summer season, he and
Varina often moved out on the outskirts of the city that
their children might have the benefit of the country air
and open spaces. It was there, Varina wrote in later years,
that President and Mrs. Pierce frequently visited them.
The President walked about with his hands in his pockets
and reminded his wife that he was in the country; played
with her children and declared that he felt more at home
than when in the city. She paid him a high tribute in her
"Memoir," in which she portrays him as "New England at
its best."

Varina had been much in Northern society, but she was
now to come in close contact with exclusive Virginia society.
This for the most part had been out of the State but
very little and, like that of much of England, was to a large
extent provincial. Though of recent Virginia ancestry herself, she had acquired a point of view and a humor that the
great body of Southern women did not possess. Their excessive pride, refinement and exclusiveness irritated Mrs.
Chesnut, but if it ever ruffled Varina it cannot be found

anywhere that she ever admitted it. Or perhaps she was too worldly-wise to resent it.

In giving her impression of the women of Richmond, she writes in the same historical manner that one would employ in portraying the manners, habits and customs of any people. There is no effort to emphasize any close, personal association, but a desire to treat her subject historically when she records, "On my first introduction to the ladies of Richmond, I was impressed by the sincerity and simplicity of their manners, their beauty and the absence of the gloze acquired by association in merely fashionable society." "They cared," she says, "little for fashionable small talk, a habit that had almost become a vice in Washington society. They were full of enthusiasm for their own people and eager to promote the good of their country." [1]   As one who had been sent to write of a certain people, not as one seeking to emphasize one's own importance among them, Varina wrote frankly: "I was impressed by a certain offishness in their manner toward strangers; they seemed to feel that an inundation of people perhaps of different standards and at best of different methods, had poured over the city, and they reserved their judgment and confidence, while they proffered a large hospitality." No one ever wrote with such impersonal, historical frankness who was in any way sensitive on one's own behalf. It is not the usual method of the snob. Your perfect snob would have claimed that the women of Virginia were the most affectionate creatures in the world, and had embraced her on first sight. Varina found no fault with the people's mannerisms, but defends them as provincialists, found in all old Southern cities; though for herself she was more cos-

[1] Mrs. Chesnut infers that this local pride amounted almost to a fault.

mopolitan and because of her lifelong residence in the
National Capital was equally at home in both Northern
and Southern society. Mrs. Joseph E. Johnston could have
written the same of the landed gentry of the lower South—
transferred Virginians and Carolinians, and even greater
sticklers for the fact—among whom one must live twenty-
five years before one would be accepted, and longer still
before one became what was termed "one of us."   Historians of that day have recorded that this same manner
was noticeable in the people of Montgomery while the Confederacy had its capital there. Reminiscences tell us how
the old Southerners shut their front doors to "keep out
the political horde that had rushed down from Washington." They were at the same time offering their whole
fortunes, if necessary, for the support of the Confederacy.

Throughout her "Memoir," Varina wrote of her life
as mistress of the Confederate White House with a taste
and discernment remarkable for its freedom from self-
exploitation. She modestly tells us that they were fortunate in finding "several old friends in the city." There, too,
we find in the scant references to herself in her "Memoir,"
was her next-door neighbor, the "handsome Mrs. Grant,"
who won her friendship and affection. It was the same
Mrs. Grant who in after years was so warm in praise of the
"kindness and sympathy with which Varina treated the
soldiers."

However, it is of a woman of more mature years that
we write when we refer to her "Memoir." At the present
time, Varina may not have done so well. She was impulsive
and highstrung and still what might be termed a young
woman. When under great provocation, though not as tempestuous as some have claimed, it is easy to believe that she

was impetuous and explosive. Her usual manner, however, was kindly and affable. Life had now become for her a daily experience of new sensations and impressions. Pallid lives subjected to an entirely new environment suffer partial or even complete change. Varina continued to be what the past had made her, strong and individualistic. As a child she had led her brother in sport, and Stockmar was never more enamored of Prince Albert than the old New England tutor was of his young pupil. As the wife of Jefferson Davis, she stood out among her sex, a forceful, compelling personality. But with all her forcefulness that some claimed verged on mannishness—a kindly critic tones it down to masterfulness—she continued to shine in the drawing-room.[1] It was this combination of accomplishments, that rarely makes a woman popular with other women, that some of her sex resented. If Mrs. Jefferson Davis was the smartest woman in the Confederacy, that was conceded her; but when Varina, in addition, drew around her all the brilliant men in the drawing-room, the jealous woman resented it. But Varina did not readily relinquish her prerogatives, or easily suppress her inclinations. It was soon discovered that no amount of interest in public affairs diminished her fondness for drawing-room triumphs, especially in these first years of the Confederacy. One discovers her taste for drawing-room life in the phrase referring to her husband, "when he liked the arrangement of the drawing-room," to know her own pride in it.

Better, perhaps, from the standpoint of her Victorian environment if she had concerned herself solely with social matters; but fate had designed her for a larger place in the scheme of things. She must live out what her aspiration

---

[1] "Wives," by Gamaliel Bradford.

called for. She would break no Victorian rule—she detested any who did—but she would interpret it at times to suit her purpose. Late in the night, after a day filled with pressing social duties and family cares, she sat up with Jefferson Davis, filled with both curiosity and a sense of duty, to go over with him every important matter concerning the army and the official departments. There was not a problem arising in either of which she was not aware. And this was no new rôle: She was doing that which she had done throughout their public life in Washington. Still, when seen in her well-arranged drawing-room with a rose in her hair and full of *jeu d'esprit,* and ready laughter, she did not appear as a mannish nor even a masterful woman.

CHAPTER XVIII

THE LULL OF WAR

AFTER Manassas, it was the general impression among foreign powers that public affairs were progressing more smoothly with the Confederate Government than with that at Washington. England was at times intensely interested though there were months at a time that the subject was not referred to in Parliament. It is true that, in addition to the press that reveled in it, all foreign secretaries, ambassadors and commissioners concerned, kept it before the world, especially in England and France. It was a duty they took to be a part of their office. At least it seemed to increase its dignity and importance. Seward was always up to his eyes in diplomatic correspondence and in the end made it work miracles in behalf of the Union. But, except for the near serious *Trent* affair, the American embroilment took the place with England only as an unfortunate foreign situation that must not be taken part in unless circumstances demanded it. Her sympathy was another matter. Comic journals, however, feed on the calamities and eccentricities of mankind wherever they may be discovered, and both the North and the South were furnishing *Punch* and other journals with pictorial history.[1] But the young Republic for the present was conducting itself in a more dignified manner than her strong adversary, and her army was daily swelling with volunteers. For a while all the

[1] "Cartoon History of Lincoln," by Dr. Albert Shaw.

praise in the quarrel between the Americans went to the Confederacy. Such witticisms as "Manassas Time," and "Yankee-Run," were heard on the streets of London and among higher ups than the Cockney. Without a doubt, the great battle had raised the Confederates in the eyes of all Europe. The self-sufficiency and assumption of the Southerners, especially of the young men, amused and sometimes astounded English visitors. Whether a Wise of Virginia, a Calhoun of South Carolina, or a Lamar of Mississippi, all were heard to make the same boast. "Conquer us, never—the South can whip the world." And yet this sounded strangely like some of the vaunt and gasconade that fell from the lips of the erudite and widely accomplished Seward. After all, as Russell observed, they were cut from the same cloth and breathed one air.

But amid all the confident talk, panoply of war, social diversion and gossip of the Southern Capital, there still were anxious days for Jefferson Davis. He knew that the end had not come and was as yet far off. Amid the seeming lull, he was aware more than any about him, of the constant sound of marching feet throughout the North. He hoped for England's recognition, but he had not put as much confidence in her Proclamation of neutrality as some had. In fact, he had not liked the expression, "styling itself the Confederate States of America" in her declaration; and he further knew that she expected the Confederacy to win its own independence. What she might do in that event was another story. While he was anxious to secure her aid, he had not depended upon it, nor had he been deluded by the hope of it. The overwhelming victories of his armies in Virginia in the summer of '62, and the stubborn resistance maintained at Vicksburg as late as November, '62, in the face of a powerful foe that, Rhodes informed us, was so strong and well equipped, is proof that the Confederacy was making no Belshazzar feast of the victory at Manassas.

At this point Jefferson Davis' skill was far superior to that of the North's, although he was handicapped by a blockade that soon passed the paper stage, and his few improvised men-of-war were scarcely above river craft. The North was feeling no such strain. That it never suffered in material progress during nor after the war is admitted. Edward Atkinson, an authority on economics, dated its marvelous progress from 1865. "Providence has placed us between two great world oceans," said Edward Everett, as early as 1853, "and we shall always be a maritime power of the first order. Our commerce already visits every sea." At the outbreak of the war the industrialism that had begun was scarcely interrupted.

A few years before the war the New York *Herald* had declared: "It must be a matter of sincere satisfaction to every American to know that in both sailing and steam vessels we have surpassed the whole world." George William Curtis spoke of the United States as "a nation whose ships could float all the kings and nobles and regalia of the world." "We have," said Clayton in 1854, "acquired a degree of skill in the construction of ships unequalled by any other nation." Hawthorne, in his "Consular Experiences," speaks of our disputing "the navigation of the world with England." Fresh from his mission to England, Buchanan, in a public speech, declared: "Our commerce now covers every ocean; our mercantile marine is the largest in the world." [1]

But the South received no benefit from this, and soon was

[1] Rhodes, vol. III.

left to exhaust its meager resources in war. However, with their success in '61, the Southern people were more eager than ever to establish their independence. The thought was intoxicating. Still they had had a taste of war, and at times their hearts were heavy. Many had perished in the hot onslaughts at Manassas, and women had not grown used to having their sons slain in battle. There was almost an edict against wearing mourning, but many slim, black-robed figures, even this early, were seen gliding about the city. The splendid armies, too, which they boasted were made up of the best troops in the world, were continually sending back to the camp fever-stricken patients. Every new regiment that arrived unloaded its sick in Richmond. Varina and her ladies soon found their places, as it were, in the ranks, and with the women of Richmond were eagerly engaged in war work. But the days for her in the main were pleasant ones.

For all the seeming lull the country, both North and South, was now fully immersed in war. In spite of the mistakes the Republicans had made, there was a ready and spirited response in the North to the call to arms. The great battle had stirred the younger generation to retaliate. Though the historian Rhodes falls into a somewhat religious strain in his picture of the gentle and prayerful people sighing for peace in the face of war, these were now springing to arms with as much readiness to fight as the Southerners. The abolitionists were furnishing the fuel for the flames, but to disgust rather than incite enlistment in New York and some places, even in New England. The New York regiments preferred Seward's "glorious union" idea. Both Lincoln and Seward had begun, more than ever, at the latter's imperative insistence, to stress the preservation of the

Union; and, too, the shame of Manassas must be wiped out —two incentives that brought forward the young men of the North. Though the radicals were biding their own opportunity, Lincoln and Seward were now acting in perfect concert. Gideon Welles bemoans the fact in a rather lugubrious strain that Seward was once more gaining an influence over the President.

These, however, were bitter days for Abraham Lincoln, as in time there would be for Jefferson Davis. Lincoln was constantly spoken of by the intellectuals of his party as a human oddity, calculated to excite laughter, a near simpleton in the matter of statesmanship, and his life made so miserable by Republican chaffing that he was found lying on his couch wishing himself dead. Russell reported to his paper that he was scarcely noticed on the streets of Washington upon which he often appeared with a red bandanna handkerchief around his neck. He had now lost the prestige that some had thrust upon him for shaking off Seward in the matter of reenforcing Sumter. But Seward had never fancied the background. If an "accident" was at the head of the government, it needed him the more. They had done things, it is true, he admitted in his usually exaggerated manner "that would have brought them all to the scaffold," but nobody now had any respect for the Constitution. Like "the race of Virginians, it had become effete," although some still sought to call upon it reverently in their speech.

The wily Secretary of State was putting aside for the time his dream of domestic solidarity, and was now to a large extent directing affairs in the Cabinet where the Blairs daily seemed to grow weaker.[1] But things generally at Washington were supposed to be in a sorry plight. As for the

[1] "A Diary," by Gideon Welles.

White House, every one was talking: there were such strange carryings on, even scandals brewing that involved a high Puritan's honor. Very discreetly and out of respect for the high station, Russell had written his home papers, and he was sincere in the belief that there was much exaggeration, that things were not half as bad as they had been described to him. One sometimes wonders at the avidness with which both sides criticised high officials at such a crisis. Although Jefferson Davis' popularity was widespread and criticism at first did not have the weight that it did in the instance of Lincoln, he, too, was this early contending with it. From the very outset, a low murmur of discontent was set up, to grow louder each day. He did not have the easy-going temperament of Lincoln in the face of serious matters of judgment, and was less afraid of opposition. Though striving for unity and coöperation, he did not fear to hold out against Daniel, Rhett and their following for what he believed to be best for the country.

In the new arrangement of the army Lee still ranked Johnston, and all through the autumn of '61 controversy of a varied nature was kept up in military circles. The President soon discovered that General Johnston and General Beauregard could not operate successfully in the same military department. Both were brilliant commanders, but self-centered and touchy. Humorously, he should have kept them together, as their own quarrels might have diverted them. Since he ranked Beauregard, Johnston was in superior command of the army at the battle of Manassas, after the two armies had united. Beauregard, however, felt that he had won the battle with General Johnston's assistance, and was far from satisfied with the thought that the honor was claimed for the latter. Before and even after he was transferred to the army of the West, commanded by

Albert Sidney Johnston, he continued to have a grievance which was increased by friends and bystanders. This difference between them was later arranged. In this, Daniel and Pollard, the editors of the Richmond *Examiner,* may have assisted, since they were always on the lookout, as in the instance of Roger Pryor, to encourage and array all influences against the President. Jefferson Davis' refusal to become their puppet early gained their ill will. They soon discovered that the man who was at the head of the revolution had a will as strong as their own and could not be controlled by every whim of others.

Conflicts of authority also began to occur early in the Virginia army. It was at first called the Army of the Potomac, but the name was soon dropped to be later adopted by the Federals. General Johnston, now in full command of the Virginia forces, let it be plainly understood that he "brooked no interference with his commands." His superiors at Richmond were soon falling under his condemnation, as may be seen in his curt disapproval of General Lee's selection of Colonel Maury for Assistant Adjutant-General, when he had chosen young Rhett for that position.[1] A former officer of high rank in the United States army, it was hard for him to acknowledge Lee's superior rank. It seemed at times to be a point between himself and Lee, though the latter seems not to have been aware of it.[2] The good, gray Knight was Virginia's pride and boast. But Johnston, too, belonged to a family that had come to the front and was widely connected, and as proud and stiff-necked as any who had ever appeared in the history of the Old Elizabethan Dominion. Pollard makes him out tall and striking; but other historians make him a little bald-headed Scotsman. Anyway, his soldiers fancied him, so did

[1] "Memoir," vol. II. [2] Chesnut.

the ladies of the Confederacy, though Mrs. Chesnut did say that it was reported that he was "backing straight through Richmond" in the spring of '62, when McClellan was advancing on the city. A very frequent flick of her whip at his constant retreatings may be found among the many things she notes in her diary. Socially he was a favorite where General Lee and Jefferson Davis were lost sight of. And neither General Lee, President Davis, Beauregard nor even the Mistress of the White House, failing to come up to his exactions, could expect to escape his marked displeasure. He was a gallant officer and had he had Lee's disposition, it is certain that there would have been harmony and cooperation between himself and the President. The South possessed many like him. The type had lingered on in Great Britain after the days of chivalry if not feudalism, and came near to a second blooming in this favored region. It was fascinating to the eye, but not conducive to the best interests of a people staging a revolution.

But, in justice to General Johnston, it should be said that he seemed sincerely unable to understand the reason why Lee had been given a higher rank than himself at the outset, since he had in a way ranked him in the United States army. It was first decided to let the old army rank obtain in the Confederacy, but this, subsequently, was changed and in his disappointment over the rank assigned him, Johnston did not take into consideration that a second law dealing with the same subject repeals the former. Besides, had he inherited his position as Quartermaster-General in the United States army, he could not have commanded troops at all in the armies of the Confederacy. No explanation nor rewards from the Virginians or courteous treatment from Jefferson Davis soothed his resentment of what he conceived to be an injustice, and he fought on gallantly with a deep resentment burning his breast like a cancer.

The controversy over rank was not only a great annoyance to the President, but was embarrassing to Virginia as well, since it involved two of her distinguished sons and she had favored Lee. Jefferson Davis had early discovered his worth and nothing could shake his belief that in him he had found all the qualities necessary to make a great general. Although the accident of Johnston's wound caused Lee to be appointed commander of the army, the credit of persistently putting him forward in the face of all opposition must go to Jefferson Davis.

Varina was quick to take in a situation. That she deplored the discord manifesting itself in the army, is seen in her letters to her husband when away from the city, in which she says that she regrets that General Johnston should feel as he did; he was her friend, and his wife was very dear to her. But if she objected to his attitude it was clear that she did not intend to take any notice of it.

While the controversies over rank had no such significance in the outcome of the struggle as has been assigned them, Jefferson Davis knew that internal dissension embittered the mind and did not help the fortunes of the Confederacy. Still, he had expected a hard road in the main and this foreknowledge became a reserved strength that lasted through the war. He knew that roses bloomed for him nowhere but at Briarfield. In all controversies, his letters stress the importance and necessity for cooperation and harmony. More of this spirit appears in his letters than in those of any of the Confederate leaders. There is little in the annals of military history more sincere, straightforward and manly than his advice to General Beau-

regard in the matter of a difference between the latter and
Judah P. Benjamin, Secretary of War. His letters to
General Johnston also make the object of winning the war
the first aim to be considered.[1] But Jefferson Davis did
not have clansmen to deal with, but "Southern gentlemen,
sir," as the London *Times* reporter soon discovered, and
sent word to England in his own phrasing. Internal dissension and bickering, however, were not at the root of
the Confederacy's failure, but only the rough spots in the
long, long road. Isolation and depletion were the two
blights that slowly sapped its strength. Its controversies
would have amounted to very little if Johnston had had
Grant's strength in '63, and if Lee had had Meade's the same
year.

In addition to the controversy over rank that had kept the
official and social circles of Richmond busy gossiping, was
the continued dispute as to who was to blame for the failure to pursue after Manassas. Both Johnston and Beauregard, sustained by the pessimistic editor of the Richmond
Examiner, were disposed to let the failure rest on the President's shoulders. A Niagarian rainfall that comes sometimes with summer heat in part explained it, but they did
not lay it all to the rain. The records are disputatious. It
is certain, however, that the condition of his army, in addition to the rain, caused Jefferson Davis to reconsider his
tentative plan of attacking Washington. The deadly set-to
at Manassas had greatly disorganized his own troops and it
is hardly fair to the Federals to say, or think, that they
would not have rallied and attacked a band of cavalry even
had it occupied the Capital. To have been captured this
early in Washington would have been a humiliating end

[1] "Jefferson Davis, Constitutionalist." His papers, letters and speeches.

for the Confederacy. Besides, it cannot be overlooked that it was not a definite policy of the Confederacy, not even a considered one, at this time to prosecute a war of invasion. The Charleston *Mercury,* that assumed to be the voice of the people, did not usually favor a move on Washington.

A rather heated defense of her husband in after years is proof that Varina felt deeply about the matter at the time. She probably expressed herself freely in the privacy of her room. An old political acquaintance of former days once said of her, in a colloquialism of the day, that she "never bit her tongue" in any matter that concerned her husband. In all controversies the editors of the Richmond *Examiner,* in a bitter, almost personal manner criticized the President, and very unwisely as well as unjustly. The Confederate government had so far sustained itself much more creditably than the Federal. Original records show that during the lull in the war, its two armies were daily being strengthened by the Provisional Government at Richmond, which was kept busy up to its dying hours in devising means for recruiting the army.[1]

But there were other differences in the summer and autumn of '61. Pollard tells us that General Johnston was at this time clamoring for the concentration of nearly all the Confederate strength in that region for an attack on the enemy. But sweeping across the Potomac, overwhelming the Federal army and capturing Washington any time during the autumn of '61, was never Johnston's method or strategy. The grim, inexorable Jackson, the shining Mars of the Confederacy, might have attempted such a feat just after Manassas—he had thirsted for some such chance, but not now in the face of McClellan's thickening legions would

[1] "Jefferson Davis, Constitutionalist." His papers, letters and speeches.

Jackson even have risked all on a venture. And, too, Jefferson Davis was not willing to tear away all of his defenses at other points and concentrate them in one command with no protection at places already endangered.

Controversy and criticism of this time also included General Lee, who was satirically dubbed the "Parlor General." The Richmond *Examiner,* a staunch admirer and supporter of General Johnston, even before it announced its open disapproval in a bitter tirade upon the President, had begun a highly satirical criticism of General Lee as a soldier. His West Virginia campaign, particularly, was a subject for satire; and now his relationship with the President and supervision of the eastern coast were subjects of caustic criticism. Varina was indignant and began to openly resent it. Pollard would lay it up against her. She had always been rather free-spoken and had not yet learned that one in her position would have to ponder every word one uttered. Her admiration for General Lee was the only point on which she and Mrs. Chesnut did not at first agree. Besides, he was the President's military adviser, and every jibe at him was resented as a thrust at the administration. Pollard was not wrong when he said that she took part in the controversies going on around her. She was not like Mrs. Woodrow Wilson who had no real inclination or desire for participation in public affairs, though forced to do so during her husband's illness. Varina was intensely interested in public affairs, and inclined to express, even contend, for her opinions. Seward could have informed them down at Richmond that she was as well acquainted with politics as she was with literature. However, if she was exerting any influence upon public matters at this time, it was of a very quiet, back-stage nature. She knew well enough that she lived in a Victorian age. Had she been oblivious of this fact, and no Southern woman of that day was, there might have been more evidence of a joint rule, perhaps of some domination. Her position thrust her constantly and conspicuously before the public and drew her into an intimate acquaintance with the affairs of the government, while the women about her could choose for themselves in such matters.

About September 7th, Jefferson Davis became very ill, and Varina was compelled to receive and welcome all callers, to discriminate as to whom to take into his sick room and whom to satisfy without having had a glimpse of the President. It was a difficult rôle for any woman; but the Confederacy at this time moved along with great flair, and she must have made few mistakes. Her manner, too, in her intercourse with the constant stream of public officials must have been pleasing since numerous old letters of the time refer to her as a woman of much charm and ready wit. The President sometimes transacted business from the sick bed. Did any one want to see him? A note was first written to Mrs. Jefferson Davis. Did any one want to discuss a very important matter?—if he could not be seen, they discussed it with her. His illness was severe, brought on by repeated attacks of neuralgia that sapped his strength for weeks, and news went abroad that he was dangerously ill. Northern newspapers made much of it. It shocked Varina to read, from day to day, repeated notices of his death in the Northern newspapers. And now that he was dead, they were suggesting his successor. Obituary notices, in some instances quite flattering, came from the enemy. She carefully kept this from him during his illness, and when he must know it, smoothed it over with some such expression as Russell records of her, "They are quite capable of such acts." Or perhaps she said more; she had great provocation, and it was beginning to be whispered that she had a temper.

Much that occurred at this time in official circles was laid at the President's door by the editors of the Richmond *Examiner* and Charleston *Mercury* to furnish pabulum for the historian fond of telling us how Jefferson Davis could have whipped the North if he had only known how. In addition to criticism of the President, the editors of the *Examiner* were now deriding the service of nearly every official connected with the Provisional Government. The suave, seemingly half-serious Benjamin, with his bland airs and enigmatic smile was a failure and Northrop, the Commissary-General, was intolerable. None was spared. There was murmurous complaint throughout the autumn that Johnston's army was in need of supplies; that the President kept Northrop at the head of the Commissary Department because he was a West Pointer and an old army friend, while the army suffered. But it is not possible that the petted and fêted army of Virginia could have suffered for anything at that early date.

For all the dissension and petty bickering, the Confederacy moved forward in a manner that won the interest and admiration of both England and France, if the pessimists and egotists at home could only have appreciated it. Its controversies, however, were mild in comparison with those going on at Washington. In both instances, though the story could not be written without them, they had but little real influence upon the issues of war, and served only to make the task harder for Jefferson Davis and Abraham Lincoln. Democracy was not through with fermentation if it is not always bitten with its own barm.

CHAPTER XIX

BRITON AND YANKEE

THE autumn was more than half gone and the blue-gold haze of Indian summer was swathing the hills and valleys of Virginia. Nowhere, after the first frosts, is the foliage more gorgeous than that in and around Richmond. Before the bewildering panorama of colors, the distant hills and gleam of water, one holds the breath in wonder at such a lavish expenditure of beauty. The season of '61 was no exception. The Southern Capital was gay with music and banners and the lighter panoply of war. Its people have been charged with continuing their usual avocations after the victory of Manassas, and with a nonchalance out of keeping with the situation. But they mistake who think that Richmond was in a state of *dolce far niente* during the fall and winter following the battle of Manassas. Besides the stream of enlistments pouring in from other states, the streets were packed and jammed with determined citizens from every section of the state, dignified and carefully groomed, it is true, since they were Virginia-bred. But while the roystering and hurrahing were left to the enthusiastic young soldiers, their elders were every whit as alert. The North and all Europe had yet to marvel at their spirit. The invaders had fixed their bayonets upon this particular stronghold of the Confederacy. They believed that its capture would put an end to the war and to what they called "the great rebellion." In all probability it would have done so, since the effect upon the Confederacy of Virginia falling into the possession of the Federals would have been appalling. Some historians underestimate the influence of the Southern Capital upon the war. Its appeal to the imagination was tremendous. Both Lincoln and Seward knew what it meant in cementing and animating the South.

The cessation of hostilities continued. The Union Army, still across the Potomac, did not seem anxious to renew the fighting. Lincoln had displaced McDowell with McClellan, who was slowly reorganizing his large army. There was little of a sanguinary nature during the autumn, and the Confederate forces were chafing under inaction and awaiting a demonstration from the enemy. The small affair of Ball's Bluff on October 11th was considered a Confederate victory, and indeed it seemed that the madcap South knew what it was about and was on the high road to independence.

The Republicans were now in constant fear that the Confederacy would be recognized by England and other European powers. This became a subject of daily discussion in Washington, and Seward boasted so much about what he would do with the situation that Welles infers that the others could not sleep at night, or something to that effect.

England's acknowledgment of the new government as a belligerent power and the victory of Manassas did really seem to pave the way for its full recognition as an independent Republic. And well might Seward be disturbed, since it is not wholly improbable that if England's main policy had not been one of strict neutrality, Victoria's spontaneous and romantic sympathies, stirred as they were at times by her greatest counselors, might have ended in recognition of the struggling young nation. Nor was Victoria the only high source in England touched by its isolation. Such rugged hearts as Carlyle's were beating faster, and one of the most promising young Englishmen [1] of the realm was valiantly defending it in the *Quarterly Review*.

It was at this time, when the Federal Union was anxiously watching the Confederacy's various efforts to win the favor of England, that an unexpected circumstance occurred that greatly affected that country's attitude toward the North. While Lords Palmerston and Russell were listening to the artful propositions of Napoleon to take some action regarding the American situation, James M. Mason of Virginia and John Slidell of Louisiana, along with the enactment of other legislation by the Confederate Congress during the autumn of '61, were appointed Commissioners to the English and French courts. The stage for the scene was quietly set. The little *Theodora* stole secretly out of the Charleston waters in the very reach of the blockade and landed its precious freight on the hospitable shores of Cuba. The transfer was successfully arranged. The British mail-ship *Trent,* carrying the distinguished passengers from Havana, was for a while unmolested. But their joy was soon cut short. On November 8th, the *Trent* was captured by the *San Jacinto,* a Federal man-of-war, and the Confederate dignitaries were arrested and conveyed to Fort Warren. Great Britain's outburst of resentment at the arrest of passengers aboard her vessel as an insult to her flag filled the minds of the Southerners with new hope of her immediate favor. The indignation in England over the affair, one wrote, "was like a sudden flow of hot lava." Charles Francis Adams, the Federal ambassador to the English Court, one of the calmest and wisest men of his time, was greatly disturbed. Seward was chesty and contemptuous. The United States, before it

---

[1] Robert Cecil, who was not then an earl.

gave in to England, "would start a war that would wrap the world in flames." Lincoln, too, was saying in homely Southern phrase to his intimates that he "would rather die than give them prisoners up." Welles stoutly abetted him. A little later England was sending regiments to Canada and preparing for war. Seward was nonplused, perplexed, and after a customary fit of heroics, cooled completely down, to Welles' perfect disgust at his "toadying and truckling to Lord Lyons and Great Britain." Russell, correspondent of the London *Times,* much to his amusement, was discovering that, notwithstanding his rash threatenings, the domineering Secretary of State could be a perfect diplomat. But chameleon though he was, he still held the spotlight in the Cabinet, though his critics were saying that "when he went in one hole, you did not know which one he would come out of." Few understood his political philosophy, and opposition kept him busy laying unfathomable schemes to carry out his designs. His present maneuvering was the very essence of diplomacy.

The South was stirred to the highest pitch over the capture of her representatives. Virginia was in a towering rage at the thought of their incarceration in Fort Warren. It would have been best for the Confederacy had they stayed there, as one historian has said. Here was the one opportunity for the South to have succeeded. War between England and the United States would have immediately raised the South among the nations. But Seward was too shrewd to let things come to that pass. He would be all things to all men if the end justified it, and certainly he took it that it did in the present crisis.

Angry threats were heard on every side in the South. If any personal harm came to its representatives, no lives of prisoners in the South would be safe. Still it elated the Southerners that the affair had stirred up strife between England and the Federal states. Jefferson Davis was anxiously watching the outcome but was less boastful. Lincoln did not know much about international matters, but knowing that Seward was an old hand at political scheming, he got rid of his position that he would "rather die than give up" the commissioners and deferred the whole matter to his Secretary of State, Welles resents in his "Diary." The latter's testy little remarks that it was disgusting the way Seward was toadying to the English was now all lost on Lincoln. If any one could save the situation, he believed it was the Secretary of State. The radicals also, for once, gave him a free hand in the ticklish matter. Seward's new schemes to bring about the renewal of friendly relations with England could not be comprehended by the frank, straightforward, somewhat dense old Secretary of the Navy. He could not see that the country was playing with fire. The would-be Premier was now deep in his favorite game of scheming. Hundreds of letters crossed the seas and many came to the English Embassy at Washington. Lord Lyons was smiling over their contents and having private chats with the war-correspondent of the London *Times*. During the misunderstanding, the Confederacy was drunk to in nearly every great house in England. But England was not as eager for war as she seemed. War was never her policy if she could do better. She was still Elizabethan on that subject. The British Lion, perhaps, had roared a little too loud, and Seward in the end would find him tamer than he had really thought he would. Still it would take some very deft handling to clear the situation. He reveled in the exercise of his natural powers. Raw Democracy had at least

produced a wilier statesman than Whitehall. The Confederate President would have had a better chance in the matter
of recognition had it not been for the man who in other days
put his arms around him and said gently, perhaps a little
shamefacedly, "I know you only speak from conviction."

Jefferson Davis feared his one-time admirer in the matter of England's position more than he did any other connected with the Washington government. Neither had his
adroitness escaped Varina who was at a loss to describe him
other than as an "inscrutable human moral paradox." [1]
She possessed as astute and thorough knowledge of all
that was transpiring regarding the *Trent* incident as any
one concerned. Aside from its political significance the imprisonment of the Confederate commissioners disturbed her
greatly. Slidell she did not know so well, but Senator
Mason was an old and valued friend. While it is suspected
that she generally liked any one who liked her husband, she
must herself be assured. Her strong admiration for
Howell Cobb had something more in it than the fact that
he was her husband's staunch friend throughout the Confederacy as much as the thought pleased her. She knew
Mason's real worth and for the "dress coat at breakfast"
she had an indulgent smile. Had Varina been a ruler she
would have taken many of the oddities of her courtiers
humorously.

An event that particularly pleased her during the November of '61 was the unanimous election of her husband to
the Presidency of the Confederacy for a term of six years.
In the strange and unexpected life she was now living she
began to feel a sense of permanency. He had been elected
without any opposition, and the fact was not lost upon the

[1] "Memoir," vol. I.

people. He had recuperated from his illness in the early autumn and was back in his office laboring with an intensity and zeal that attracted the attention of foreigners in the city. Despite controversies over rank and other matters, he was still very popular. People broke into cheers whenever he appeared on the street. Although he cared little for public show, for their delectation he sometimes rode the white Arabian horse that had been presented to him. It was a sight that set Varina's nerves tingling. She remembered in after years the gallant figure he made as he rode through the streets with "his staff clattering on behind." They continued to note that he rode with a military air and bearing not equaled by any of his generals. Joseph E. Johnston did not have sufficient height and General Lee's seat appeared slightly unmilitary. Placed at the head of the army in a conquering mood, Jefferson Davis might have crossed the Potomac, captured Washington and reconstructed the old Union on a resumption of Constitutional liberty; but the Fates had made him President of the Confederacy.

Along with other things, both important and trivial, that occurred in the autumn of '61, the subject of public entertainment at the Confederate White House became one of heated discussion. Since her removal to the White House, Varina had been deeply interested in all plans for the entertainment of the army. She was fond of entertaining at times. The fact, however, of prospective motherhood had kept her somewhat in retirement during the latter part of the season. Still, while women were fastidiously squeamish in the matter of appearing in public at such times, motherhood was not regarded as the social handicap that it seems to be today; women looked upon it as a natural condition that needed no further comment than one woman's confidences with another. Large families were the rule, and much honor was attached to the fact. Queen Victoria, herself, had set the example for all Christendom, and the Victorian ideal was in full vogue in the South at the formation of the Southern Confederacy. Perhaps it had taken a deeper root here with women in sex matters than anywhere else on the globe. At least from the time of Sir William Berkeley of Virginia.

It was during this first year in the Executive Mansion that Varina's fourth son was born on the 16th of December. The child was given the name of William Howell for her father.[1] The event was one of much interest throughout the South, and women began counting up to find out whether there were more children in the Confederate White House than in Buckingham Palace.

The delicate health of the President interfered at times with social entertainment at the Executive Mansion. Physicians in Washington had already advised care in the matter, and his severe illness in September had kept the Mansion quiet for several weeks. But Jefferson Davis could recuperate rapidly from any illness and the one thing more than another that prevented him from taking more interest in social life was his utter absorption in his official duties. This had become the one thing that gave him entertainment. Both luncheon and dinner got cold or went untasted if the Committees were meeting or the horses ready for him and his aides. His iron will, throughout, triumphed over his lean, aching body.

But as Christmas approached, people began to complain more frequently of the lack of social life at the White

[1] Another date had been given; but this was taken from a memorial window to his memory.

House. It belonged to the public and there was no social entertainment provided for either the young or the old. The editor of the *Examiner,* always on the alert for the slightest point of attack, was soon writing caustic paragraphs—that satraps reigned in the Confederate White House, whose dignity did not permit them to condescend to the level of the "common herd." And if not that interpretation, then they were getting rich on their income, when it should be spent on public entertainment. But while Jefferson Davis ignored the petty fling, Varina resented it for him. He was now responsible to the public, not only for everything that he did, but for every seeming attitude in which he was placed. The biting pen of the editor of the *Examiner* could do him a world of harm in the eyes of the masses, who are always swayed by petty charges. She was not as happy at times as she had thought to be. Life was not as rosy as it had been in the old Washington days. Still she was resourceful. Although her child was scarcely two weeks old, she began to arrange for public entertainment, and took upon herself the principal responsibility of it to shield the President, since so much else of more importance demanded his attention. Could not the people she resented, at least the editors of influential papers, see how petty it was to make serious comment upon such unimportant matters? She was full of a quick, impatient satire when confronted with petty faults in men. It was enough for women to possess them, she could forgive women but expected more of men. It was a Southern attitude that sometimes crops up today. However, between them, Varina and her husband arranged the social matter for the coming winter. She would assume the heaviest part of the entertainment. It meant much contact with public life, and even this early in the Confederacy, she was becoming closely acquainted with all public affairs.

CHAPTER XX

THE autumn had passed but with Manassas still to point to Richmond continued confident. Although it was winter the streets at all times of the day were lined with eager, smiling faces. Handsome carriages drawn by sleek, well-groomed horses and filled with beautiful women from all parts of the South, moved in a continuous stream to and from the hospitals and camps. One could be certain that Mrs. Jefferson Davis was among them. Mrs. Chesnut preserves us a pretty picture of the Confederacy's First Lady on her way to the reviews in her handsome landau drawn by spirited bays. She had not this soon put her coachman and other servants in livery, but some said that they felt sure she would do so. Mrs. Randolph and other social leaders must have thought it the proper thing since the editor of the *Examiner* noted that the ladies of Richmond joined Varina in various social excesses and love of display. His criticism that the President was "hoarding his salary," may have had something to do with Varina's effort to spend it, though he criticized her for her love of display. But in the face of all adverse comment, handsome carriages continued to roll through the streets, some emblazoned with the family crest and coat of arms.

The winter of 1861-62, in the matter of fine clothing and luxurious living, was perhaps the most brilliant period of social life in the Southern Capital during the war. The

Southern Confederacy was now enjoying much prestige, if not actual power, among European nations and England was still demanding the release of Mason and Slidell. No special failure so far had been experienced. President Davis' unanimous election to the Presidency and his coming inaugural were subjects of daily discussion in both American and foreign papers; and there was about the newly-established government an air of old-world dignity that charmed the courts of both London and Paris. Neither dreamed how fundamentally democratic it was. But the social life of the Southern Capital and of the state generally was aristocratic. Possessing wealth and fond of display, both men and women were regal and haughty in their new rôle of independence of the old Union. The presence of the army added to the gorgeousness of the daily scene and gave the capital an air and touch of medieval chivalry. There was no question with women, in the first proud days of the Confederacy, of what one should wear at any social function —fine feathers, jewels, satins and laces were seen everywhere.

It was a day, it is true, of narrow limitations for women; but it was also a day in which sex appeal had little to do with a woman's fascinations. Mincing women in styles décolleté in the extreme would have resented it had any man glanced admiringly at their bodies. Paradoxical as it appears, her airs and graces, voluminous skirts and wasp-like waist, were the things that bound the genial cavalier to her feet.

Numerous visitors enlivened the social life of the city during the winter of '61. Among them was the occasional arrival of some titled subject of Great Britain, peeping about the new states of America to see, as Lincoln expressed it, "what all this fuss was about." The coming in the fall of Sir James Ferguson with his suite had seemed an occasion of a deeper significance than social. Many thought he came with negotiatory powers. But as it turned out he was only making a tour of the country, and wished to spend a few days in Richmond before joining a party of friends farther south.

The winter festivities of '61-'62 had brought to Richmond, with numerous other young women, the beautiful Cary cousins, as they were called. Constance came from Alexandria, and her cousin Hetty, a brilliant blonde beauty and heroine, from Baltimore. Refugees, they humorously called themselves. Hetty was just out of jail where her loyalty to the Confederacy had placed her, and for that fact, every man, woman and child in Richmond adored her. The cousins occupied rooms at the old Clifton Hotel where they dispensed a war-time hospitality, of which many delightful stories have come down in history. They belonged to the best families of Virginia and occupied a high social position. Some thought them unduly haughty and full of family pride. But be it as it may they were among the most popular young ladies in Richmond society. The President's young secretary, Burton N. Harrison, was soon in love with Constance. From the first their attachment promised to be a love match, to form one of the most charming romances of the war.

The Confederacy covered a portion of the Union where the social had always been greatly stressed. Numerous patriots of other countries who had espoused the Southern cause were amazed at the flair and flame of society, and wrote back to their friends at home that it equaled anything in European courts. It is an instance in which one might wish there had been an effusive society page in the daily papers.

Though much has been preserved of the social life of Richmond at that period by participants and other observers, women do not seem to get much mention in the newspapers of the day except in a general way. We find few daily reports of social activities. Brief mention occasionally occurs in the scant space not filled with war and foreign news. Several women, Constance Cary particularly, wrote a great deal for various papers, but their writings principally concerned the general situation, and personal social mention was brief. Memoirists, however, made up for it in after years. The author of "Richmond during the War" wrote of Mrs. Jefferson Davis that, "she was of a tall, commanding figure with dark hair and complexion, and strongly-marked expression which lies chiefly about the mouth. With firmly set yet flexible lips, there is indicated much energy of purpose but all beautifully softened by the unusually sad expression of her dark, earnest eyes." The writer continued: "Her manners are kind, graceful, easy and affable; and her receptions are characterized by the dignity and suavity which should very properly distinguish the drawing-room entertainment of the Chief Magistrate of a Republic." Numerous writers stress her power to amuse and entertain. There was still, at the age of thirty-five, a youthfulness of gesture and manner, and an abundance of gay, infectious spirits that a crowd, or a room full of people invariably emphasized. At such times people said that she was both beautiful and fascinating. Women more artistically beautiful were often overshadowed by the natural charm of her manner. The lively and charming Mrs. Chesnut seems to have felt no spirit of rivalry in connection with the brilliant Varina.

One sometimes gets the impression that she enjoyed watching her in the part of playing first lady in the vast Confederacy which was becoming the talk of foreign powers.

While it is certain that Varina was not always as charming and delightful as her friend Mary Boykin found her in some "moods," nor as "mannish and dictatorial" as Pollard has described her, there was a frank and gay humor and a quick ready wit and responsiveness that attracted and held people of all stations. Her manner towards the poorer and less fortunate class was one of her best, and these felt its charm as many incidents in her life show. Both servants and workmen found her always ready to hear something of their lives. But withal, there was a touch of dignity and reserve in her bearing that could not be ignored except intentionally. "Imagine Mrs. Jefferson Davis' being overlooked in her own drawing-room," wrote Mrs. Chesnut, as if one could well divine the consequences. If Varina in her resentment of a discourtesy burst into a passion, and on one occasion it is recorded that she did, this was not often enough for it to be set down against her as a habit. Conduct brought about by unusual circumstance is one thing and habit is another.

But if she expected some deference from those about her, she felt it was due to her position; at any rate the few who withheld it intentionally did not go unrebuked, and sometimes received a cut that smarted like a burn. Varina had her critics and sometimes envious ones. A jealous tongue had early remarked, "It was something to be the first lady in all this great Confederacy." The glamor of it, too, was beginning to appeal to her pride as nothing hitherto had done. The pleasure she took in it offended the editor of the Richmond *Examiner,* who made it his duty to watch both the Confederacy's first lady and her husband. "Who was Varina that she should assume such airs?"

But Varina put out of her mind any misgivings as to the future. With Jefferson Davis' name ringing in the courts of Europe, shouted up and down the streets of Liverpool and London by swarms of shrill-voiced newsboys, and all the South, even the grim, unemotional Jackson crying, "Hurrah for the President," she could forget the editors of the Richmond *Examiner* and Charleston *Mercury*. Besides, there were the people to offset the impressions these sought to create; and as long as they cried their hurrahs for Jefferson Davis, she was satisfied.

By the first Christmas, troops from every state in the Confederacy had arrived in Richmond, and despite their noise and rostering Virginia was proud of them. Women's eyes filled with tears as the gray legions filed through the streets day and night on their way to camp. All Richmond society gave itself up to the entertainment of both officers and privates; "Po' White," as well as aristocrat, received his silver goblet of foaming eggnog from the hands of the fairest women of the city that first Christmas in the Southern Capital. His awkwardness and blushes only increased the kindly attention paid him.

The spectacle was one of war with its incessant marching and drilling, but they laughed and said that there seemed to be no enemy on which to turn their guns. Would the Federals never make a move? Lincoln, who was manifesting some of Seward's nervous impatience, complained that McClellan had the "slows." But McClellan had typhoid fever which was vastly equivalent. Left to the lull in war, throughout the first winter, in the Southern Capital, while women continued their work in the hospitals with devotion and meticulous care, the entertainment of the army continued on a large scale. Both Jefferson Davis and General Lee, though they took little part in it, approved of it. While they were sorting out and cementing varied elements —slaveholder and non-slaveholder, Cotton King and poor white, that were to become one of the best armies in the history of mankind, women must relieve the *ennui* that settles down upon the spirit of war as well as upon that which rules the exploits of peace.

No woman in the capital city gave herself more freely to the entertainment of the army and all official circles than the mistress of the Executive Mansion. If Jefferson Davis was not physically able to keep up with social duties and administer government at the same time, she would fill the breach for him. The Confederate White House soon became noted for its lavish and easy hospitality. "People of all official ranks," and "every one not in mourning," wrote the facile author of "Recollections Grave and Gay," attended the reception. No personal sorrow came to Varina the first year of the Confederacy, and, surrounded by kindred and friends, it is suspected that she was never happier at any time during the war than she was during the winter of '61. Her household, besides her immediate family, now consisted of her young sister Maggie and her husband's young secretary, Burton N. Harrison. Young Harrison was regarded as a member of the family, and Mrs. Harrison records years later that he was a son to the President. His devotion to Jefferson Davis was of the priceless stuff of which romance is made. The Davis household was devoted to him. Various "Memoirs" relate how Varina and her young sister Maggie on one occasion put aside everything to fashion a costume for him out of an old Indian regalia

MRS. JEFFERSON DAVIS AT THE AGE OF THIRTY-FIVE.

that had belonged to Jefferson Davis during his youthful days in the West. The young Secretary had been induced to shave and take part as an Indian brave in a certain theatrical they were getting up for the soldiers' entertainment. The theatrical form of entertainment was much in favor with Mrs. Randolph and other ladies of the city for the amusement of the army. Reminiscences and diaries devote many gay pages to it, and some of it, from accounts, would have entertained Joe Jefferson himself. Varina sometimes induced the President to witness the performances—their children often had a part in them—and it has been stated that he himself was once persuaded to take part in one. Pollard says satirically that he starred with a "great blonde beauty who represented Maryland," which leads one to believe that it was the dashing Hetty Cary.

In their social entertainment, Varina and her sister Maggie were constantly assisted by Mrs. Chesnut, and it is from her diary that one gets a pleasing glimpse of Maggie. This particular sister had been under Varina's care since early childhood, and she always spoke of her as her adopted daughter. Varina was now interested in numerous young people about her. The Cary cousins, of whom she was fond, were constantly at the Mansion. Hetty was her ideal of feminine beauty, and a warm friendship existed between them. Everything at the White House, including the carriage and horses, was at the young people's disposal. Later in the war Hetty was married to the gallant Major Pegram, and a funny little story is told that on her wedding day, Varina's horses balked so miserably that the bride was compelled to make use of an old ramshackle barouche. As yet, with the exception of the large, formal receptions that every one attended, entertainment at the Mansion centered around the official circles of the government.

During the first winter of the Confederacy, the White House at times became extremely gay and festive. The young army officers, whom Varina encouraged in all sorts of pleasant attentions to the young ladies of the city, swarmed around her to be early transferred to them as escorts. Besides, Varina herself was young. As well versed as she was in statecraft and public affairs, she was feminine to the core and liked the general admiration of the crowd around her. She herself cites instances in which the young soldiers brought her banners from the war, some of which she kept long years afterwards. But Varina was Victorian, and obsessed with the one love of her life. She would as soon have practised the arts of the coquetry of that day upon the grave Rector of St. Paul as upon the fledgling heroes who gathered around her.

All was now well with the Confederacy on its Northern borders, and as yet no calamity had been reported from the Western front. Still the Federals were casting covetous eyes at the far Southern cotton lands where they were striving to get a foothold. But, while the war rested lightly on the Southern Capital this first Christmas, Varina knew that it did not rest lightly on the heart of Jefferson Davis. How to help him carry the load, either by giving receptions and dinners, or writing notes for him, or entertaining with diverting stories the hundreds who swarmed in and out of the Mansion, this was her chief concern.

CHAPTER XXI

As the first lady of the Confederacy, Varina was coming more into public notice each day. Eyes at times were fastened as critically upon her as upon her husband. She was now being closely observed by people interested in both the civil and military branches of the government, and the inquiry was often made concerning the influence she would bring to bear upon her husband in appointments. She did not look like a woman, they said, who would be contented to stay in the background. Varina, however, continued to grace her salon with an ease that won the praise of the most critical.[1] While it is easy to believe that she made indiscreet remarks at times in moments of deep feeling, she recovered herself with her characteristic alertness and shrewdness. She was now playing two rôles, one as leader of the official social life of the new government, and the other as a deeply concerned, if silent, partner in its councils. She was her husband's confidante concerning all official proceedings. This was a habit they had formed during his public service in Washington. But outside of official circles, which were large, she had so far drawn around her but a small circle of friends. And while this was composed of the best families in the city there were many in its social circles that she had met only on formal occasions.

As has been observed, the Richmond papers, now reduced

[1] "Grave and Gay," by Mrs. Burton Harrison.

in size and devoted almost exclusively to the proceedings of the Confederate government and foreign affairs, reported very little social news. Among the *Examiner's* occasional references to social affairs is one of a general reception before the inaugural which Varina was unable to attend on account of a recent illness. At this time even her maiden name did not seem to be generally known to the public, as her young sister, Maggie Howell, was often referred to as Miss Howard in the city papers. On the day of her husband's inaugural, to which she had looked forward with keen interest, she was in a highly agitated mood. Several small mishaps in the arrangements for the day had a share in her perturbation. She had always been used to display, even fond of it, but without ostentation, to which she was averse, painfully so at times, and the stately and somewhat absurd manner in which she was being conducted to the Capitol to witness the inaugural ceremonies, with her coachman and footman in white gloves and moving as if in a funeral procession, struck her as being ridiculous in the extreme. She must have been greatly annoyed since her first impulse was to order them away. Although she later took a humorous view of the pompous manner in which she had been driven to the Capitol, one may believe that at the time she displayed the usual amount of disapproval attributed to her on such occasions. In temperament she was like neither Mrs. Alfred E. Smith nor Mrs. Herbert Hoover, both of whom in a like position would have meekly accepted the situation whether they approved it or not; but Varina was not a meek woman, and with all her diplomacy found it difficult at times to conceal her disapproval of things that annoyed her. Arriving at the Capitol, she regained her poise somewhat and was elated over the ceremonies in the Hall of the House of Delegates. These were greatly to her taste, which was fastidious in any matters relating to her husband. Of the inaugural proceedings in the Hall, the daily Richmond *Examiner* for Saturday, February 22d, and Monday, February 24th, carried, not editorially, but in the reporter's columns, the following brilliant account: [1]

"It was a grave and great assemblage. Time-honored men were there, who had witnessed ceremony after ceremony of inaugurations in the palmiest days of the old confederation, those who had been at the inauguration of the iron-willed Jackson; men who, in their fiery Southern ardor, had thrown down the gauntlet of defiance in the halls of Federal legislation, and in the face of the enemy, avowed their determination to be free, and finally witnessed the enthroning of a Republican despot in our Country's Father's Chair of State. All were there, and silent tears were seen coursing down the cheeks of gray-haired men while the determined will stood out in every feature. The President in plain black citizen's clothes was very pale, and although his emotions were slightly visible, showing how deeply he felt the responsibility resting upon him, yet there was on his countenance that great will and determination, which gave proof that he was fully equal to the exigency of the times.

After these ceremonies the procession was then formed and moved according to programme to the stand erected at the Washington Monument in the Public Square. This platform was a segment of a circle extending from the pedestal in front of the statue of Mason to that in front of Jefferson and held comfortably about a dozen persons. The press of the crowd was very great, and the aides of the Marshal were obliged to open the way with their horses for the proces-

[1] Copies made from newspapers on file in the Richmond Confederate Museum.

sion, and afterwards for the band. The assemblage was
called to order by Mr. Lyons of Virginia, Chairman of the
House Committee on Arrangement. A most solemn and ap-
propriate prayer was then offered by the Right Reverend John
Johns.[1] On the coming forward of President Davis, he was
greeted with cheer after cheer, so that some moments elapsed
before he could proceed with his address."

The day which, according to Mrs. Chesnut's Diary, must
have opened fair down in South Carolina, turned out to be
a dreary one in Richmond with the skies sullen and gray and
a constant downpour of rain that alternately slackened and
quickened. Of the occasion the *Examiner* further recorded
in its reportorial columns: "Notwithstanding the drenching
rain, beginning Friday night and continuing throughout
Saturday, before ten o'clock Saturday every street and avenue leading to the Capitol Square was thronged with
pedestrians, and by noon the Capitol building and every
available space in the Square were occupied. The Square,
as one viewed it from the Court House, looked like an
immense plantation of giant mushrooms. Neither legs nor
bodies of the crowd were visible, nothing but a nodding and
waving grove of umbrellas." Varina's depression grew.
Her husband's pale face, she says, distressed her. Would
the people be impressed with the message he would bring
them? She never doubted his capacity, but there was a su-
percilious air in the manner of the young men on the Richmond *Examiner* that she did not like. The platform upon
which she sat was small and cramped the few who occupied
it. There was no one about her but her sister and a few gentlemen, most of whom were strangers to her. Her naturally
pale face became pallid as she held her breath in dismay

[1] Bishop of Virginia.

at the persistent downpour of rain. The President, the Bishop and the Committee in their wet clothes stood not far from her. The damp, raw air was bitter cold and many shivered. The great throng below them endeavored to look up from under a trembling, swaying canopy of umbrellas upon which the rain streamed in a noisy patter, sometimes drowning the voices of the speakers. It was a dismal sight and there were the ever present wag and the pessimist to make significant and prophetic comments. The fear of, if not the actual belief in, signs, trifling or serious, still to an extent engaged the mind of many at that day. Did Varina, too, not like the sign of the rain, or was she thinking of what Pollard would say tomorrow in his paper, or was she vainly turning over in her mind how best to bring about amicable relations between her husband and the disgruntled military leaders, or was she distressing herself on account of his pale face? That some such thoughts flashed through her mind a biographer may be permitted to say. Certainly the editors of the Richmond *Examiner* at times were in her thoughts. With such a brilliant and unappeasable coterie, she felt that they were there to condemn and criticize. They had been like sleuths upon the track of the tall, pale man who, despite all opponents, was bringing to the ears of the people a message that would thrill and animate them for four years, years full of deadly warfare which his strong unbending will alone prolonged. It was a message to which Whitehall and all Europe later listened with the deepest respect, a circumstance that should have put to shame the editors of the Richmond *Examiner* and Charleston *Mercury*.

Not since their arrival at the Spotswood had Varina felt that an occasion was more in the nature of a first appear-

ance. One gets the impression from her "Memoir" that it
was one of the most painful experiences of her life during
the first years of the Confederacy, which, in the main,
held for her happiness and honors. After another glance at
her husband's pale face she was so overcome that a faintness
seized her, and fearing that she might attract attention,
she made some excuse and slipped away. Years afterwards, describing the scene, she wrote as if the pain
still lingered, "Then began my husband's martyrdom."
Reaching the Executive Mansion, she was exhausted, and
also apprehensive as to the impression his message would
make upon the people. In the past she had not feared
the public, but she knew that her husband already had critics who were misleading the people. But Jefferson Davis
had an iron will that even she had not fathomed.

Varina's temperament was one that quickly rallied from
depression. By evening she was relieved of the sudden
faintness that had seized her during the day, and with
the help of her sister Maggie and the servants, got the
Mansion ready for their reception. They had intended
having the inaugural ball in the city hall, but later decided to have the great coming together at their beautiful
new White House. Varina had left nothing undone to
make the occasion a notable one. People said that she
looked very beautiful as she stood beside the President
in a gorgeous white silk evening gown with a flower in
her dark hair. She was now making merry over the solemn
and majestic air of her white-gloved attendants of the
day. But the main thing that had restored her spirits was
the word brought her through the day—and still on every lip,
that Jefferson Davis had captured the hearts of all Richmond with his noble utterances; that the rain-soaked audi-

ence hung on his words breathlessly and thousands had shouted his name through the streets. This had made her happy. The editors of the *Examiner* might carp and indite vitriolic editorials but as long as the people were on his side, she felt that all was well. She had discovered that fact from their political life in the past.

The inaugural reception proved to be a brilliant success. A city paper carried the following notice of the reception:

As announced in the papers on Saturday, the Presidential Mansion was from 8 to 11 P.M. thrown open for the reception of visitors. Mrs. Davis did the honors of the occasion with rare grace and unaffected dignity. The President, though pale and somewhat worn from his recent indisposition, appeared cheerful and in good spirits.

But Varina's elation was not to last. The Richmond *Examiner*, the next day, came out in the following pronounced criticism of the President:

The Inaugural Address is a well-written document, but does not require or invite much comment. It throws no light on the real condition of the country, and gives no indication of the President's probable policy. It might have been omitted from the ceremony had not custom required that the President should say something on such an occasion. The public expects a much more important communication from the President than this, and it is the hope of every rational man and disinterested patriot that he would create a cabinet of the ablest, best informed and most experienced, especially of the most active and energetic men. Men of strong characters, men who know the affairs of the nation at large. Under the present régime, the so-called Secretaries are mere clerks and not one of them is a statesman of calibre equal to these times or any other time. They seem to have been selected with reference to the geographical sections of the Confederacy. The life and future of the whole country depend upon the central government, and in the selection of the Cabinet nothing but intellectual capacity, general public information, patriotism, activity and courage should be the tests even if the greatest men of the country were all from one county, that circumstance should not weigh a feather in the choice. The President has hitherto been the Departments, but it is impossible this system should go on. A little Joseph in the house of Pharaoh might have been sufficient for peaceful Egypt, but in modern governments even the Napoleons have seen the necessity of dividing this power with the best men they could get; and in a government like ours it is useless to expect one head to suffice for the design and execution of the complicated affairs. Any candid observer can see that the Yankees have outwitted us in the art in which we are supposed to be superior, the art of government. The Confederacy has had everything that was required for success, but one and that one thing it was, and it is, supposed to possess more than anything else, namely —*talent*. We have permitted the magnificent armies of last year to dwindle into imbecility and insignificance, the most puerile partiality has been displayed in the treatment of officers. Little lieutenants and colonels have been erected into major-generals without achievement or justice, and it would seem the government was afraid of genius and will, so sedulously has it kept at a distance individuals of lofty intellect, knowledge and energy.

The scathing effusion, patriotic and enthusiastic, for the author was all that, but indicating deep personal animosity as well as crass ignorance, fired Varina's heart. It was the first fierce pricking of the thorns that were to become so plentiful.

"Of lofty intellect, knowledge and energy"—who were they? Where were any better than those already employed in the service of the government? Blind, selfish egotist! Did he not see that such criticism would injure the Confederacy in the eyes of the world? She said something like this, perhaps more, as her private letters often contain comments of a highly satirical nature. And many might ask today why the government did not suppress an organ that was doing the Southern cause such deadly harm. The fact that foreign statesmen were praising the Confederate President for not infringing upon the liberty of the press did not cure the matter.

By this time Varina had a very clear idea of the attitude of the prominent men of the South. She read carefully every issue of the American and foreign papers that came to Richmond. While it was a constant source of irritation to read what the former were saying about her husband, it kept her in close touch with everything concerning him and the new government struggling to make a place for itself among the nations of the world. The bitterest pain came from the internal criticism. She told friends in long years after, with a little tremulous smile that, while it had in it much of forgiveness, was tinged with bitterness, that there were times when she hated Daniel, Pollard and the elder Rhett more than she ever hated any Republican in Washington. She was now ready to exclaim angrily and bitterly, "A house divided against itself." What did they expect to accomplish?

But Jefferson Davis had fired the hearts of the people on his inaugural day with new zeal. The Confederacy continued to flourish, rising over every criticism and beating down every obstacle in its path. Still, with all the fair outlook in

Virginia, there had been pallor on his face as he spoke of his losses at Fort Donelson and Roanoke Island. But it was only a momentary spasm that clutched him, for his strong will was suited to such a quest as he followed. One thing was certain, he would need more troops to contend with the great army that Rhodes tells us was opposing him in the spring of '62. The volunteers were splendid but not ample enough to contend with the numbers that he, better than any about him, knew would face them. The Constitution under which he lived had plainly provided for the contingencies of war. There it stood in the written law, "in time of war to raise armies." He would point this out to Congress, would make it see the necessity of defense, to withstand the numbers that Grant was taking into the very heart of the Confederacy. But the captious, stubborn ones would not have it so, and declared him a dictator and despot like the other in Washington. Had he been less strong he would have quailed before the "hard and pompous men" that Russell saw throughout the South, but his will was stronger even than theirs. The civil liberties of men were dear to him, the *ultima thule* of all for which he was contending, and not one would be taken from them that the Constitution did not grant in its provisions for war and Congress did not approve; but this much, in the face of the "hard and pompous" ones, he would demand. The editors of the Charleston *Mercury* and Richmond *Examiner* might have taken a few lessons in statecraft and diplomacy from Seward.

CHAPTER XXII

SPRING OF '62

JEFFERSON DAVIS did not employ sordid mercenaries in his armies but a number of young patriots came to him from Europe. In the spring of '62, numerous young foreigners figure prominently. Many of these belonged to the titled families of Europe and served in the Confederate armies with distinction. After Russell was prevented by Stanton from following McClellan's army, the London *Times* and several other European papers kept representatives in Richmond. Young Edward St. Maur was under fire at Frazier's Farm and several distinguished young Englishmen were with Lee at Gettysburg. The gallant, giant-statured cavalryman, Colonel Heros von Brorcke, the Lafayette of the lost cause, seems to have been one of the most admired. At times he was Stuart's right arm in the defense of Richmond. He was, they said, "the life of any social gathering," and both men and women honored him highly. The South fascinated him—everything about it, including the homespun dresses of the Virginia country girls. They tell a funny little story that the troopers who could never get his name right always called him "Major Bandbox." Thus war stories accumulated that would fill many volumes. Of fancy costume parties, suppers, luncheons and dinners, tableaux, charades and dancing in the Southern Capital, we have innumerable reminiscences. All such entertainment was encouraged by the grave heads of the army. The need of

251

it throughout the war is apparent.   In answer to the harsh criticism of it by the editor of the *Examiner,* one could say that it was a highly valued feature of the World War.

Jefferson Davis was socially inclined in a quiet way, but showed a decided preference for official duties, a disposition that grew upon him.   Still he was interested in the affairs of the young people about him, as numerous stories preserved in various volumes show.   He was deeply attached to the women who had drawn close to him during this period of his life.   It is an accepted fact, however, that he remained unsusceptible to any who sought to arouse in him any admiration other than he would have bestowed upon a sister.   While Pollard makes him out attractive to women, he goes no further.   Mrs. Chesnut records a slight scowl upon his face in disapproval of some attempt at coquetry with him on the part of a lady she does not name. No hint even of salacious gossip ever found its way on the tongue in connection with the White House of the Confederacy.   Here was sacred ground that all trod with care. Not Albert and Victoria had set up a higher standard of propriety in family life than the master and mistress of the Brockenbrough Mansion.   The people pointed to it with pride.   The family court of their Confederacy at least would go down in history without a breath of scandal. But that women regarded it an honor to receive some attention from the President is seen in such remarks by one who, next to Varina, was nearest to him, "The President sat by me on the sofa," "The President walked with me," "The President gave me his arm when the loveliest women of the city were near." [1]

For the most part the entertainment fell to Varina.

1 Chesnut.

She was, however, daily growing more absorbed in public affairs. She early began to be haunted with the idea that the whole responsibility of the war rested upon her husband—all the world, all the North, all the South, seemed to her to be taking the position that success or failure rested with Jefferson Davis. The thought daily grew more intense, and often caused her tears of anger. And could they not see his many difficulties—the proud, self-centered but gallant and heroic spirits about him who had never bent their wills to any authority, to any discipline? While Lincoln was molding a far different people, one taught in the main to conform, to comply, Jefferson Davis was contending with a class of leaders every one of whom it was said thought of himself as "a king in his own right." And he must have labored with a skill far greater than the prejudiced eye can discover to have molded and shaped into one great whole the dazzling, heterogeneous mass of men, masters and overlords, that daily lined the streets of the Southern Capital. "If they all labored as hard as the President," an English observer exclaimed on noting his thin, upright figure pass as he went to and from his office, "the country would be better off."

Sunday afternoons were the only hours that Varina and her husband had to themselves. In the seclusion of the old Brockenbrough garden, terraced and fragrant with flower and fruit, with their children she relaxed with something of her pleasure in the old Briarfield days. It was a pretty picture of restful home life, with the woman holding her baby in her arms, the man silently drinking his tea, little Margaret and her associates playing dolls under the cherry trees, and the little boys, Jefferson and Joe with their playmate

"Jim Limber," [1] pelting some object they called the Yankees, or staging a mock battle between the Hill Cats and the Butcher Cats.

These names were given to the children of the aristocratic families on the hill and the children of the working class who lived below the hill. A feud of long standing, growing out of social antagonisms, existed between them and sometimes broke out in small riots. The Davis' children with their negro playmate, Jim Limber, were sometimes involved in the fights and Varina with a zest for preserving little stories of the people tells us a humorous story of the battles between the two clans; also one of the house painter at the Mansion who confided to her that before his new position in the city, he was a Butcher Cat.

But was Jefferson Davis drinking his tea in silence? It may rather be believed, that there was anxious talk about the war and the Confederacy; still it was the few fleeting moments of the privacy and seclusion, Varina tells us, to which she, with all her love of stir and action, had looked forward. [2] The manner of her early education had left this impress.

How much her thought and opinions in regard to public matters were now affecting Jefferson Davis' actions is still much of a conjecture; but it must always be believed that she was never inarticulate. A few thought that her strong will, which dominated so much about her, included him. And yet when one sees recorded much later than at the orchard teas, "You never liked to have me advise you in such matters," one feels that there was no undue yielding on Jefferson Davis' part. Still Varina was tenacious,

[1] A small negro boy they had rescued from a vicious caretaker.
[2] "Memoir," vol. II.

though she admits that he always decided, and often at her own solicitation, much of the momentous for her. Such expressions as "The President thought it best for me to leave Richmond, though I was reluctant to leave him," are too frequent not to have a meaning. While it is certain that she expressed herself freely about many matters, one point stands out prominently—there was always close co-operation. Of this, numerous instances speak, not only during the four years of the Confederacy but throughout life.

It was during the winter of '61 that Mason and Slidell, the Southern Commissioners to the English and French courts, were released from imprisonment at Fort Warren. While this spread relief throughout the Confederacy, it did not elude the Southerners that it might restore peace between England and the Federal Union. It would have been a stroke of good fortune, it may be repeated, for these to have remained in prison; but Seward had come down off of his high perch long enough to save the Union from a war with England. That it was his diplomacy none can dispute; but instead of getting praise for it, he got actual abuse from Gideon Welles and other Republicans. The sensitive, sympathetic Southerners had worried over the fate of the Commissioners. But while it pleased them that they had been released and the Union crest had been cut to the bone, Jefferson Davis feared the new rôle of diplomacy that Seward was so shrewdly playing. There had been tottering days for the Union, and the Democrats of the North had used every effort to keep public feeling quiet. A thousand rumors had flooded the South that several dozen of the most distinguished Southerners would go to their death with Mason and Slidell. Jefferson Davis was considered the prime offender and rumors were daily heard that a speedy death would be his fate. Rhodes naïvely gives the credit to England that the country was spared an orgy of blood that would have shocked civilization. But now that the Commissioners had safely arrived at their respective courts, the exciting topic passed out of the day's conversation. How the self-respecting old democrat, "Jeems" Mason, was to get on with Lord John Russell was the next worry. In Virginia people called first on strangers.

Though England negotiated the *Trent* affair, the Confederacy continued confident. The Federals had not made any particular advance; still news that their preparations were on a prodigious scale reached the Southern Capital. The war spirit in the city had not cooled. The young blood of the South, still exulting over Manassas, was champing its bit for another trial at arms, and still another declaration from the cotton barons came that the South could whip the world, England or no England. Jefferson Davis, however, was settled in the belief that the Federal Government was preparing, if possible, to subjugate the Confederate States if they continued to resist. A large army to withstand this was more and more his daily concern. Without that, he knew that the Confederacy would go down in this very year of '62. One is again struck with Seward's keen insight that here was the brains of the revolution.

Though the North seemed slow in renewing hostilities, preparations had been made on an immense scale, and the unlimited resources of that section in the matter of factories and materials were now lavishly used to equip the army. The editor of the Richmond *Examiner* was shrewdly taking note of the continued industrial and mechanical progress of the North; but made no allowances in Jefferson Davis' instance for the different economic systems of the two sections, and the isolation that was slowly getting a stranglehold upon the South.

Reverses had stung the North's pride. Seward was also beginning to be fully conscious of the spirit of contest, and conferring, Welles says, with Lincoln every minute in the day. Twitted slyly as he had been by the London *Times* reporter, his really good intentions at the outset misunderstood in the South, he was growing more ardent each day in his efforts to "put down the rebellion." Lincoln and the Cabinet now had little trouble in arousing the battle spirit in him towards the "rebel states," that he had thought to woo home after a day of wrath.

While the Southern army remained inactive in the winter and spring of '62, with Johnston, who had left Manassas, awaiting development, the soldiers grew impatient and many were beginning to complain of the monotony of camp life. The Richmond *Examiner* was placing the blame upon the administration, especially its weak cabinet, a body it never lost an opportunity to deride. The public situation, however, had in no way, except as food for light and irritating gossip, affected the preparations for war, nor had criticism had any appreciable effect upon military matters. The war spirit in the army was daily growing stronger and the desire to come to arms with the enemy was at white heat. Daily outrages were reported from the regions infested by the enemy. Loyal Southerners were forsaking their homes and bringing with them tales of plunder and sacrifice that fanned the fires of sectional hate. It was scornful comment among the youthful Confederates that the Yankees would not fight regular battles but preferred slipping down and foraging upon the country, engaging in loot of a petty nature, such as appropriating watches and ladies' rings. The Federals, in turn, were scoffing at the soft, white hands of the young lords of Slavonia. Northern poets and preachers were naming them in biting satire, "Lords of the Lash." The enmity of both sides left a deadly sting that burns sometimes even today.

The winter was passing. Diminutive grass spears were thrusting up their shining points upon sunny hillsides. The two armies still continued to eye each other, and Richmond was this early feeling the strain. The city was not only the central ground for the army, but for all refugees from Maryland and the other border states. Strangers of every land were found in the hotels; spies by hundreds were also secreted in the city and peddlers of many nationalities were hawking their cheap and tawdry wares on the streets, smuggled through the blockade—Yankee toys for children, beads for the negroes, perfumed soap for society. Greed and trafficking went hand in hand at all times and everywhere. But this was scarcely noticed in the roar and confusion of the gathering army. One cannot well imagine at this far and fair day, the stir and excitement that shook the city, with regiment after regiment coming up from the towns, villages and open country of the deep South. Many brought with them the charm and presence, as it were, of tender, soft-voiced women, jasmine and white magnolia; others bespoke largely of animal thirst and cravings; but all had the battle fire in their eyes. The grave people of the city made no complaint. They had made it their war and had determined to accept the full responsibility, let it fall upon them as heavily as it might. Their beautiful city had been converted into a pandemonium of war activities. Their lawns, their flower gardens, their homes and all they possessed were placed at the command of the government with smiling faces. Yes, it was their war, and not a woman in all the disheveled, noise-wracked city would have drawn back from dressing the wounds of the dirtiest soldier out of the far South.

As is the fate of all nations in times of war, vice of every kind was beginning to show itself in places. Still the spirit of the Southern Capital remained strong and unterrified. If it were now not actually gay, it was proud and self-sufficient and constantly indulged in emotional transports that approximated joy. The newly-elected Confederate Congress had assembled and both England and France were praising Jefferson Davis' messages. Though no note of bluster and braggadocio was heard, still there was perfect assurance in his outlook. Neither Boyce nor Foote, nor the dozen or more like them that later yelped at his heels, had as yet developed their indecent craving for notoriety by opposing the President; their only chance, a contemporary has said, for attracting attention to themselves.

For the Confederacy the outlook in '62 was fair. Jefferson Davis had managed well. They might have their differences, and did among themselves, but it was a solid front that they turned to the foe. The indiscreet, carping editors of the *Examiner* were just as ready to die for the cause as Jefferson Davis. For the South these were proud days, engaged as it was in a high, adventurous and romantic exploit for conviction, the zeal and fervor of which approached that which marked the Holy Land exploits of Cœur de Lion. At least more than one proud romanticist thought of himself as "crusader for the right." Their zeal, too, had in it much of religious fervor. But, though living in a day intensely and traditionally religious, humankind found its objective mainly in physical truths.   Mystical apprehension in its higher, more enthralling cognizance opened no vistas, and spiritual consciousness was largely material. God, for all their awe of Him, was almost as much a bodily presence as themselves, not certainly a carved image, but an invisible, sentient, solemn giant they had glorified and before whom much kneeling would secure favor.   But it was His favor and blessing in matters of their temporal welfare and protection that they craved, as Israel had done before them.   As they optimistically and joyously conceived God to be, few generations since the nomadic march of Joshua acknowledged His presence more in battle.

CHAPTER XXIII

THE TEST OF ARMS

THE Federal government now had large armies everywhere at its command and continued to gather recruits. It is true that angry women in New York City continued to throw rocks at the recruiters, and the demonstrations against war at times were much like revolutions in themselves; but the martial spirit once stirred is difficult to quench. The North had decided to make of the struggle a test of arms and Seward shrewdly kept proclaiming "for the preservation of the Union." It, however, was taking a rather unfair advantage in naming it a "test of arms," since the Federal army generally outnumbered the Confederates three to one, and in some instances historians have said as much as six to one.[1] The war with the Republicans was only a matter of "high tariff and hurt vanity," was a satirical remark of the time, but the "preservation of the Union" was a slogan that never failed to enlist the young men of the North. Slavery in some quarters was constantly stressed as a cause of the war to impress England and France and the regiments from the abolition strongholds in New England. It had its weight, but neither Bright nor Cobden could make England believe that the South was fighting for anything but its independence. "Slavery counts for little with the South in the quarrel, commercial antagonisms for much," said the London *Times,* an authori-

[1] Pollard.

tative organ so dreaded and hated by the Republicans. "The watchword of the South is 'independence,' " declared the neutral London *Standard* and *Herald;* and other influential English publications like the *Quarterly Review* were voicing the same sentiment. The *Index,* edited by the devoted Southern patriot, John R. Thompson, as expected, was outspoken in behalf of the Southerners' declaration that they were fighting for their independence. Russell, too, was constantly writing to his paper that "It continues to be improbable that the South should be conquered and impossible that it should be held in subjection." England's sympathy, though she had waived war, was largely with the South, but it was never strong enough of itself to cause her to be willing to become involved in the revolution. A recognition of this fact would do away with much contention as to why the South neglected her opportunity. The opportunity was never really presented. Too, that the North, from the hour Lincoln issued his call for 75,000 troops after the attempt to reenforce Sumter, was determined upon a war of invasion and subjugation should also be recognized. It had determined that it would not give up what it considered a portion of its territory. That, as much as anything else, kept England quiet since she felt the same way about her own. Also, twenty million people, irrespective of the patriotic idea of preserving the Union, would never have consented to be whipped by seven million, especially when one side had guns and the other had none, and one side had cotton and the other had factories that would have been idle if their adversary had won. As it was, the operatives in them, in many instances little children, were already half-nourished and overworked. Work must be provided them in future even if it took war to procure it. It had been said at White-hall that the South already had been sucked like an orange by the North, but the fruit was still juicy and sweet to the tooth. Still the North thought it had a right to retain what it believed was its own. Seward had let no opportunity pass to paraphrase Webster's burning climax, "one and indivisible, now and forever."

It was a large well supplied but unwieldy army that the North sent against the South in the spring of '62. In February, McClellan began moving down from the Potomac with a view of an advance later on Richmond. The Federals, as has been seen, had met with success in the South and the Southwest, and had won conceded victories in February. There was a hard line about President Davis' mouth whenever he referred to them. His strong will was often seen in the compression of his lips, a habit that, with the loss of some of his teeth, thinned the gently shaped mouth that his early pictures show.[1] But while the lordly Southerners left it to the historian to discover the thin lips, the *Mercury* and *Examiner* were accusing him of despotism and military dictatorship. The people had caught the spirit of complaint that was going on at Washington, and while they would have indignantly resented the accusation, there was much imitation of the adversary across the Mason and Dixon line, in the matter of condemnation of public officials. They did it in the North, why not in the South? Shrewd eyes had detected their strong likeness to each other. But the Southern carpers could not see that the difference between the policy of President Davis and President Lincoln was that the former

[1] See picture at the age of 32 in volume I of "The Rise and Fall of the Confederate Government," by Jefferson Davis.

did nothing without the consent of Congress.   In the matter
of the Conscript Law, which he recommended in the face
of a falling off of volunteering, when New Orleans was in
imminent danger and the Atlantic seaboard always open
to invasion, Congress was the means through which he
acted.   But the law had in it something of a far-off relationship to a National Army, so condemned and dreaded by
the Southern Colonial group, who, in the trenchent phrase of
the historian, "read Macaulay and swore by Hampden."
Its leaders could not realize that the country was at war
and its independence depended upon keeping a large army
in the field.

But Jefferson Davis got his way, and the great armies
that he raised in defense of the Confederacy should have
stopped the mouthing of Governor Brown of Georgia
and others who, whatever were their other deserts, did not
know how to make war.   Though historians have sought to
make much of Jefferson Davis' seeing his "strict construction" policy go to pieces, it is perfectly clear that there was
no real infringement of States' Rights in the Conscription
Act, since the state in time of war gave the power through
the Constitution to raise money for the common defense, to
declare war, to raise and support armies, to provide and
maintain a navy and to govern and regulate both land and
naval forces.   The following letter of Jefferson Davis to
Governor Brown is a perfectly clear interpretation and explanation of the whole matter.

"The Constitutional question discussed by you in relation to
the conscription law had been duly weighed before I recommended to Congress its passage; it was fully debated in both
houses, and your letter has not only been submitted to the

Cabinet, but a written opinion has been required from the Attorney-General. The constitutionality of the law was sustained by very large majorities in both houses. This decision of the Congress meets the concurrence, not only of my own judgment, but of every member of the Cabinet, and a copy of the opinion of the Attorney-General herewith enclosed develops the reasons on which the conclusions are based.

"The war powers granted to the Congress are conferred in the following paragraphs: 'No. 1 gives authority to raise revenue necessary to pay the debts, provide for the common defense and carry on the governments, etc. No. 11. To declare war, grant letters of marque and reprisal and make rules concerning captures on land and water. No. 12. To raise and support armies but no appropriation of money to that shall be for a longer term than two years. No. 13. To provide and maintain a navy. No. 14. To make rules for the government and regulation of the land and naval forces.'

"It is impossible to imagine a more broad, ample and unqualified delegation of the whole war power of each state than is here contained with the solitary limitation of appropriations to two years."

Two bitter calamities befell the Confederacy in the middle spring of 1862—the death of Albert Sidney Johnston at the battle of Shiloh on April 6th, and the capture of New Orleans by the Federal fleet on April 30th. The Confederate losses in the middle and lower South affected Jefferson Davis and Varina deeply. The gardens of Briarfield were dear to them, but it was not of these they were now thinking. Their sorrow and regret over the death of Albert Sidney Johnston, the heaviest the army had thus far sustained, was also personal. Varina wept bitterly. They had lost a friend when friends meant much. In his death, the

Western army suffered a loss from which it never recovered. Jefferson Davis winced under the heavy blow, but his lips tightened.

The Federals were now claiming success at New Orleans, Mill Springs, Forts Henry and Donelson, Nashville, Shiloh and Island No. 10, and had in their possession a large portion of the state of Missouri. Much of this, however, was questionable. Still the historian Rhodes notes the fair outlook of the Southwestern campaign and boasts of the tremendous armies that the North was at that time massing in the middle South. At the same time he asks us to meet General Grant. The Mississippi was still in the control of the Confederates and the eastern interior to the Atlantic coast was largely Confederate territory, although its scattered battalions would not, all combined, have made one large army. But its spirit was one that would yield only to superior forces. If the North now thought that a single victory by McClellan would end the war, they had yet to test the temper of the Confederate President. The writer claims exemption from the accusation of sentimentality in these passing interpretations of Jefferson Davis. If the critic desires an object to whet his derision of the sentimental upon, let him turn to the volumes of Rhodes, Channing, Nicolay and Hay and innumerable others and mark the sentimental rhapsodies, all sincerely inspired it is granted, over President Lincoln. Any, too, who would carp at the repeated references to the Confederate President in the story of the wife, should remember that Strachey, one of the best of modern biographers, in his life of Victoria gives a fair-sized portrait of Albert.

The losses in the lower and middle South, while they gave Jefferson Davis sleepless nights, were not considered permanent. Grant had yet to fail in his first awkward if not lugubrious attempt on Vicksburg, and Van Dorn was still unfurling the "Constance Cary" banner in his face. The people, of a naturally sanguine temperament, had little fear that the North would win the war. Joseph E. Johnston, they prided themselves, was opposing McClellan, and all Richmond believed that Manassas would be repeated somewhere when the silence along the Potomac was finally broken. The fires of patriotism had never burned higher in the Southern Capital than on the first anniversary of the bombardment of Fort Sumter, not even the Fourth of July had stirred more enthusiasm. Throughout the day the women of Richmond were on the streets and Varina kept open house. But the spring crept on with much inaction in both armies on the northern borders of the Confederacy. "All quiet on the Potomac" began to sound like a humorous jeer and scoff at the Federal army. The one stirring event was that of the victory of the ironclad *Virginia,* formerly the United States frigate *Merrimac,* in action with the *Monitor* of the Federal fleet in Hampton Roads. It was such a battle as the Olympic gods might have longed to take part in. Women with knitting in their hands rushed bareheaded to the Mansion to get news of the victory. The reports upset all Washington. Lincoln's Cabinet gathered for grave consultation in the White House and Stanton trembled for fear that the *Virginia* was on its way to Washington. A shot at any moment might pierce a window near the table where they sat. That the *Virginia* had destroyed the *Congress,* the sloop-of-war *Cumberland* had defeated the hated Federal *Monitor* and silenced the guns of the *Minnesota,* were eager phrases crowded into one breath as people rushed up and down the streets of Richmond. Their joy was

turned to mourning when, after another desperate battle
with a newly-arrived ironclad *Monitor* from New York, the
gallant vessel was disabled and later destroyed for fear it
would be captured by the victorious enemy.   Pollard and
his followers are full of harsh criticism of the President,
but its destruction was one of the bitter necessities of war.
Its capture would have sent depressing news abroad for the
Confederacy and in addition would have supplied the North
with another ironclad vessel.   The Union flag captured by
the *Virginia* in its first engagement was brought to Varina.
It was a compliment the commanders often paid her.

With all their spirit and patriotism, Southern women were
easily affected by the calamities of war, even if those of their
foes.   Varina wrote that she did not think that she could be
touched by any misfortune that befell the enemy, but when
they brought her the flag, and she found it wet with
blood, as proud as she was of its capture, she went to
her room overcome by the horror and tragedy of war.   She
had not yet become hardened to such painful sights and
beneath her strong personality was the underlying emo-
tionalism and tenderness usual to woman.

By the middle of March, McClellan had begun his Peninsular campaign, which included his settling down in April
on a long siege of Yorktown.   It was not until May that his
army, now proudly christened the Army of the Potomac, began a serious offensive against the Southern Capital.   He
faced a none too strong Confederate line which covered a
number of miles between the York and James rivers.   Break
it by all means and forthwith were Lincoln's instructions
from Washington, and the old General of Cossacks also had
assured him that "all roads are bad in war."   But McClellan

had not been idle. Although coming out of a spell of typhoid fever, he had busied himself in fortifying his army in the best possible manner. It was pitched forward many miles and Jefferson Davis anxiously watched the claws that reached for Richmond. The withdrawal of McDowell's whole corps was a severe loss to McClellan, and one from which he never rallied during the first part of his campaign. General Johnston, now the pride and hope of Virginia, was in command at Yorktown with 53,000 of the South's best trained troops, the early picking of the Cavaliers. On May 3d he had thought best to withdraw from Yorktown, and the army, after several fierce encounters with McClellan's forces at Williamsburg and other places, fell back fighting its way towards Richmond. McClellan was at last taking the offensive.

The war was staged once more on Virginia's soil, to continue there until its wooded vales, green fields and blue and purple hillsides were battle-scarred in a thousand fierce encounters. Here in the land of Washington, almost in sight of the spires of the Southern Capital, an Ilium-like struggle had begun. Washington, they boasted, had he been living would now be leading Virginia in a cause similar to the one in which he had won independence for the American Colonies. Was Scott, the unhappy old Virginian, thinking of this when he let it out in Paris that the Republican administration had ordered the arrest of Mason and Slidell?

On May 9th, it was well known that the Federals were preparing to carry out their designs against the Southern Capital. President Davis insisted that Varina should take their children to Raleigh, North Carolina. On the eve of the 9th, there was a large reception at the Executive Mansion to bring together in close fellowship the notables of

both the military and civil governments. Varina had
consented to go to Raleigh, and would leave in a few days,
but said nothing about it to the callers. Her heart was full,
and at first she had rebelled. She did not want to leave
Richmond, and wanted to delay the matter; but we gather
from her "Memoir" that after they had argued it out she
finally agreed. She realized that it would relieve her husband of great anxiety concerning his children at a time
when all his efforts were centered on the defense of the
city. At such times he depended upon her to take care of
them, and the care of the four with a constant change of
nurses and maids fell rather heavily on the mother. Her
sister Maggie remained with Mrs. Chesnut and Mrs. Preston, and later left with them for South Carolina. The
Mansion, with the exception of the President's quarters
and rooms for conferences, was practically closed. The city
was in a state of intense excitement, and many were leaving
for points farther South. Such dreadful communications
as "McClellan is on the Chickahominy!" "The enemy's gunboats are ascending the river," were constantly received.
Some thought they could see them from the landing below
the rapids of the James. The fear of the gunboats surpassed the dread even of the army. Would the obstructions
on the river prevent their ascent? Could they hold in the
face of the fleet? Who could say. As yet the Confederate
Capital had had little that was deeply tragic, and in all the
grim business of war, despite conditions, the serio-comic
frequently intruded. People everywhere were doing unexpected things. Varina could not restrain her laughter when
a lady, who she infers was something of a social celebrity,
rushed into their midst in the dining room and falling on
her knees prayed aloud, "Lord, have mercy upon me." The

prayer seemed very self-centered with so many other lives to be considered and the fear stamped upon the woman's face at the thought of her own safety struck Varina as highly ludicrous. The comic and droll, even when of an ordinary and everyday nature, afforded her amusement. This was often held against her and critics sometimes charged her with a want of the solemnity so approved of at that day by Southern women. But Varina was reverent in her attitude towards the deeper things of the spirit. Like all the women about her, she was full of the fundamental faiths. She might find an outlet for her humor in any singular or queer behavior of men or women; but throughout life the name of God was held so reverently that she called it with a tinge of awe in her voice; and even when they had reached adult age, she did not approve of her children calling it carelessly.[1]

It was at about this time when she was to leave the President that she was made very happy. She had, for some time, earnestly hoped that he would connect himself with the church, and before she left Richmond, Jefferson Davis was received into the Episcopal Church at the Executive Mansion by the Reverend Charles V. Minnegerode, rector of St. Paul's, after his confirmation by Bishop Johns. The Richmond *Examiner* satirically described the occasion as "the telling of beads," but it may be recorded here that Jefferson Davis, like all the people of the South, was religious. About the same time President Lincoln was received into the Presbyterian Church at Washington. Many of that day believed that a soul that had had no church connections was, in death, cast into a lake of fire or in some way punished. But henceforth, none could have any qualms

[1] Contemporaries.

about either the Confederate or Federal leader's religious status, since each had proved that he was orthodox in the most approved and conventional manner.

The Confederate President was at this time in better health than usual. He was strikingly handsome and with the bright outlook for the Confederacy, he might have enjoyed some sense of ease had not one burning purpose deadened all other sensations. In the eyes of the world, he was the embodiment of a great leader and a foe to be feared. The Richmond *Examiner* still carped, but the *Whig* affirmed that Jefferson Davis made no mistakes. He was now very active and during McClellan's advance on the Southern Capital, had the affairs of the Confederacy well in hand.

While McClellan was moving forward, Banks and Fremont were contending in the Shenandoah with the grimly determined Jackson. The latter's campaign in the famous Valley, with a force but one-third as large as the enemy's, reads like a succession of the miraculous feats of the armies of the Israelites. Through the little valleys of the great Valley, with such gallant spirits as Ashby, he harried the Federals for days, finally to drive them above the Potomac. This had prevented a concentration of forces that would have lent such strength to McClellan as the Confederates would not have been able to withstand. Characterized at Washington as priggish and perverse, he was ready at retort and there was constant derision of Lincoln and his Cabinet. His army was now in splendid shape.

Johnston continued to watch the blue columns pressing towards the Southern Capital. As they drew nearer his martial spirit rose to its highest pitch. He would gratify his chafing legions that had longed to be led against the foe.

On the last day of the soft Virginia spring, when the May bloom was thickest in the valleys and on the hills, the Southern army furiously attacked McClellan's advance corps at Fair Oaks with a signal victory. This had but one shadow to mar it—General Johnston, in the midst of the battle, was severely wounded. It was a circumstance that of itself should have been sufficient to raise the morale of the Union army. But as the lynx-eyed correspondent of the London *Times* had earlier recorded, there were many foreign troops in the Federal army. The Confederate army was to a man composed of troops fighting for their homes and firesides. With Johnston wounded, all Virginia was in alarm. Who would take his place? Would it be Lee, or would they send for Beauregard? The Richmond *Examiner* had something to say in ridicule of the former, but Jefferson Davis, after going himself to see General Johnston, with perfect confidence in General Lee appointed him to take command of the army. The Confederate President was a better judge of men than Lincoln who was feeling about in the dark for a general without a clear knowledge of what it took to make one.

CHAPTER XXIV

No sooner had Lee assumed command of the Southern forces that were henceforth to be known as the army of Northern Virginia than a secret order went to Jackson in the Shenandoah. Had Jackson arrived in time, Jefferson Davis believed that the Confederates could have overwhelmed and captured McClellan's whole army. It was one of his bitterest disappointments, and malicious critics about him attempted to turn his disappointment into some disaffection for Jackson which had no foundation whatever. He had steadily and rapidly raised Jackson from a minor position to where he commanded a separate army, and his faith in him was not in the least impaired by his failure to join Lee, as much as he regretted it. Not even Lee himself mourned the tragic death of the great soldier more sincerely than the President.

McClellan was now facing the spirit of Virginia and the whole South. The opening battle had been staged on the Chickahominy.[1] In the oratory of the day, "the tumult began that, with shock after shock, shook the very walls of Richmond." When McClellan, after the Seven Days' Battle, began his retreat towards the James to be protected by the gunboats, there were many explanations—the lack of reenforcements, the broken, hilly, well-wooded country, the rain that filled the Virginia roads knee-deep in places with mud and water. But the bickering continued, and the

[1] Battle of Gaines Mill, June 27.

"young Napoleon" whipped out that the Republican cabinet was nothing more than a "flock of geese."

Throughout the better part of the summer from Fair Oaks to Malvern Hill, the Confederate colors flew victoriously. Another victory on Saturday, August 30th, on the historic Bull Run, in Prince William County, where the Federals again lost large quantities of equipment, seemed to make the spot, indeed, the "Lucky Ground" of the Confederacy. "Within the sound of the guns," Henry S. Foote in a convivial mood told them down at Richmond, "Mrs. Jefferson Davis' great-grandfather [1] was buried" whom he, as a child, remembered. It is thus that surprising little bits of history are sometimes preserved.

The fame of Lee and Jackson's victories heartened the Confederacy throughout the South. Varina had not been in Raleigh long before people swarmed around her asking news of the army. The place had rapidly filled up with friends from Richmond, "arriving daily," she says, "without anything except the clothes on their backs in a piteous jumble of pain and worry." During her stay in Raleigh she was in constant correspondence with Jefferson Davis. Her infant who had been sick on her arrival became worse, and its life for a time was despaired of. She would have liked for her husband to have come to her, but she did not expect it; not even when she thought the child would die did she ask it. If he slept on the battlefield, she would sit alone by their dying child. Jefferson Davis was now constantly with the army. Both had necessarily been separated a great deal in the past and knew how to make sacrifices. The bond between them was strong but there was no such weak dependence upon each other in the matter of affection

[1] Dr. George Graham.

as has been suggested by Pollard and his following. Months, extending into years, when the necessity called for it, they spent away from each other. Jefferson Davis had always regarded her as an intelligent being interested in all that concerned him. And if any might doubt that Varina did not comprehend the situation of the country, they have only to read the correspondence that passed between Jefferson Davis and herself, just after the repulse of the army of the Potomac.[1] The communications show her to be in as close touch with affairs as any member of the government. Besides, no one could have written her "Memoir" who was not intimately and profoundly acquainted with every detail of the Confederate struggle.

Varina had fretted over her absence from the city. She liked action and wanted to be in the midst of it. With some improvement in her baby's health, she left the other children with friends and returned to Richmond. By September, she had brought the whole noisy brood back to the Capital. Her infant was well again and soon became known as the "pretty White House baby." Numerous writers inform us that her children were much petted by the people of the city. Mrs. Chesnut, Mrs. Clay and Mrs. Harrison, all preserve charming stories of them in their Memoirs.

Varina found the Executive Mansion in bad condition. Jefferson Davis was never of a domestic turn, and was now more than ever oblivious of household matters. Portions of the house had also been used during the summer for council rooms. Her ability to create order and system in the midst of confusion had always been a marked characteristic. In a short time she again had her household affairs running smoothly.

[1] "Jefferson Davis, Constitutionalist."

The victories in Virginia and the dogged resistance to Grant on the Western front had restored every one's confidence. The Mansion was again opened for general receptions. Varina was once more in the midst of entertaining, and her gayety and *esprit* drew about her a brilliant company of men and women besides those of official circles.

The future of the Confederacy seemed secure. Jefferson Davis, perhaps, was never more confident and despite all difficulties had everything in his grasp. The Conscript Act had gone far to help the country, but irreconcilables like Governor Brown of Georgia continued to be critical. With Lee and Jackson defending Richmond, the President was more cheerful about the Southwestern situation where, in the following November, he placed General Joseph E. Johnston in command after his recovery. Everything now seemed to point to success for the Confederacy. Many foreign papers were noting its recent victories. Varina was elated when she read the following editorial in a London paper relative to her husband's message after the Army of the Potomac had failed in its Peninsular campaign against Richmond:

"If any fault has been found with the late message, save by those who cannot think that the South can do any right or the North any wrong, it is that it speaks almost too coldly and indifferently of the glorious achievements of this summer's campaign—achievements which would have wrung an ample meed of praise from the haughtiest and most reserved European statesmen. There is a Roman, almost a stoical, sternness in the manner in which the Confederate President accepts, as matters of course, the victories which have saved the capital; and the army might almost be disappointed did it not know how thoroughly a ruler, himself a distinguished

soldier, appreciates the exploits which have signalized the
soldiership of the South.   Never was anything further removed from bombast or boastfulness than the language in
which Mr. Davis announces triumphs which would have excited enthusiasm even in phlegmatic England, and done honor
to the veteran armies of France. 'Mr. Davis' temper does
not fail him, even when he has to speak of the wanton bar-
barities suffered by the districts that have been visited by
the invaders, and of the unexampled outrages on the laws
of civilized warfare which reflect such signal infamy on the
Federal Army and on the Federal Government.' He speaks
strongly, no doubt, but in terms of just and measured repro-
bation, of the crimes which have rendered a cause, bad to
begin with, utterly detestable in the eyes of the civilized."

As the autumn of 1862 advanced, the victorious Southern
army pressed into Maryland.   But among the middle classes
Lee did not find the Hetty-Cary-Land that he had dreamed
of.   Still, with the exception of the Battle of Antietam, he
was triumphant.   Some historians have thought that this
partial failure of the Confederates checked England's recognition of the Southern Republic.   But England had had a
good example set her in Elizabeth's thirty years of dodging
war, and the stanch old Palmerston was gallantly following
in her footsteps, even boasting of it.   Still the Confederacy
had received much benefit from English sympathy.   This
was expressed in many ways.   British vessels, as best they
could, kept up a limited business communication with the
Southern Republic.   British consuls in the blockaded states
stayed on for years and were, in many instances, sympathetic.   The North accused England constantly of ignor-
ing her neutrality laws in the interests of the South.   For a
romantic episode with a touch of comedy, nothing in all his-

tory is so good as the story of the construction in Liverpool of the powerful man-of-war *Alabama*. One can imagine the thrilling tale that Masefield, rhythmic narrator of romantic sea stories, could have made of it. When the great warship eluded detention and sailed away from Liverpool on July 29th, to pick up her arms farther away, the North accused Her Majesty and her ministry of "conniving with Mr. Jefferson Davis in the escape." Lord John Russell smiled and said little, but Adams suspected him and wrote as much to Seward. The former was in much fear that the capricious Earl, of whom none could say what he would do around the corner, left to his own impulses, might at any moment encourage Her Majesty and her aged Premier in some move in recognition of the young nation. But as time passed nothing definite came of his attitude. His country's good intentions, having let slide numerous good opportunities, were beginning to be questioned by the dictatorial editor of the Charleston *Mercury* and the most hopeful of the Cotton Kings around Charleston. These, and not Jefferson Davis, Russell tells us, had hardly been discreet in the matter of recognition by England.

Although they were beginning to suspect that the High Lord Chancellor would not exchange his woolsack for a cotton bale, any unfavorable condition of the cotton situation in England was everywhere hailed with delight by the Southern planters. In some quarters, the cotton question continued to be one of great moment in England, and the South had many friends at Manchester. But if England got her cotton from the South, she got her wheat from the North; and people can do without clothes longer than they can bread. Jefferson Davis' face hardened. The South would have to stand alone. In a hundred speeches, he told his people the stern truth and no word ever fell from his lips to delude them with the assurance of recognition, nor had he depended upon foreign favor for the success at Fredericksburg.[1]

The war was now the whole thought of the people. The citizens of the town had assured the President that they would personally make themselves responsible for any expense that occurred in efforts to protect the Southern Capital. The Confederacy as yet was in good shape. The Southern Capital had distinguished guests from all parts of the country. Even the cautious M. Mercier strolled across the Potomac to keep the *Quai D'Orsay* informed. The Richmond *Examiner* and the Charleston *Mercury,* for the moment, had little to complain of. They grew sympathetic enough at times to print portions of the President's speeches. In Virginia all was well with the Confederacy and all might have continued so had not the eyes of the Federal Government been focused for the second time upon Vicksburg. Grant's first campaign against it had failed and the authorities at Washington were sending many of their best troops into the heart of the Confederacy. Though the South had a handful of successes to its credit, and to all appearances was victorious, the North was slowly gaining the vantage ground.

[1] The frequent references to this subject on the part of Jefferson Davis and to Seward's position in the preservation of the Union are necessary since they are closely associated with the progress of the war.

CHAPTER XXV

SOCIAL LIFE IN THE CONFEDERACY

PEOPLE walking or riding by the Executive Mansion on pleasant afternoons during the autumn of 1862 often saw Mrs. Jefferson Davis with a group of women sitting on the gallery, either knitting socks or platting straw to make hats for the soldiers.[1] The war spirit among women in Richmond grew more pronounced each day. Women of all classes were now organized for services of a varied nature. Their lips daily grew more compressed as they fashioned stacks upon stacks of coarse socks for the soldiers. The whole social order had undergone a change, especially for the women of the ruling class. Women of the most exclusive circles were coming in daily and kindly contact with the coarse illiteracy of the South, one good that would be felt in its future civilization. They were saying in England that the women of the Confederacy as much as the men were keeping the war going, and in a way it was true. Nothing they possessed was withheld from the army. The most laborious tasks were gladly performed, such as sewing, cooking, superintending the farms and plantations, and by women who had hitherto led a life of luxury and ease. Private homes were turned into hospitals and delicately bred women vied with each other as to how much nursing they did in the hospitals.

[1] Publications of the Southern Historical Society.

Hardship accumulated but the war spirit back of the guns burned on. Soldiers in the Northern army could hardly account for its intensity, and often stood dumbfounded before it. A Federal officer compared it to a "forest fire." Nothing renewed it more than the Emancipation Proclamation, covering the Confederate States, which had been issued on September 23, 1862, to take effect January 1st, 1863. It was a subject for bitter denunciation, not so much for the loss of the slaves as for the spirit which they believed had prompted it. "They do not want to see them free any more than we do," exclaimed a South Carolina woman. They had not this soon recognized its full force, and boasted that the negroes would never take up arms against the South, but the Proclamation greatly intensified their hatred of Lincoln, also of Seward who they believed had done much to initiate it. The fact was not recognized that Lincoln was only carrying out the mandates and policies of his party. The Emancipation was not Lincoln's idea. As far back as the summer of '61, the abolitionists grew so insistent in the matter that the radicals seized upon it as a war measure.[1] A circumstance that inflamed the war spirit of the women, more perhaps than any other thing, had been Butler's orders relating to the women of New Orleans. The notorious affair had stirred them as nothing had during the war. They were overjoyed that the whole English press, Victoria, her ministers, and even the House of Commons, had denounced the infamous order. No wonder the London *Saturday Review* compared it to the deeds of the "bloodiest savages" and the acts of the "loathsome yahoo of fiction." Seward had Butler removed, but having no love for Seward, they

[1] See Bancroft, "Life of Seward," vol. II.

had overlooked the fact. The blockade was a subject constantly discussed, sometimes humorously, and again with an anxious and often repeated enquiry, "Why does not England force them to lift it?" It was not because they wanted silk from Paris or London, as a Northern historian seemed to think, for records prove that they gladly wore their own finery four years, remodeled and made over many times. It was guns, not silks, they prayed for.

The Federals' partial success at Antietam had created the deepest anxiety among them, but as bitterly as they regretted it, there were still Lee and Jackson's superb victories throughout the summer to point to.

It was of such things that women in the Southern capital talked as with feverish energy they knitted and platted straws or made coarse, heavy garments for Lee's army. And such women as they were, some beautiful, some young, some pale and thin, some with white hair, but all with one purpose in their eyes! It surprises one to find from the diaries and memoirs of the time, how much they knew about public matters. Though few of them held any public position, and the majority would have blushed had one been offered them, they talked as incessantly as the men did about the affairs of the Confederacy. After they had wrapped up the unfinished socks for another day's hard knitting, they walked home from their meeting places, some to prepare dainties for the sick in the hospitals, others to dance with the restless young army officers far into the evening. They had danced a great deal in their lives, danced gracefully in softly-lighted ball-rooms. Anywhere where there were lonesome soldiers they danced now. "My boys must be entertained," the good, Gray Knight had told them more than once. He, himself, sometimes came to their informal parties

at the Executive Mansion, and the gay and shrewd Mrs.
Chesnut was daring enough to record a little story in which
he figures with a bit of gallantry, the color of which, however, at this day seems faint and fugitive. The President, of
whom every one stood a little in awe, rarely attended the
informal parties, was sometimes not even seen at the grand
receptions: but Mrs. Chesnut has him present on several
occasions. It is also recorded of him that he sometimes
indulged in a little playful raillery and banter with very
young ladies; young couples visiting the Mansion were
charmed with his interest in them.

Such were the delicate, restrained, social relations of the
day. Here and there one less repressed broke through established customs and sent gossip flying from mouth to
mouth; but the Confederate woman, in the main, was
squeamishly Victorian. "The trouble about being nice
to these handsome South Carolina men is that they are
such ardent admirers," was a comment among them. A tart
criticism of each other, however, was as prevalent as at
any other period of history. Varina herself indulged
in it and was sometimes the subject of it. But scandal, she plainly warns her friends, she would have none of.[1]
Comments about her of the following nature, which the
writer has no desire to withhold, are found in numerous
records and reminiscences: She was handsome, but arrogant and self-assertive; her figure was all out of shape;
her receptions, after all, were not such wonderful affairs,
and her children literally took the Mansion. There was also
the story about her getting angry with the laundryman and
the one about her not forgiving a caller for not speaking
to her at her own reception. All such, in substance, one

[1] Letters.

finds recorded in the histories of the time. Varina may have laughed at, or denounced, the idle chatter with criticism just as tart, but she rarely nursed her grievances. From Mrs. Chesnut, one gathers that such criticism originated in and was mainly confined to official circles.

Pollard's intimation that Varina was hoarding the President's salary was still pricking her. She now kept open house for the society people of the city, among whom she was beginning to number numerous friends. At times she was as gay as any among them. She often had them at the Mansion to share the dainties that the daring blockade runners sometimes brought in. However, the great number of vessels captured daily by the strong blockading squadrons was gradually cutting off the South from contact with the outside world. The Federal maritime power at this time was getting to be one of the strongest upon the ocean, while the Confederates' was a mere makeshift. Although the runners still dashed across the seas with their precious freight, as many as six vessels loaded with arms, steel, tin and zinc for the Confederate States were destroyed at a time. So Varina's luncheons were not always ample spreads, nor was a third of the needs of the Confederate armies supplied when the United States blockading squadrons once got command of the ports and seas. Of their efficiency Welles had early boasted.

The change in the social life was never more evident than in the music and songs of the South, and music it would have, the army often marching, hungry and barefoot, on its battle-songs. Johnston of Richmond and Blackmer of New Orleans and Vicksburg, the chief music publishers of the South, furnished stacks of popular Southern airs composed for the New Republic. The standard composers

were no longer in demand in the parlors or public halls
where they had been held in such reverence. Nothing was
now allowed upon the streets but Southern airs. Not only
such favorites as "Dixie," "My Maryland" and "The Bonnie Blue Flag," upon which the army went into battle, but
Confederate marches and Palmetto waltzes were heard
throughout the South. "I'll learn this piece, Ma'am, if you
will let me learn the Jeff Davis march next," a small pupil
implored her English music teacher.

But even amidst all the saturnalia of hate and strife,
ties of blood and friendship in numberless instances bound
the two peoples together. One finds Mrs. Pegram of Virginia telling her friends that she did not fear that her
captured son would be mistreated in prison. Nor was she
surprised when he was permitted to go to the Pennsylvania
springs for his health. Would that all the prison stories
could have been as beautiful. And General Scott! Deride him as a traitor, as the haughty, loyal men and women
of the state constantly did, they intuitively knew that
his heart was with Virginia. Historians have difficulty in concealing the truth that the old General was in
love with both sides. And certainly Beauregard in the
thick of the fight would pause to give aid to a Northern
friend he discovered wounded amid the débris of the battle.
Many instances could be cited as proof of the ties that
bound the two sections together; though there was now hate
between them such as Russell, who had witnessed the em-
broilments of many nations, had never before encountered.
Still, the hate here more often took the form of wild and
incoherent denunciations of each other. There was beneath
it the lingering sense of unity. Northern soldiers, even
when going into battle, said that the people were committing

a great wrong in making war upon each other.[1] They had become so closely allied in colonial years that in more instances than history will ever give any account of they were related by ties of blood. Although in many things one people, different economic and social conditions had produced two distinct types. "I'd like to kill a thousand Yankees," a young girl exclaimed as she watched an Illinois regiment pass by in their new blue uniforms, while she mended her brother's ragged, gray coat. "You might kill the grandsons of your grandmother's twin sister, then," her mother replied with a pained look in her eyes. "When we came farther South along the Carolina route, our Aunt Mary went over the Alleghanies with her husband and children into Illinois. Some of her family must be in Grant's army today."

While military action was taking place at the various seats of war, many such incidents were occurring in the social life of the people that bear upon the history of the Confederacy. All reveal the nature of the people. The Southern woman was both enthusiastic and sacrificing. Women everywhere in the South were fashioning home-made articles to help out the small factories in operation at various places. While countries do not suddenly change their industrial system in times of peace, and never in war, all the people's brave endeavors, though the returns were scant, deserve mention. For the first years they did not realize the falling off in their yearly agricultural products, but more and more they discovered the inadequacy in maintaining the conflict. Among other things the Confederacy was soon found to be in dire need of cannon and an insistent appeal for brass and old iron had gone up from

[1] Grant is quoted by local citizens as saying as much in the last Vicksburg campaign.

Beauregard. Patriotic poems calling upon the South to "melt its bells for the sacred cause" appeared in the papers. Iron and brass of every description were gathered to be shipped to places where they could be molded into cannon. Soon the entire South was responding to the call. School children waited impatiently for the hour of recess to hunt old iron. Brass andirons, brass heads of shovels and tongs and even handsome brass fenders and dinner bells were thrown into the pile with old and new iron.

The story of a bell in a Presbyterian church at Woodville, Mississippi, is a kindred story of many that could be told of communities throughout the South. The bell had been sent to Woodville as a present from the Presbyterian ladies of Boston when the church was built, with the molded inscription: "Presented to the Presbyterian church at Woodville, Mississippi, by the ladies of Boston, Massachusetts." "The people had learned to love its silvery peals, but they unfastened it from the steeple early one Sabbath morning and it fell with an angry crash to the ground." Next morning a car loaded with bells, iron and handsome brass household furniture and ornaments stole out of Woodville on its way to Richmond to be cast into cannon. Nearly all the Southern towns were supplied with Northern spies, who had some way of keeping the army posted about matters going on among the people, and before the car reached its destination, it was followed and captured by a detachment of Federal soldiers. The great bell went back to Boston, or somewhere beyond the Mason and Dixon line, to disappear from sight forever. But of more consequence is the spirit that brought it to the South and the spirit that sacrificed it for conviction.

CHAPTER XXVI

As the war progressed, slavery loomed up in larger guise in Republican circles to become an outstanding issue with the radicals. The Emancipation Proclamation had not had the effect intended for it after Antietam, and Fredericksburg had made Lee an adversary to be feared. Still the Proclamation could be made to serve as a war measure for the future. Despite the harsh criticism it had at first received in England, it had the appearance of a humanitarian effort in the eyes, at least, of such men as Cobden and Bright, and Lincoln had got over his dismay at having issued it. He was even willing, on occasions, to leave the ethics out of it and admit to Horace Greeley that it was to save the Union. It greatly elated the Garrison brand of Abolitionists when, to cause a new sensation, it went into effect on January 1st, 1863. These, however fanatical they may have been, had always been zealous and active in the matter from an ethical standpoint. The Republican party, also in time, shrewdly began to stress the ethics of the Proclamation in order to present its side of the war in a better light to the outside world. Its reputation abroad had greatly suffered. Among other things, the Butler stories had been rehearsed and denounced at the firesides of the English aristocracy. The Proclamation of September 22d had not been much better received. Still the institution of slavery had injured the South abroad. Its evils had been

magnified, and its good controverted by Northern agencies
sent abroad for the purpose.   Numerous misrepresentations
of the institution are recorded by an authoritative British
subject, residing at that time in the South and engaged in
making a careful study of the condition of the negroes.[1]
The institution, however, had been discarded by the civilized world, and the North was getting the benefit of it.
But the claim that is made for emancipation as an ethical
measure appears manufactured and ulterior.   There had
been several efforts, at the beginning of the revolution, in
the Federal Congress favored by Seward and Lincoln for
reconciliation between the two sections, based on the continuation of slavery in the South.   The notable speech
Seward made on January 12th, before the Confederacy was
organized, was filled with grants and concessions sufficient
to have cooled Southern ardor had the mere ownership of
slaves been the main issue.

In the discussion, thousands of records accumulated to
furnish a very sea of material in which the historian finds
himself prepared, to establish any contention that he has
espoused.   None, however, can show that there was desire
or effort on the part of the South to make the ownership
of slaves, in itself, the basic cause of secession.

Some historians have been so thoughtless of the ethical
claim they make for the Emancipation Act as to reproachfully declare that the South had everything to make its
position secure—slavery proposed within its borders by
constitutional act, double representation through population
and even the right to take its slave property into the new
territory, at the risk, it is true, of losing it in a territory on
its being admitted as a free state, but the right nevertheless.

[1] "Life in the South during the War by a Blockaded British Subject."
S. L. G.

In addition to these proposed concessions, it had the advantage of being strong if not in full control of both branches of Congress, which would have given it power in the Republican administration at least for a number of years. What, then, was it but a desire for independence that actuated it in the winter of 1860-61 after all just compromises had failed?   W. H. Russell, the coolest critic of the day, read this in the hearts of the people throughout the Confederacy. He felt convinced that the great body of the people was moved by the one desire for separation. It was not a question of slavery but of national independence, he was constantly averring.

It is hardly fair of Rhodes, seeking to be open-minded in some things, to infer that the motive for the provision in the Confederate Constitution prohibiting the reopening of the African slave trade was placed there simply to conciliate England and the other foreign powers.   A careful study of the slavery question reveals the fact that the South itself was earnestly seeking a solution of the problem; was growing sensitive about it.   As has been noted, Jefferson Davis is upon record in a clearly defined statement made years before the war, that he looked forward to a day when slavery would be a thing of the past. He, furthermore, predicts for the negro a future and the full enjoyment of freedom, if permitted to come naturally into his estate.[1]   If historians seek to find expressions in his writings that seem to contradict this position, one must reply that contradictions relative to the negro's future may be found in Lincoln's writings. No harsher outlook for the slave, as the Abolitionists viewed it, is recorded by any Southerner than that of Lincoln's assertion that the negro could never be given even so

[1] Speech on the Oregon question.

much as political equality with the whites. However, Lincoln's ethical point of view relative to slavery improved a great deal in such close contact with the Garrison ideals, but never to that point that the question could not be used for political purposes. One has only to study Welles and other sources, but particularly Welles, to know that ethics had no part whatever in the Emancipation Proclamation that went no farther than a declaration to free the slaves alone in the Confederate States.

The war had been in progress nearly two years with the Southern armies for the most part victorious and the Confederacy attracting the admiration of all Europe when Lincoln was constrained to say something like this to members of his Cabinet: "We will have to set the niggers free—the war can't be won without it." [1]

Seward had never really liked the idea and when it was first proposed exclaimed "Don't do it *now,* for God's sake. It would sound like a last shriek on the retreat. Bear it on the 'bayonets of an advancing army, don't drag it in the dust of Fredericksburg,' " was his florid oratory.[2]

That it was a party measure is seen in the fact that every member of the Cabinet favored it, except Blair, who was a native of Maryland and objected to it as unnecessary. The thing was to take effect on January 1st of 1863. Welles tells us that Lincoln told him it was necessary to win the war. Rhodes admits that Lincoln hesitated, but found his party too strong for him. With Seward, who despite other influences swayed his intellectual thought, Lincoln yielded to the combined demands of the radicals and reformers. Seward who had dodged and hedged in the

[1] Welles.
[2] Bancroft.

matter of the Proclamation now based his hopes on the thought that Jefferson Davis might be induced to give up his struggle for independence. He had arrived at a high point of diplomacy and both Great Britain and France were beginning to feel and recognize his subtle power. His greatest alarm was the danger of a servile insurrection that might, he said, follow emancipation. Besides his genuine horror at the thought, he felt that it would be sure to cause the intervention of foreign powers. Not having been able to defer, or do away, with the proclamation altogether, he now must make England and France believe that it was a wise measure. What Southerner's oratory "ever scattered more star dust" than the message he sent to Dayton, October 20th, 1862, upon the subject? It was the policy of the administration, he reasoned, and had to be sustained. Perhaps his pathway would not have been so devious had he not known the nature of his enemies. The Republicans, generally, were pleased with the Proclamation. Sumner and Stevens, long heard in Congress, and Stanton and Chase had all clamored for it; even good old Welles became excited and emphatic.

The Proclamation was now decided upon for an early spring war measure, and was claimed to have been the fruits of Antietam. It shrewdly left the slaves alone in all Federal Southern territory. They were emancipated only throughout the Confederacy, or as it was expressed, "in states that shall then be in rebellion." But was there any ethics in this? The South claimed that it was a gross usurpation of power on the part of the Republican President to issue such a Proclamation. Aside from the Constitutional inhibition in a way the South was right, since if the Confederacy was a belligerent power, and England had recognized it as one, the Federal government had no authority to meddle in its domestic affairs, whatever right it might have to subdue it by conquest. The Republican administration, however, never openly recognized the Confederacy as a government, and vainly endeavored to act from that standpoint, to make a farce of it, since there were many instances in which it did recognize it as a separate power. The Republicans hoped that the effects of the Proclamation would disorganize the domestic life of the South and bring about an immediate surrender. But alas for them, they were to find that the measure had the opposite effect—that of uniting it in a more determined effort to establish its independence. This was expressed nowhere more determinedly than in Virginia and South Carolina, states that were now doing much of the South's principal thinking. But eventually the Proclamation got in its work. "The infamous war measure," "An instrument of darkness," were phrases on every tongue in the South. The names of Lincoln and of Seward, for the latter was thought to be at the bottom of all the mischief hatched in the Republican administration, became a hissing and byword throughout the South. The radical Republicans, who were just as bitter and vindictive as they ever were after the war, were lost sight of while these two outstanding figures were being denounced; Lincoln because he was at the head of the administration, and Seward because he was regarded as Lincoln's mouthpiece.

But the Proclamation continued to be criticized even in the North. New York especially condemned it. Foreign countries questioned the morality of such a measure. To free a slave and arm him against his former master was unheard of in civilized warfare. Numerous English papers denounced it and members of Her Majesty's ministry had disclaimed any kinship with a race that would perpetrate such an act of barbarity. It was a crime even if it had been legal. So indignant had these become, that but for "Seward's cringing flatteries" of the world powers, as Welles calls them, this and the Butler stories really might have brought about intervention. But the Secretary of the Navy tells us that Seward was flattering them *ad nauseam*. Bancroft, too, notes the wiles and artifices of the arch manipulator of all matters pertaining to foreign relations.

One of the most amusing instances of Seward's foreign policy occurred in the spring of '63 in connection with the captured Peterhoff mails in which Seward, Welles, Lincoln and Sumner all figure. The Secretary of State finally triumphed and his liberal views in the matter of the much discussed mails brought incense from England to the Union, to Welles' utter disgust. That good old Puritan was still talking about "those two bad men, Palmerston and Napoleon." We do not know whether that exact phrase is found in the Diary or not, but if it is not, we beg pardon for quoting it. Welles could not see that Seward, in the matter of the mails, was using a bland diplomacy to keep the Federal Union on terms of good will with England. The Secretary of State must, at times, have greatly irritated him, since he accuses him of meddling with the other departments to any extent he pleased, and with Lincoln's full approbation. "They were always off somewhere in a corner talking." The Secretary of the Navy, however, was suspicious of all foreign powers and contended that Palmerston and Napoleon were as much the enemies of the Federal Union as Jefferson Davis.

CHAPTER XXVII

THE SUNDERED TIE

THE tie between master and slave had been in a manner sundered and the South was soon to feel the strain of the disruption of her domestic life. The effects of the Emancipation Proclamation on the economic affairs of the Confederate States in time began to be disastrous in the extreme. While the Republicans did not immediately realize from it all that they had hoped for, it slowly began to do its work and by '64 had done much to disrupt and demoralize the economic life of the Southern States. At first the negroes received it with apathy and resisted orders to take up arms against their own people. The tie between the two was stronger than the Abolitionist had supposed. The negroes were still primitive and but half civilized but they were happy, were gradually attaining civilization and were, in many respects, cared for far better than the white labor in the North.[1] However, after the Proclamation had been broadcast among them and constantly discussed and explained by the soldiers and numerous secret agencies, negroes in large majorities left household service and many refused to work in the fields. With the exception of the best element they became a care to their owners, and, in many instances, were of substantial aid to Federal armies as surreptitious couriers and spies. To the white women of the South much credit is due in retaining, to a large extent, the

[1] William E. Dodd, on "Factory Labor in the North."

negroes' allegiance during this deplorable setback in their passage from savagery to civilization. The bonds of reverence and affection, amounting to superstition for those they felt to be superior to the Northerners, held when all others had been sundered. But for this the Proclamation, with all sorts of inflammatory literature flooding the South, coming at such a crisis when the manhood of the country was with the army, might have brought about conditions hardly paralleled in vandal history. What the race lost in self-respect and moral restraint by the manner in which it was freed, cannot be estimated. It is certain that it had begun, before the war, to develop as commendable traits as are possessed by any race. In the gentler amenities of social life such as certain gracious forms of politeness, benignity and kindliness, few races excel the pre-war negro. The women of the South trusted implicitly the burliest and most uncouth among them in the matter of their protection. Often left alone on large plantations with their children, they felt as safe as if they had been guarded by troops. A mistress on one occasion when the Federal raid included her home, asked her servants why they had stood so near her, to receive the reply, "If any of dem so'gers had 'ove tetched you, they'd hed to kill us fust." Mrs. Jefferson Davis, on one occasion, found herself a mediator in a wrangle between one of her angry slaves and the overseer. In the effort to bring about peace between the two, she would sooner have feared the temper of the undisciplined white man than that of the black man who grinned and confided to her afterwards, "I wasn't gwine to hurt him, Miss Vrena. I jus' wanted to skeer him with this," showing her a huge knife handle that had no blade.

But soon an unsettled condition was noticed among the

negroes, especially in the larger cities of the South where they came in closer contact with the messengers sent among them to explain the Proclamation. While such means of warfare seem of little consequence in comparison with battles, they are of more value than is supposed. Disarrange the domestic life of a people and in time you weaken their ability to defend themselves. We hardly agree with the historians who seem to think that emancipation coming during the war did not work irreparable evil to the Southern Confederacy. Richmond, sooner than any other city, became a hotbed of all measures taken to disaffect and arouse the negroes. Clubs were organized by leading freedmen under the supervision and fostering care of Northern white men and women sent secretly into the city for that purpose. One special device of the clubs was that of rewards paid every colored servant that quit the service of white families. As an ironical twist of fate, the larger number of contrabands became a heavier burden on the Federal government than it cared to shoulder. The Northern soldiers too objected to any association with the camp followers.

The Executive Mansion of the Confederacy was the special object of attack by the clubs. People close to the President's family recorded more than once that they feared for its safety, although Varina believed that if any harm came to them it would be the work of spies and not of negroes.[1] The servant question, however, became one of a serious nature, not only in the Executive Mansion but in many households. Mrs. Robert E. Lee and others moved to the city on account of the disorganized condition of house servants. As negroes in droves began to follow the armies, Richmond was full of helpless negro waifs and whole

[1] Chesnut.

families left by camp followers sometimes became public wards. A story that evinces a great canniness on their part is the one where a lazy camp follower, on being admonished by a Federal officer for neglect of his family, said with utter unconcern, "Nor sur, I ain' skeered ter leave my chilluns. De white folks ain' gwine ter let 'em suffer for nuffin."

Under the influence, however, of overzealous Federal authorities and the lower element in the armies, negroes were encouraged to manufacture stories of the most damaging nature about their owners. William L. Yancey wrote home from Europe as early as '61 that England and other European countries were ringing with the most absurd slanders that could be invented against the slaveholder for the purpose of damaging the cause of the Confederacy. Literature such as that written by Stowe, Olmsted, Kimball, and the famous "Crisis," was in every bookshop reduced in price or else given away. The idle remarks of the most irresponsible and unreliable authorities were measured against the great missionary work of civilizing and Christianizing a savage race. The hot-headed, passionate Southerners had their say, and denounced all such writings as inspired by malice, hate and envy of the South. "What will the Republicans put upon the South next?" Catherine Hopley, a blockaded British subject was constrained to ask. Heated accusations and replies filled the conversation of the day. Lurid and intemperate language was used everywhere in the country in both its speech and press. An able historian has observed that the right in Washington to openly call even the highest authorities in the land "imbeciles," was a divine one in the eyes of both the military and civil population. This was a favorite epithet applied to Abraham Lincoln, and one may come across a similar one of Jefferson Davis in the columns of the Richmond *Examiner* or the Charleston *Mercury*.

There was more Lincolnesque in the country's speech than is admitted. It would make racy reading if all that the refined gentlewomen and ministers of the Gospel throughout the South said on the occasion of the Emancipation Proclamation could be gathered in one volume. However, it is certain that it was not called forth by the thought of losing the negroes. The South, both its men and women, everywhere was growing tired of the institution, and to give the negro freedom through sound and peaceful measures was a growing inclination on their part. And why question it? Had not the North arrived at the same conclusion in the past? Why should any have acted on the principle that the South would not follow in the footsteps of other nations? A spokesman for the vast realm of slaveholders in South Carolina wrote at the time, "This war was undertaken by us to shake off the yoke of the invader, so we consider our cause righteous." In biting satire she continues, "The Yankees have discovered that they are fighting to free the slaves. They do not want to see them free any worse than we do." [1]

With the great body of the people it was not the loss of the slaves that stirred their resentment. It is true that they resented the interference with any institution in a country recognized as a belligerent by England and other European nations. There might have been here and there a few, like an old kinsman of the writer, whose hair, it was said, turned white in one night at the thought of losing his one thousand slaves. But there was a deeper cause for resentment at the

[1] Chesnut.

Proclamation coming at this particular time. For two years the negroes had in many ways been urged to assert their freedom; their affections in many instances had been alienated from their owners and some dangerous leaders had arisen among them. Many of the South believed, in bitterness of heart, that Lincoln had issued the Proclamation with the hope of destroying the white civilization of the South. England also had her suspicions of it, and said some very lurid things upon the subject. It took much of Welles' despised toadyism on Seward's part to explain it to certain high sources in European courts. But there is not the slightest proof to show that Lincoln had other in his mind than that of an economic disturbance in the South that would force it to surrender. Thaddeus Stevens and his kind might not have deplored such a disaster, but both Lincoln and Seward would have stood aghast before it. Still, all knew the advantage of their famous war measure. Negroes freed in great numbers, officers in the Federal army told a British subject, would cause a great number of Confederate soldiers to stay at home. One intelligent officer said, "With our superior numbers, nothing then could save the Confederacy."

While Jefferson Davis regarded the Proclamation as wholly unethical and an unwarranted usurpation of power, he told his people that it cleared up one point: "The Proclamation will have a salutary effect in calming the fears of those who have constantly evinced the apprehension that this war might end by some reconstruction of the old Union, or some renewal of close political relations with the United States." This point he knew was one that the North had as well to recognize. His will was fast becoming implacable, inexorable, and his quest consuming. Varina wrote that "the effect of the Proclamation on the people of the South was unmistakable. It aroused in them a determination to secure their independence, if anything, stronger than before." But while this was for Jefferson Davis the one good to be had of an ill wind the crops of '63, and especially of '64, were proof that the shrewd war measure had struck a vital point.

CHAPTER XXVIII

WITH the victories of Lee and Jackson and the continued resistance to Grant on the Western front, the outlook was fair for the Confederacy in the winter of '62-'63. England and France were never more sympathetic with the Southern cause, and the neutrality laws were laxer than ever. Gladstone was in open admiration of Jefferson Davis' success in establishing his government. It sent Francis Adams to Lord Russell with a bitter complaint. Adams, they admitted, was of the peerage, not a Salisbury or a Palmerston, but the type that one did not expect to find in any great numbers in the States. Socially, they ranked him higher than Mason, whose democracy Palmerston could not make out any more than he could measure the universe. Still the favors all went to the Confederacy to puzzle the accomplished Adams.

France, beginning to grasp at empire, was daily showing signs of intervention to greatly raise Slidell's hopes. To seat Maximilian and the delicately-nerved Carlotta upon an American throne, even if it had to be among the aborigines, was in accordance with the first Napoleon's policy of placing rulers here and there. But England would keep her own and every other alien finger out of the quarrel as long as Seward pelted the foreign office with flatteries such as the arch manipulator was learning to concoct. This was seen in the nervously quick way that Great Britain withdrew her

troops from Canada, all forgetting that she had ever demanded a salute.

Still England had not exactly liked the cocky manner in
which the audacious Secretary had acted in the matter. The
London *Times* refused to print some features of it, and it is
said that Seward laughed heartily about it. However, his
finesse and subtile skill in appeasing England continued to
be of great advantage to the Federal Union. There was
much, however, to increase the South's optimism, and social
life in Richmond continued active and seemingly as brilliant
and elaborate as ever during the winter of '62-'63. Women
were still clad in jewels and remodeled satins, and rode in
handsome equipages behind high-stepping horses. Mrs.
Jefferson Davis, critics said, was not democratic in her
tastes, and with other society leaders was engaged in all
sorts of "frivolous amusements." But one must see that
the main purpose for which Varina and the women of the
city were now indulging in social amusement was the entertainment of the army and the official circles of the
government. With the exception of a few, high officials
were as little inclined to do the society act as the President
himself. The gifted and oracular Secretary of War, Benjamin, it is true, could often be depended upon and could
still charm a brilliant circle at dinner parties where good
food was served with a grace as much lost to the world
today as Apollo's arms. But generally, all social effort was
made with an eye singly to the entertainment of the soldiers.
The privates received nearly as much attention as the officers.
Richmond was the base of supplies for the entire Army of
Northern Virginia and the rendezvous for troops of every
rank. Mrs. Chesnut records that Varina sat up far into the
night at the Executive Mansion and exerted herself with

humorous quip and laughter to entertain the officers and others who called while the hard-pressed President sought a few hours' sleep. "Mrs. Davis said something funnier than ever and everybody laughed and forgot their troubles."

Among other favors sought of the occupants of the White House, people both in and out of the city expected to be entertained. Jefferson Davis had little time for it. Every ounce of his strength was put in the struggle to keep the army fit. The entertainment had long since been referred to the wife, and at times the crowds were difficult to handle. There had always been misunderstandings in the matter of social rules and forms in the new government, and Varina, who was never averse to taking the initiative, decided on a systematic plan of entertainment. There must be, she contended, some rules and etiquette for official circles. She had always been systematic and logical in her methods and rebelled at the haphazard manner in which official entertainment was being conducted. With victorious armies defending it, the Confederate states of America was a government that was now attracting the attention of the courts of Europe, and the time had arrived, she decided, that some serious thought should be given to the matter of social forms and rules. And now the city rang for days with the story that Mrs. Jefferson Davis with a number of other ladies of Richmond were attempting to outline rules of etiquette and procedure for the Confederate government in keeping with that which she had known at Washington.

It was reported that Varina had put her servants in livery and was assuming the manners and airs of a great lady; some said she sought to ape royalty. The editor of the Richmond *Examiner* was infuriated and made a note of it for his future "Secret History of the Confederacy." Varina had, in her new set of social rules, reserved to herself the right not to return calls. It was a disgrace to a democratic administration! If the Confederacy could not remain democratic; if it was to be turned into an "unrepublican court" by frivolous women, it was already a failure. Mrs. Chesnut had recorded that Mrs. Jefferson Davis was one of the most brilliant and cultured women of the country, but some were whispering that the mistress of the Confederate White House was a willful, imperious upstart and snob who was seeking to rule every one about her. Others said that she longed for the brilliant drawing-room life she had known at Washington. Some, more kindly, thought that perhaps she had grown tired of all the jealousy and jabber over military rank as to who should have been appointed first to this or that place, and was determined in social affairs, at least, to settle all the debatable points by hard and fast rules.

One does not know whether she got her way entirely about the matter, but it has come down that she was persistent about it. Pollard says it all wound up in a sensation little short of a scandal. He neglected his tirades upon Jefferson Davis and caricatures and detestations of Abraham Lincoln long enough to take note of what he termed the frivolities of Richmond society. That frivolous society, which always includes a large portion of the *élite,* was so deeply involved in Varina's scheme, is evidence not only of her influence with it but of the need of some fixed rules for public entertainment. However Varina soon found herself involved in an endless controversy. In the furor created by her attempt to introduce a new set of rules in the official social life of the government some went so far as to whisper that she was a Northern woman, had not come of a slave-holding family, and had actually done housework. The gossip, however, was invariably confined to official circles in which it was said "two courts" had been established in the Confederacy. Fashionable society, however, continued to sustain the new social code and in reality, as the editor of the *Examiner* charged, were a part of it. But Varina was charged with initiating it, and it was further whispered in official circles that she was a Western woman full of social assertion and snobbery. Varina felt outraged. It was her first experience in having her social position questioned. She expressed her indignation freely, and for the first time told her critics what she thought of them. The city took sides. But Varina had drawn about her many of the best families in the city. Still her pathway was now growing thorny and with all her poise and good humor, as the winter waned, there was a slight sharpness in her tones which people took for hauteur. With the Rhetts still bitterly disappointed that the family had not been recognized for the Presidency of the Confederacy, with Beauregard married into the Rhett family, with Joseph E. Johnston refusing to believe that he should not have ranked Lee, and all in some way attached to Pollard, who complained that Jefferson Davis did not like him,—powerful forces were closing in around the first Lady of the Confederacy as well as around her husband.

Varina was gifted and resourceful, and all admitted possessed undeniable charm, but could she, with all her deftness and suavity, cope with such a difficult situation? Like circumstances have filled many famous women of history with frustration.

But Varina was not easily thwarted in her purposes. She persisted in enforcing her new rules. Her receptions became grander, stiffer and more formal than ever.

Besides, "one had to be on time, and leave on time,"
it mattered not who they were, though Solomon and the
Queen of Sheba." [1]   Varina had succeeded, and "all society not in mourning" went to see how the new rules
worked, and to rejoice over their victorious Confederacy.
The army for which everything was planned was there; the
President was present and Varina was radiant.

It was a self-confident and sometimes haughty and satirical woman who measured lances with her critics that last
brilliant Christmas in the Confederate Capital.   Varina, at
this period, though wedded to the Southern conception of
the "eternal lady," was growing more assertive.   The
time, however, favored the expression of such qualities.
Pollard informs us that she joined in much of the frivolity
that Richmond society indulged in during the first and middle years of the Confederacy.   In that staid Victorian age,
any slight deviation from its fixed rules was noticeable, and
the mere fact that women were no longer cooped up in the
four walls of their homes excited suspicion.   As brilliant
and flashy as his intellect was, the editor of the *Examiner*
could not see that the social needs of an army made up
from widely scattered territory were many, and to meet
them it demanded the greatest exertion, ingenuity and self-
sacrifice on the part of the women of the city, now representing every state in the Confederacy.   There was little
provision made by the Confederacy for the entertainment
of the soldiers such as is thought necessary in modern warfare, and upon which large sums must be expended.   The
obligation and responsibility of furnishing entertainment
for the large army that marched in and out of Richmond
devolved upon Varina, her ladies and the women of the

[1] Chesnut.

city. This was all lost upon the brilliant associate editor of the *Examiner.*

In time it became Varina's turn to play critic. With the fires of her own nature burned down to a steady flame, writing in a calm, dispassionate manner of the incalculable harm the Richmond *Examiner* did her husband in his efforts to encourage the people, she says, "The *Examiner,* as the exponent of the critics, foretold every evil for the Confederacy." But however criticism may have raged at home, at least for the Christmastide, with its garniture of swords and holly, Jefferson Davis had the authorities at the Federal Capital, in a manner, terrorized. And what praise young Robert Cecil was bestowing upon the new Western Republic in the London *Quarterly Review!* The London *Times,* too, printed articles at times that caught Seward's disapproving eye. Still he was feeling his power.

CHAPTER XXIX

SOME CHARACTERISTICS

EVERYTHING concerning the family that occupied the White House of the Confederacy has been eagerly sought by historians but the following story concerning Varina has been to a great extent overlooked. So staid and important a person as Gideon Welles, Secretary of the Navy in what was humorously called President Lincoln's "Compound" Cabinet, was not averse to listening to any story that disparaged the first family of the Confederacy. Along with chronicling much that is amazing of both Lincoln and Seward, he turned his attention from serious matters long enough to gossip a bit with his colleague, Edwin M. Stanton, Secretary of War. Among other irrelevant subjects that took the place of Cabinet discussions was the story told at the close of the war that Mrs. Jefferson Davis, while living in the Mansion, gave one of her servants a vigorous slap whenever he displeased her. Stanton, whom Welles despised but nevertheless quoted, had seen the young negro and got the story from him.[1] Varina was usually what they called easy on her servants, but all servants at the Mansion were not among the valued house-servant class. For his own good, this particular one, given many privileges according to the custom of the day, may have needed correction. She little thought that how she regulated her household would become a matter for discussion in the Federal Cabinet. It was

[1] The negro boy "Jim Limber" who was carried to Washington after the capture of Jefferson Davis.

her ill luck to become mixed up in a petty story with a body of worthies whom she detested, but she must pay for her high distinction.

The Cabinet gossip in time seeped back to Varina to greatly mortify her, but "Small talk and gossip," she flashed contemptuously, "was one of the vices of Washington."

As for the Cabinet story, to chastise an obstreperous youth of any color was not objectionable at that day. Everywhere in the South young white boys, nearly grown up, were whipped prior to '61, and by Yankee teachers of both sex.[1] It is significant of the time, however, that the stanch old Secretary of the Navy, who had no faith whatever in his informant, in his doubts of the story's being true used the word "perhaps." It is noticeable that he does not use the word in any other reference to Stanton. In connection with the Cabinet story, it is a well-known fact that household service in the Executive Mansion, where a large number of servants, for various purposes, must be employed, soon became a difficult problem with which its mistress had to deal. One catches, all through the minor records of the time, allusions to the mysterious comings and goings of the servants and employees at the Confederate White House. Thefts, attempts at incendiarism and the discovery of propaganda of a dangerous nature introduced by Northern agencies were frequent. Mrs. Chesnut gives several accounts of such occurrences, some of which happened even during public entertainment. More than once she expresses her anxiety about the safety of the family in the Mansion. She says, with some amusement, that "Mrs. Davis had such

[1] The South had many Northern teachers before the war, some of whom were notably strict disciplinarians. These were considered highly necessary, but while treated with respect were not considered social adjuncts.

faith in some of her maids that she could believe no evil of them. It never crossed her mind that some of them would leave her, only to find later that they had been induced to do so by unknown parties." Varina usually made light of her domestic difficulties and often amused her guests, even the grave Rector of St. Paul's Church, with humorous accounts of the negroes' naïve replies when questioned about the Northern agents seeking to alienate them. One especially good story was of a devoted maid who received so many handsome presents from the Northern agents that she wanted to divide them with the family.

The Davis home continued to be the object of the agents' activities throughout the war. During the entire four years of the Confederacy, threats of putting Jefferson Davis to death were heard in the North and in the Federal army, and but for Varina's skill in the management of her household, the sense of duty impressed upon her servants and the affection with which they usually regarded her, there might have been a more successful attempt on the life of the Confederate President than the one suspected at Montgomery. While it is believed that she managed her household affairs with order and system, there are too many instances of the good will that existed between her and her servants for the Stanton story to have any weight.

But there were critics at home. With all her efforts to be the diplomat in difficult situations she was not on occasions as tactful as some thought she should be. Varina usually punished her critics, to forgive them on the first sign of any change in her favor. While this trait was kindly in the main, it was not without a certain indifference, possibly a degree of selfishness that served as a protection against the self-injury that comes of harboring revenge and malice.

However she might strike back at times, she would never risk her main purposes. Sometimes unable to deal with her critics with wit and good humor, after an evaporative outburst, she dismissed them as unworthy her notice. It was a favorite method, more often assumed than was realized, with the haughty Southerners of disposing of the enemy. But with Varina, it became a practical philosophy. Only in rare instances was she unable to apply her creed. For the most part she was a creature of good will. Her deepest and bitterest resentments had been brought about in defense of her husband. In this middle period of the Confederacy, she still ruled her Court with grace and ease. Numerous editors throughout the South visiting the President's home, and falling under her spell, came home to write in their scant weekly papers, often now printed upon the reverse side of wall paper, that she was a "gracious and charming hostess, one fitted in every way to preside over the White House of the Confederacy."

With youth still on her side and, at times, handsome enough to be readily called beautiful, she was in the spring of '63, notwithstanding some adverse criticism, the center of a brilliant circle, the most sparkling and intellectual of her sex within it. From numerous memoirs and reminiscences and such friends as the Carys who were constantly, in the most informal manner, at the Mansion, one is led to believe that Varina was at this time a very impressive woman. Criticism of her, as has been observed, was generally traced to official sources. Differences between Jefferson Davis and any public official soon involved the women concerned. Some of these, Mrs. Chesnut records, were already scolding and "poking fun" at Varina's receptions, even at her figure; but as the mother of two children born in the White House, this fact should have put to shame the critics. Some were doubting that the President was ever as sick as she reported. It was all "buncombe" got up for effect. In several supreme efforts, Varina had succeeded, or thought she had succeeded, in pouring oil on the troubled waters, to gain her friend Mary Boykin's amused approval. She had the offended ones to spend the night with her at the Mansion and constantly rode out with them to the camps to cheer the new regiments that were daily arriving. While one is not given the right to say what Varina and her friend talked about it is certain that they referred with some merriment to this *coup de grâce* in the art of diplomacy. No one better than Varina could feel for the weaknesses and vanities of her critics. While she resented criticism if it made things more pleasant and comfortable she could ignore it, even forget it.

The offishness that some thought they discovered in her manner towards Mrs. Joseph E. Johnston was now anything but covert tea-table talk. She continued to ignore it and the author has failed to find any confirmation of it on her part. Gossip, however, had it that perfect good will did not exist between the two, and there might have been strained relations as the disagreement over military matters progressed, but it was never to the extent that she could not play the part of the gracious lady upon public occasions. Besides, it is believed that she really liked Mrs. Johnston. We find them frequently in the early years of the war riding out together. On one occasion, both were thrown from the carriage, and both injured, but "bore themselves with much fortitude." It was known that they had been "warm friends in the past and would miss each other." [1]   And one cannot forget that Varina, though Pollard says that she reserved the privilege of not returning calls, went in the most friendly and loving manner to see both General and Mrs. Johnston when he was placed in command of the Army of the West. None could doubt that she had their interest deep at heart. Still there continued to be hints and insinuations that she had something to do with Jefferson Davis' inability to get on amicably with Joseph E. Johnston; that it concerned the men and dated back to old Washington days.   So Varina, whether it was true or not, had this to confront her.

It is certain, as has been seen, that she was never as close to any of the wives of the military and civil branches of the government during her reign in the White House as she was to Mrs. Chesnut.   In this friendship, she was particularly fortunate.   One finds them visiting each other informally at any hour of the day, conferring with each other upon all sorts of subjects from costumes to recent battles.   When one considers the very frank and shrewd manner in which Mrs. Chesnut wrote of every one—her numerous sharp observations that General Joseph E. Johnston was always retreating, her humorous caricatures of Richmond ladies as they appeared in war work, her puzzled surprise at their squeamishness in the matter of fearing that their social standing would be injured if they were seen with plain people; her smart take-off of General Lee—when all this is considered her general portraiture of both Varina and Jefferson Davis is remarkable for its absence of any disparaging criticism.   At times these fall under her half-

---

[1] Many of these facts and impressions have been gathered through the courtesy of the officials of the Confederate Museum in Richmond, from the Richmond *Examiner,* and also from various papers, memoirs and reminiscences.

humorous animadversions, but one feels, throughout, the affection and confidence with which she regarded both. However she might use her rapier upon others, these were spared. There was a touch of reverence in her manner toward Jefferson Davis. He understood better than any one the conditions that the Confederacy faced; his voice was the most calming sound that reached her ears in a world of strident, raucous war noises. These and other kindly references we find in her Diary. She observed both very closely during these years and sometimes doubted if Varina found in her high station all that she thought she would.

Did Varina herself sometimes recall if not in a way pine for the old Washington days before the dreadful cataclysm had torn the friends from her that she had known since girl-hood, friends whose children, she says, she had "seen grow to manhood and womanhood in the National Capital"? One cannot say and cannot account for all the vagaries that infest the mind to be instantly discarded, leaving not the slightest conscious trace behind. In lighter humors she was fond of telling some of her friends that her children at first thought that they were still living in Washington and were indignant when told that the Yankees had taken away their beautiful city. But the most groundless statement that has ever crept into history is the one which tells you that she had been influenced in her rearing by her Northern kin. Aside from having heard that her father's people were among the first families of New Jersey, a fact of which she was always proud, she knew but little of them. William Burr Howell, like S. S. Prentiss and all the young men who located in the prosperous little city of Natchez, was completely won over to the Southern attitude, customs and habits. His children were reared as those of other slaveholders and Varina knew nothing of housework nor even of housekeeping until her marriage. The insinuation that she had done housework had no truth whatever to sustain it, although historians continue to wrestle with the allegation. We have gone somewhat out of the way in this volume for the sake of historical accuracy to repeat what was stated in the first volume. That some of her philosophy, as well as erudition, was absorbed from her New England tutor is true. However, it is a fact, though humorously stated, that Northerners coming South in time, like all new converts, were more rabid than the natives in its defense.

Varina's children, no sooner than they had in a vague way comprehended the situation, became belligerent young Confederates, playing soldier, with every room and hall of the Mansion ringing with defiant laughter. She records the pretty story that the little boy Jefferson, whenever the guns roared on the James, strenuously insisted when asked to join her in prayer that he should be allowed to first go and help his father fight the Yankees and pray afterwards. With all her cares and responsibilities, she continued to keep her children close to her. She constantly had them at their prayers, and at any time in the day; and often she and her husband knelt in prayer. Knowing Varina as we do, this might seem to be an affectation on her part, did not one take into consideration the fact that great store is set by form in the service of the Church of England. It was these forms and ceremonials, not to say elegancies, that adherents believed to be not only essential to spiritual life but necessary to good breeding. Lenient in many things, she was at the same time careful of her children's standards. Even to extreme old age, she is found writing an article for the New York *World* on the care of the young child.[1] Though Mrs. Chesnut draws for us no such portrait, Pollard thought her assertive and masculine. There may at times have been what one might take to be an air of these things about her, but beneath were qualities purely feminine, and sensitive to the least indelicate conduct on the part of others.

She had acquired in her association with the political leaders of the day much of a man's outlook, and it is quite probable that at times the woman's view, during that narrow scope and prospect for her sex, seemed to her small and inconsequential. If there were nothing else to prove it, her "Memoir" reveals the fact that she was better acquainted with public affairs than any other woman of her day in America. She read at pleasure all her husband's correspondence and corresponded with him on all sorts of important subjects when away from Richmond. She was accused of listening at the door to sick-bed conferences at the Executive Mansion. But this she could have done without any bad meaning attached to it, since she was freely admitted to all executive conferences that took place in her husband's sick room; was entirely at home in the midst of the informal councils held in the Mansion. No one there would have kept back a thought because of her presence. Some would have discussed matters with her. She herself records that she frequently overheard conversations about public matters in the Executive Mansion. She speaks often of meeting General Lee and others in these conferences with no feeling of intrusion on her part. We find her offering him a cup of tea on one occasion before the consultation began.

[1] Contributed to the New York *World* at the age of 80.

But with all her disposition to take part in public affairs, Varina was a good model of the prevailing Southern type. One finds her often seeking to cover up her more profound knowledge with all the light touches of wit and humor and other certain feminine graces. One often hears from a guest at the White House that she was a "delightful hostess," a "social Queen," even when her weekly receptions had grown tame from frequency.

She had much skill in meeting difficult situations and little deep-seated animosity. She could antagonize one day and forget it and make others forget it the next. It has been said that she quarreled with Clement Clay and at times with the whole Toombs family and many others, and yet we find her chummy afterwards with Senator Clay and entertaining the families of disaffected leaders for a night over at the Mansion. In any estimate of Varina, it should be remembered that her antagonisms were for the most part brought about largely by political differences between her husband and the coterie that opposed him. Left alone with men and women, she seems to have managed many of them with a great deal of skill. To extreme old age, she could attract a roomful of men about her and this without a particle of sex sentiment, but a certain intellectual charm that when mixed with lighter graces has a wonderful fascination. It is suspected that she understood how to play upon their small vanities.

At times a sudden blitheness captured even her women friends. Mrs. Chesnut calls it "mood" and infers that it came and went, but when "in the mood" she did not know a more delightful person. But Varina had a variety of moods, one in which she, though only thirty-five or six years of age, thought of herself as old. In her letters,

with all her vivacity and youthful spontaneity, she frequently refers to herself as "an old woman." In Varina's
time, however, thirty-five was dangerously near to being old.
But it is certain that she did not relish being described as a
"handsome, portly, middle-aged lady," the description of a
country editor, unacquainted with a defter speech. She
liked better Russell's comment in the London *Times* that
she had a "good figure."

She was now being closely observed, to continue to be so
throughout the four years of the Confederacy. Today
many are still asking if she was not a more forceful woman
with a keener desire for a fuller realization of herself than
has generally been accorded her. What was the nature of
her influence upon the fortunes of the Confederacy, is a
question that piques the mind after reading Pollard's diatribes in which he portrays her in Elizabethan outline. One
also reads over and over again that sentence in William
E. Dodd's life of Jefferson Davis, "She assisted him in
the discharge of all his public duties."

In all such studies and estimates of her one must first
consider that the "womanly" was so firmly implanted in the
feminine breast at that period of American history, that let
a woman's powers and ability be what they may—even
equal to that of the men about her—she was certain to feel
the restrictions and customs that had molded her sex for
generations. There was, unquestionably, ability on her part
to have governed, and had she been the ruler of some
country, she would in all probability have given history a
vivid personality to number among its famous women. It
is very certain that she rushed forward in times of dire
crises to offer advice with a swift tongue in matters of
state; but hedged in by social environs, it is also certain

that she drew back with a sense of having overstepped the fixed bounds allotted her sex. Ridicule, she knew, of certain fastidious grand dames was sure to be her portion if she were found taking an open part in public affairs; and no frost on young leaves was ever more blighting than the disapprobation of a Victorian grand dame of one of her sex. Even on occasions as *chargé d'affaires per interim* of her husband, as she sometimes humorously claimed to be, she must not forget her boundaries. At times, however, when public matters reached a crisis, so strong and clear were her perceptions and judgment that she risked the limitations, forgot her evening dresses, her *bon mots* and charms. At these times, her manner may have had something in it of masculinity and Pollard's eye was quick to catch it. But if Varina was a mannish woman, she did not wish to appear so. Even when one finds her offering advice to her husband, she does it with a tact and consideration that disconcerts the eye of such deep-sighted probers as the seerish Bradford.

So the lesser critic cannot go farther, nor does the writer believe that the probe would find anything beyond a desire to cooperate with her husband, or any fault more than with the times that demanded of Southern women that if they ruled at all, they must do so with diplomacy, perhaps intrigue. In saying so, I may lay myself open to the charge of having failed as a biographer since it seems to be the impression that if you fail to find the stain-spot, no matter how you have studied your subject and noted its absence, you have proved that you are not a true analyst. Finding the flaw is the only proof that you are an expert, though you have applied as much skill in discovering its absence as in discerning its presence.

Admitting then that the wife of Jefferson Davis, whose historical fate like that of Carlotta and the Empress Eugenie was hanging in the balance, possessed frailties and weaknesses common to all humankind, not one distinguishing bad quality stands out. Pollard, with all his railings against her, never once included her in his dark insinuations against war-time society in the Southern Capital. From his own account, scandal might camp at the very gates of the Confederate White House, but it never entered them. The relations between husband and wife are said, by all writers and observers, to have been marked by devotion, and a high purpose. If she and Jefferson Davis sometimes quarreled, it was not of a nature to affect their happiness; besides they lived for the most part in public and this gives a good account of them. All through the records one comes across incidents of happy family relations. In this she was not selfish, for she continued to be surrounded by various members of her family. Amid all household interruptions, with extra bedrooms to be constantly prepared, extra plates put down, one hears no word of complaint. The woman that Pollard painted as self-willed and dictatorial, with a tongue that could lash like a whip, must have possessed much patience and nobility under the top layer of arrogance and *hauteur* to have carried so gracefully all the burdens and demands of family and social life, and, as some claim, of public affairs. It is well known that Jefferson Davis, with his many aches and pains, was something of a "parlor boarder." One particularly likes her consideration of him in such expressions as "Everybody must keep quiet when the President is sick." [1]

[1] Chesnut.

The household at the Executive Mansion regarded him with a mixture of pride and affection in which there was a slight feeling of awe. Varina herself was not entirely free of this attitude towards him but felt a secret pride in the thought that the grave, still handsome man to whom every one deferred could lie in her living room on a sofa near her with his children frolicking over him. And admitting, to please the psychologist, that there was a faint, deleterious influence exercised by the wife, one might ask if it did not come of too much mothering rather than dictation. How this could come about, if it did—and it is not the sway of the selfish, arbitrary woman—is puzzling when one considers the great difference in their ages. But even this might hold some proof of Varina's desire for domination. Her efforts, however, seem to have been concerned in assisting and defending him, not so much in directing him. If there were some instances in which she acted as an adviser, she went about it in a very charming and helpful manner: "If I am intrusive, forgive me for the sake of the love that impels me." One, too, cannot fail to be charmed with the faith she expressed in him in the hour of his supreme failure, "I have seen you stir men up when every one else failed."

CHAPTER XXX

MILITARY operations carry us back to the autumn of '62. The success of the Federals in the early autumn, and the boastful claims that were made to the victory of Antietam served only to make the Confederates more determined to drive the Union army out of Virginia. If they said in the flowery language of the day, that "no invader should tread its sacred soil," it sounded much like some of Seward's phrases in connection with the Union. Roger Pryor and hundreds of stanch Virginians had reiterated it a hundred times in fiery speeches throughout the South. The Federals by this time had begun to find out that the "effete race of Virginians" had become astonishingly virile. Throughout the spring and summer of '62, Lee and Jackson had contended in victory after victory with the Army of the Potomac, now commanded by Burnside. McClellan, who had been relieved, and restored after Pope, a pet they said of President Lincoln's, had failed in the Virginia Campaign, had won the battle of Antietam on September 17th. It was the greatest success so far of the Federal army. The Republican Cabinet, however, veiling its jealousy, some have thought, of the rising young Democrat, continued to stress his failure in the early advance on Richmond. For very little recent cause, he was summarily removed and Burnside placed in command of the Army of the Potomac.

324

Some changes had been made in the army by the President of the Confederate States, but while historians have sought to criticize Jefferson Davis for what they call interference with his generals, nothing in all history compares with the rapid displacement of commanders that took place in the Union army. Certain historians, to sustain the administration, have stressed a point to condemn some of the officers, especially McClellan. Though these have sought to minimize it, there was less harmony between the executive and military branches in the Federal government than in the Confederacy.

After his appointment, Burnside began to reorganize his large army of something over 113,000, and in the late fall was on the north bank of the Rappahannock opposite Fredericksburg. By December 12th, he was ready to meet Lee and Jackson. The rain fell in torrents at times; the roads were knee-deep in mud in places, and a dreary mist constantly enveloped the Virginia landscape, blurring the hilltop distances. The forests were gray and gloomy and the scant brown leaves hung heavy and sodden on the naked branches. With approaching winter, both armies had become active, but Lee's men were in high spirits. The number of their victories was so encouraging that in summing them up Antietam passed out of their minds. The famous battleground of Manassas again seemed a good stand for the Confederates. Lee, however, discovered a stronger position near Fredericksburg on the Rappahannock, and posted his army on Marye's Heights out from the town. It was encircled with batteries and fortified on the side facing the town with a stone wall lined inside with infantry. This gave the Confederates something of the same advantages that the breastworks at the battle of New Orleans gave Andrew Jackson. The Confederate commanders were sanguine though far outnumbered. The authorities at Washington were discovering by now that the Confederate President knew how to make an army. With far less resources to draw upon, he kept a good army in the field years longer than the North believed it could be done. One who wrote in all fairness has said that the slender economic resources of the South were no match for the mighty strength of the nation that opposed it.[1]

Burnside, after much consultation with the authorities at Washington, began his attack on the 13th with a loss of fame that went down in a total eclipse in the horrors of Fredericksburg. Again the Confederate army was victorious and with Virginia many of the states of the Confederacy won unfading laurels. Mortified over their defeat, the Republican leaders were also disputing among themselves, with both Chase and Seward threatening to resign from the Cabinet. It was a radical intrigue all around, and it seemed for the time that Seward would get the worst of it; but his hold upon Lincoln was as mysterious, Welles says, as ever.

Lincoln accepted, with much relief, the resignation of Burnside, to make another mistake in appointing "Fighting Joe Hooker" to succeed him. Hooker was to go to a worse fate in the Wilderness passes. The Federal affairs were never in a worse plight. Lincoln was bitterly censured, but, like Jefferson Davis, held steadily to his purpose in the face of all criticism. His reliance upon Seward, Welles affirms, was increasing, still his viewpoint was becoming more national. While the removal of Hooker might have been wise, it will remain a point of dispute why McClellan

[1] "Division and Reunion," by Woodrow Wilson.

was removed after Antietam unless it could be explained in the political controversies and intrigues that were going on at the time.

The Army of Northern Virginia was now at the height of its fame, and few armies of history have displayed more skill. Still the victory of the Confederates at Chancellorsville was mingled with gloom in the loss of the great Jackson, believed to be, by some historians, the most superb commander developed by either army. To find the place where best to strike the foe had always been a favorite strategy with him, and while reconnoitering to discover a point of vantage, he was taken by his own men for a Federal and shot, receiving a wound that proved fatal. Many have seen in it a forecast of the dark fatality that marked the Confederacy. Notwithstanding this great misfortune the Army of Northern Virginia under Lee went from victory to victory, until the world rang with its story. Battle after battle had been won to the amazement of all Europe. But winning battles at the expense of the army which was dwindling in numbers and against a government that had money, bounties and population to sustain it, must have an end. Sooner or later it must yield to the overwhelming forces against it. Such is the inevitable law of conflict, nor can man outwit it. But at the present, flushed with victory, with the final but reluctant approval of President Davis, General Lee decided to take his army into the rich state of Pennsylvania where it was said the people were tired of the war. With a signal victory, too, he hoped to overwhelm the enemy and in all probability bring the North to terms of peace. The fighting quality of his troops had so far proved unquestionable, and that feature held no fears for him. But their equipment and supplies were getting to be a serious matter. With a victory he could clothe and fit out his army in a rich territory. Jefferson Davis had perfect confidence in him. He would risk it. The unexpected offensive might draw some of the North's attention from the middle South. It was good tactics if the feat could be accomplished. The army, blithe and confident, began its march on the shrill blast of "Dixie."

The Republicans were in alarm. Lee was on his way to Pennsylvania where the people were denouncing the "cruel, inhuman war." Some one was to take Hooker's place and the Republicans had been casting about in the dark for that individual. General George G. Meade was the next victim who, like McClellan, was to be displaced without full recognition or explanation. It became a custom in humorous after-war speeches in retaliation of Northern criticism of Jefferson Davis, to call the long roll—"McDowell, McClellan, Pope, Burnside, Hooker and Meade." In view of the numerous displacements, it might be asked, "Where was the shrewd almost mystical insight into men's fitness and ability said to have been possessed by Lincoln in comparison with that of Jefferson Davis, whose occasional displacements of officers have been so constantly the theme of critical Northern historians?" The author is only contending for fair play among the historians.

With the victories of '62 and early spring of '63, General Lee had won a popularity superior to that of any officer engaged on either side. He now planned his grand offensive upon a larger scale than his campaign into Maryland. No one could dispute the psychological effect of carrying the war successfully into the enemy's own country. That he intended to capture Washington is not a matter of record, but it was a logical sequence at this time with the Confederacy taking a decided offensive, a policy that it had not considered practical, or even desirable, at the beginning of the war. The Confederacy had now reached the zenith but the finger of fate pointed low to the nadir. One might say that here was the greatest mistake of the Confederacy. A strong army at home continually strengthened might have proved a Chinese wall that eventually would have worn out the spirit of the North. Still, if it was the settled policy of the North to subjugate the South, nothing in the end could have saved the Confederacy, since the disparity in numbers between the two sections was quadruple if not greater. With Gettysburg the tide in the fortunes of the Confederacy receded.

The story of Gettysburg and the valor with which the Southern army conducted itself against a strong and determined foe, belongs to a more purely military history. Though General Lee assumed entire responsibility for the failure, students of history have agreed that lack of cooperation, especially of that of his cavalry and of Longstreet, went far to ruin the campaign. Still in view of the fact that the man power and all resources of the Confederacy were dwindling, even had the Federals lost Gettysburg, the North, without a doubt, would have continued the struggle. Its leaders knew that the South was growing weaker every year and that it was now only a question of time when it would have to furl its battle-stained banners. After Gettysburg England to some extent began to stress her neutrality laws and no more shipbuilding went on in her ports though thousands of hearts in her realm still sympathized with the struggling young nation. France, too, whispered that the United States could do anything it pleased so far as she was concerned. The Quai D'Orsay wanted to smoke. Why not ignore the Confederacy altogether and bring home her many hogsheads of tobacco stored in Richmond.

At the same time that the Army of Northern Virginia suffered defeat in Pennsylvania, the war in the South ended disastrously for the Confederate armies. Grant's two years' campaign against Vicksburg had at last been successful. After his rather dismal failure to capture Vicksburg, the prized Confederate stronghold, from a northern approach in the autumn of '62, he had, in the spring of '63, conceived the idea of crossing the river above and moving a portion of his army down the Mississippi to attack the city from a southern direction. With this purpose in view, he used the entire Federal fleet, commanded by Admiral D. D. Porter, to protect his transports while they ran the batteries at Vicksburg. Some historians have thought that had General Johnston attacked Grant after he crossed the Mississippi he could have cut him off from his headquarters. Leaving Sherman on the Yazoo attacking the Confederates at Snyder's Bluff and other places by April 30th, under the protection of the fleet Grant carried five transports, a gunboat and twelve barges down the river. These he landed at Bruinsburg, west of Port Gibson, leaving at the former place a number of troops to protect his batteries. The Confederates under Bowen faced the advance of the Federal Army four miles from Port Gibson where a severe battle was fought. It was in favor of the Federals, but not until their killed and wounded covered the battlefield.

Grant then brought his army from Port Gibson to meet the Confederates under Gregg near Raymond where another severe battle was fought on May 12th. While the victory, from the standpoint of valor, belonged to the Confederates, they were finally overcome by the superior Federal forces, and were compelled to retreat, followed by Sherman's army to Jackson. Grant chose the Clinton Road to Jackson and moved with Sherman on the Capital. On May 14th, both arrived at the same time and took possession of the little city, which Grant had planned to wreck before he attempted the capture of Vicksburg. General Joseph. E. Johnston was at Jackson with a view to defending the city, but feeling that he was unable to do so with his forces, moved out of the place and retreated toward Canton where he concentrated his troops. This left Grant to contend alone with General J. C. Pemberton, who had his headquarters at Edwards between Jackson and Vicksburg, with troops stationed at Bolton and other points throughout the battle area.

After sacking and burning Jackson, cutting off all railroad connections and isolating it, Grant collected his forces at Clinton and moved against Pemberton. From that time on skirmishing, fierce encounters and cannonading took place between Grant's and Pemberton's forces which were meeting everywhere on the roads, making the whole country between Jackson and Vicksburg a battle scene. Grant was ready now to meet Pemberton in the main battle at Champion Hill or Baker's Creek. Johnston was to have joined Pemberton here, but feeling that he was not strong enough did not come.

The Confederates were now slowly yielding ground when a dispatch was captured and carried to Grant that acquainted him with Pemberton's movements. After one of the fiercest battles of the campaign, Pemberton's forces moved back towards Vicksburg by way of his headquarters at Edwards. At Big Black River, a few miles from the city, the Confederates turned again and fought desperately. It was then that a Federal officer said that on looking up he saw facing him no one but boys and old, white-haired men. Grant's stronger forces pressed them so furiously they finally withdrew within the lines of Vicksburg.

But the prize was not to be won for many terrible days. Grant himself was appalled at the price he had to pay for it. The old people remember that he was kind. The distressed and excited people were attributing his recent victories to various causes. Some laid it at Pemberton's door; others said that it was caused by Johnston's failure to cooperate with Pemberton. Neither was spared the severest censure. Not all the harsh denunciation common to the hasty, impatient Southerners was reserved for Jefferson Davis. Throughout the middle South and up through the Carolinas, Johnston was being bitterly criticized for his weak defense of Vicksburg and its territory, and sudden retreat towards Canton out of the way of the Federal army. Gossip of it reached Jefferson Davis a hundred times after his return from Vicksburg where he went to inspect the army. Old soldiers, hardened to war, without any awe of their commanders, were saying of Johnston, "Retreat, I should say so! He can do nothing but retreat." Humorous ones were picturing him as "an old maid who must have things just so before he could fight a battle." One gathers many such impressions from a careful perusal of the Chesnut Diary. Old inhabitants, also, inform us that the country was full of complaints of his disposition to retreat.[1] This was constantly reaching the ears of Jefferson Davis who was anxious for him to take the

[1] Conversations with contemporaries.

offensive. One feels sure that this constant complaint and gossip had much to do with his placing Hood, at a later period, in command of the Western army, though, as has been pointed out, Hardee had been his first choice.

In Virginia the army had been noted for its aggressiveness and Jefferson Davis had always favored that method when on Southern soil. It was difficult for him to bear patiently with any other. He had been a soldier himself and knew what aggressiveness meant upon the battlefields. He did not possess the stolid temperament that eased Lincoln over rough places in his pathway. Yet from a careful, impartial study it is clear that he exercised self-control in his intercourse with those with whom he differed. In all official relations with him, Varina tells us in her "Memoir," that she never heard President Davis say anything derogatory of General Johnston, though they held entirely different views of military strategy. Rhodes, who sustains Johnston, still states that with the reenforcements he received, he had an army as large as the one Grant reserved to meet a rear attack. Rhodes also says that Pemberton in one instance endeavored to obey Johnston's orders to get with him, but was met by Grant's army and given battle. Other historians have stated that Pemberton never once tried to unite with Johnston; others that Pemberton urged Johnston to make a rear attack while he repelled Grant in his assaults on Vicksburg. Thus, Johnston was pictured as a constant retreater, and Pemberton a presumptuous, stubborn subordinate. The general arraignment and denunciation engaged in at the time indicates to what lengths men go in criticism whenever there is failure.

There is more reason for Johnston's failure than that usually given. The situation in the middle South was that

Grant, by two years of what he called "attrition," was wearing out the army of the West. The heart of the South, trampled for years by invading armies, the land was scarred and seared with battlefields upon which green corn did not simultaneously grow. The real trouble with the Confederacy was that while it had two good armies, despite all Jefferson Davis could do neither was strong enough to indefinitely overcome the horde that was gathering against them. It became more a question, not of whether by doing this or that they could have won, but whether the North was or was not determined to keep the South in the Union. With its constantly failing resources, isolated as it was, it could not have withstood a determined North, growing stronger in war material and more prosperous in many ways each year. The wonder is that it lasted so long, and refused to quit until it had written its Homeric epic in American history. This was the corona surrounding its fame.

Grant and Sherman now held the spotlight in military circles in Washington. The latter was more inflated, it seems, over his success than the Westerner, for later we find him preparing to march up through Georgia, with something of the spirit of a conqueror, to finally bring upon himself the charge of seeking the dictatorship of a reunited Union.

There were now sleepless nights in the Executive Mansion, of the bitterness of which the world knew nothing. Added to the shock at the defeat of the splendid army at Gettysburg and the fall of Vicksburg, wrangling was going on over many matters in Congress and the insistent and destructive criticisms of the Richmond *Examiner,* the Charleston *Mercury* and other disaffected papers broke out afresh. All through his administration, Jefferson Davis had just such foolish talk to contend with as the Governor of Louisiana's saying that he was sorry that his state had not gone alone in its struggle for independence. An old veteran told the author that Governor Brown of Georgia and a dozen loud-mouthed, noisy railers almost disrupted the Confederacy after Lee's defeat at Gettysburg, and set on foot schemes to cut it up. Nothing but the iron will of Jefferson Davis held it together until he had exhausted its wherewithal to make war.

There was gossip now about the town that the Richmond *Examiner* was not respected at the White House, that Varina was refusing to read it and was expressing contempt for its editors. The whole city was talking. Who knew the truth about it, or was it one of those false rumors that, once started, is never silenced, like whispers that live on when grievous, open scandals are forgotten. But it could have happened without any great reflection upon her. The provocation was strong enough in view of their bitter diatribes upon the President.

Varina with all her diplomacy and efforts to be discreet was gaining the reputation of a "martinet." But was not the Chesnut Diary there to exonerate her? Not a stinging criticism appears in the Diary where so many sharp thrusts at others are found. That one at least of the embittered editors of the *Examiner* would get even with the haughty woman in the White House, needed only time to prove.[1] The vitriolic criticism that he made of the husband would in future include the wife, and Varina was to number him among her bitterest foes. One, however, must discredit his criticism of her since his denunciation of Richmond soci-

[1] "Secret History of the Confederacy," by E. A. Pollard.

ety was still harsher.   In time she treated him with a cold,
studied indifference.   Some thought that she should have
found some way to appease him.   But Varina, though tactful and wise enough in many things, refused to overlook
his unjust attacks upon her husband.

Nothing had pleased the President's enemies more than
to witness the strife between himself and the brilliant, indiscreet editors of the Richmond *Examiner.*   It became
town talk.   The criticism became harsher after Gettysburg.
At times Varina was filled with anger and when deeply incensed was given to tears.   It was not the life she had
intended to lead.   It had been her sincere desire to be on
terms of good will with those about her.   She loved nothing
better than a great stir where every one worked harmoni-
ously together.   It is barely possible that Jefferson Davis
would have preferred that Varina should not have been so
resentful of criticism in public matters, but he knew that
her intentions were good and his faith in her was strong.

She was now giving her whole thought to the success of
the Confederacy, but how much she was seeking to influence
state affairs at this time is still a surmise.   It is very
clear that she believed that Jefferson Davis was the most
capable, invincible and blameless spirit in all the unhappy
Revolution.   Through the autumn of '63, and on through
the dreary winter, she gave him her constant thought.   With
the women of the city she worked with more feverish
energy and selflessness than ever.   Social activities, though
still kept up, had lost their glitter.   Women were beginning to feel the bitter pinch of poverty.   They were now
dyeing their clothes, making shoes out of pieces of old
parlor carpets, ink out of oak balls and pokeberries, molding candles and tallow dips and eating their corndodgers

and pea soup with smiling faces.[1] Their silks and satins, all that had not been made into flags, were threadbare. Besides, it was not now considered good taste to wear rich colors. Some still did on state occasions with a kind of proud defiance that the Southern woman displayed throughout the war. It is not recorded whether Varina wore homespun or not, but one can believe that she wore cotton materials. Her last picture taken a short while before the fall of Richmond shows her in a rather cheap muslin evening gown. The President's salary in Confederate notes, after the expense of entertainment, did not provide more than the necessities of life during the waning years of the Confederacy, and her own clothes and those of her children were from many accounts improvisations of old finery. The extortioner, too, like the sneaking moth that knows its own seasons, was with them. One had to pay enormous prices for the simplest article of clothing. Notwithstanding Pollard's acid comments, Varina still kept up a limited entertainment. She might even have to give up this, but she persisted in it now as a part of the effort by the women of the city to divert and hearten the soldiers. The Mansion continued to be the favorite resort not only for all social purposes, but for the hundreds of visitors and callers bent on missions of importance or else seeking it through curiosity. Open house, now, for the most part informal, was kept for soldiers of all ranks. They came and went at will. Writing at this time about the spirit of the women of the South, Varina records in her "Memoir," "The close relations that fellowship in danger bring about are sweet memories, and are harder to relinquish than those of courtly ceremony or triumph."

[1] "Recollections Grave and Gay," by Mrs. Burton N. Harrison.

She records with great pride that "Mrs. Robert E. Lee and her daughters furnished one hundred and ninety-six socks and gloves to Posey's brigade, and this when Mrs. Lee was confined to her chair, a hopeless victim of rheumatism, and her daughter's time was largely consumed by nursing in the hospitals."

"It is a proud memory," she tells us, "that our people rose in their might and met every emergency with industry, ingenuity, self-sacrifice and a reckless daring, worthy of their noble cause."

The historian Rhodes has sympathetically observed that when one thinks of the lavish life in the South and now reflects upon the suffering its people were enduring—sacrifice and hunger, the spirit its women exhibited has few parallels in history.

CHAPTER XXXI

THERE were now distressed and anxious faces throughout the Confederacy. The Southern Capital was wrapped in gloom, and women cried as if their hearts would break. General Lee had brought his army back to Virginia and was in correspondence with President Davis from his headquarters at Camp Orange. Varina was in despair. The news of the fall of Vicksburg coming with the disaster to the Army of Northern Virginia filled her, she says, with horror. At times she yielded to her grief, but resisted it and gave her whole thought to her husband and the many grave problems confronting the government. She had often heard him singing about his work when he felt that all was well with the army; had seen him playful with his children; but now he toiled silently at his tasks. An expression of settled sadness in his eyes troubled her. Any reflection upon General Lee was resented by both. How much Jefferson Davis' estimate of him had always influenced her is not known. Although she generally liked those that he did, she relied on her own judgment in many matters. In the instance of General Lee she was outspoken in his favor.

Though in perfect accord with her friend, Mrs. Chesnut, on most points, they at first had differed in their opinion of General Lee. Mrs. Chesnut had never seen him until she came to Richmond. From her Diary one gets the impression that on first acquaintance she did not admire him. She ob-

jected, it seems, to a certain coldness and aloofness, if
not impenetrableness in his manner, giving it out that she
liked his kinsman better. Who could get close to the other?
To Varina, who had been accustomed to her husband's
somewhat taciturn manner, this slight reserve and reticence
on the part of Lee increased her admiration for him. That
he was sometimes formal, even a little shy and stiff, in his
efforts in ladies' company to be urbane and social, afforded
her a tender amusement, while it ruffled the proud South
Carolina dame who demanded that all men should be of
the Chesnut and Manning type in their manner toward
women. Varina had often heard the claim of aloofness and
reserve made against Jefferson Davis, and knew how to estimate her friend's first impression of General Lee. Her
views on closer acquaintance would change, she felt sure;
and it did as the impulsive, generous-hearted diarist informs
us with much emphasis and elation.

Of the private conferences held in the Executive
Mansion between Jefferson Davis and General Lee, to
which Varina was admitted—"merely overlooked," she
laughed and told friends in after years,—one wishes that
more had been preserved. But there is enough saved to history for one to know that perfect sympathy existed between
the two great Southern leaders in their constant intercourse
with each other. Though unlike in nervous temperament,
their ideals, conceptions and beliefs were the same, and the
harmony with which they worked together throughout the
long struggle in which they, more than all others, bore the
heat and burden, make some of the most impressive pages
of its history.

After Gettysburg, Varina sometimes found her husband
sitting at his desk where he toiled incessantly, rereading

the lines in General Lee's communication which said, "You have done everything in your power to aid me in the work without omitting anything to promote the general welfare."

She saw his lips tighten and his lean and haggard face take on grimmer lines. These, she knew, were the signs of his determination to renew the struggle. But, though the dream had not faded, the long shadow had fallen and was slowly enveloping the land. Could he meet the enemy again in '64? It was a heavier task than he looked for but he set himself to it with a fierce energy.

The repulse of the Army of Northern Virginia at Gettysburg and the capture of Vicksburg, coming together, as if fate were making sure of her decrees, had filled the country with the deepest gloom and depression. With the Mississippi in possession of the Federals, Texas, which was one of the principal sources for the supply of meat and horses for the army, was cut off as suddenly as if it had been transferred to Asia. A chicken sent across, they said, could not evade the blockade. In addition to the lost lands of Texas, Sherman's army was still in the heart of the South, not only living upon the country's produce of '63, but making plans to rob the homes and lay waste the fields of Georgia and the Carolinas in '64. The cotton lands were never a prolific source of food supplies at best, and not even patriotism could make three stalks of corn grow in a hill. It is not the truth of the situation to say that there was any great amount of food to be had in '64 even if it could have been transported to the army. The agricultural and economic situation daily grew worse and in the gloomy prospect men's spirits sank. The South was slowly becoming paralyzed in all its activities. The valiancy and glory of striving was lost upon them in the bitter realization of defeat. It was the first admission that failure might overtake them. Could Jefferson Davis' iron will and impassioned plea reanimate them? He believed that a loss of spirit had not been felt in the army; nor among the great body of the people to an extent that it could not be aroused.

In high places the harshest criticism of both himself and General Lee was now indulged in both openly and surreptitiously by the leaders in all branches of the government, and even more openly by the public journals. None were more caustic and destructive than that of the Richmond *Examiner*. Benjamin could do more than smile and ordered the *Examiner* suppressed, but Jefferson Davis had always upheld the freedom of the press and would not sign the order, to win from Lord Campbell a eulogy that Englishmen did not often pay Americans. But amidst all the censure, as bitter at present of General Lee for the failure of the Maryland and Pennsylvania campaigns as of Jefferson Davis, nothing disturbed the Confederate President's peace of mind as much as Lee's wish and offer to resign from the army. The Army of Northern Virginia had become indissolubly linked with the name of Lee—the great Lee without whom Jefferson Davis could not see his way. This, he felt, would be the most irremediable blow that could befall the Confederacy, and it must be averted.

Varina, who was now in the closest touch with all that transpired, understood her husband's pain and perplexity when he read "the following letter" from General Lee at Camp Orange, dated August 8th, '63.

Mr. President: Your letters of July 28th and August 2d have been received, and I have waited for a leisure hour to reply, but I fear that will never come. I am extremely obliged to you for the attention given to the wants of this army, and the efforts made to supply them. Our absentees are returning, and I hope the earnest and beautiful appeal made to the country in your proclamation may stir up the whole people, and that they may see their duty and perform it. Nothing is wanted but that their fortitude should equal their bravery, to insure the success of our cause. We must expect reverses, even defeats. They are sent to teach us wisdom and prudence, to call forth greater energies, and to prevent our falling into greater disasters. Our people have only to be true and united, to bear manfully the misfortunes incident to war, and all will come right in the end.

I know how prone we are to censure, and how ready to blame others for the nonfulfilment of our expectations. This is unbecoming in a generous people, and I grieve to see its expression. The general remedy for the want of success in a military commander is his removal. This is natural, and in many instances proper. For, no matter what may be the ability of the officer, if he loses the confidence of his troops, disaster must sooner or later ensue.

I have been prompted by these reflections more than once, since my return from Pennsylvania, to propose to your Excellency the propriety of selecting another commander for this army. I have seen and heard expressions of discontent in the public journals at the result of the expedition. I do not know how far this feeling extends in the army. My brother officers have been too kind to report it, and so far the troops have been too generous to exhibit it. It is fair, however, to suppose that it does exist, and success is so necessary to us that nothing should be risked to secure it. I, therefore, in all sincerity, request your Excellency to take measures to supply my place. I do this with the more earnestness because no one is more aware than myself of my inability for the duties of my position. I cannot even accomplish what I myself desire. How can I fulfil the expectations of others? In addition, I sensibly feel the growing failure of my bodily strength. I have not yet recovered from the attack I experienced the past spring. I am becoming more and more incapable of exertion, and am thus prevented from making the personal examinations and giving the personal supervision to the operations in the field which I feel to be necessary. I am so dull that in making use of the eyes of others I am frequently misled. Everything, therefore, points to the advantages to be derived from a new commander, and I the more anxiously urge the matter upon your Excellency, from my belief that a younger and abler man than myself can readily be obtained. I know that he will have as gallant and brave an army as ever existed to second his efforts, and it would be the happiest day of my life to see at its head a worthy leader; one that would accomplish more than I could perform, and all that I have wished. I hope your Excellency will attribute my request to the true reason, the desire to serve my country, and to do all in my power to insure the success of her righteous cause.

I have no complaints to make of any one but myself. I have received nothing but kindness from those above me, and the most considerate attention from my comrades and companions in arms. To your Excellency I am specially indebted for uniform kindness and consideration. You have done everything in your power to aid me in the work committed to my charge, without omitting anything to promote the general welfare. I pray that your efforts may at length be crowned with success, and that you may long live to enjoy the thanks of a grateful people.

With sentiments of great esteem, I am very respectfully and truly yours,

R. E. LEE, *General*.

To His Excellency Jefferson Davis,
    President of the Confederate States.

It was the most critical period in the history of the Confederacy. The effect of General Lee's resignation upon the army and the people, coming immediately after the failure of the expedition, would have been disastrous in the extreme. The *morale* of the army was still good and the people were as eager as ever to establish their independence. With Lee Jefferson Davis felt that he could repair the loss. But what confusion and disarrangement, even disaffection would have to be overcome before he could again get ready for the main work of fighting battles. If not to Lee to whom could he intrust the Army of Northern Virginia? Lee himself had suggested a younger man which was conclusive proof that he felt that none of the old commanders would answer. It was now that the skill and leadership of Jefferson Davis rose to its highest peak and his firm position in the matter of General Lee's resignation and his knowledge of the necessities of the whole situation compare with any action recorded in history. He knew the worth of Lee to the Confederacy and it was his strong will in retaining him that prolonged the struggle and preserved to the story of the Confederacy some of its most heroic pages. On August 11, after a calm and fixed determination to do what he knew was best for the country, he sent General Lee the following reply to his letter, and the gods of battle must have clapped their hands:

General R. E. Lee,
    Commanding Army of Northern Virginia.

General: Yours of the 8th instant has been received. I am glad that you concur so entirely with me as to the wants of our country in this trying hour, and am happy to add that, after the first depression consequent upon our disasters in the West, indications have appeared that our people will exhibit that fortitude which we agree in believing is alone needful to secure ultimate success.

It well became Sidney Johnston, when overwhelmed by a senseless clamor, to admit the rule that success is the test of merit, and yet there is nothing which I have found to require a greater effort of patience than to bear the criticism of the ignorant, who pronounce everything a failure which does not equal their expectations or desires, and can see no good result which is not in the line of their own imaginings. I admit the propriety of your conclusions, that an officer who loses the confidence of his troops should have his position changed, whatever may be his ability; but when I read the sentence, I was not at all prepared for the application you were about to make. Expressions of discontent in the public journals furnish but little evidence of the sentiment of an army. I wish it were otherwise, even though all the abuse of myself should be accepted as the results of honest observation.

Were you capable of stooping to it, you could easily surround yourself with those who would fill the press with your laudations and seek to exalt you for what you have not done, rather than detract from the achievements which will make you and your army the subject of history, and objects of the world's admiration for generations to come.

I am truly sorry to know that you still feel the effects of the illness you suffered last spring, and can readily understand the embarrassments you experience in using the eyes of others, having been so much accustomed to make your own reconnaissances. Practice will, however, do much to relieve that embarrassment, and the minute knowledge of the country which you have acquired will render you less dependent for topographical information.

But suppose, my dear friend, that I were to admit with all their implications, the points which you present, where am I to find that new commander who is to possess the greater ability which you believe to be required? I do not doubt the readiness with which you would give way to one who could accomplish all that you have wished, and you will do me the justice to believe that, if Providence should kindly offer such a person for our use, I would not hesitate to avail of his services.

My sight is not sufficiently penetrating to discover such hidden merit, if it exists, and I have but used to you the language of sober earnestness, when I have impressed upon you the propriety of avoiding all unnecessary exposure to danger, because I felt your country could not bear to lose you. To ask me to substitute you by some one in my judgment more fit to command, or who would possess more of the confidence of the people or of the reflecting men in the country, is to demand an impossibility.

It only remains for me to hope that you will take all possible care of yourself, that your health and strength may be entirely restored, and that the Lord will preserve you for the important duties devolved upon you in the struggle of our suffering country for the independence of which we have engaged in war to maintain.

As ever, very respectfully and truly,

(Signed) JEFFERSON DAVIS.

Even if there were not so many other evidences, after a close study of these two letters, it is difficult to see how any historian, unless he writes with an ulterior purpose, could infer that the closest cooperation did not exist between these two most distinguished heads of the Confederacy. In view of all that passed between them at this crisis and all that had taken place between them in the past, it would be unfair to General Lee to infer that he was not in the closest sympathy with the man who had not only discovered his great worth, but in the face of criticism at various periods of the Confederacy had openly expressed the deepest faith in his ability.   Before the Confederacy, as War Minister of the entire country, it had been Jefferson Davis' pleasure to appoint him to the high position of Superintendent of the West Point Military Academy.   This of itself was sufficient to have created a bond between them. But from the very outset of the Confederacy he had shown his faith in General Lee and after the latter's somewhat fruitless campaign in West Virginia that others were not slow to pronounce, even to denounce, as a failure, he placed him in a position next to himself in authority.   And now though Gettysburg was lost and critics were plentiful, Jefferson Davis knew that Lee was the Confederacy's greatest asset.   But for his iron will in refusing to accept his resignation, the Confederacy would have collapsed years earlier than it did and necessarily with a marked loss of prestige that General Lee now enjoys, since his resignation following failure would have cut short much of the fame that his noble achievements in '64 and '65 won for him.   Historians, and strangely enough, young Southerners who seek so industriously to attune their writings to suit Northern ears by finding fault with what they deem Jefferson Davis' autocratic control of every branch of the Confederate government, must readily appreciate his strong will in refusing to accept General Lee's resignation of his command.   Such historians should realize that the best critics only want the truth about Jefferson Davis.   An affectation of dislike for him on the part of an author to gain their ear more often than otherwise offends them.   An able and keen-sighted Northern critic has recently remarked that it seemed that a Northern man would yet have to write the life of Jefferson Davis.   Already it is beginning to be the opinion of some Northern historians that the Confederacy owes its long life to him. The subtle and keen-sighted historian Bradford has observed that with the means he had he did better than any other could have done in his place. All historians must agree that he had the strength and judgment of the great ruler, and the insight of the seer in refusing to accept General Lee's offer to resign from the army. Nor did Lee make it in any spirit but that of serving his country better, as he thought, by relinquishing his place to a younger man. No historian, seek as he may, can ever separate and antagonize the efforts of these two great leaders in the prosecution of what both believed to be a righteous cause. When the Constitution that bound the Federal States together was disregarded, their faith in the right to establish an independent nation was the same, as much as both may have regretted the necessity for so doing. General Lee's real opinion of the right of the South to secede has been colored and distorted by so many historians that, in some instances, they have even convinced Southern historians that he fought for a cause in which he did not believe and fought alone in defense of Virginia. General Lee had under him the soldiers of every state in the Union, and he felt that it was not only for Virginia that he was seeing these go to their death but for the entire Southern Confederacy.

One who early referred to the people of West Virginia as "traitors" certainly felt the moral right of the cause he espoused. The feigned, sweetish adulation with which some historians have sought to honor Lee by insinuating that he had some doubts of the right of secession, should be rejected since it places him in a false light to posterity. These make it appear that he was willing to sacrifice the troops of Alabama, Louisiana, Georgia and the other states of the Confederacy in a cause that he owed no allegiance to except that it had been espoused by his own state. In the following letter written by General Lee to R. S. McCulloh after the war, he clearly and concisely states his views of the constitutional right of the South to secede and the right of the Southern Confederacy to establish its independence.

I am very much obliged for the kind sentiment felt for the South & the sympathy extended to our people. Every brave people who considered their rights attacked & their Constitutional liberties invaded, would have done as we did. Our conduct was not caused by any insurrectionary spirit nor can it be termed rebellion, for our construction of the Constitution under which we lived & acted was the same from its adoption, & for 80 years we had been taught & educated by the founders of the Republic & their written declarations which controlled our consciences & actions. The epithets that have been heaped upon us of "Rebels" & "Traitors" have no just meaning, nor are they believed in by those who understand the subject even at the North.

CHAPTER XXXII

WAR was slowly eating away the heart of the South. Grant's army, to his regret at times it has been said of him, had devastated thousands of miles of fair country. But the worst had yet to come. As in any great body of swirling waters, a vortex gathers somewhere, the army on the Western front, tossed and battered for years by superior forces, was soon to reach a whirlpool of disaster. The only light that illumined the dark sky was Bragg's splendid victory, August 20th, over Rosecrans at Chickamauga, a noble one for which he should not be begrudged at least one good green bay. Although his fame was eclipsed, it should not be forgotten that after Vicksburg the Confederacy gathered under him its broken ranks to hold the enemy at bay. If failure lowered his standard, who among that illustrious company did not at times face it? It was upon this scene that Grant arrived, covered with the fresh laurels of Vicksburg. With his well-equipped, eager brigades, he instantly retrieved Rosecrans' losses, to later plant, with the boasted battle above the clouds, the Stars and Stripes upon the highest peak of Lookout Mountain. The flags of Chattanooga, a rebel center, had been lowered, still Tennessee had not yet given up.

But lowering skies hung over the South. On August 21st, the long bombardment of Charleston began that ended on Christmas day. It had not been an easy feat and of the stubborn resistance of the city Varina wrote proudly that "after withstanding for nearly a year the most formidable bombardment from land and naval batteries ever directed on one fort the Confederate flag was still flying on Sumter."

Grant had now become the hope to which all eyes at Washington turned. Throughout the North there was a constant call for him; soldiers grasped his saddle skirts and clung to his bridle reins. Motley wrote that a messenger from Heaven had announced the coming at last of the right man. The historian Rhodes tells us that while Grant was hailed as the savior of the Union, Lincoln at the same time was being denounced by the radical leaders of his party as totally unfit for the Presidency. These still eyed Seward with suspicion, and the Abolitionists could never get over the fact that he told all Europe that they were worse than the revolutionists. Although the radicals of his party made no more attempts to have him removed from the Cabinet, there was never a time that they did not fear and resent his influence upon the President.

In the North such fulsome praise of Grant continued that friends implored the public to desist, since even a Napoleon could hardly stand such adulation without becoming inflated with a self-importance that bred fantastic delusions. But Grant, whatever were his other qualifications, was too heavy and dull to be swept off his base by flattery. He knew better than any of the fawners about him that he had won no easy victories; what Vicksburg had really cost him and how long it had taken him to reduce the small river city. He, furthermore, remembered with a grim smile that in '62 they had classed him with Hooker and other failures.

But his severance of the Confederacy at Vicksburg and his brilliant exploits at Missionary Ridge had dazzled the eyes of Washington. In many respects it meant more than the victory at Gettysburg. He was ordered to come to Washington to receive a nation's honors. But Sherman implored him, "if he loved his country for God's sake to stay away from Washington and the Republican administration, that cesspool of politics and intrigue." Grant, nevertheless, stayed at the Capital long enough to receive his appointment as Commander-in-Chief of the United States Army to in person command the Army of the Potomac. Meade had sauntered all too slowly in pursuit of Lee from Pennsylvania to please the Federal administration, and was to be added to the long list of displacements in the army. It seemed, to use a famous phrase, the slow attrition by which the Federal government had found the right man to command its armies.

But we do not agree with Rhodes that Lincoln was now entirely put aside for Grant. The truth of the situation was that Seward was getting the stronger influence over him and Lincoln himself had developed a certain degree of leadership, not of the first quality, but far better than that of the radicals who sought to control him. Welles, who witnessed the daily scene, informs us that Seward was still directing matters, and largely did so to the end. How much, one will never know. But Welles in his resentment did not realize that Lincoln had gradually adopted Seward's policies and now felt more confident that the little nest of radicals could not injure him politically since they themselves were fast losing influence with the masses on account of their rabid views of public questions.

In purely political maneuvers, Lincoln was and always had been since his early days shrewd and adroit, and more so now than the intelligentsia dreamed him capable of.

With all his handicaps he makes a far better figure in history than any of the radicals with whom he had to contend. He had little party animosity, though pressed by the radicals about him he sometimes appeared to have it. At first he was overawed by them, but he had at last taken their measure. Politically, he had managed well and in the October elections of 1864 defeated McClellan. How far his friends went in voting the army for him will continue to be a controversy among historians. But his election was not a brilliant triumph and in New York the race was closer than anywhere else in the North.

Nothing could have exceeded the criticism of Lincoln in the North during the campaign. Seward was for him, decidedly so. Not that Seward believed Lincoln to be a great man, but because he well knew that he himself was unpopular with his party and he could influence Lincoln better than he could any other Republican. It now was believed in the North that the Confederacy was exhausted and it is not too much to say that Seward was even then looking to the restoration of the South in the Union. As late as '64, Welles says that Lincoln was yielding everything to him. He also accuses Lord Lyons of helping Seward run the government. Foreign affairs under the Secretary of State's wily manipulations were running smoothly. Welles notices a better temper in the winter and spring of '64 in England and France, but gives Seward no credit for it. But England was still given to a characteristic subtlety in the matter of her cousins across the sea, and of late her attitude had taken a rather humorous turn. Lord John Russell sent a nice letter to the deeply anxious James M. Mason that said in substance that it was the opinion of Her Majesty's government that any proposal to the United States to recognize the Confederacy would hurt the feelings of that government, and any proposal of the Southern States to return to the Union would hurt the feelings of the Confederacy. In time, she wiped her hands of the whole matter.

Although the Republican President was not now as unpopular as the radicals thought him, it remains a fact to lament that both Abraham Lincoln and Jefferson Davis suffered immeasurably from the harshest criticism throughout the war. "A despot reigned in Richmond and another in Washington," is the manner in which the two were described by the editor of the Richmond *Examiner*. It was not true of either, though their methods were different. Jefferson Davis was stringently put to it to raise the great armies that contended for four years with a far stronger foe. If he at times became drastic, the situation demanded it. At every step he had to contend with men who had themselves shown little ability.

After Gettysburg and Vicksburg, malcontents and sulkers daily increased. To add to the general depression the poor people of the city were really hungry and when Richmond had its bread riot and neither Governor Letcher nor any of the city officials could disperse it, Jefferson Davis went out in the street and quieted and pacified the people. It was such work as Pollard, as their fellow townsman, might have assisted in. Lincoln, too, was having his difficulties, among them a draft riot in New York, a veritable mob pronouncing maledictions upon "Old Abe" and his administration and threatening to hang Horace Greeley on "a sour apple tree." But the country was big, and for the greater portion American born from which Lincoln had to draw his legions. With renewed energy that held him to his task he persisted in gathering recruits, and Horace Greeley was not hung on the tree that was later picked out for Jefferson Davis.

The outlook for the Confederacy was now dark, but the South came forward again, determined to win its independence, preferring death to submission, which is shown in its response to the last call. It was now giving all. Its waning resources were getting to be a mere dribble when it came to sustaining a war that had already lasted three years. Although the people were refusing to believe it, the Confederacy was shattered in all but spirit. Surrounded by armies and hemmed in by a formidable fleet, it was in a more helpless condition than its people realized, and but for the fire in their hearts, they would have given up the struggle sooner than they did. The path was a difficult one for Jefferson Davis, but his spirit was never more relentless. Varina tells us in her "Memoir" that he, at no time, wholly despaired of success and in the correspondence relative to General Lee's resignation it is clear that neither believed that the end had come. Still he knew that obstacles had multiplied.

Besides Dahlgren's plot to surprise and destroy the city and capture and kill Jefferson Davis, and Sheridan's raid that strained the nerves of the inhabitants for days, there was actual suffering among the people for the want of food and clothing. There never was a greater misconception than the one that sometimes creeps into history that the South was, after three years of intensive depleting warfare, upon its own soil, prepared to continue the struggle. The army that Jefferson Davis raised and equipped for the campaign of '64 was made up of the last resources in men and materials the South possessed. It was his policy and that of the people generally to make light of this condition, but it existed and Northern leaders and generals had discussed it among themselves. Welles tells us that they were already discussing the manner of the restoration of the States.

The gradual falling off in the production of food supplies from the very first was noticeable. It grew more pronounced each year until by 1864 there was very little more produced than was needed for home consumption, especially since the people had been hurt by one failure of the corn crop. Two armies also had lived in the country. At first the older men and women with the slaves, the latter not as yet demoralized, managed to produce more supplies than were needed; but even then as compared with the lush crops of the antebellum South it was as a drop in the bucket. But by '63, much of the land was fallow and overgrown with sprouts and sedge. The remainder was half cultivated by still older men and distressed women, with what little assistance that could be had from the now thoroughly demoralized negro labor. Corn planted in the spring of '64 throughout the Carolinas and Georgia could not feed armies at a distance, however relishing it might have been for the army of invasion. Besides thousands of green fields already in silk were destroyed by Sherman's armies.

The domestic life of the South was wholly disorganized. Negro laborers were now quitting their crops on the least provocation and old mules were falling dead in the plow. Little children, especially among the poorer whites, were half nourished, stunted in growth and dying in great numbers. It is a stark fact of history that half the people in the South were undernourished during the last years of the Confederacy. While the women of the better class bore their hardships and deprivations in silence, women of the "poor white" districts, innocent of the effect of their letters, were constantly writing to their men in the army telling them that their children were dying for the want of medicine. Thousands of such letters flooded Lee's army to cause frequent desertions.

These conditions faced the Confederacy in the spring of
'64. Grant's army had lived in the heart of the South since
'62 and people do not thrive in their domestic affairs with
the cannon roaring in their ears and the expectation of
raids which, when they did occur, robbed the farms and
plantations of their last plow horses, small stores of meat
and corn and everything valuable that could be found in the
homes of the people. Still the Southern people everywhere
were willing to share their scanty store with their army,
and their passionate devotion to the cause makes some of
the noblest and most pathetic pages of its history.

There was criticism still of the system of impressment indulged in by disaffected parties, and unworthy natures took
advantage of it. While Jefferson Davis was using every
effort to assure and animate the people, and was busy collecting supplies for his last great armies stationed at various
places of defense throughout the South, in the dingy walls
of the old State House at Richmond there sat men, without
discretion or discernment, engaged in the most venomous
criticism of his efforts. The words *conscription, impressment,* by mouthing malcontents since '62 had been tortured
into a thousand untrue meanings in which were mingled
interrogations of why Lee did not win Gettysburg, and why
Jefferson Davis still looked to him as his chief dependence.

It would not be the truth of history to say that Jefferson
Davis was always patient with such ill-advised censure. He
at times expressed his disgust, especially at the repeated
allegation that he was a dictator and a tyrant. Imperialistic
fancies stirred his brain as little as they inflamed that of
the kindly Minnegerode who, the editor of the Richmond
Examiner boasted, knew every thought in the President's
mind. This fact alone clears Jefferson Davis of any autocracy.

But amid all the petty jealousies and feuds, Jefferson Davis labored on and by the winter of 1863-64 had raised and equipped, as best he could, a noble army. Lee found it one of the best he had ever commanded. The new army made a brilliant show and the proud old war-worn city once more took on a martial air as it faced the first dark Christmas it had ever known. In the face of it, women still bore themselves with a proud dignity that won the admiration even of the enemy. Varina records in her "Memoir" a long list of women who impressed her with their rare fortitude and nobility. Although the Christmas passed with little of its former display and brilliancy, women, she tells us, strove as never before to cheer and sustain Lee's army. Parties, dinners, midnight suppers for belated officers, were arranged for their diversion. Every tempting morsel of food that came into their hands was withheld even from their families for the soldiers—both officers and privates, who went in and out of Richmond. "Our deprivations were far less," Varina wrote with the fine candor characteristic of her "Memoir," "than those of persons not holding as high positions, but they were many." The following from her pen gives a clear insight into the real condition of the country. "Women made a substitute for coffee out of parched sweet potatoes and corn, and also of the grain of rye; for sugar they used sorghum syrup. They wove cotton cloth for blankets, and sewed up coverings for their feet out of old carpets, or rather such bits as were left after cutting them up for soldiers' blankets."

Varina was generous with everything at the mansion that could be used for the public good. Her carriage and horses were held for the general use of friends. On all public occasions some one used the Davis' carriage. Although she, at this time, chaperoned few gay parties, she was still the dominant spirit of the social life of the Confederacy. As grave and serious as life had become, her natural gayety at times asserted itself and no discouraged visitors nor callers at the Executive Mansion found her dull or unentertaining. However all that she did now was with the thought of helping her husband. She remained close by his side during these last hard years of the Confederacy and it went far to keep him fitted for his task.

It was about this time that she was to experience one of the bitterest sorrows of her life. Jefferson Davis now spent but a few hours at the Executive Mansion, and remained at his office through the entire day. His work had grown voluminous. At times he was ill and Varina was greatly concerned. He insisted on having his midday meals sent to the office and finding that he often left his food untasted, she began to carry it to him herself, thinking that a reminder from her would induce him to partake of some light nourishment. She had sometimes, when they lived in Washington, carried him food, "a little beef tea" or "a bit of tempting fowl" to refresh him after a strenuous debate in the Senate. Under what changed skies she now anticipated his needs. Any caller at the office, from General Lee down to the most insignificant army officer, was invited to share the President's luncheon and with many of these Varina discussed the situation in the army. They liked to talk to her and she was always at ease with them. There were subtleties in her nature that reflected both feminine and masculine qualities not so pronounced in either as to be injured by contrast; but presenting a constant intermingling of grace and strength. She impressed both men and women throughout life with this singular power.

It was on one of these occasions when she was with her husband at his office that a messenger rushed in with news that little Joe, their second son, had fallen from an upstairs balcony or gallery at the Mansion to the brick pavement below. Leaving a white nurse with her baby and other children playing in her room, she had just entered her husband's office with a basket of food when the servant came for her. When they reached the Mansion they found the child dead. He was a favorite with the people in the city. They had been struck with his great beauty and promise and his marked resemblance to the President. Varina herself thought that more than any of the children he resembled Jefferson Davis and when away from Richmond often wrote him, "Joe is as manly as ever and makes me think of you." The sympathy of the city was widespread. There were immense crowds at the funeral and flowers were brought by every child in Richmond. "I could see nothing," Mrs. Chesnut wrote, "but the form of little Joe and his broken-hearted mother. The father's footsteps, as he walked the floor the livelong night, sounded in my ears." Again at the grave, "The bereft mother stood back in heavy black wrappings and her tall figure drooped. The immense crowds, the flowers, the children, the procession as it moved, all come and go, but these two dark, sorrow-stricken figures stand. I can see it all now. That night with no sound but the heavy tramp of his feet overhead, the curtain flapping in the wind, the gas flaring, I was numb, stupid, half-dead with grief and terror."

Varina's grief over the tragic death of her child filled her with frustration for days. The Executive Mansion was closed to the public except in instances when visitors were compelled to have conferences with the President. His own grief was deep and bitter; but silently and patiently with the assistance of his faithful young secretary, Burton N. Harrison, he resumed his duties.

There must have been some suspicion as to the manner in which the child came to his death. So many mysterious fires and robberies had broken out at the White House that one was ready to believe anything. Many believed that spies, bent on mischief, constantly went in and out of the Executive Mansion. At Mulberry Place, where Mrs. Chesnut went later in the summer to join her husband, removed from all excitement, with these dark hints still in her mind, she asks in her diary, "Whom will they kill next of that devoted household?" Throughout her diary anxiety is felt for the safety of the Davis family. Her loyalty and devotion to the President of the Confederacy and his family was strong and tender during these last stormy years of the revolution. It deserves to be further noted for the consideration of those historians who have in such strong terms commended her rare insight and judgment that of the many whom she now and then took a little covert delight in stripping of all grandeur, these were never once the subjects of her humorous and often satirical comments; nor could she suppress a passionate resentment at any disparagement of them.

On one occasion when the editor of the Charleston *Mercury* was seeking to entice her with the tempting bait that Colonel James Chesnut, among others mentioned, would make a better President than Jefferson Davis, she met it with a criticism and ridicule of his judgment that must have sounded to him more like a rebuke than any pleasure at the compliment. Her condemnation of the editor of the Richmond *Examiner* and all others whose attacks she felt were injurious to the success of the Confederacy places her in prestige next to Varina in the official household of the Confederacy.

CHAPTER XXXIII

In the face of all reverses and hardships the spirit of Lee's army in the spring of '64 was strong and eager. Virginia still looked for victory. Dispatches from Lee's headquarters announced that "practically every regiment had reenlisted for the war." Once more the Southern Capital was jubilant. There was a note of tearful hysteria in the rejoicing, it is true, for there had been much sorrow and mourning in the city. The streets and hospitals were filled with women clothed in some kind of black, and there was scarcely a family that had not given two, sometimes three, names to the casualty lists. It was with an effort that Varina now took any interest in the social life of the city. The tragic death of her child had darkened her life. But Jefferson Davis needed her, and though overwhelmed by her loss, she was constantly at his side, watching eagerly with him for news of the armies. Every victory elated and animated them. Finigan's and Colquitt's success in driving the Federals out of Florida, and every brilliant dash of Nathan Bedford Forrest in the middle South gave them fresh hope. If the rugged and resourceful Forrest could have come sooner to the front some chapters of the war might be other than what they are. But he came on too late. With the exception of Van Dorn and possibly Morgan it is probable that he had never even seen Stuart nor Hampton, the great cavalry leaders of the Confederacy.

363

But for all Johnston's strategy and ability to keep a good army at his command the lower South was really in the possession of Federal forces. In the Virginia campaign Lee now was to meet Grant, the new idol of the Federal government; and somewhat abashed Grant was to meet Lee. Who was this King Arthur about whom he had heard so many wonder tales? Somewhat gingerly he took command of the Army of the Potomac on March 17th. Massed on the Rapidan it numbered 141,160 well trained troops, many of whom were veterans. The sight of it must have reassured him. To meet it, Lee's strength did not exceed 64,000, with a slight reenforcement later at Hanover Junction. On May 4th, with flowers blooming and birds caroling along its pathway, not as ignorant perhaps of men and their affairs as we suppose, Grant's army stirred, unwound its heavily coiled units and commenced to march. The road, a wilderness one, over which he came, though not strange to some of his troops, was new to him. He had rarely, if ever, set foot in Virginia; had always stood somewhat in awe of it. He must get acquainted with it by degrees, though not in the *sangfroid,* confident manner with which he had entered the Mississippi country. Still, that had been no easy victory. But now he was facing the unknown with a dangerous adversary. Advancing cautiously through the Wilderness, he unexpectedly received a blow from Lee that for the moment staggered him. Somewhat compelled to fight, he got ready for the battle which lasted two days and exhausted both sides. Both Lee and Longstreet, whatever may have happened at Gettysburg, were now at their best. Grant flinched, realizing as McClellan had in '62 on the Chickahominy, that he had met his superior in battle. But there was a grim, imperturbable expression upon his somewhat saturnine countenance that hid its own secrets. He was discovering that Lee's army in comparison with his own was half-clothed, half-fed and poorly equipped. No wonder they fought like demons. But such regiments could not fight forever, and Grant knew it. Throughout the engagement in the Wilderness the battle at times raged so furiously that fearing his trusted legions might grow confused and waver, General Lee rode twice to the front to lead them in person. Not a man would advance until he returned to a place of safety, and all up and down the lines was heard the fierce burst of Southern emotion, "Lee to the rear and we'll send them to hell."

Again fatality seemed to take a hand in the affairs of the Confederacy, for just as Lee for the second time was nearing victory, and in the thick of the fighting, he was robbed of his able corps commander. In an almost similar manner that Jackson was shot, Longstreet was accidentally wounded by his own men and borne from the field. Still Grant seemed afraid of Lee. His next movement was to try and possess Spotsylvania Court House, but Lee gained the place at the same time and the head columns of the two armies entrenched. Grant was now faced with the necessity of fighting, and on May 8th began his favorite method of attack, his men cheering and shouting, "On to Richmond." Assaulting the Confederate front, he was repulsed with heavy loss. Both Grant and Lee were now urging their lines, and it was during these intense, unequal conflicts including the burning salient—"The Bloody Angle" —that the Army of Northern Virginia won again and again its right to the Valhalla.

With everything in Grant's favor, he remained cautious and waited six or seven days for heavy reenforcements.

Even then he declined battle, and for a while Lee pursued
him.   Had their forces been to any extent equal Grant
would have been driven out of Virginia.   As it stood, he
knew that he could by "hammering away," as he expressed
it, "all summer," wear out the thin gray regiments of Lee.
At Hanover Junction, General Lee picked up the reenforcement that Jefferson Davis had gathered and sent him, and
the two armies next met at Cold Harbor.   Grant here took
a decided initiative and assaulted the Confederate lines entrenched behind a slight breastwork.   Although he assaulted again and again until his exhausted men refused
to go forward, he was repulsed with heavy loss.   A little
confused as to what to do, he turned towards the James
River with a view, in time, of capturing Petersburg.   In
this he was held up by Beauregard.   After assaulting Lee's
lines with fruitless efforts, he finally decided to settle down
south of Appomattox in a slow siege of Petersburg at
which place Lee had entrenched his army.   His losses had
been fearful as compared with a like campaign of McClellan's.   It became the tale of the country and Grant was
losing some of the lavish fame he had won at Vicksburg,
while Lee had fully regained his former prestige.

Every state in the Confederacy shared in the victories,
but the gaunt, gray army besieged in Petersburg was
more threadbare and exhausted than the country realized,
though Jefferson Davis and General Lee themselves were beginning to be torn with anxiety.   Richmond, which had been
throughout the spring threatened by cavalry raids, continued to be the coveted jewel; but its people still believed
the city to be the impregnable Holy Ground of the Confederacy.   Still there was bitter mourning in its midst, and
hunger so frightful that the 13th Virginia regiment at times

fasted to send it rations. But more bitter even then its hunger was the loss of the beloved and gallant Stuart, who died in its defense. But the spirit of the people continued strong. In its midst was still heard brave laughter and cheerful speech sprinkled with wit and raillery, the grace of which is only possible to races, facing evil fortune, that have attained spiritual confidence and poise.

Among other criticism, the summer found the people complaining that the Mansion was closed too much for the public good. Although Varina had taken but a few weeks for her grief, she consulted Jefferson Davis about opening it again to the public. It had been closed for social purposes following the death of little Joe. The birth of baby Winnie on June 27th had also kept her in retirement. Born amid the victories that had saved the city from the enemy, it was thought to be a happy augury, and General Lee came and held the infant in his arms.

With the birth of her last child, who was to become the most noted of her children, Varina's health became impaired. She lost her robust figure and did not regain it during the war. Her last picture taken in the winter of '64 shows her face and figure gaunt in comparison with the robust woman of the first years of the strife. The hardships and bitter experiences they had endured told visibly upon both herself and the President. Both had aged in appearance. Varina, though still young in years, at times looked like an old woman. White strands were beginning to show in the hair about her temples. Still, from old letters and records of the day, one finds her striving in many agreeable ways to popularize her husband's administration. But there were a hollowness in her eyes and a droop in her figure never seen there before. But one gathers from Mrs. Chesnut that she was always cheerful. They were now constantly together, walking, driving or spending the day with each other. In all her bitter disappointment and heartbreak Varina still bore herself proudly, scornful at times of her critics, but ready to forgive and ignore the past if it served a useful purpose. And it is with a many-sided and highly developed personality that one has to deal in any appraisement of her worth. One moment we see her in the rôle of a contented, devoted wife and loving mother; and in the next we find her with her husband perhaps appointing brigadier-generals, or removing some. Who knows? Though the records usually are silent, there is the strong appeal to her husband in which she implored him not to appoint "B. B." to command in the early spring of 1865, although she bases her plea on "intestine feuds."

Was Varina more given to politics than her husband? Although engaged in domestic and social affairs that usually interest women, if Pollard is to any extent to be believed, it was now an influence in governmental affairs that she craved and sought. Quoting the idle gossip that oozed daily out of the closed doors of Congress he records her flaming up with the retort that she was the one with whom President Davis should advise. Idle gossip also ran over the town that on another occasion she gave way to a great burst of temper, going so far as to say that if she were in her husband's place she would be "hung" before she would submit to the efforts of Congress to humiliate him. It was a strange and what was termed a "common" expression for any elegant Southern woman of that day to use. But travelers in the country have recorded that they often heard expressions like it from numerous squeamishly refined Southern women in moments of anger, or even excitement.

It was a frequent expression of the day with men, and women sometimes resorted to it for extreme emphasis. However, Varina was known to be a stickler for the "lady-like" and for her to be found using a favorite expression of Abraham Lincoln's was a rich discovery for the editor of the Richmond *Examiner* who bided his time to record it against her.

But one has only to read the diaries and reminiscences of that day to find that the Southern woman, though not approving of what she regarded as the indelicate if not indecent doctrine of "Woman's Rights," was now, though scarcely conscious of it, feeling faint pulsations of her new freedom. And but for the long period of Reconstruction that returned her to her four walls, she would have emerged sooner from her seclusion than she did. Throughout the war, she made a gallant figure and even now with Lee's army besieged in Petersburg and the Confederacy in mourning, she was still undaunted. An earnest Richmond woman went so far as to speak at a public meeting of women. Of the circumstance the editor of the *Examiner* later took occasion to say that Southern women were now overstepping their bounds.

With such feelings they faced the summer approaching its solstice. The parks and gardens, where a riot of spring bloom had been, were now a solid monotonous green. The weather was intensely hot and much sympathy was expressed for the sick and wounded throughout the country. Jefferson Davis, amid all his cares, worried over the condition of the Federal soldiers in several of the prisons. The Northern press continued to blame him for all failures to care for them properly and his life was constantly threatened by unknown parties. At the same time the leading

papers of the Southern press were ridiculing his great concern for the enemy. The situation, too, in the army in the
far South filled him with the deepest concern and anxiety.
The dates in the Chesnut Diary are sometimes wrong, a
fault that the author admits with charming *naïveté,* but if
the table talk and gossip that went on about her had any
truth in it, the severe criticism of General Johnston for
constantly retreating had more to do with Jefferson Davis'
placing another in command than any personal ill will.
Varina was now defending her husband and it was easy for
others to think that she influenced him in the matter of
General Johnston's removal. Mrs. Chesnut continued to
indite jibes in her diary that she had heard relating to his
disposition to retreat. It is certain that the two women
conversed frequently about the matter, and if Varina carried
news to Jefferson Davis, she only repeated the common talk
of the day.

The summer passed by filled with anxiety for Varina and
her husband over the sad plight of the Confederacy. While
hope still glimmered in the dark skies they could not divest
themselves of the gloom that hung over the country. With
all of Lee's victories they knew that their armies were
growing weaker each day. Sherman was moving against
Atlanta, and Grant was holding Lee at Petersburg. It is
true he would not leave Lee to capture Richmond, but
its capture was looked forward to by the Federals as much
as it had ever been at the first Manassas. The soldiers in
the Federal army had always been told that this was the
grand strategy. At a day when psychological influence and
effect are stressed, it is strange that a historian could think
that the capture of Richmond would not have weakened the
Confederate chances of success. Its importance in the

scheme of things is shown in the constant efforts to capture it as much as in the efforts to defend it. From Manassas down until the last campaign, the Federal army directed its efforts in that direction. While Grant followed Lee and feared to leave him, it was his final aim to take the city as a signal that the war was over; and the Federal army was never satisfied until it marched into it. It is certain that had Grant been prevented by Confederate forces from entering the Capital, Johnston would not have thought it necessary to surrender his army. As soon as the army occupied the city, Johnston's army immediately lost all hope and there was not the reluctance to surrender that was found in Lee's army.

Varina must at this time have feared that the capture of the city was inevitable, even though Lee's army could free itself of Grant. Mrs. Chesnut records that "Mrs. Davis is utterly depressed. She says the fall of Richmond must come. If it does, she will send her children to me and Mrs. Preston. We begged her to come too." But Varina had determined to remain with her husband, and but for his wishes in the matter would never have left the city. For herself, she had little physical fear. The safety of her children, however, since he persistently stressed it, was the main motive that controlled her movements. Both Mrs. Chesnut and Mrs. Preston were now constantly with her, and in all dire crises she seemed to have turned to these two intimate friends. They often talked of sharing each other's fate if the worst should come. Providence had not decreed that they should leave the city together, but before the final débâcle, Varina placed her young sister Maggie in their care.

Varina was now as implacable in the matter of any surrender as her husband. Her letters show that she would be willing to contend with him to the bitter end. Her absorption in the success of the Confederacy had been more gradual than his but it had now become as selfless as his own. She had a full knowledge of all that was transpiring in each of the branches of the government. But as deeply as she was concerned about public affairs an item in the Chesnut Diary about this time shows her in a purely woman's mood. The death of little Joe had made her more lenient with her children, and at times they stood badly in need of correction. "I drove out with Mrs. Davis and all the infant family. Wonderfully clever and precocious children, but with unbroken wills. At one time there was a sudden uprising of the nursery contingent. They laughed, fought and screamed. Bedlam broke loose. Mrs. Davis scolded, laughed and cried." In the next moment Varina was putting shrewd and earnest questions to her friend about an important matter connected with the government. When separated, letters frequently passed between them dealing with public affairs and these show that her mind dwelt feverishly on the fate of the Confederacy. With Jefferson Davis, she was catching at every straw the winds of war blew in their favor.

Early's invasion of Maryland in July, with its gesture towards Washington, had elated them. This, however, was displaced with the gloom of Phil Sheridan's presence in the Shenandoah where Grant had told him to destroy the growing crops and everything else that a people could subsist on. As the winter approached, Varina could see that Jefferson Davis was feeling the strain of the unequal conflict. Her whole thought was now centered on him and the cause for which he was contending. In these last desperate efforts it seemed to her that in the eyes of the whole world the struggle had grown to be his alone, and the bitterness of failure had a double torture for her. Nor could Jefferson Davis with all of his stern composure hide the troubled look in his eyes over the situation. Varina grew more solicitous of him each day, and her very solicitude may have helped to lay her open to the charge that she was becoming his adviser.

The bitter criticism, too, of him by disaffected members of Congress angered her. She could not be hard enough, she says, not to feel the studied slights that coarse and thoughtless critics offered him. But Varina, although they were whispering that she was now taking part in her husband's councils, was a highly social creature and felt the need at times of having her own sex about her. In a letter to a friend one finds this candid, somewhat humorous observation, "You know it is absolutely necessary to have a woman to whom one may confide a woman's thoughts about other women."

She had now formed numerous friendships in the city and was more popular than she had ever been. Even as late as the autumn of '64, her luncheons were pretty affairs "with more people at them than ever before." [1] Social life in Richmond still held together and women held their heads up to the last. When not nursing in the hospitals or knitting or sewing for the soldiers they spent their time in preparing luncheons for army officers, and government officials and sometimes their tables were filled with a scant supply of delicacies from the blockade, for their Majesties must make something out of foreign war.

They called it "manna sent down from Heaven," but they

[1] Chestnut.

scarcely attributed it to the same God to whom Abraham
Lincoln, the historian Rhodes tells us, was with the divine
fervor of the Hebrew leaders having prayers offered up.
God must indeed feel at a loss when both sides of war
appeal to Him. It was on such occasions when the blockade
had remembered them that the ladies gave their luncheons
and these were given more often than otherwise to army
officers. Varina records, and others of her day confirm her
statement, that the women of Richmond practiced the most
rigid economy among themselves. With the army, to which
they sent boxes of food daily, they were lavish whenever
they possessed the means. Entertainment too of a varied
nature was kept up to amuse the soldiers as late as the winter
of '64.

Varina's receptions continued up to the last weeks of
her stay in the Mansion, while it was whispered around
her that the Confederacy was crumbling and Jefferson
Davis the cause of it. Throughout the reception hours she
was forced to listen to the irrelevant chatter about her; to
engage in it herself when she knew that her husband was
overwhelmed with the knowledge that Grant had Lee besieged at Petersburg and Sherman was devastating the
eastern half of the Confederacy.

Still the White House kept open. Generals were there for
breakfast in company with other officers, sometimes on business, trampling the white carpets with muddy boots. But
who cared for white carpets now? Sunday dinners, too, became fashionable for church visitors from a distance; every
one wanted "to drop in." Society was relaxed, a little giddy.
Women had grown daring enough to coquette a little with
the officers as their share of the entertainment. Still it was
a Victorian atmosphere that one breathed at the White

House of the Confederacy, and any serious breach would instantly have been frowned upon by both the mistress and master.

It was at about this time that Varina lost one of her most intimate and trusted friends in the departure from Richmond of Mrs. James Chesnut. How sorely she must have missed her! A selfish woman would have urged some appointment that would have kept her near. But no, if Mary Boykin's husband could best serve the Confederacy away from Richmond, Varina would see her go with him and make no complaint. Letters continued to pass between them, and in one is recorded this generous estimate of the woman with whom she had come in close contact for much of the four years of the war. "Providence has seen fit that I should know three great women and Mrs. Jefferson Davis is one of them." Also her feeling cry that Varina was one woman for whom her heart ached in all this tragedy. One gets a close-up view of Mrs. Jefferson Davis in the Chesnut Diary. Her quick resentment at any adverse criticism of President Davis, her profound respect for him and devotion throughout all the vast tragedy of war, her passing mistakes, her fortitude and courage, and the grace and charm of her unusual personality all are portrayed and make estimates that are well worth recording in the life of the woman who held the highest position for women in the Confederacy. Besides her sincere affection for her, she could never forget that Varina was its First Lady, and it was in this light that she always regarded her. One gathers, too, that Varina always looked like a First Lady to the keen-eyed diarist.

As winter in the Southern Capital drew on, Lee's half-starved and ragged armies were still at the mercy of Grant's flushed, well-fed brigades. Sherman, after his blighting march to the sea, was crushing his way through the Carolinas, destroying the land to its very roots. The South had its back to the wall. The region which was to have kept Lee's army supplied had been laid waste. The Confederacy was bleeding at every pore. The naval affairs, what little there were of them, were all in favor of the North. In some instances, the small navy had been important to the country as affecting commerce, if not in any way affecting battles. The disaster in the summer, off the harbor of Cherbourg, in the English Channel, in which the famous *Alabama,* in a fierce, unequal duel with the stronger *Kearsarge,* went down, added to the gloom of '64. Well might Jefferson Davis' face be pinched and blanched these wintry days as another Christmas approached. Throughout the Christmas season, sadder and darker than the one before, Varina shed bitter tears that she constantly strove to hide from others. There might have been some truth in the criticism that she grew careless of her appearance; had lost her poise, was no longer beautiful, no longer the proud, self-confident woman who not only graced her salon with a queen's air and ease, but seemed, herself, capable of commanding a regiment.

Varina had had her day. One studying her closely at this period will discover that there was some frustration, but not of purpose, since that was deeper laid in the woman than any dreamed; but of behavior, of manner and poise. Besides the loss of her child, much had happened in official circles that had destroyed her peace of mind. She had had trials and disappointments of her own, but it was of Jefferson Davis that she was now thinking. Her love for him had never been stronger. All its psychic chords had been strung.

MRS. JEFFERSON DAVIS IN THE WINTER OF 1864.

CHAPTER XXXIV

On January 12th, 1865, the White House of the Confederacy was carefully set in order for the arrival of a distinguished visitor. There was an unusual flutter in the preparations. Everything wore an air of expectancy within the pleasant rooms where cheery fires burned in large open grates, and fresh flowers scented the air. The children were freshly bathed, combed and dressed. He would be certain to want to see them. Margaret and little Jeff he had seen often in his own home. And Varina herself! It had been four weary, distracting years since he had seen her in Washington—the youthful, proud and winsome wife of one of the most distinguished officials of the National government. Would he find her greatly changed? Varina went over the part she was to act several times in her mind, but was nervous as she assisted her husband in welcoming their visitor, who was none other than the famous Francis P. Blair, said to have had great influence with Lincoln in the reenforcement of Fort Sumter. He came with a scheme to induce Jefferson Davis to uphold the Monroe Doctrine by heading an expedition against Maximilian in Mexico.

While his visit to Richmond was made in some respects in a spirit commendable enough, it was attended with features hardly fair to the honor of the leaders of the Confederacy. In Washington, and later in Richmond, it is well known that the popular Blair, a Southerner and Democrat himself,

anxious to stop the slaughter of the country's manhood both
of the North and the South, gathered about him hundreds
of civilians and minor officials, representing all portions of
the Confederacy, and talked peace with many alluring advantages to the South. Such offers now constantly emanat-
ing from the government at Washington did have an influence upon the weaker and more selfish spirits of the
South. There were some also who had become inert from
hardships and weariness, and were willing to accept peace
at any price. This is seen in the fact that desertions became
more frequent in the winter of '64. Peace overtures were
welcomed and often proposed by the Confederate government. But when peace was to be attended with a
forfeiture of Southern independence, the great body of the
Southern people stubbornly held out unaffected by any offer
the Federals made it. Jefferson Davis declared that they
would fight on for independence until the last straw was
placed on their back. If it broke, their honor would at least
be secure.

The credit for these negotiations for peace (what there
was in them) should go to Seward, who had harped upon
this policy for four years with all sorts of fantastic propositions and warnings. His ethical ideas in the matter were
superior to any of his party. His mistakes, grotesque
enough in some instances, seem to have come about from
lack of authority. But the motive behind them is the thing
to consider. Lincoln had come closer to him during their
trials, and their ideas for the restoration of the South had
become practically the same. It is highly probably that if
Seward could have kept his influence over Lincoln and
they had been given full power to perfect a policy, they
would have preserved the Union without war. It is true

that both agreed to harsh war measures to retain what Seward had been fond of calling "this magnificent portion of the Union," but one feels sure that animosity did not prompt them. It is certain that both had something to do with the proposition that Blair made to Jefferson Davis to take part in the Mexican situation though records may not confirm it. Blair knew that Jefferson Davis in the past had been a prominent military figure and suspected that there was a romantic vein somewhere in his makeup. That the scheme of acting with the Union in enforcing the Monroe Doctrine in the matter of the French occupancy of Mexico might have struck his fancy with the independence of the South guaranteed is probable. But it is certain that he would never have relaxed his efforts to establish a Confederate States of America, independent of any scheme in connection with the overthrow of the Bonaparte-Hapsburg dynasty in Mexico.

The blandishments of Blair were extended to Varina. Their families had been warm and intimate friends in Washington. He knew the sway that women like Varina have over the men of their households; knew that she was fully acquainted with the nature of his mission. He must have told her of his proposition to her husband since he told others; must have had hopes that it would appeal to her when he told her that Jefferson Davis would become a second Washington or an Andrew Jackson in leading triumphant armies against Napoleon III in Mexico. How this might have affected her independently of any requirement that the South would have to give up its dream of independence is not known. But the project did not in the remotest appeal to her when it was accompanied with the proposition for the South to give up its struggle for independence and return to the Union. She was now as deeply immersed in the struggle for the independence of the South as Jefferson Davis. She received Blair with smiles, put on her best dress for him, set her table with her finest china and plate and poured for him perhaps the last of the good tea the blockade runners had sent her; but in reply to all his blandishments, with a fleeting return of the old gayety, irony and finesse that he remembered so well, she told him of Dahlgren's orders to sack the Southern Capital and kill Jefferson Davis, adding with a humorous smile that a government that could tolerate such orders could not be trusted in any matter. He demurred. It was impossible. He was sorry, but could not refrain from laughing a little at her gallant artifice and strategy to outwit him.

The visit of Blair brought about the famous Hampton Roads Peace Conference on February 3d. For the Conference, though critics said he had no tolerance for those opposing him, Jefferson Davis appointed his opponent, Alexander H. Stephens, whom he had also selected to head the Gettysburg peace commission. The Conference ended without satisfactory results for either side. When it was found that Jefferson Davis would not yield the independence of the South for any scheme, the peace promoters realized that they had played their last card; that there was nothing left but for Grant to reduce and destroy Lee's army. Seward at the opening of the conference was full of urbanity and asked after the health of Jefferson Davis with something of genuine interest. Some might argue that Jefferson Davis was wrong in not accepting some one of the likely terms offered him to put an end to the struggle; but whatever may be said in behalf of the peace efforts of Jacques, Gilmore or Blair, it will have to be conceded that Jefferson

Davis filled all the requirements of what the historian of all ages has pronounced a hero; one who alone yields to the foe when overpowered. In language that sounds strangely like the impassioned speech of a French patriot during the World War, he told them, "I desire peace as much as you do, but the war must go on till the last man of this generation falls in his tracks and his children seize his musket and fight our battles unless you acknowledge our right to self-government." And again, "We are not fighting for slavery, we are fighting for independence. You have already emancipated nearly two million slaves, and if you will take care of them you can emancipate the rest, and you may emancipate every one in the Confederacy, but we will be a free people. We will govern ourselves." Such a spirit was full worthy of victory. These burning declarations of freedom were constantly his answers to the various peace overtures after blood between the two sections had been shed. Every year made him more determined on independence, more infatuated with the dream of liberty. Still he wanted peace and was ready at all times to treat in a liberal way with the Federal government upon terms of equality which meant, he always specifically stated, "two countries."

President Lincoln was disappointed at his failure to make terms with the Commissioners. On finding that the Emancipation Proclamation that he, the historian Rhodes affirms, had been pressed by the radicals of his party to issue did not create the widespread demoralization among the white people of the South hoped for, he hurried back to Washington with a brand-new scheme. This was to propose to Congress to pay the slaveholders of the states engaged in the struggle an ample price for the loss of their slaves if they would lay down their arms. It was a fair, even kindly proposition, and in keeping with a line of policy that he was considering; but he must have known it would never meet with the approval of the radical wing of the Republican party, whose policy was to subjugate the South and impoverish the slave-holders as much as possible. The spirit of Reconstruction was but the continuation of that of Thaddeus Stevens and his rabid associates during the war. Lincoln had little power with this element in Congress. With Seward he was now grasping at any means of stopping the war. Though often overridden by the radicals of his party and forced at times to reverse himself, he was now with Seward thoroughly infatuated with the thought of a restored Union, with as little reconstruction as possible.

But there had also been shrewdness in Lincoln's proposition aside from a natural desire to deal generously with the Southern people. Coming at the hour when the Confederacy was weakest, discussion of his proposition reached the South to cast a damper on the efforts of some who, weary of the struggle, were ready to yield to motives of self-interest.

Although he would not publicly admit it, each day the task of supplying the army became more difficult for Jefferson Davis, and private communications of General Lee continued to anxiously refer to the many desertions through the winter of '64-'65. The war was slowly drawing to its close. The South was exhausted. In his reports, Grant sent word that the South "had robbed the cradle and the grave" to fill its army and there were none left for replacements. With unflagging spirit Jefferson Davis still held out, and even after the Hampton Roads Conference gave to the world his memorable pronouncements of freedom and national independence.

Varina strove with him. Although she had borne herself

with a proud distinction in the presence of her Northern visitor, her eyes were red with weeping throughout the winter and spring. She had shared all her husband's hopes, unnatural in their brightness, and his disappointments more bitter than wormwood; had herself become infatuated with his dazzling quest for independence. But though covered with failure there was no stain upon their brief dynasty. Francis P. Blair, who had come from the sordid atmosphere of corruption in Washington, found the Confederate government, though torn by hopelessness and *intestine feuds* withal, as free from moral corruption as were ever the seats of the Revolutionary sires. Knowing all the dark intrigue and shameful lack of integrity and honor that marked public affairs at Washington, he must have winced as he noted the difference.[1]

[1] "History of the United States," by James Rhodes, vol. V.

CHAPTER XXXV

FAILURE was closing down upon the worn-out Confederacy. The Southern armies for months had fought with only an occasional victory that cost them almost half of their entire strength. For four years Virginia had been the object of the enemy's persistent attack. The Federals were determined, and it had always been their aim, to capture this stronghold of the South, believing that as soon as it fell into their hands the Confederacy would go to pieces. It is true that Grant followed Lee to Petersburg but it was with the ultimate aim of lowering the flags on the Confederate Capitol. Lincoln never felt secure until he had sat in Jefferson Davis' chair. "We will join Grant in Richmond" was the constant cry of Sherman's cavalry as it raided the Carolinas. Richmond's evacuation was only a matter of a few days. The news of coming failure spread like a death-plague throughout the country. The bitter, loathsome truth was on every tongue and was reaching the ears of the soldiers. President Davis was constantly charged, by a coterie of embittered spirits, with the fate that had overtaken the country. The North continued to accuse him of cruelty to the prisoners; the Richmond *Examiner* taunted him with failure to retaliate and in the most prompt manner for the mistreatment of Confederate prisoners, thinking that the severest retaliation would put a stop to the cruelties that were reported in Northern prisons. It

384

was the old, old story in warfare of each side accusing the other of deeds of the most monstrous nature.

The days were dark ones for the occupants of the White House of the Confederacy, and Jefferson Davis' strength of purpose was all that now sustained him. Distant cannon daily told of the presence of the Federal army. At old St. Paul's Mrs. Jefferson Davis and every woman in the church on one occasion stood up on the benches in terror at the sound of the heavy guns. The deepest depression was visible on the faces of the people. These kept within doors, and with benumbed thoughts and paralyzed energies awaited the final blow. The streets wore a gloomy, deserted air and those who met upon them exchanged little else than sighs for greetings. As the days passed Varina sat alone with her children gathered around her, and waited for her husband's daily return from the office. Her health had not improved. There is hollowness and sadness in the eyes of the faded photograph made of her in the winter of '64. Some said that she had never recovered from the sudden death of little Joe. But there was more that had darkened her life.

During the winter and early spring she gave her whole attention to her husband. His wasted form and pale, anxious face filled her with anxiety and pain. At times, she says, it seemed that her heart would break. It was, she tells us, when she sat alone in her room that he came in, calm and erect, but with ashen face; she knew at one glance that all was lost. His frame shook as he put his arms around her, but suppressing his feelings he told her that the worst had come; the capture of the city was daily looked for; that she must take their children to a place of safety somewhere in the far South, and await news of his future plans. He would struggle on with the foe; would remove his government to some other place in Virginia. The thought of being separated from him shocked her. How could she leave him, perhaps to some horrible fate? Both feared she says that they were looking in each other's faces for the last time in life. The thought of all her goodness and devotion rushed to his mind—but he was firm. If he must hurry his government away from Richmond there would be no time nor place for the care of four young children. He confided them to her care, and she must put her trust in the Providence in which both believed with the trusting faith of their day, even though it was to all appearance cursing them. Verily Job had many disciples in "Slavonia."

After long hours of painful perturbation Varina finally agreed to make the flight. The suppression of self was noticeable throughout their public life. Before they separated she says that he gave her a purse of money and showed her how to use a small pistol if it became necessary. The little boy Jefferson cried bitterly to remain with him, and his young daughter Maggie clung to him in tears. His children's affection and loyalty touched him deeply but he was firm in his decision that Varina should take them away and leave him to his task. His quest was not to be attained, but he would give proof to the world that liberty was not dead. What the separation cost the two unhappy beings is a province that the novelist claims, but the biographer retains domain enough to set down in their behalf that there were always in their every thought and act the sense and dignity of a clean purpose. This was never more sustaining than at the present.

In the first dark hours of her flight from Richmond hardships for Varina immediately set in. The worn-out engine of a dilapidated train broke down no sooner than they were out of the city. There was nothing to do but to sit all through the night waiting for some assistance that they were hardly sure of receiving. There were no arrangements for sleeping, and if there had been she would not have slept. In the horror of all that was happening, the fear for her husband's safety and the care of her four young children, one an infant in arms, there was no time for rest of mind nor body. After a wretched trip following their night's delay of twelve hours, in which they got no further than Danville, Virginia, they halted for a few hours and friends insisted that she should rest there for several days. But having her husband's advice still in mind, under the care of his young secretary, Burton N. Harrison, she pressed on to North Carolina. She was grateful, indeed, she says for the good will manifested by the people at a time when good will and kindness meant so much to her. Her car on the next journey was a crowded sleeper even worse in the way of general comfort than the day train. The baggage car where she stored her clothing at times leaked streams, and the berths where she and her children slept were damp and sometimes wet. A steady rain fell with little intermission for a week before she reached Charlotte, North Carolina. Through it all she made no complaint, but continued to care for her children with the steady purpose that throughout life was an underlying force of her seemingly easy-going nature. Still, she was filled with anxiety. Every breath she says, was a prayer for the safety of her husband left in the menaced Capital of the Confederacy. It was now that her religion meant much to her, and not only Varina but women everywhere throughout the South found solace in it. Whoever they did blame for their bitter misfortunes they did not blame God. They took their defeat, however, with less grace if that were possible than their men. Some, it is true, had in letters plead with them to return to their unprotected families, but Southern women as a whole were unyielding and would have sent them back to fight again. Stanton said at the close of the war that they would never become reconciled.

Varina had been separated from her husband in the past, but under no such circumstance as this. She now realized that it was best for him not to be encumbered with his family in the event that he had to leave Richmond and take the government to some other place. They would constantly correspond, as was their habit when separated, and in that way she would keep advised of all his plans. With such thoughts consoling her, with a singularly adaptable nature she set her face resolutely towards any circumstance that might overtake her. Still it was a bitter and dangerous situation that confronted her. The country was infested with foraging troops and bummers from Sherman's army, hungry and rapacious, and in some instances brutish and bestial-minded. Her young sister Maggie was with her and even little Margaret was large enough for her to fear violence from the stragglers of his army. A horrible story had already reached her from South Carolina.[1] "Universal consternation" she says prevailed, and mixed with her fears was the unhappy thought that when seen with people she was compromising them in the eyes of the enemy. Though hiding it she could but become sensitive. She was Mrs. Jefferson Davis, the one woman of the whole Confederacy about whom the Federal army, and the people of the North generally, were most curious. Everything that

[1] Chestnut.

related to Jefferson Davis was the object of their ill will. One harboring any of his family, she knew, would be especially singled out for punishment. The Federal Cavalry Commander Stoneman had made it an order.

With the bitter thought that sometimes deepened into horror at being captured she kept bravely on, in an attempt, at least, to carry out the plan upon which she and her husband had agreed. She avoided as much as possible friends and acquaintances for fear of injuring them with the foe. Still, it was bitter to deny herself at such a crisis the friendly aid and sympathy that she so desperately needed. Many, she gratefully records, dared any fate to aid and protect her, but there were enough blank faces, if not positively cold ones, to assure her that their owners feared to be seen with her, or any of her family. The selfish did not seem to reflect that here was a lone, imperiled woman suffering from the effects of having been their representative and subject to the heaviest penalty of the North for having occupied the highest position of any woman in what it called the "Great Rebellion." She was the object of persecution not on account of anything she had done more than other Southern women, but that she was the wife of Jefferson Davis. If Varina gave any thought to this, the bitterest thought was that her husband far more than herself was the object of condemnation, and for what all the South had been a party to; for what Lee and Johnston and Toombs and all that array of Southern manhood had sanctioned and fought for. She was too shrewd an observer and thinker not to know that he, more than all others, was held responsible in the thoughtless mind of the North for the revolution. And now, as absurd as it was, an embittered coterie of his own people were charging him with its failure—he whom she had seen wear his heart out for its success, and while others were losing hope held on to the bitter end.

It was not her first painful experience in this respect. She had felt the long and continued criticism of him in the past. But even now, when it was more consorious than ever, she was too proud to admit that it was true only in the instances of a few disaffected leaders. She avoids in her "Memoir" as much as possible any reference to her feelings on her flight. Still her tremulous overflow of gratitude for the simplest kindness extended her told one of her sharp grief at its absence. Of a kindly old Jew who had retained through centuries the benignant characteristics of his race she wrote in her "Memoir," "This acknowledgment of his kindness is to some extent a relief to my heart that has borne his goodness in grateful memory for twenty-five years." And there were others of whom she wrote in after years who revered the name of Jefferson Davis, for despite defeat his name still thrilled the hearts of the Southern people. She heard it everywhere on her journey in the old familiar accents of pride and reverence. At such times her heart grew lighter and she gave her thought to the care of her children. This was all that had been left them of the vast débâcle. She knew how bitter his thoughts must be and to comfort him wrote from places along the road, "They love and honor you here. I meet your friends everywhere."

Settled for the time at Charlotte, Varina awaited news of her husband and the Southern army. In the event that all was well with him she would linger here until she could counsel further with him. For several days she heard nothing definite. She knew from her lifelong study of his nature and temperament that he was not one to give up readily. That he would struggle on she felt certain. This might lead to violence of his person should he be captured. She put the thought from her, and strove to be cheerful in the presence of the excited people around her. That all hope was dying in their breasts was evident on their faces. She could perceive it also in every word, message and paper that reached her. It cut her like a knife to hear it admitted on all sides that it would now be a miracle should the South win its independence. Jefferson Davis, she knew, was not of that number; her heart ached at the thought of what it would mean to him. There were many, however, who had not lost hope; the fatal word "surrender" had not yet passed their lips. Varina could not bring herself to utter it. As the days passed she grew restless. Heavy April showers had been incessant since her arrival in the town. The weather was depressing and the sparse news coming to her over broken and tangled wires kept her nervous and excited. In putting broken bits of rumor together she feared that disaster was fast overtaking Lee's army. The sad news had reached her that General A. P. Hill, one of General Lee's ablest corps commanders, had been killed at Five Oaks. Then came the horrible rumor that General Lee could no longer hold the lines at Petersburg. This would mean the capture and evacuation of Richmond. With the enemy's assaulting columns advancing daily on the city she knew that her husband's life was in momentary danger. All past history told her that all rulers in a revolution were held responsible for the acts of the people. Though spared in person the painful details of the capture of the city, her anxiety and fears were more distressing for her absence. The hours dragged by. Then came fresh news: first, rumors, then reports, none authoritative, none verified. But none doubted it when Lieutenant-General John S. Wise brought the news that General Lee was retreating from Petersburg; that Richmond had been evacuated; that the President had removed the government to Danville and was putting the town in a state of defense; was collecting stores and waiting for Lee to join him. "He was fertile," she wrote, "in all expedients to supply deficiencies." Still she could form but little idea of what was taking place.

The main features of General Wise's report were true. From Petersburg, on April 2, General Lee had telegraphed President Davis that he could no longer hold his lines and would leave that night which would necessitate the evacuation of Richmond. The Federals, elated by their recent victories, were pressing the siege with vigor and on these last days the firing upon Lee's lines had been incessant. This was returned with such spirit that it drew the enemy's fiercest fire. With nightfall Grant's activities ceased and Lee began to quietly remove his army. "At 12 o'clock," Varina wrote in her "Memoir," "the last man and the last gun of the brave army that had defended the lines of Petersburg for twelve months passed over the pontoon bridge and the retreat began that ended at Appomattox." With the Federal infantry pressing them, and large cavalry forces constantly attacking, the Confederates were facing a last crisis. Daily pressed by overwhelming numbers and hedged about with every difficulty, General Lee advanced toward Amelia Court House. The whole country was now in the hands of Federal forces. All letters and communications were captured and no concert of action could be had between the Confederate armies and the government at Danville. It was the President's wish that Lee should bring his army there and unite with Johnston's, but when the exhausted army reached Amelia Court House it was near starvation with only parched corn to relieve its hunger. The soldiers, it has been claimed by eyewitnesses, ate the young shoots that were putting out on the April trees to cool their fevered bodies. "For the first time in all history," Varina wrote, "soldiers were reduced to such a necessity." On April 5th, hoping to unite with Johnston's army, Lee began to retreat in the direction of Danville, and had he been fortunate in this there still might have been another chance of meeting the enemy in a great but hardly decisive battle. The heavy Federal lines, however, were closing down upon the retreating Confederates in such vast numbers that at Jetersville Lee was compelled to turn towards Lynchburg. On April 7th he reached Farmville, and here for the first time since leaving Petersburg provisions were issued to the hungry army. As the enemy continued to press them the Confederates began to burn their wagons and other equipment rather than have them captured. At the railroad bridge a large Federal force engaged the retreating army which caused it to turn in a last desperate repulse. But the vast horde pressing it was too much for its wasted strength. "On the evening of the 8th," Varina wrote in her "Memoir" with a pathos that the years only intensified, "with his army wearied and diminished in numbers, with men falling by the wayside who had never before abandoned their colors but were now unable to keep up with the retreating columns, General Lee decided, after a conference with his corps commanders, that he would advance the next day beyond Appomattox Court House, and if no stronger forces were confronting him than Sheridan's cavalry he would disperse it and continue his march to Lynchburg."

On the final surrender of the Army of Northern Virginia we will not dwell since the gloom that it cast upon all things hangs so heavily over succeeding chapters.

Although fair in all her statements and writing, without prejudice or animus, one suspects that Varina took intense pleasure in recording years later that, "There were 7,892 of the Army of Northern Virginia who had arms in their hands at the surrender. The total number, including those who reported afterwards, was between 26,000 and 27,000. Grant's army numbered 162,239." Rhodes agrees to the Confederate estimate but places the Federal estimate at 113,000. Other historians vary it slightly.

The provisions of the articles of surrender upon which General Lee and General Grant agreed make strange reading when one considers the ten years of military rule and tragic method of reconstruction to which the South was subjected after the war. That this benign policy for the restoration of the conquered States would not be accepted could have been decided at the time by a close study of the radical wing of the Republican party. At one time, however, it seemed that the worn-out, tired, and scarcely happy Seward would at last get his way, since Lincoln was now thoroughly in accord with the conciliatory policy that the Secretary of State had so persistently recommended in '61.

CHAPTER XXXVI

A REMARKABLE CORRESPONDENCE

AFTER Jefferson Davis left Richmond on April 2, 1865, and had established the government at Danville, Virginia, the following correspondence took place between himself and Mrs. Davis and covered much of the time of her flight southward. It is brought together in one chapter, as it best tells us all that was passing in the minds and hearts of these two distressed, but still courageous, souls in their hour of defeat and ill fortune. They were now condemned and pursued in the usual manner in which the unsuccessful heads of great revolutions and the wars growing out of them are treated. The great Washington would have suffered approximately the same fate had he failed.

There is said to have been numerous other letters, notes and telegrams that passed between Jefferson Davis and Varina at this time which were intercepted and captured by Federal orders along with other correspondence. Out of the number, this valuable collection was fortunately preserved for posterity. With its pathos and charm and historical significance, it forms one of the most dramatic and charming correspondences of all history.[1]

The letters were found among the private papers of Edwin M. Stanton, Secretary of War in the Lincoln Cabinet,

[1] A number of the letters appear in "Jefferson Davis, Constitutionalist," His Letters, Papers and Speeches. To some extent the author has followed the arrangement made by Frank G. Carpenter, correspondent of the New York *Times*.

after his death. The fact indicates how well he understood their value, or else, that he was so thoroughly hypnotized with their charm that, however he might have desired to do so, he did not have the heart to destroy them. The letters were written spontaneously in moments of intense anguish and distress and with no thought that they would ever be seen by another. Still they retain the innate grace and charm that characterized every thought and action of the man and woman who indited them.

The first letter of the correspondence was written after the evacuation of Richmond while Jefferson Davis was still at Danville with his government and Mrs. Davis and her children had in their flight south reached Charlotte, North Carolina. The originals may be found in the Library of Congress, and the Confederate Museum of Richmond.

There had been numerous discussions between them as to what would be best to do in the event of the capture of Richmond. Varina had constantly urged him, should that befall the city, to take with him all that he possibly could carry for use in establishing the government at some other place in Virginia. She had always been somewhat more thrifty than her husband and the last four hard years of self-denial and economy had made her more so. She was, she confesses with a naïve charm that frees the thought of any selfishness, not unlike other women. "All women like bric-à-brac," she wrote, "which sentimental people call their 'household gods,' but Mr. Davis calls it 'trumpery.' I was not superior to the rest of my sex in this regard."

She even wanted to take with her, on her escape from Richmond, some flour that she had hoarded pound by pound, for fear, she says, that her little ones might at times suffer from hunger. To this he had objected. As long as there were hungry soldiers and a government to be sustained, even his own flesh and blood must trust to fortune. Although he had little taste for practical domestic affairs, he had striven earnestly to save and remove such things to Danville as they would need in establishing the government. At this time it is evident that he did not contemplate the[1] dissolution of the Confederacy. Nor did Varina realize it as her letters show. The letters are addressed and signed in a guarded manner, since all correspondence was likely to be captured.

"Danville, Va., April 5, 1865.

"My Dear Wife: I have in vain sought to get into communication with Gen. Lee and have postponed writing in the hope that I would soon be able to speak to you with some confidence of the future. On last Sunday I was called out of church to receive a telegram announcing that Gen. Lee could not hold his position longer than night and warning me that we must leave Richmond, as the army would commence retiring that evening. I made the necessary arrangements at my office and went to our house to have the proper dispositions made there. Nothing had been done after you left, and but little could be done in the few hours which remained before the train was to leave.

"I had short notice and was interrupted so often and so little aided that the results are very unsatisfactory.[1]

"The people here have been very kind, and the Mayor and Council have offered assistance in the matter of quarters, and have declared their unabated confidence. I do not wish to leave Virginia, but cannot decide on my movements until those of the army are better developed.

---

[1] She had greatly prized a bust of him and the famous picture, "The Valley Heroes"; these he tried to preserve for her.

"I hope you are comfortable and trust soon to hear from you.   Kiss my dear children.

"I weary of this sad recital and have nothing pleasant to tell.   May God have you in his holy keeping is the fervent prayer of your ever affectionate

"HUSBAND."

From Charlotte, North Carolina, Varina sent the following letter to her husband.   She still employed the fanciful term of endearment which she had so frequently used in the old Briarfield and Washington days.   She now used it designedly, not only to deceive the Federals but with the desire to comfort him with the thought of her love and faith in him in his bitter hour of adversity.

"April 7, 1865.

"*My Own Dear Old Banny:* Since my arrival here I have been so busy as to have only the evening to write in, and then but one room where the children 'most do congregate,' so I have written you but one disjointed letter.

"The news of Richmond came upon me like the 'abomination of desolation,' the loss of Selma like the 'blackness thereof.'   Since your telegram upon your arrival at Danville we have nothing except the wildest rumors, all, however, discouraging.

"I, who know that your strength when stirred up is great, and that you can do with a few what others have failed to do with many, am awaiting prayerfully the advent of the time when it is God's will to deliver us through His own appointed agent.   I trust it may be you, as I believe it is.

"It would comfort me greatly if you could only find an opportunity to write me a full, long letter.   As soon as we are established here I am anxious to leave Mrs. Chesnut the children and bring Li Pie [evidently the baby] to see you. I do not know how soon that may be. God grant it may be soon. The gentlemen I have seen here (the officers of the post) are exceedingly kind, and have offered me every civility in their power.

"The Surgeon General was also very kind in his offers of service. Col. Johnston with his wife called to see me. Mrs. Joe Johnston is here living with the cashier of the bank and family, and keeps a very pretty fancy carriage and horses. I have not seen her, but I hear she is going out of town before long to some watering place or other. Mrs. Semmes went off yesterday for the South. I did not see her. The Wigfalls are staying, I believe, with Mrs. Johnston also. They arrived yesterday.[1]

"I heard a funny account of Wigfall's interview with Beauregard. It seems he went to see him on his way to this place, and when the news of the evacuation of Richmond came, and that the enemy had not yet entered the town, the General said, 'Oh, they do not understand the situation! It is, or ought to be, a plan of Lee's to keep between Richmond and the enemy. If Grant attempts to throw troops between his army and Richmond, Lee can whip them in detail.' With this plan Wigfall was immensely satisfied.

"I cannot judge of the moral effect of the fall of Richmond. The people here were about as down . . .[2] as they could be, as I infer from little things, but, upon the whole, I do not think the shock is as great as I expected.

[1] In the breach between President Davis and General Joseph E. Johnston the Wigfalls sided with the latter.
[2] Several words effaced, evidently "in spirit."

"We had a digest of your address to the people today, and I could not make much of it, except an encouraging exhortation. Am anxious to see the whole thing. Numberless surmises are hazarded here as to your future destination and occupation but I know that wherever you are and in whatever engaged it is in an efficient manner for the country. The way things look now the trans-Mississippi seems our ultimate destination.

"Though I know you do not like my interference, let me entreat you not to send B. B. to command there. I am satisfied that the country will be ruined by its intestine feuds if you do so. If your friends thought it best I should feel helpless, but resigned; but even those who hope for favors in that event deprecate it for you. If I am intrusive forgive me for the sake of the love which impels me, but pray long and fervently before you decide to do it.

"Mrs. Chesnut wrote me a most affectionate letter from Chester today. She is staying in two rooms very badly furnished, and furnished with food by her friends there. As I shall have a spare room, she will come over and stay a few days with me. I have carpets, some curtains, some window shades and three pictures, and some lovely volumes of books belonging to a man in Augusta—a marble table, brocatelle chairs, nice china and nice tin basins and buckets. I am very well off and very kindly treated by the Jewish man, Wiele, who owns the house—with the delicacy and hospitality of a gentleman. Major Willis has offered every attention and so has Major Echols—Harrison has been more efficient and attentive than I thought he could be, and very affectionate and kind. I really regret to see him go tomorrow, which is the day he proposes to leave.

"The Trenholms left yesterday for Chester, with Col.

Trenholm. Our little ones are all well, but very unruly, or else the small house 'makes me sensible' of it. Li Pie is sweet and pink and loving, her hands and gums are hot and swollen, and I think she is teething. Billy is well, but bad. Jeff is unremunerative, but behaves well in the main. Jeff is very much exercised about his pony, Maggie about her saddle—Margaret about her saddle—Ellen about her child—Washington (who is a fine boy) about his $2,000 left in his master's hands with his clothes and I about my precious Old Ban, whom I left behind me with so keen a heartache.

"Write to me, my own precious only love, and believe me as ever your devoted wife—

The following letter refers to one that Mrs. Davis evidently never received, since her reply shows that she is still ignorant of the country's situation. As it does not appear in the correspondence and has never been found, it is probable that it was intercepted by Federal soldiers and lost. The second communication that reached her reads:

"Danville, Va., April 6, 1865.

"Dear Winnie: Many thanks for your letter giving me an account of your situation at Charlotte. In my letter of yesterday I gave you all of my prospects which can now be told, not having heard from Genl. Lee and having to conform my movements to the military necessities of the case. We are now fixing an executive office where the current business may be transacted here, and do not propose at this time definitely to fix upon a point for a seat of govt. in the future.

"I am unwilling to leave Virginia and do not know where

within her borders the requisite houses for the Departments and the Congress could be found.

"I hope our dear children will be well when they have recovered from the effects of their journey. Enclosed please find two letters. As specimens of deep feeling and idle speaking they might stand for extremes in their classes.

"Love to Maggie, little Maggie, Jeff, Billy, and little Winnie. Farewell, my love. May God bless, preserve and guide you.

"HUSBAND."

Mrs. Davis in her flight southward hurriedly left Charlotte, North Carolina, where rumors of a Federal raid were on every tongue. The country was believed to be infested with Sherman's troops. Her next point was Chester, South Carolina. The letter does not indicate whether she knew or not that her husband had left Danville and was making his way southward. However, in her "Memoir" she says that this was at that time his intention, and the correspondence later confirms it. From Chester on April 13, 1865, she wrote the following letter which was found in the Stanton Collection. Jefferson Davis with his Cabinet had left Danville for Greensboro, North Carolina. Both he and Varina were now upon the road, uncertain of each other's destination and their painful Odyssey continues:

"Chester, April 13, 1865.

"*My Dear Banny:* The rumors of a raid on Charlotte induced me to come south, and a threatened raid here induces me to leave without making an hour's unnecessary stay. I go with the specie train because they have a strong guard and are attended by two responsible men. I am going somewhere, perhaps to Washington, Ga., perhaps only to Abbeville, S. C. I don't know. Just as the children seem to bear the journey will I decide. Gen. Chesnut seems anxious, as is the author of the letter you sent me to Charlotte, but oh, so moody that I am wordless, helpless. The children are well as are Maggie and I. Would to God I could know the truth of the horrible rumors I hear of you. One is that you have started for Gen. Lee, but have never been heard of. Mr. Clay is here and very kind. He will catch up with my train and join me tomorrow.

"May God have mercy upon and preserve your life for your dear wife."

The reply to Varina's letter reached her the next day through loyal private soldiers who knew the country and generally the whereabouts of the Federal army, disjointed columns of which were scouring the country. From signatures and missigned letters it is evident that they were seeking to evade a capture of their communications.

"Greensboro, N. C., April 14, 1865.

"*Dear Winnie:* I will come to you if I can. Everything is dark. You should prepare for the worst by dividing your baggage so as to move in wagons. If you can go to Abbeville, it seems best as I now advise. If you can send everything there, do so. I have lingered on the road and labored to little purpose. My love to the children and Maggie.

"God bless, guide and preserve you, ever prays, Your most affectionate

"BANNY."

"P.S.—I sent you a telegram, but fear it was stopped on the road. General Bonham bears this. His horse is at the door and he awaits me to write this. Again and ever yours."

It was from Abbeville, South Carolina, that Varina wrote her husband the following letter of anguish and despair. Her grief over the failure of the Confederacy filled her with horror and consternation and bitter words burst from her lips; and bitter words were on the lips of thousands of Southern women who could not realize that the Confederacy had failed.

"Abbeville, April 19, 1865.

"My Dear Old Banny:

"The fearful news I hear fills me with horror. This is that Gen. Lee's army is in effect disbanded, Longstreet's corps surrendered, Mahone's also saving one brigade. I do not believe all, yet enough is thrust upon my unwilling credence to *weigh me to the earth.*

"Where are you? How are you? What ought I do with these helpless little unconscious charges of mine are questions which I am asking myself always. Write to me of your troubles freely for mercy's sake. Do not attempt to put a good face upon them to the friend of your heart.

"Since I left Richmond no such heartfelt welcome has been extended to me as the one I received here—they will hear of no change of place for the present, and urge me with tears in their eyes to share with them the little they can offer. People call promptly and seem to feel warmly. Mr. Burt really seems to feel tenderly towards us, pets the children, and does every kind thing in his power to me. Mrs. Burt is more than affectionate.

"Jeffy D. was taken quite ill on the cars and is here sick at Mr. Trenholm's, who lives just across the street. He is better, but not well. He and Joe both had very badly swollen throats, with high fever. Joe was nearly well and went on with the train which left here yesterday evening, having arrived in the night. I hear it has been stopped nine miles from here by a rumored raid below here. I do not know how true this is. I shall wait your further directions here. Do write every day and make the staff send the notes (I do not expect more) by officers coming this way—I am so unhappy and anxious.

"The children are well and very happy, play all day. Billy and Jim fast friends as ever. Little Winnie the sweetest little angelic thing in the world—she rode along in the wagon as we bumped over the horrible roads, making noses at everything—the children seem to improve under it.

"Mr. Clay passed through here today, but did not stop long enough to see me. I felt quite disappointed, because he was so very kind to me at Chester and Charlotte; he sent me word he would see me at Washington in a very few days.

"Wigfall made a descent upon Mr. Burt the week before I came, and spent uninvited a week with them but left the day before I came. Hood and he went on together.

"Do remember me affectionately to the staff and Mr. Harrison and tell them if you cannot always write they can, but don't.

"Margaret sends you her best love, little Pollie sends hers, and the boys—your little pet would, I know, feel for you if she hoped to find you.

"May God in His mercy keep you safe and raise up defenders for our bleeding country prays your devoted wife."

"24th.

"My Own Dear Old Banny: The dreadful news, with its dreadful confirmation, has rendered us very wretched. I long for one word from you. I will come to you for a day or two if this truce is really so—i.e., if you cannot come to me. The children are all well. Jeff has gotten well.

"May God in His mercy have you in His holy keeping prays your devoted wife.

"P.S.—How comes it that my dear Joe did not go to you as soon as paroled? Everything is mystery."

This letter and her reference to Clement Clay indicate that she had grown sensitive about the attitude of others towards them at this time.

When Jefferson Davis reached Charlotte, North Carolina, he sent Varina the following lengthy letter which, to a great extent, explains the condition and situation of the Confederacy and its armies before the final surrender. Negotiations had already begun between the armies. The letter shows that he now had but scant hope of reorganizing the army but was looking forward to an escape westward to there determine his future course.

"Charlotte, N. C., April 23, 1865.

"My dear Winnie.

"I have been detained here longer than was expected when the last telegram was sent to you. I am uncertain where you are and deeply feel the necessity of being with you, if even for a brief time, under our altered circumstances.

"Govr. Vance and Genl. Hampton propose to meet me here, and Genl. Johnston sent me a request to remain at some point where he could readily communicate with me.

Under these circumstances I have asked Mr. Harrison to go in search of you and to render you such assistance as he may. Your brother William telegraphed in reply to my inquiry, that you were at Abbeville and that he would go to see you. My last dispatch was sent to that place and to the care of Mr. Burt.

"Your own feelings will convey to you an idea of my solicitude for you and our family, and I will not distress you by describing it.

"The dispersion of Lee's army and the surrender of the remnant which remained with him destroyed the hopes I entertained when we parted. Had that army held together I am now confident we could have successfully executed the plan which I sketched to you and would have been today on the high road to independence. Even after that disaster if the men who 'straggled'—say, thirty or forty thousand in number—had come back with their arms and with a disposition to fight we might have repaired the damage; but all was sadly the reverse of that. They threw away their arms and were uncontrollably resolved to go home. The small guards along the road have sometimes been unable to prevent the pillage of trains and depots. Panic has seized the country. Johnston and Beauregard were hopeless as to recruiting their forces from the dispersed men of Lee's army, and equally so as to their ability to check Sherman with the forces they had. Their only idea was to retreat. Of the power to do so they were doubtful, and subsequent desertions from their troops have materially diminished their strength and, I learn, still more weakened their confidence. The loss of arms has been so great that, should the spirit of the people rise to the occasion, it would not be at this time possible adequately to supply them with the weapons of war.

"Gen. Johnston had several interviews with Sherman and agreed on a suspension of hostilities, and the reference of terms of pacification. They are secret and may be rejected by the Yankee Government. To us, they are hard enough though freed from wanton humiliation and expressly recognizing the State Governments, and the rights of person and property, as secured by the Constitution of the United States and the several States.

"Genl. Breckenridge was a party to the last consultation and to the agreement. Judge Reagan went with him and approved the agreement, though not present at the conference. Each member of the Cabinet is to give his opinion in writing today, 1st, upon the acceptance of the terms, 2d, upon the mode of proceeding if accepted.

"The issue is one which it is very painful for me to meet. On one hand is the long night of oppression which will follow the return of our people to the 'Union.' On the other, the suffering of the women and children, and carnage among the few brave patriots who would still oppose the invader, and who, unless the people would rise *en masse* to sustain them, would struggle but to die in vain. I think my judgment is undisturbed by any pride of opinion.

"I have prayed to our Heavenly Father to give me wisdom and fortitude equal to the demands of the position in which Providence has placed me. I have sacrificed so much for the cause of the Confederacy that I can measure my ability to make any further sacrifices required, and am assured there is but one to which I am not equal—my wife and my children. How are they to be saved from degradation or want is now my care.

"During the suspension of hostilities you may have the best opportunity to go to Mississippi, and thence either to sail from Mobile for a foreign port or to cross the river and proceed to Texas, as the one or the other may be more practicable. The little Sterling (money) you have will be a very scant store, and under other circumstances, would not be counted, but if our land can be sold that will secure you from absolute want. For myself, it may be that our enemy will prefer to banish me. Or it may be that a devoted band of cavalry will cling to me, and that I can force my way across the Mississippi, and if nothing can be done there which it will be proper to do, then I can go to Mexico and have the world from which to choose a location.

"Dear wife, this is not the fate to which I invited you when the future was rose-colored to us both, but I know you will bear it even better than myself, and that of us two, I alone will ever look back reproachfully on my past career. I have thus entered on the questions involved in the future to guard against contingencies. My stay will not be prolonged a day beyond the prospect of useful labor here, and there is every reason to suppose that I will be with you a few days after Mr. Harrison arrives.

"Dear children, I can say nothing to them, but for you and them my heart is full, my prayers constant and my hopes are the trust I feel in the mercy of God.

"Farewell, my dear; there may be better things in store for us than are now in view, but my love is all I have to offer, and that has the value of a thing long possessed and sure not to be lost.

"Once more, and with God's favor, for a short time only, farewell,

"YOUR HUSBAND."

Varina was still at Abbeville when she sent the following letter to her husband.

Her letter indicates that she was still willing to go on with the conflict if there was any possible chance of success—would put her "children in school and join him in Texas" in any attempt that he should make to reorganize the Confederacy, though she had as little hope as he expressed of its being attended with success. That this strong tenacity of purpose was a natural one it is easy to believe but long association with him had deepened and strengthened it. Her letter evinces the natural charm that all of her letters possess.

"Abbeville, S. C., April 28, 1865.

"My Dear Old Husband: Your very sweet letter reached me safely by Mr. Harrison and was a great relief. I leave here in the morning at 6 o'clock for the wagon train going to Georgia. Washington will be the first point I shall unload at. From there we shall probably go on to Atlanta or thereabouts, and wait a little until we hear something of you. Let me beseech you not to calculate upon seeing me unless I happen to cross your shortest path toward your bourne, be that what it may.

"It is surely not the fate to which you invited me in brighter days. But you must remember that you did not invite me to a great hero's home, but to that of a plain farmer. I have shared all your triumphs, been the only beneficiary of them, now I am but claiming the privilege for the first time of being all to you, now these pleasures have past for me.

"My plans are these, subject to your approval. I think I shall be able to procure funds enough to enable me to put the two eldest at school. I shall go to Florida if possible, and from thence go over to Bermuda, or Nassau, from thence to England, unless a good school offers elsewhere, and put them at the best school I can find, and then with the two youngest join you in Texas—and that is the prospect which bears me up, to be once more with you—once more to suffer with you if need be—but God loves those who obey Him, and I know there is a future for you. This people are a craven set, they cannot bear the tug of war.

"Here, they are all your friends and have the most unbounded confidence in you. Mr. Burt and his wife have urged me to live with them—offered to take the chances of the Yankees with us—begged to have little Maggie—done everything, in fact, that relatives could do. I shall never forget all their generous devotion to you.

"I have seen a great many men who have gone through —not one has talked fight. A stand cannot be made in this country! Do not be induced to try it. As to the trans-Mississippi, I doubt if at first things will be straight, but the spirit is there, and the daily accretions will be great when the deluded of this side are crushed out between the upper and nether millstones. But you have now tried the 'strict construction' fallacy. If we are to acquire a Constitution, it must be much stretched during our hours of outside pressure if it covers us at all. I am much disappointed at Joe's going to New York—however, I hope it was to get home sooner—Gen'l McGowen says he was in pretty good spirits. Haskell says he and many other young officers desired to escape, and that the argument used was in his case put by Longstreet thus: 'Is it possible you would desert your men? If they cut their way out, if the surrender is not accepted upon honorable terms, would you fly your share of the conflict?' Genl. Lee said there was no hope—Young Haskell insists upon my going to his father's in the morning to take lunch—he has been more than polite to me—so have all the people here—it is like old times—

"I have a very painful thumb, a runround has caused it to ache violently, so I must close. Maggie says in the anticipation of her journey she was forced to go to bed. She sends 'a thousand loves,' and says Pie C. is sweet as can be. She is really now too playful to suck. Billy and Jeff are very well. Limber is thriving, but bad.

"Be careful how you go to Augusta. I get rumors that Brown is going to seize all Government property, and the people are averse and mean to resist with pistols. They are a set of wretches together, and I wish you were safe out of the land. God bless you, and keep you. I have wrestled with God for you. I believe He will restore us to happiness.

"Devotedly,

"Your Wife."

Among the last letters of the famous correspondence is the following, located and copied from the original in the Confederate Museum of Richmond, Virginia. From her repeated words of warning and caution it is evident that she feared he might be captured at any moment. Varina was now at Washington, Georgia.

"Washington, 9 o'clock,
"Monday Morning.

"My dearest Banny,

"The young gentleman who will hand you this is just going by Abbeville and I cannot refrain from expressing my intense grief at the treacherous surrender of this department. May God grant you a safe conduct out of this maze of events. I do believe you are safer without the sentry than with it, and I so dread their stealing a march, and surprising you. I left Abbeville against my convictions, but agreeably to Mr. Burt and Mr. Harrison's opinion. Now the danger of being caught here by the enemy and of being deprived of our transportation if we stay is hurrying me out of Washington. I shall wait here this evening until I hear from the courier we have sent to Abbeville. I have given up the hope of seeing you but it is not for long—Mr. Harrison now proposes to go in a line between Macon and Augusta, and to avoid the Yankees by sending some of paroled escort on before, and to make towards Pensacola, and take a ship or what else I can— We have a very gentlemanly escort—among whom is Capt. Moody who says he will see us through—there are also some Mississippi teamsters— We are short of funds, and I do not see why these trains of specie should be given up to the Yankees, but still I think we will make out somehow. May the Lord have you in his holy keeping I constantly and earnestly pray—I look at the precious little charge I have, and wonder if I shall with it see you soon again. The children are all well. Pie was vaccinated on the roadside, as I heard there was smallpox on the road —she is well so far—the children have been more than good; and talk much of you as does big Maggie; Harrison too is kind and attentive.

"Oh my dearest precious husband, the one absorbing love of my whole life, may God keep you free from harm.

"Your devoted wife."

The following touching letter, though complete, is not dated:

"My own precious Banny.

"How disappointed you are I know—may God give us both patience against this heavy trial. The soldiers were very unruly and had taken almost all the mules and horses from Camp. More of Wheeler's Cavalry are expected, as were the Yankees, so we thought we had better move for fear our transportation would be stolen and moving felt it best to cross the railroad before nightfall. We will make a march tomorrow of 25 miles to pass beyond the point of positive danger between Mayfield & Macon by day after tomorrow. I did not receive the letter sent by courier, only the one sent from the Saluda river. Every letter, I thank God for anew. Col. Chamburg and Dick Nugent will give you this and tell you more than I can with more time. I think they will be useful knowing all the crossings of their departments, & I have as many as is necessary—Mr. Harrison is quite sick tonight or I would get a note from him— Do not try to meet me, I dread the Yankees getting news of you so much, you are the country's only hope, and the very best intentioned do not calculate upon a stand this side of the river. Why not cut loose from your escort? go swiftly and alone with the exception of two or three—

"Oh! may God in his goodness keep you safe, my own— The children send pipes—Maggie, dearest love, says she has your prayer book safe. May God keep you, my old and only love, As ever

"Devotedly, your own

"WINNIE."

There are several other letters to her husband, some mere fragments found in the Stanton Collection, none of which are dated. Varina was now suffering great anxiety for his safety, but continued to cheer him with news of herself and their children. This was the one solace left him out of the wreck of all things for which he had so earnestly and tenaciously striven.

The following is a fragment of one of her letters:

"All well, with Winnie sweet and smiling. Billy plenty of laughter, and talk with the teamsters, keeps quiet. Jeff is happy beyond expression. Maggie one and two quite well.

"I have $2,500, something to sell, and have heart and a hopeful one, but above all, my precious only love, a heart full of prayer. May God keep you and have His sword and buckler over you. Do not try to make a stand on this side. It is not in the people. Leave your escort and take another road often. Alabama is full of their cavalry, fresh and earnest in pursuit. May God keep you and bring you safe to the arms of

"Your devoted,
"WINNIE."

Throughout the days covering the correspondence with her husband Varina was filled with pain and horror over the fate of the fallen Confederacy. She still clung to the hope of a future somewhere with her husband. The thought aroused her to further action when her strength at times seemed scarcely equal to the dreadful situation in which she found herself. In these efforts she might make mistakes; might at times say bitter, scornful, perhaps indiscreet things of those who were placing at her husband's door all the blame for failure. But she was sound in all her being and full worthy of the tribute paid her by

Pulitzer, editor and publisher of the New York *World,* that "here was a great woman of whom all America might well be proud." In addition to the heroic qualities that the correspondence evinces, it furthermore reveals a distinctly feminine charm that holds fast a lover. She had drawn closer to him each day in his adversity, had witnessed his triumphs and failures, and had now only words of praise for his efforts, and thoughts of his safety and welfare.

CHAPTER XXXVII

INTO THE UNKNOWN

DURING her correspondence with her husband Varina was also in communication with Mrs. Chesnut, who was at her Mulberry estate near Camden, South Carolina. Well might the latter have said that "Dear Mrs. Davis is one woman for whom my heart aches in all this tragedy." She had insisted that Varina, in any crisis, should come to her and bring her family, and at one time Varina had thought of sending her children and sister Maggie to her, but dreading the separation, she kept them with her. It was on her flight that she met Mrs. Chesnut again at Chester, South Carolina. "We went down to the train to meet Mrs. Davis. She is brave and smiling as ever." [1] "I went down to the station when she left. My heart was like lead, but she did not give way. It was but a brief glimpse of my dear Mrs. Davis and under altered skies."

On April 17th, Varina wrote to Mrs. Chesnut the following letter without which any biography of her would hardly be complete:

"Do come to me, and see how we get on. I shall have a spare room by the time you arrive, indifferently furnished, but, oh, so affectionately placed at your service. You will receive such a loving welcome. One perfect bliss

[1] The death of Mrs. James Chesnut occurred on November 22, 1886. On some of the last pages of her famous Diary she pays high tribute to Mrs. Jefferson Davis.

have I. The baby, who grows fat and is smiling always, is christened, and not old enough to develop the world's vices or to be snubbed by it. The name so long delayed is Varina Anne. My name is a heritage of woe.

"Are you delighted with your husband? I am delighted with him as well as with my own. It is well to lose an Arabian horse if one elicits such a tender and at the same time knightly letter as General Chesnut wrote to my poor old Prometheus.[1] I do not think that for a time he felt the vultures after the reception of the General's letter."

At Chester, Varina had decided to go with her brother, young Jefferson Davis Howell, who was moving with the Confederate treasure train out of the country. She would, at least, go as far as Abbeville; beyond that she had formed no plans but the vague one of getting out of the country. She would go out of that portion where both armies were foraging, meeting in daily conflicts and engaging in many acts of lawlessness. For her journey, after much effort, she secured an ambulance for herself, her sister Maggie and the children. A wagon was provided for the baggage. With many fears, she again began her flight southward. Travel over country roads at times was difficult, and fear of scattered bands of robbers and bummers, with which the country was infested, kept her nervous and anxious. With every mile the roads grew worse. The spring rains had flooded them with a bed of mud and water. The lower branches of the trees and the grass and weeds along the dismal roadsides were spattered with mud and slush. Here and there, to relieve the dreary sight, a flowering bush starred the wet

---

[1] Jefferson Davis' saddle horse had been taken from Colonel Chesnut's plantation by Sherman's army.

spring woods with splashes of color, and birds sang. The ambulance in which she was riding with her family mired at times in the deep mud. To lighten the load she threw out all baggage that could be spared. As the maid was panicky and feared to leave the vehicle, Varina took her youngest child in her arms and walked behind it five miles through mud and water. The treasure train had advanced too far along the road to help them and was itself laboring and floundering in deep mire.

Her children, she says, the little boy especially, were happy and full of frolic. The infant in her arms, too, she says, "cooed in delight," and the sweet babble of her children and thoughts of their safety gave her strength to seek some place of refuge, where, out of the way of harm, her husband could join them. This was all she now desired. That she would ever have found herself in such a predicament was hard at times to realize, but the child was heavy in her arms and the road in places ankle deep in mud. The physical strain kept her senses alert. At many of the small, ramshackled villages they passed they were told that the Yankees infested the country, and foragers, some from the disbanded Confederate armies, were appropriating everything they could find. With the unhappy thought that her husband perhaps at that moment was suffering even a worse fate than herself, she directed the party to move on as fast as possible, hoping to come up with the treasure train before night! At one o'clock, to her relief, they came up with it at a small country church.

Once more with her brother near her, she put out of her mind the terrible experience through which she had passed. Her little family was made as comfortable as possible for the rest and sleep she knew they must have in order to take up the flight in the early morning. She found many of the party already asleep on the floor of the church. The communion table had been left for her by a thoughtful woman who had accompanied her husband, but Varina, whose sense of the incongruous was keen even in this extremity, took in the situation with a smile and decided to lie upon the floor. One gathers from her story that she reflected in some derision that, at a time when all things else were being profaned in Christian America, she at least would not include this emblem of its civilization.

As she lay on the hard floor of the church unable to sleep, her thoughts, she says, were constantly of her husband. Where was he? What were his final plans? How would all this horrible plight they had found themselves in end? At times she gave way to a burst of bitter passion, as she realized that the South had failed, and covering her face with her hands, wept all through the night. After several hours of fitful sleep she aroused her small party and got her children ready for the next day's journey. The treasure train moved ahead to attract as little attention as possible. Then a situation more serious than any they had yet encountered faced them. Food of every variety was scarce.[1] "Forage on the country liberally," Sherman had ordered, to be slyly reminded of it when he discountenanced its excess by a great lout with his mouth dripping with honey and his body weighted down with hams and chickens. There was now scarcely enough food left to appease hunger, and people parted with it reluctantly. Whenever they did, the price was enormous. The small hostelries and even private homes charged as much at times as a hundred dollars in Confederate money for a single biscuit and a glass of milk, which

[1] "Memoir," vol. II.

indicated that they were losing faith in its monetary value. Sometimes even this could not be procured at any price.

Varina was unknown to the people and this she preferred; but so pressing was the need of assistance at times that she was compelled to make herself known to the better class of Confederate soldiers. In such instances she says she was pressed to share all they possessed. In an exhausted condition she reached Abbeville, and the treasure train, without halting, moved on without her to Washington. With many apprehensions, she realized that she would, in traveling, no longer be near her brother Jefferson. Some insisted that she should rest on her journey. There were daring spirits among the people of the little town despite the presence of Federal soldiers, and Varina and her little family were taken to the hospitable home of Mr. Armistead Burt, to whom she refers in her letter. It was here that she heard of the assassination of President Lincoln. Though the Confederacy had failed and the fate of her husband was unknown, she wept, she says, at the thought of what the dreadful tragedy must mean to the stricken wife. The stabbing, too, of Seward, brought up recollections that filled her heart with the keenest pain at his fate. It would not be the truth of history to say that the Southern people generally were grieved, as some historians have inferred, at the news of Lincoln's death. Many who had lost every male relative in their family and had suffered the deepest wrongs from the presence of the Federal army, believed that a tyrant had been removed from the world, and some clapped their hands. Many throughout the North felt the same way about Jefferson Davis. A world gone mad!

As the days passed, Varina found herself thinking of the effect the tragedy might have upon the future for the

country. The deed had been committed by a young actor of
a famous Southern family. It was actuated by a fierce,
fanatical impulse to avenge the South. The act was committed in the same spirit in which John Brown sought to
secretly murder the Virginia slaveholders. Many such examples of fanatical patriotism, the effects of a disordered
brain, appear in history. It was murder in both instances—but would the North, that had condoned John
Brown's deed, burst forth at John Wilkes Booth's act in a
fierce passion of retaliation against the South? Would any
lives be safe in the Confederacy now that it was in the possession of the enemy? She was filled with fears. Her last
communication with her husband had not told her anything
definite of his future plans. She sent a note to be handed
him at the Saluda River where they said he was crossing.
It said that she would meet him in Texas if he decided to
make a stand. It is certain that this had been his intention
before Johnston determined upon surrender. It was the
spirit of Washington who went even further and advised
guerrilla warfare against the British as long as that nation
opposed the Colonies. Varina's note was not received and
Jefferson Davis rode hurriedly to Abbeville to find that she
had moved on with her family. He immediately sent his
Secretary, Burton N. Harrison of his staff, after them with
instructions that if he himself did not come up with them,
for young Harrison and a small party to see them safely
out of the country. Jefferson Davis did not himself expect
to meet with any clemency from the foe, and, but for his
family, seemed indifferent to his fate, as his refusal to leave
it in the country unprotected shows.

Mr. Harrison brought Varina the news that the enemy
had rejected the proposals of the Confederates and had

ordered active operation to be resumed in forty-eight hours. When she reached Washington, Georgia, she found the town and surrounding country in the wildest state of excitement. Men were cursing their fate and swearing to never yield to the foe. Others were giving up everywhere; men who had never faltered during four years, looked blankly into space when questioned about the future. Her correspondence with her husband had ceased and hence, on her journey through the beautiful April woods, continued to be one of hardships. Flowers greeted her eyes everywhere but how could flowers be so heartless as to bloom at such a time? But no, in the strong faith of her day the thought tugged at her heart that "God did all things well." Although she was in the deepest distress, this thought had power to comfort her.

As yet she did not quite understand the situation of the Confederacy; whether war would be prolonged or that the Confederate government would or would not accept the terms of the victors. Giving way to a fierce burst of passion at the thought of the South's surrendering, she sometimes cried out to her sister Maggie, "I would die a thousand deaths before I would give up." She was now facing many difficulties, some in which her fevered mind was filled with the most tragic apprehensions. A weaker spirit would have collapsed, overcome by the horror and dangers of her situation. Daily they met rabble hordes of the enemy, who saw them only as lonely women and accosted them with lascivious glances. In Washington, she tarried only for a day determined now to go in the direction of Florida, and moving sometimes against Mr. Harrison's advice. When not influenced by her husband, she usually decided issues for herself. This keeping his children out of his way in certain crises had been his policy heretofore, and now she, too, felt that his family would only attract attention to him and make his escape more difficult. Still she sometimes reproached herself for not waiting for him to join her. How bitterly disappointed he must have been on not finding her at Abbeville. But no, it was best for him not to be encumbered with his family in eluding his enemies. Every one too along the route to whom she became known urged her not to join him, but to let him travel alone and as quietly and speedily as possible.

The ground was hard and cold for her those April nights, and the fear that bands of marauders would steal upon the camp and surprise them constantly harassed her. In all her gloom and perturbation an unexpected happiness awaited her. In the Georgia country she met General Robert Toombs, who finding to his distress and dismay that the wife of the President of the Confederacy was making her escape through the Federal armies, forgetting all personal differences and expressing the warmest admiration of her husband, immediately offered her every protection. This affected her so deeply that she burst into tears, which would indicate, the psychoanalyst would say, that in her flight she had often felt the sting of neglect. How much she and Jefferson Davis both suffered from it during the waning days of the Confederacy was their own well-kept secret. It is well known to all that they turned calm and smiling, and, the writer came near saying inscrutable, faces to the world in after years.

The human mind, like the wind, bloweth where it listeth. There in the dark woods in an army tent on the lonely roadside infested with every conceivable danger, as realistic as all things were, did Varina in some vague way feel that she was linked with remote and unfamiliar things that still held lines of association with the present. It was at Caerleon, King Arthur's own land in the far-off county of Monmouth, England, before they went into Wales, that history says her race began. Did she at times wonder what they were like in those days? Had there always been warriors among them? Had there always been clans and great battles to prove that liberty was not dead? What seed had been scattered in America to keep the great world tourneys in lance for right? Varina had not made Jefferson Davis a leader but there was that in her blood which helped him to be one. There was much of the spirit that brooded over Caerleon in old Richard Howell of New Jersey.

More probably there was nothing of this in her mind, but had there been, her restless children, *enfants terribles,* she had sometimes playfully called them, drew her mind back to the tent, the hard cot and the wet ground. They tossed, kicked each other and had to be covered up many times through the night. Sometimes, she said, she could hear her sister Maggie sobbing. Was she, too, thinking of those bloody revolutions of other days, where people had been overtaken in flight and hideously murdered? If they could get out of the country, a gallant ship, it was whispered, awaited them on the coast of Florida.[1] If they could only reach it! But no, if he should gather his army beyond the Mississippi she would be with him.

Varina slept little on her journey. With the warm bodies of her children pressed against hers and the infant held to her burning heart, she was at times conscious only of her misery. Writing of it in after years in the one chilling

[1] "Memoir," vol. II.

sentence, "more dead than alive," she conveys all that she must have endured in the horrible experience.[1] But with all her fears and misgivings she still possessed an intelligent sense of her situation. She had little physical fear. The woman who struck Pollard as being masterful and brawny was at times stamped all over her. They would in all probability capture herself and family and all with them in keeping with the usages of war; but she felt that it was not herself, nor her children they wanted, but Jefferson Davis, the President of the fallen Confederacy, the object of their deepest venom and wrath. In her distress she had turned over in her excited mind every circumstance that might be attached to his probable capture, but not for an instant did she desire that he should seek any favor at the hands of his foes. They were surrendering all around her and in some instances expatiating, in a language that caused her lips to curl in scorn, upon the kind treatment they were receiving from the enemy by their diplomacy. As terrible as was his predicament, she had no desire that he should pursue any course but that in keeping with his convictions.

Not hearing anything after the third night of their journey, the little party prepared for another day's hard travel. Where to, Varina hardly knew, but out of the region occupied by the Federals. On the Georgia roads they found Confederate soldiers returning to their homes, half-shod, dirty, lousy men, their clothes stinking with the wear of many days, but with tears in their eyes over the thought of failure. Varina could not restrain her grief whenever she met them. All along her desperate flight she picked up the ragged stragglers of the disbanded Confederate armies making their way into the deep South. At her urgent request

[1] "Memoir," vol. II, and in many conversations with friends in after life.

the most feeble and broken rode in the wagons. Sometimes they would carry the baby for her.[1] The sight of their maimed limbs filled her with anguish. With her own hands she treated their wounds and sores along the road. Defeat was stamped upon their faces, but in all this story of victory and black disaster they had their place.

But not all the Confederates straggling home after the surrender of the armies were as Varina would have liked them to be. A spirit of rowdy lawlessness was noticeable among the lower element. In many instances organized bands of Confederate gangsters sought not only food but loot of any kind. Varina's little party was on one occasion overtaken by one of these bands who took them for a part of the quartermaster's outfit in charge of the treasure train. They had come, they said, "to have a divide." [1] On another occasion she says, when they had halted for the night, a party came up to the campfire. The commander of it recognized her. She had dressed his wounded arm in Richmond. After expressing shame and regret, he gave the little party safe conduct to pass by another party which they soon met at the crossroads. Touched by their rags and hunger she offered them her few groceries, but even had this been money, she says, they assured her that they would not have taken it from her.[2]

As they traveled on, strange appearances in the road attracted their attention. Branches of broken trees, as if signs had been placed there with a motive, marked the roadside. It gave Burton Harrison and Colonel Johnston great uneasiness. They informed Varina that they believed they were being followed by some enemy. "At last, after a long day's journey, we halted," she says, "about sundown, and

[1] "Memoir," vol. II.   [2] *Ibid.*

my coachman went into town for some milk. A party of men took the mule that he was riding and told him that they would have all the mules and horses that night. Our dread was great of being left helpless in the woods without transportation." Upon hearing this, she says, that the gentlemen parked the wagons and tied the horses and mules inside. They divided into two watches so as to meet the robbers before they could make an assault.

Little did Varina, or any of the party with her, think that Jefferson Davis was on the same road with them. But rumors of her danger had reached him and he was now determined to satisfy himself as to her safety. Only a few of the government officials, at his own request, continued with him. Jefferson Davis had no desire to include any one in his ill fortune and had spurned any provisions for his safety at the final surrender. At Varina's hysterical request in her correspondence with him, he had reduced his escort and rode with only a few companions. Others also along the road had counseled him to do so. Out from Washington, Georgia, he came up with the commissary and quartermaster's train, having in charge the Confederate archives, and on seeing that they were ignorant woodsmen, he selected four experienced men from his escort and instructed them to convey the valuable papers out of the war region.

As dark as was his own fate, and he knew that the enemy intended him every harm, his mind dwelt anxiously upon the safety of his wife and children. After several days of hard riding he sought news of them along the road. He knew that he was traveling in their direction but people told him different stories. They had seen a lonely woman and several children with a small party camping out in the woods. Others said that she had been seen walking behind the wagons with a year-old baby in her arms. Still others brought him news that they knew exactly where she was, that a band of desperadoes was stealthily pursuing her with the intention of attacking the party for the purpose of robbery. The only ray of hope that flickered in his heavy gloom was that his young Secretary, Burton Harrison, was with his family. If any man would know what to do in a fearful crisis, he would be that man. But the younger man, too, had never surrendered and was liable to capture.

Changing his direction slightly and riding day and night with Secretary Reagan, and two of his personal staff, Jefferson Davis came up with the party about daybreak. The camp had already attracted a number of foraging and pillaging bands hiding in the woods, but of which army they could not say. Varina and her sister Maggie with the children had laid down without removing their clothing. The children slept soundly, for which she was thankful. "*Our* gangsters at least are quiet," she whispered to Maggie with a wan smile as she covered them up. She told friends in after years that neither she nor Maggie slept, but waited with strained ears for morning to break. The faintest sound caused them to spring up. When the moon went down, they had been told, the attack would begin. It was now slipping below the treetops, leaving only shadows behind when the sound of horses' feet was heard. Varina was up and had aroused her sister and the children when some one came to the tent and told her that President Davis and his party were outside. As dangerous as his course was in not making a speedy flight out of the country she was overjoyed. What better plan had miscarried, they knew not, but they were with each other, to face any fate that might overtake them. His presence brought her a sense of security that she had not felt since she left Richmond. Her bitter fate seemed to have lost some of its harsh austerity.

The little party now traveled quietly on for several days. The children were happy and frolicsome, but in little Maggie's eyes could be seen an understanding of all that was taking place. Her small face had a grave, pinched look as she eyed her parents and strove to quiet her noisy young brothers.[1] Jefferson Davis and Varina talked of their future. All they now had left were their children; they would go somewhere and forget the past. It stung her dying vanity that she could no longer speak of him as the President, and it pleased her greatly when others persisted in giving him that title.

Before Johnston surrendered his army, Jefferson Davis had thought of raising an army in the West, in Texas, the land that he had served with such passionate devotion and ardor in young manhood. With this, if the army here would unite with his efforts, he would once more defy the conquerors of the South. But the Confederacy was no more; it had in fact gone down with the occupation of Richmond by Grant's army. It was hard for him to understand that there was no longer any hope of its success. All about him forgot their own pain in the presence of the anguish that wrung his soul at its dissolution. After the final surrender he had determined to find his wife and children. Their safety was now his supreme thought.

As they traveled on the little party grew more composed. Maggie Howell and young Harrison began to talk of their friends in Richmond. He was deeply in love with Constance Cary, and Maggie Howell was his friend and con-

[1] "Memoir," vol. II.

fidante. In the last days of their journey they seemed to have reached a less disorganized region and Jefferson Davis rode ahead, but in the midst of a terrific storm rode back in the night to see if they were safe. If things looked favorable he would leave the following night.

He now felt that he could leave his family under the protection of Burton Harrison, Colonel Johnston and young Jefferson Davis Howell. Only a small band would accompany him. Varina and all in the camp were eager for him to leave the country as soon as possible and to go alone. In after years she bitterly reproached herself for having begged him to use a smaller force. His horse was saddled and hitched in a clump of woods near the camp and all was in readiness for his early start as soon as the moon went down. It was about this time that one of the staff rode up from a neighboring village with the news that there was talk that the camp would be raided at any time. The information determined Jefferson Davis to remain longer with his family, but he kept his horses still saddled and his pistols in the holsters for any emergency. Reduced in strength and more wounded in spirit than he would let them see, he lay down in an effort to rest.

CHAPTER XXXVIII

VARINA could not sleep. The least noise, the twitter of a
bird, or a squirrel leaping from limb to limb in a tree, caught
her ear. A sudden quick firing of guns near the camp
startled her and she sprang up and aroused the others.
Her sister Maggie had the older children with her in a tent
close by. Little Winnie slept upon her mother's cot. Robert, the coachman, had told them that he had heard firing
that day below the camp, but they did not think that it
specially concerned their party; but this last firing could
not be mistaken. It sounded like an attack and both Burton
Harrison and Colonel Johnston believed that it was, and
notified President Davis of the danger. Varina looked
cautiously out of the tent, but could only hear horses' hoofs
approaching through the dark. Against her wish, Jefferson
Davis stepped out thinking, he said, to see and conciliate
the band of raiders and marauders, who he supposed were
searching for food on their return from the disbanded
army. Varina was greatly excited and agitated, but Jefferson Davis must have been unknown to fear, or else
indifferent to his fate. He was aware that reckless Federal
cavalry was scouring the country everywhere with a view
to his capture. The troopers that met his eye through the
half light he knew were not Confederate bands straggling

home but United States cavalry. They were well mounted and their voices were full of rough authority. Stepping back into the tent, he told Varina that Federal troops were attacking the camp. She herself had discovered that a guard was now standing at the door. Affecting great fright at his presence she implored him to ride away.

So completely had her ruse worked that Burton Harrison actually persuaded him to ride a few paces away. She then agreed with her husband that he should go out quietly and began to help him get ready. Threatening voices some few yards away and the knowledge that his horse was tied up on the very path by which the troopers had approached made them both nervous. In the dark tent she helped him throw on a large waterproof coat that they took for his own. Snatching a shawl from around her shoulders she endeavored to cover up as much of his person as possible, recording years afterwards in her "Memoir" that she would have done more if by that means she could have averted the fate that awaited him. She had followed him to watch the direction he took when she was accosted in loud threatening tones by several troopers. These believed that he was still in the tent, and roughly demanded of her to know. Jefferson Davis had started for his horse but was seen by another trooper who ordered him to halt. When he did not, the man began cursing and pointed a carbine at him. Determined if they shot him to die with him, Varina ran forward and threw her arms around him. She had forgotten her children, her helpless young sister and her own danger. His safety was all that she now cared for. Out in the wild night, among angry, cursing men and trampling horses, she remained by his side. There was some comment to the effect that it would have turned out better for them had they acted differently. But they had acted naturally and in keeping with the unexpected circumstance, and had Varina remained cowering within her tent and awaited results, her story would not have been worth telling. Though nervous and believing he might die at their hands at any moment, Jefferson Davis did not show the slightest fear. His capture was no more than he had expected, but he longed to take his captors by the throat as a last gesture of contempt for the government they represented. "God's will be done" he said to his wife as they walked back to the tent.

The morning found Varina undone. "More dead than alive," to use her own speech, she faced the future. Following the capture, the camp was plundered, the trunks burst open and all valuables, they said, "quarreled over, as dogs would at a feast." A faint smile came to her lips when one trooper in his effort to open a trunk touched off a pistol inside that exploded and wounded his hand.

The story of the capture, so often garbled and misstated, flew far and wide. Northern papers carried caricatures of Jefferson Davis disguised in Varina's clothes, hoops and all. But so near was the raincoat he wore like the one that Burton N. Harrison saw him wearing in the rain on his way from Danville, Virginia, that he always contended that the Confederate President wore his own. But Jefferson Davis would not have it so. He had, in the dark, taken Varina's, which was the same size, for his own and expressly states the fact in his autobiography. There was nothing in Jefferson Davis' life that he wanted to hide. The same Northern papers that had carried accounts of what they had termed Abraham Lincoln's cowardly secret journey to Washington, shut up in a box car with a Scot cap pulled down over his face, made an exciting story of Jefferson Davis' capture. In both instances there was little disguise; each had only sought to take some ordinary precaution. But the Lincoln story was abroad in the land and the country must have one about Jefferson Davis to offset it.

The North grew very hilarious over the capture of Jefferson Davis. Newspaper reporters from the large cities swarmed like flies upon the spot. The same of whom W. H. Russell had said that more than half were "the worst liars" he had ever known in all his wanderings through foreign countries. No one could be certain that a thing they wrote was true. But humor was at a low ebb in American life and the best that could be achieved was a story of Lincoln hiding his face and Jefferson Davis his legs to escape death by a probable assassin when the country was engaged in a revolution.

After his capture Jefferson Davis realized the futility of further resistance and calmly conducted all interviews requested by the Federal authorities. In his dire extremity he still knew what to do. He asked that his family, the youngest an infant in arms, should be taken North by a water route. This was granted. He also requested that those of the party who had been paroled might retain their horses. But all persons captured with him were later considered prisoners, and their horses were parceled out among those who had quarreled over them at the time of the capture. Their owners, however, were permitted to ride them at present. Among them was the war horse of General Albert Sidney Johnston, a splendid animal, which his son, Colonel William P. Johnston, who accompanied the party, was riding.

Jefferson Davis and Varina were now prisoners of war and their small party amid cursings and blustering had been ordered to pack up and turn back on the road to Macon, Georgia. The manner of their captors was loutish and disrespectful, but on repeated orders of Colonel Pritchard they had as yet refrained from any threat that suggested violence. Varina exonerates Colonel Pritchard a number of times in her "Memoir," though, she says, he himself could not hide his glee at the capture. That the troopers held Jefferson Davis responsible for the war and all the ills it had brought upon the country was evident, and it is certain that they would have shot him had it not been for higher authorities. These had been cautioned that as recognized belligerents, the two governments, in the eyes of the world, were on an equal footing.

With stoical faces the prisoners maintained a proud silence and quietly obeyed all orders. Varina was no longer hysterical, but her white, drawn face showed what she was suffering. Her children, placed with her sister in another vehicle, were noisy and in tears. Maggie, the eldest, she says, had taken in the situation with almost a woman's comprehension. With her small arms clasped tightly around her father she eyed every gun pointed at him in rowdy, mirthful sport. Their most distinguished captives were placed at the head of the line of march. Burton Harrison, John H. Reagan, young Howell, Colonel Johnston and Governor Lubbock, with the rest of the party, moved behind in a column, and with smothered oaths of indignation, watched every movement of their captors. In this plight they turned back over the road they had traveled the day before. They had not been upon it long when broken contingents of the Federal army joined the party. Occasionally they met a number of ragged, barefooted men who they immediately knew were Confederate soldiers straggling home from Johnston's army. The sight was like a dagger to Jefferson Davis' heart, and Varina wept bitterly as she gazed on their dejected faces. As their party passed a noisy Federal cavalry camp, a brass band in a large wagon drawn by two handsome horses was playing the popular airs near the roadside. These must have known of the capture, since no sooner than the vehicle in which Jefferson Davis sat came abreast with the wagon, the band suddenly began with a loud clatter of cymbals to play "Yankee Doodle." Hooting voices were heard in the camp as the party passed on.

Beyond the camp, with the loud, harsh music sounding in their ears, they rested for a few moments for a hasty luncheon. Varina ate nothing and had not slept but in fitful moments for many nights. But the final blow had yet to come. The Georgia woods were marvelously beautiful with the May bloom everywhere. The grass was like velvet beneath their feet and the blue sky without even a gossamer cloud. Here and there a stately magnolia flaunted an early white bloom and a bird's song reached them from the trees. But Varina saw and heard nothing that the spring time offered her. Jefferson Davis was calm and seemingly stoical, but she could divine much that was passing in his mind. Sitting in a little huddled group, they were startled when a Federal trooper dashed into the camp, waving a paper over his head and shouting in loud tones that it was a Proclamation by the President of the United States offering a reward for the capture of Jefferson Davis and other Confederate leaders charged with participation in the assassination of Abraham Lincoln.

After his announcement, in stiff, curt tones, the bearer handed the paper to Jefferson Davis. His revenge had come at last—Andrew Johnson, his ancient foe, had risen as it were out of the past—the humble tailor who had sat squat upon his legs stitching fine clothes for finer dandies, and Jefferson Davis was one of them. But they did not at the time know that the thing had been concocted by Stanton and Holt. Johnson alone was held responsible for it at the South, as he would be for much else of the evil of his administration. As sensitive as he had been about his humble beginnings, he was without barbarity. Like Lincoln he had been for the time over-powered by the radicals about him. The President of the Confederacy could only see in the terrible injustice the hand of his one-time enemy.

Varina could bear no more. The final blow had been dealt them. She shrank from the cursing, jibing crowd about her. No sooner than the proclamation had been read and explained to the various squads of soldiers guarding them, the rougher element, in spite of Colonel Pritchard's orders, became more boisterous and insolent, using language, she says, of the most vile and abusive nature.[1] These were not altogether to blame for their attitude since they believed what had been circulated among them. In the face of the base accusation Jefferson Davis remained silent. He had begun to take the measure of his enemies at Washington. He now knew with what he had to contend. He suppressed his own feelings to comfort the distressed woman at his side—the woman who had kept close to his side in all that "devil-may-care" throng the night of his capture. As they moved along the road they noticed that the proclamation continued to affect the man-

[1] "Memoir," vol. II. Conversations.

ner of the guard which was hourly increasing. At times it seemed that their curses and threats would lead to mischief. Burton Harrison and Colonel Johnston determined at any cost to protect the two illustrious captives, and kept a watchful eye on all the movements of the soldiers. As they were nearing the town of Macon the guard halted the party, drew up in line on either side of the road and ordered it to pass through. While standing at ease as the vehicle in which Jefferson Davis and Varina were riding passed they hurled epithets and execrations upon them in language that was, she says, unfit for women's ears.[1] Long years afterwards she wrote in her "Memoir" with a lingering feeling of the resentment and bitterness that she had earnestly striven to live down, "The insults they heaped upon us were hard to bear."

At Macon they were carried to the Lanier Hotel. The town was in an uproar. Men and boys, white and black, crowded the streets. The captors, joined by numerous contingents of the Federal army loafing in the place, were in a wild, hilarious mood. At the hotel a strong guard was placed about the entrance. Varina with her husband and children and sister Maggie, guarded by troops, passed to the rooms that had been assigned them. The faces of the people in the hotel were full of sympathy and concern, and tears were in the eyes of many who watched them. Though closely guarded they were given comfortable quarters. This on the part of the Federals might have been an accident as it came about through a Northern man who had lived in the South for many months. Any manifestation of kindness or sympathy affected Varina deeply. The sight of a bunch of Georgia roses placed with the dinner served

[1] "Memoir," vol. II.

to them in their room brought tears to her eyes. "I put 'em there," said the negro waiter, with a tear glistening in his own eyes. "I could not bear for you not to have some flowers with your dinner." Aside from the thoughtful kindness that had made her weep, Varina had a perfect sense of conservation. Her trunks were always full of mementos and other tokens. The roses were pressed between the lids of her Bible among the Psalms, and served in after years for the topic of many conversations. On the negro's part it was a strong racial trait that had been nurtured and brought to flower in his contact with as gently-bred and gracious civilization as has ever been known in the history of mankind.

Throughout their stay in Macon, every device that could be imagined for the humiliation of the distinguished captives was resorted to. Nor is it strange that the common soldier should have displayed that spirit since the Northern newspapers were reeking with such headlines as *"The traitors, Jeff Davis and Bob Lee, should be and would be hung."* Immediately taking their cue from the sentiment higher up, such threats were made by the common soldiery on every side. Hooting and cursing were heard everywhere up and down the streets. Small boys were hailed with such taunts as, "Hey, Johnnie, we've got your President." It was too much for one small freckle-face who shouted back, "And the Devil has got yours." They tell many such stories of the day, for it was an embittered and unreconciled land.

When the party was leaving Macon the various detachments of Federal cavalry dashing about the town gathered and surrounded the hotel where it had been held under a heavy guard. They formed into two lines at the entrance. The citizens, those who would view it at all, made no effort to conceal their indignation. Women behind rose-wreathed doors wept in bitterness of soul. Some clenched their delicate white hands and made a vow never to forget, a vow that they piously kept down to the grave. The Federal soldiers had been told so often that the "blue-blooded Southerners" despised and looked down upon the Northern troops, that these gloated over every opportunity to humiliate their scoffers. Varina was to come in for a principal share of their revenge. "Mrs. Jeff Davis has done this country more harm than forty women," a noisy young officer of Sherman's army exclaimed.[1] She, too, must be kept under military restraint.

As the party came out of the hotel, the troops grew more boisterous and insulting. Varina and her husband with their terrified children and frightened young sister were now ordered to enter battered, disused vehicles, which had been secured on the outskirts of the town and rigged up for the occasion. These were drawn by rawboned horses that could scarcely pull their light burden. The weather-beaten old barouche in which Jefferson Davis and Varina were placed wobbled from side to side; the gaunt horses stumbled with every step. When Burton Harrison, with his face flaming with indignation, stepped forward to ride with his Chief, resolved to follow his fortunes to the end and determined to honor him in the eyes of his tormentors, the gruff guard interfered. A prisoner of war himself, young Harrison was forbidden to ride with the Confederate President. Little in all history or fiction portrays an instance of stronger loyalty and devotion than that expressed for the President of the Confederacy by his faithful secretary. Throughout the war, their souls had been knit to-

[1] Letters.

gether in the struggle for independence. There was a difference of many years in their ages and the feelings that existed between a father and son had grown up between them. Varina in her "Memoir" wrote tenderly of the affection that existed between the two men while numerous others have noted it.

With the great masses of people Jefferson Davis was never unpopular. His name, in spite of his critics and detractors, held a fascination that the name of Abraham Lincoln, with all his gifts of good fellowship, did not inspire. England was swayed by it and France acknowledged it. Seward felt it when he told the war correspondent of the London *Times* what kind of man he would find when he went down to Montgomery, the newly-established Capital of the Confederacy. That the astute Secretary of State also knew of his warmth and power is seen in his irritable remark that "Jefferson Davis had stirred up all this confusion in the South!" At the North the Confederacy was constantly called Jefferson Davis' Dominions.

But the Fates had been too malignant for Jefferson Davis. At last they had foiled him. His face was ashen-gray, pallid as the faded Confederate suit he had worn so long that it bagged about his thin body, as he sat erect within easy touch of his captors. His deep concern was now for his wife and children. While his delay in leaving the country before his capture might make it seem that he was somewhat indifferent to his fate, it would be unreasonable to think that he did not wish to live for his wife and children.

Amid cursings and revilings and between armed cavalry they moved towards the station. The threats at times grew so violent after the party entered the car that Burton Harrison drew up his small force of a half a dozen, ordered the car doors closed and notified the guard that if a man boarded that train, he would do it at the loss of his life. "Of the horrors and sufferings of that journey," Varina wrote in after years, "it is difficult to speak."

CHAPTER XXXIX

JEFFERSON DAVIS and the entire party captured with him, were taken directly from Macon to Augusta, Georgia. The night ride was one of mental anguish and physical discomfort for all. The children, Varina says, slept, but on waking cried. To the party at Macon had been added Vice-President Alexander H. Stephens, Senator Clement C. Clay and General Wheeler, all under arrest, and in addition to their mental distress, sick. Jefferson Davis was suffering with neuralgia that affected his eyes and also had fever. He was exhausted and in need of sleep. Throughout the entire journey, neither Alexander H. Stephens nor Clement C. Clay was well.

At Augusta, the prisoners, haggard and worn, were transferred to a light craft to be taken to Savannah. Here was discomfort more pronounced. There were no chairs nor seats of any kind for the exhausted passengers and they were compelled to sit about on their baggage. Jefferson Davis, they said, was nervous and restless and walked about a great deal. The scenery along the river, more beautiful for its spring bloom, attracted his attention. At times it seemed to soothe him with a peace as of the laying on of hands. He pointed it out to them several times on the route. Though not a Pantheist in the strict sense of the term, he was still a worshiper of nature, although roses for him had ceased to bloom and there was nothing left but the "innumerable thorns" to pierce his hands. It hurt them to note how old and broken he looked. They did not mistake. Only the invincible spirit reduced to a single glittering spark remained. But there was still that about him that compelled the eye. Of her family, Varina alone remained well enough to give aid to the others. Her sister Maggie continued sick and the children fretted and cried constantly. Mrs. Clay, who was with her husband, was sympathetic and helpful. During much of the journey Jefferson Davis continued to suffer intense pain. "He never used drugs," Varina wrote, "and cologne water had little effect." As she held his head against her breast, her heart ached. She could never forget that the last days of her flight, though pursued by his enemies, he had ridden back to her camp through the stormiest night she had ever known to satisfy himself of her safety. He could have ridden out of the country as she had implored him to do; could have hurriedly made his way to the Mississippi, or else made a dash for the Florida coast where a ship awaited him. Others had escaped.

On the 15th of May the Confederate prisoners were removed from Savannah and put on the *Clyde,* a large ocean steamer. They were shortly borne out into the Atlantic with the guns of the *Tuscarora,* an escorting man-of-war, turned upon them day and night. The battle-axes and every means of defense had been removed from the *Clyde.* The spirit, if not the armored hulks, of the *Stonewall* and the *Shenandoah* pervaded the now placid waters. Varina saw a heavy shiver pass over her husband's thin frame. She knew that he was recalling other scenes. The *Tuscarora* kept a watchful eye on the prison ship. Tugs from Port Royal

and other ports at times came out filled with jeering Federal
soldiers and some women. It was a great day for Grant
and Sherman. Besides their victories, both were thankful
that the war was over. The prisoners passed Fort Calhoun.
By its name, if there were no other record, one would
have known that Jefferson Davis had it built while he was
the country's war minister. His keen glances took it in and
in the thin arms clasped to his sides as he walked about the
deck, there seemed yet to be a mighty blow that he longed to
deal his adversaries. On May 20th the *Clyde* anchored at
Hampton Roads in waters off Fortress Monroe. They then
knew that they would not be taken to Washington as they
had at first thought. They were now almost certain of their
destination.

It was a strange world that opened to their view. The
ships of England and France with many Union vessels and
smaller craft flaunted their banners in friendly wise, but
nowhere on land or sea could be seen the ensign that
wrapped their hearts in its folds. Napoleon was waiting
to come up the James and bear his forty hogsheads of
tobacco home, and M. Mercier could reaffirm to Seward
that the Emperor was no longer interested in Jefferson
Davis' Confederacy. The crafty Secretary of State had
won, but there was a bitter taste in his mouth.

The prison ship, still guarded by the *Fourth Michigan,*
lay in anchor a few days before any further action was
taken. Jefferson Davis' manner, though he was suffering
with fever, was composed, but Varina knew that his
thoughts were painful. Once he took his baby in his arms
and tried to talk to her, but his voice was dry and husky.
The little party hovered closely together, endeavoring to
comfort each other. There had been differences, but none

heeded them in the presence of a great common sorrow. It was still a calm and unafraid band that faced their fate.

On the morning of the 21st, the separation began. Varina and her sister Maggie were the first to suffer the fiery ordeal through which all were to pass. The dreaded fortress in the estuary of the James could be seen in the distance. From the shore a tug was seen approaching and in a few moments their young brother, Jefferson Davis Howell, a paroled midshipman, "taken," she wrote, "without arms and engaged in no act of violence," came to them and whispered a few words. The fine young creature in the first bloom of manhood, she says, advanced with a cheerful countenance, and throwing his arms around them whispered, "They have come for me. Good-by. Don't be uneasy." The separation was bitter for Varina; but she controlled herself to comfort her sister. She had constantly had the younger members of her family with her and often referred to them as her children.

Writing of the scene long afterwards, she recorded of the young brother that his "cheery smile as he went over the vessel's side haunts me yet." After this the tug was sent back and forth to take others in their turn to their destination. First General Wheeler, Governor Lubbock and Colonel William Preston Johnston were sent to Fort Delaware. A few hours later Alexander H. Stephens and John H. Reagan were transferred to the war vessel *Tuscarora* for Fort Warren. The latter was a warm and devoted follower of Jefferson Davis' but the former had not always been his friend. Still, in after years, Varina said that when they took from the ship, under arms, this singularly frail bit of humanity, though mighty in power and intellect, her husband's face grew ashen gray with indignation and her own heart seemed to be bursting with pain. And strange indeed that it was thought necessary to keep under the guns of a monster warship such a handful of delicate, exhausted creatures. It is not believed that Commander Frailey, who had personally known Jefferson Davis and others of the distinguished party, had anything to do with the execution of the orders.

By the 22d, only Jefferson Davis, Senator Clay and young Burton Harrison of the party were left on the *Clyde*. It was an unintentional kindness that Jefferson Davis' young secretary was left with him as long as he was, but it meant much to the unhappy man who now knew that Fortress Monroe was to be his destination. They frequently discussed their situation. Unless assassinated by some unknown party in the first days of the surrender of the Southern armies, he did not believe that they would be summarily dealt with by the government, since the South had been declared a belligerent power by foreign nations and any violence on the part of the Federal government would have outraged the whole world. Holt and Stanton and other Republicans at Washington, knowing that their power was limited, had sought to fix upon him some connection with Lincoln's assassination to excuse the unwarranted methods they pursued.

On the 22d of May, as the reserved climax of the high drama, a tug from the shore came alongside the prison ship with orders for "the transfer of Jefferson Davis," its most distinguished prize. Varina was filled with terror and at first could not control her grief; but at his request and thinking that it would enable him to better bear the separation, she strove to be calm. He spent the brief time counseling with her as to the future. Dreadful as was his own predicament the fate of his fallen Confederacy was still in his thoughts. She was to tell the various agents and authorities of the government for him to use all monies in their possession to pay off the debts of the Confederate states; she should ask Mr. O'Conor of New York City to defend him. A letter, however, was on the way in which he had already volunteered his services. In the separation, Varina with her children followed him to the deck, too wrapped in her sorrow to heed the crowd about her.

Jefferson Davis was not well and was suffering with a fever when he left the ship, but continued to be master of himself. But with all his composure his frame trembled and his face grew deathly pale as he parted with his family. The sight brought tears to the eyes of the sailors as they stood about the deck.[1] A guard who endeavored to soothe Jefferson's cries of distress could not suppress a smile when the little boy cried in a passionate outburst that when he got grown he was going to kill every Yankee in the country. As the boat bore her husband away Varina strained her eyes for a last view of him. In after years, she wrote proudly that "he seemed like a man of another and higher race." When she returned to her cabin she gave herself up to her grief. "The bitter wailing of women and children," one present wrote, "told them everywhere that he had left the ship."[2] Varina shrank from the fate that had become too dark for her. Not even Mrs. Clay, who had been with her constantly, went to disturb her. She herself, a devoted wife, was undergoing a fiery trial of her own as Senator Clay had been taken from the ship at the same time. Young Harrison, too, who had burned his sweetheart's

[1] "Memoir," vol. II. Conversations.
[2] Mrs. Clement Clay.

letters and picture to keep them from falling into the hands
of the soldiers, had been transferred for imprisonment in
the National Capital. The building where he languished
was recently torn down to give place to the Supreme Court
building, but his manly conduct within its walls has been
preserved in a memoir by his lovely and gifted wife.

The women and children were all of the party that now
remained on the ship. The faithful servant, Robert, who
was attached to Varina's maid, continued with them. Their
emancipation as yet had not made the negroes suspicious
of the Southern people and in this particular instance, happy
in each other's affections, they were proud of serving those
they thought superior to the Northerners, notwithstanding their misfortune. This attitude and a natural affection
springing from long association account for much of the
loyalty that many of the negroes exhibited for their owners
throughout the war. Varina had always held the affection
of her servants, and the devotion of the two faithful friends
who remained with her meant much to her in her misfortunes. She was now alone with a very sick sister and four
helpless little children. For the first days of her separation
from her husband, she could not think of anything but his
dark fate. The thought was bitter that kept intruding—
she had grown very sensitive—that there was none to do him
justice but herself. Even some among his own people who
were now seeking the favor of the Federal Government
were censuring him.

But criticism founded upon both fact and falsehood was
rampant everywhere in the restored Union. While some in
the South were condemning Jefferson Davis, many Republicans were regarding Abraham Lincoln's death as fortunate for the country, and were already condemning his views

relative to the future restoration of the Southern States. Seward was lying at the point of death and unable for many weeks to get in touch with President Johnson. About June first, the Cabinet meetings were held in the White House for his benefit. It was a scrawny, pinched-faced little old man who reassumed the duties of Secretary of State, but he was shrewd, egotistical and autocratic as ever. It was always a mystery to Gideon Welles, who never leaves off complaining about it, how he managed to keep his hand upon two presidents; but while the fearful wounds were healing the sick man's brain had been busy with tangled schemes, in the main to fail, to peacefully reunite the country.

In the instance of Lincoln, public leaders were to change their opinion and Varina and Jefferson Davis, in time, were also to have their hearts eased. But now, what others withheld from him, she would give in lavish measure. She sat in her cabin giving vent to her grief. As long as there was action she could think, plan. Now all was chaos. Mrs. Clay could not quite understand why the proud, high-spirited woman she had known in Richmond could no longer hold her head high; could not give word for word with her tormentors. But Varina was crushed. The horror of what had taken place had overwhelmed her. Mrs. Clay wrote that "it was a mistake to ever let her see the newspapers," where threats against Jefferson Davis' life were constantly appearing. Her sister Maggie said to friends in after years that her sister's grief was the most painful thing she had ever witnessed. Mrs. Chesnut, perhaps of all women of that day, comprehended better what this tragic ending must mean to the woman who for four years she had seen by the side of Jefferson Davis; the woman who had so earnestly and heroically helped him to establish the Confederacy through good and evil report.

It would not be the truth of Varina to say that she was calm and composed in the separation from her husband. She had forced herself in some measure to be so when parting with him because he had requested it. She, too, was filled with resentment for the wrongs they had done him. There was no response to any perfunctory kindness on the part of her captors. Varina was no easy adversary. In after years her heart softened, but she was never as bitter towards the North at any period of her life as she was for the next few years. Her sister continued desperately ill. The separation from the young brother had prostrated her, and steadying herself, Varina became both her nurse and physician. She had made an effort to secure a physician from the shore but failed, to find later that none was allowed on board.

She was now subjected to the closest scrutiny by the Federal authorities. Jefferson Davis had been but a little while taken from the ship when a raiding party visited it for the purpose of searching her trunks. Among other things, including her letters and papers, they demanded of her her waterproof coat and a small shoulder shawl, claiming that these had been used to disguise her husband at the time of his capture. It may still be seen in some museum of the country, probably in one in Washington. Everything captured was turned over to Stanton, Secretary of War, and this accounts for his having the correspondence between Jefferson Davis and Varina among his personal papers. The boy, "Jim Limber," already referred to in earlier chapters, was with the party when Jefferson Davis was captured and he too was sent to Washington. Stanton's statement that the boy was one of Jefferson Davis' slaves and had been brought from Briarfield is untrue. There were no Briarfield negroes among the servants at the mansion.

CHAPTER XL

VARINA was still under military restraint, and with her children, her sister Maggie and Mrs. Clement C. Clay, was returned to Savannah, then held by the Federals. It was a rough journey, and but for the kindness of a young Lieutenant Grant of the 14th Maine, the exhausted women and children could hardly have endured its many hardships. At Savannah, the people met her with the deepest sympathy and anxiety and offered her every assistance, but she was detained at a hotel in which detectives had been placed. No sooner than the names of herself and children became known than they became objects of aversion to the wives of the soldiers who were flocking South to be with their husbands. Besides the numerous petty indignities with which she herself, as the wife of Jefferson Davis, was treated, the daily manner in which her children were taunted kept her nervous and alarmed. Finding that it was dangerous for them to play upon the street, she requested the authorities to permit her to go into Canada with her family, but was curtly informed that if she were permitted to leave the country at all, it would be with the edict that she would never be allowed to reenter the United States.

It was at this time that she read the story, carried in the newspapers everywhere, of the fettering of Jefferson Davis in his cell at Fortress Monroe. It was a horrible story,

454

written in a coarse, unfeeling vein. Varina was shocked and her grief kept her in her room for days. She had begun already to make vague plans in behalf of her husband's release, and the inhuman deed increased her efforts to arouse the people, both in the South and the North, to a sense of the injustice that he suffered. The rigorous treatment, that was in a sense actual torture, to which he was subjected during the first part of his imprisonment under the direction of General N. A. Miles, will always find condemnation in the North as the assassination of Lincoln does today in the South. It is not set down here in malice, but as something of a "touchy" reply to the brilliant Stephen Vincent Benet's execration of Henry Wirz,[1] that many people of the South would have at the time rejoiced at the sight of the blatant and brutal young jailer of Fortress Monroe "hanging high and dry." However, it is very meet and well that our volcanos have burned out.

That Jefferson Davis conducted himself in the most manly and heroic manner in all the physical and mental torture through which he passed at this dreadful crisis in his life, is too well established to need averment here. Despite the many unworthy efforts to rob his figure of its greatness, if somewhat gloomy because of its tragic setting, it continues in heroic size. Any derision of it by historians stands in a pitiable contrast with the impartial writings of Macaulay and Carlyle relating to the great historical figures who helped to make the story of the British Isles.

Varina now had her task clearly set before her, and at no period of her life does she appear more convincing than during her efforts in behalf of her husband's release from imprisonment. A number of her letters are given here as

[1] "John Brown's Body," by Stephen Vincent Benet.

they acquaint the reader, better than any biographer could
do, with her finesse, spirited manner and strength of purpose; her humor, too, becomes more tart.   While she
herself was a prisoner at Savannah, Georgia, she managed
to pass them through the inspectors.   The following letter,
dated July 14, 1865, was written to George Shea, of New
York City, who had offered Mr. O'Conor his services in
defense of Jefferson Davis.

"My dear Sir,
   "Your kind letter of the 3d inst. was duly received, but
must have met with a good deal of detention upon the road,
perhaps in the 'circumlocution office,' for a copy of Mr.
O'Conor's letter to me, which you enclosed, and which he
had dispatched through a channel which I suggested to him,
reached me some days earlier. I forwarded Mrs. Clay's
letter to her immediately; I am sure it will be very welcome.
   "Please believe I feel a deeper gratitude than language is
granted me to express for your disinterested desire to serve
Mr. Davis.

<blockquote>
'The poor make no new friends,
But oh they love the better far
The few their Father sends.'
</blockquote>

Measure my thanks by my forlorn condition and helpless
womanhood.
   "I perceive that you concur with Mr. O'Conor in the
belief that Mr. Davis may not have a trial at all, but eventually may be pardoned, or transported, or something, perhaps a long imprisonment.   The prospect is not inviting.   I
inferred from Judge Bingham's reiteration of the charge

---

[1] Letter from Mrs. Jefferson Davis to George Shea, copied from the
original, in the Confederate Museum, Richmond, Virginia.

that Mr. Davis was accessory to Mr. Lincoln's assassination, made in closing his argument against the prisoner before the what is it? that the government would certainly proceed to indictment, and trial for the crime. Perhaps it is proposed to pardon him this punitive crime because the real assassin *slain before a confession of his accomplices could be made,* did not kill Mr. Lincoln's alternate. I have little patience with the false accusers, or their hollow pretences of magnanimity. If he is saved from an inquisitorial tribunal, it is only because the people would not have submitted to such a violation of the dearest right of a freeman. The manacles showed the animus of the government. Again, if Mr. Davis is tried for treason, and should happen to prove by that obsolete instrument the Constitution, that the federal government could not coerce a state, because all the powers not ceded to the federal government in the Constitution were reserved to the States, Mr. Johnson would find it awkward to pardon him for (if you choose to so characterise our secession) an inexpedient assertion of an undeniable right. For the rest—he has not even $20,000 left now, and has stolen the property of no person living or dead, nor yet of any fat corporation, consequently he is utterly contemptible, and beneath a pardon. How long oh Lord, how long! Falsely accused of every baseness and inhumanity which could disgrace mankind without a shade of proof, a brave soldier, a devoted patriot, and honest gentleman lies in prison awaiting the next veer in popular opinion. In that helpless condition he has been insulted by a personal enemy who is now by accident 'dressed in a little brief authority.' Col. Pritchard's report of Mr. Chase's answer to his question, 'What will be done with Mr. Davis,' was 'I do not know, it remains to be seen what the feelings

of the people will indicate.' Not whether he was guilty
but how the people would decide to dispose of him. I was
gravely asked if I thought I could find counsel for
him! I do not think the Administration know any more
than you do what they are going to decide upon. They
are mousing among the Archives of our government
for something upon which to support accusations, and it
depends upon their success whether Mr. Davis is done to
death by ill treatment, a 'military court,' or a public trial—
And combining business with pleasure, Quidnuncs are pol-
luting with their unhallowed gaze the precious records of
my few happy hours, and turning an honest penny by selling
garbled extracts from my husband's letters, and mine to
those papers whose readers needing a gentle excitement, are
willing to pay for 'readable matter.'

"Mr. Stanton's assertion that he knew of no ill treatment
is disgusting. What is his standard of decency? Mr. Davis
was taken from his family, every male protector having
been previously withdrawn from them, and sent to different
prisons; he was not advised that his was a final separation,
put upon a tugboat with a high fever upon him, and placed
in a casemented cell, though he had been forced while Sec.
of War to remove strong men from those very casemates
because they died of diseases superinduced by the dampness.
He was then offered coarse food, such as a healthy man, in
constant habitual exercise might become hungry enough to
consume, but which a sick man, immured in a dungeon
could not eat. I know this is so because Genl. Miles told
me that he received soldier's rations, and would be allowed
to buy nothing. The destination of his helpless family was
kept a secret from him as from them—and when mental
and physical agony exerted themselves in impatience, he was

manacled like a felon or a madman. The opinion of the world compelled Mr. Johnson and Mr. Stanton to feed his body better, but his mind is given over to their tender mercies. In looking forward to his future, I pray that 'the wicked may cease from troubling,' but I know that if they do not very soon cease 'the weary will be at rest,' and then the strength and glory of my house will have passed away, but 'as thy day is, so shall thy strength be,' watching and praying as one whose only hope is in the God of Justice, and love. I know he doeth all things well, and though he slay us yet will I trust him.

"Ever since Mr. Davis' incarceration I have been detained here. I was brought here against my will, had never been here before, and knew no friend to whom I could turn. Left with no other support than the small sum which the cupidity of the enemy, our captors, had failed to ferret out and steal—I have been forced to spend as much in one month as I could have lived upon in a cheap place for a year or until Mr. Davis' case could be decided. Denied the comfort of telling him how his baby prisoners are, or of sending one word of love to him. When his life was apparently hanging upon a thread the government had not the humanity to send me notice of it, but every agony of his was published accompanied with jeers of the valiant editors, and hawked about the streets in extras. I applied three days ago to go to Augusta to see my family, leaving all my children in Savannah, but was refused permission, because a prisoner within the limits of Savannah. Yet the government does not pay my expenses. I am accused of no wrong, yet am I confined here without redress, as I was conveyed here guarded by men armed with Spencer rifles, and bayonets, and up to the hour of leaving Fortress Monroe, they

guarded my door. If not relieved from this coerced visit to
Savannah I fear I shall bury one of those precious ones
who seem to cumber the ground now that their dear Father
is no longer able to protect them. My infant who came here
rosy and gay is now drooping and suffering from the
whooping-cough contracted here where it is epidemic—All
the children are failing as well as I. Can Mr. Greeley do
nothing for me? Can it be that the name of the unarmed
helpless sufferer in Fortress Monroe is 'worth a thousand
men'? Is it sought to prevent me from communicating with
the outer world lest the plea for justice may not be over-
powered by the cry of 'crucify him'? For our down-trodden
people I crave the 'amnesty' whatever that may be, it is
Protean and I cannot define it, unless it is their Adamic
legacy confirmed to them by President Johnson—permission
to breathe God's air, and to gain their bread by the sweat
of their brows.

"But as for me, and for mine, we crave no amnesty. We
have been robbed of everything except our memories—
God has kept them green. Friends, brothers, husband,
home, strength, hope, even the graves of my dead children
do not belong to me. There is no bond uniting us to the
Northerners—a great gulf of blood rolls between and my
spirit shrinks appalled from attempting to cross it. I am
strong to suffer, but quite unable to offer friendship, or
receive amnesty at the hands of the Federal 'many headed
monster thing' which has usurped the place of our grand old
compact. If we get justice I desire no favors. Mr. Johnson may pardon us as like the Revd. Mr. Chadband whether
we wish it or not, but he will never be asked.

"Byron somewhere describes my sensations as I look at
the swarms of armed negroes and Yankees who are stand-

ing like 'the abomination of desolation' where they 'ought not'—I quote from memory, and perhaps do not quote aright—'It is as though the dead could feel, the icy worm around him steal, without power to scare away, the cold consumers of the clay'—If I am bitter against your people, it is because not only my men have been slain in battle, but one of my women kin has been deliberately murdered. However enough of this, I am unhinged by sorrow, and forget you have not lived in an invaded country, and that consequently your ire has not been lighted at the funeral pyre of friends, and homes lost forever.

"Living in the closest friendship with Mr. Davis, I am cognizant of a great deal relating to his official conduct, and where I cannot speak from personal knowledge, could tell you in most instances where to apply to those who participated in his action. I have also a very valuable record in his letter book, but it is impossible for me to trust that in the Federal reach as it is now the only record which he has left of his official life—Files of the Richmond papers will best show the falsity of the accusations of cruelty to prisoners—for they contain one unbroken tirade against him for not consenting to emulate the Federal government in such atrocity.

"Please if you write direct your letters on the first envelope to Carrie Belle, on the next to W. F. Sergeant of this place, and I will certainly receive them speedily, and intact.

"If so illustrious a combination of talent, energy and good will as yours with Mr. O'Conor's fail to extricate Mr. Davis, vain is the help of man.

"Confident of your whole power being exerted in the case, satisfied if justice can flow from a rock, that your rod will open the way, grateful beyond expression for your manly outspoken sympathy, pray consider me in any event,

"Yours gratefully and sincerely,

"VARINA DAVIS.

"P.S. The only injunction of secrecy which I intended to impose upon that kind and fair-minded old gentleman, Mr. Greeley, was that the newspaper people about his office should not see my letter, and cause me to be further persecuted by the powers that be."

The following letter, marked *private and personal,* and dated June 22nd, 1865, was addressed to Horace Greeley, editor of the *Tribune.*[1]

"Hon Horace Greeley.

"*Sir*—Not that you may blush for your people, but only to give you an idea of how I am tormented in my imprisonment here, I send you an article clipped out of the Savannah *Republican*—one of the many which have been published for my benefit daily, about the man of all others I most reverence. How can the honest men and gentlemen of your country stand idly by to see a gentleman maligned, insulted, tortured and denied the right of trial by the usual forms of law. Is his cause so strong that he must be done to death by starvation, confined air, and manacles? With all the archives of our government in the hands of your government, do they despair of proving him a rogue, falsifier, assassin and traitor—that they must in addition guard him like a wild beast, and chain him for fear his unarmed hands will in a casemated cell subvert the government. Shame, shame—he is not held for the ends of Justice but for those

[1] Copied from a letter written to Horace Greeley by Mrs. Jefferson Davis, in the Confederate Museum, Richmond, Virginia.

of torture. There is not a man I will venture to say among the better class of your people who in his heart believes Mr. Davis guilty of the crimes so falsely imputed to him. Is no one among you bold enough to defend him? Will no one of influence stand forth and demand where the money is with which he was found running off to a foreign country. Where the elaborate disguise in which he was arrayed? What benefit he expected to accrue to him from the assassination of a kindly man about whom he knew nothing, and the substitution of a bitter enemy in his place? where are the commissions which authorize the hotel burnings—the St. Albans raid—and all the other 'villanies' of which he is accused? Is reiteration to be substituted for the truth? What counsel has he been allowed to see; is it intended to precipitate his counsel unprepared upon a mass of undigested matter thoroughly sifted and *expurgated* of all vindicatory matter, by the prosecuting counsel? Even now I see extracts of his letters to me in the papers; letters which were never written—and which they profess to have taken from me at Fortress Monroe—I will tell what they did take. My husband under circumstances of brutality, my friends and protectors, servants, money, clothing and liberty—last not least my good name and that of my family. When I reached Savannah my children had to be clothed by contributions from our poor dear impoverished people, until I could have some clothing made for them. In the new lexicon a free Confederate woman 'under no restraint' means a woman confined to a town in which she never set foot before, free to pay the heavy expenses of a large family at an expensive hotel. Magnanimity means refusal to prosecute an honorable man upon untenable and villainous charges, but to pardon him as guilty, and so on to the bitter end.

"Now I have important documents which I could cite if necessary. I have not got them with me but I could produce them if needs be. I have also important evidence which I could give if summoned—*I demand to be summoned upon Mr. Davis' trial,* if the means used to slay him do not succeed before that time. I know you can feel for the sorrows of the oppressed. Will you ask why I alone am denied the privilege of sending a word of affectionate greeting to my husband—why he is debarred from the fresh air which is accorded Mr. Stephens upon the plea of delicate health? Is it because Mr. Davis *believed* in the cause he advocated; is it because he served for love the country of his birth instead of holding office in it for expediency's sake?

"Will you take pity upon a helpless distracted woman and find out how Mr. Davis is for me, and put the exact state of his case in your paper; so that I may see it? The commander of this post Genl. Biege has done what he could to relieve my mind, but can find out little—If he is on a monitor where is his cell? Is his food such as will support the life of a man of such delicate constitution? How is he? Let me implore you to cry aloud for justice for him, with that I shall be content. With the hope that you will not show this letter but feel for me and aid me I am

"Very respectfully yours,

"VARINA DAVIS."

After writing her famous letter, Varina sadly awaited some development that might arise from it. She knew not what, but she was a creature of hope, which is always strong in those whose energies of mind and body are keen and active. Fearing that her children's natures might be injured, that they might even suffer bodily harm in their contact with the rowdy element—both Federal and Confederate—that met in daily conflict upon the streets of Augusta, she had sent them with her sister into Canada to join her mother. Though not permitted herself to leave Georgia, she received permission to remove to a country place near Augusta. She wanted to be where she and the baby Winnie could have the advantage of fresh air and be under less restraint. Her letters to her friends reveal a highly nervous state of mind, extracts of which are given, not only to show the trend of events but the more voluble, even light and frivolous style in which she indulged when writing to her own sex. Her wit and humor drop into a nonsensical vein at times, but her letters still contain shrewd observations about people and books. Here and there they contain bitter and hopeless paragraphs indicating deep distress and anxiety. To a large extent she withheld her troubles from others. It was a frequent remark with her that, "One had no right to burden others with tales of one's own woes." Though she made herself believe that she was benefited by her country seclusion, her letters show a craving for news and contact with the outside world. "Write me—write me everything. Drag your nets and let me have the news, even gossip, but mind you, no scandal," one often finds in various phrasings throughout her correspondence with her women friends.

From Mill View, near Augusta, on August 18th, 1865, she wrote,

"My dearest Martha.[1]

"I was most affectionately received by Mr. Schley, and

[1] Mrs. Phillips of Savannah.

have been most kindly urged to remain to 'try persuasion'
upon the authorities. I have never been to town, nor do I
intend to go, so that I *risk nothing* by staying here—but I
am starved for a little chat with you. How is it that I do
not hear something? Are you 'sick or sad, dull or mad,
light, tight or airy'—or have you become in the ever elegant and momorable diction of the beloved Barnes 'a case'?
'Who fights, who flees'? Certainly my own brave Martha
has stood her ground; so we may regale ourselves with those
who do not. I hear the officers here are exceedingly cut because the women will not associate with them. I fear they
are very pronounced here too in the expression of this
aversion—and a very indignant officer a day or two since
who had occasion to berate some ladies who with their
Father had gone to take the oath, said that there was no
knowing how badly the little girl of fifteen who demurred
at taking the oath, might grow up, and how much injury
she might do,—'Just look at Mrs. Jeff Davis,—she has injured the United States government more than forty
women.' "

To the same friend she wrote a few weeks later: "Do
people's thanks bore you, dear good friend? They do me;
when I am sure they are the overflowings of true feeling I
would rather have them understood, than expressed. But
how with the town, and river between, can I make you understand how I thank you for your kindness—unless I tell
you. I quite choked when I came to that part of your letter
when you spoke of pawning your watch for 'Jeff's release.' [1]
Is the irrepressible conflict worse than an irrepressible family? If they go on assisting me in my weary pilgrimage like
Milbrook's page I shall cry out:

[1] Young Jefferson Davis Howell confined in Fort Warren.

" 'Now by the Lord Harry I shall have nothing to carry.' [1]
Do be explicit." . . . [Her letter at this place grows vague
but seems to have something to do with paying out money.]
"It is hard to spare it, but I cannot consent to be a
heritage of woe to the Savannah people—The Yankees are
perfect Sangrado's, they get us into hot water and then
bleed for a cure—and like Gil Blas I am afraid of the
practice. . . . Do read the 'Pilgrim's Progress'—it is both
honorable and remunerative—This is not a letter but a
fantasie—a pot pourri—So don't expect Wittilesly's universal dovetailedness throughout its parts. Don't ask me
to stop your 'portable engine' Crane—I like him for having
the modern improvements handy—Somebody ought to cry
if perchance I might cool my burning tearless eyes with their
tears. I have cried, through much 'divine despair' and
oh how I realize every hour that 'the tender grace of a day
that is dead can never come back to me.'—

"Now my dear do you wish to know what ails me tonight? Why I am wellnigh worn out with the heartsick-
ness of hope deferred, and if I could see you I should cry
myself quiet again—I do so long for the touch of his vanished hand, . . . Don't let us read any more except every
day books—Miss Braddon's, or Miss Somebody's who does
not feel down deep for the fine fibers."

In a later letter, of which excerpts are given, she tells her
friend of her great happiness in being allowed to correspond with her husband. "Now for your delectation I have
kept the bonne bouche—I have a long letter from my husband—he tells me that I must be reconciled and writes in

---

[1] The various members of Mrs. Davis' family were at this time closely
observed. All they said and did were constantly being reported in the
papers, much to her annoyance.

an angelic strain of pious resignation more delightful to me
than I can tell—he is now allowed to write to me, and I
to him about personal matters without restrictions except
that the Atty Genl reads the letters—he has been removed
to better quarters also—I wish you would turn Christian
so that you might thank God with me."

In answer to an invitation to visit her while at Mill View,
near Augusta, Varina sent the following letter, dated Sept.
9, 1865, to Mrs. Howell Cobb:

"My very dear friend,

"I have been waiting from day to day to find out when
I should obtain leave to quit Georgia, and that point ascer-
tained, to decide and write to you at what time I could be
able to go to see you at your home to which you invite me
in your own sweet affectionate way; but the authorities so
far do not vouchsafe to me an answer and I do not like
to leave here until it is received. I am so racked by anxiety,
so unhappy between hopes and fears. At present released
from imprisonment 'within the city limits of Savannah,' I
am permitted to go at large in the State of Georgia. Think
what a roaring lion is going loose in Georgia seeking whom
she may devour—one old woman, a small baby, and nurse;
the Freedmen's bureau and the military police had better be
doubled lest either the baby or I 'turn again and rend them.'
But I will not talk of these things lest I say more than is
right. Let me tell you rather of the 'leniency,' 'humanity'
or what not which has been evinced towards me. I am
now allowed to correspond with my dear husband under the
supervision of the Atty. General strictly upon family matters, and the permission has relieved me of the dreadful
sense of loneliness and agonizing doubt and weight of re-

sponsibility. I may ask his advice instead of acting upon my own suggestions, and above all I may know from him how he is. I know, dear friend, you will rejoice with me over this change in my unhappy circumstances and pray with me that God may bless me yet more by softening their hearts to let us meet. He writes in such a spirit of pious resignation and trust in God's faith with those who put their dependence upon him that he has comforted me greatly.

"The children who were so large as to remember their father and the Confederacy I was forced to send out of the country. Their sensibilities were so wounded that I felt it could not be well for them to share my durance, and so sent them to Canada with my mother who will put them [in] school there.

"Mr. Schley's family who reside about five miles from Augusta are very kind to me and urge my remaining here a few weeks longer. Then after a short visit to Mrs. Burt (if I can get permission to go to Abbeville) I will return and pay you and Col. Willis of Greensboro each a short visit. I so much desire to see you before I leave the country. I want to see your children and your kind husband once more. Is Mary Anne near you? Mr. Davis says she has changed but little.[1] How queer it seems for your boys to be married,—they seem little to me yet as memory spans the many happy hours of the past. Do give my best love to them.

"I would rewrite this miserable scrawl but then I am anxious to save this mail.

"My dear old friend, may God add all unto you which now seems denied to our poor people, and if it is not his

[1] Jefferson Davis saw the family on his last trip through Georgia. The friendship between the two families was strong and had been strengthened during the vicissitudes of war.

blessed will be assured you will ever have the most affectionate sympathy of your sincere friend."

CHAPTER XLI

AFTER a detention of many months in Georgia by Federal authorities, Varina was finally permitted to go to any place she pleased except Fortress Monroe. With the purpose of securing permission to visit her husband in prison, she decided to first go to Mississippi and Louisiana. She wanted to see the Briarfield place and learn conditions on the plantation. She was destined to find the famous place in the custody of Federal military authorities stationed throughout the state. They also would raise cotton with negro labor. She had partially recovered from the shock of her husband's capture, but contemporaries have said that she was at times greatly depressed, and gave way to her indignation at the injustice he was suffering at the hands of the Republican government. Reverdy Johnson, describing her at this time, says that she was "a tall, rather stout, handsome woman, with great strength of purpose stamped on her face." Though in early middle age when most women are at their best, she had lost much of her freshness and gayety of manner. Her nervous system had been ravaged and touched at vital points and it took months, even years, to restore the damage that had been done. Though she had grown stout again, and claimed in a letter to a friend that it took one full yard to make herself a belt, there was still a gauntness about the face and eyes that comes of severe mental shock and suffering. It is evident that Varina, with all

471

her fortitude and courage, wept a great deal at this period of her life, and it could now be said in all truth that there was a melancholy expression in her eyes. "There was little left," people said, "of the light-hearted woman of other days." She looked old at times and her mouth was often drawn, in a bitter curve.

With the exception of Montgomery, Alabama, she was better known personally in Vicksburg, Natchez and New Orleans than in any of the cities in the deep South. She visited these places before making further plans to join her mother and children in Canada. From Mr. Joseph Davis, now old and infirm, she learned that Briarfield and the Hurricane had been plundered by Grant's army and now were confiscated property. She knew that meant great deprivation for her family in the future. Though greeted everywhere with the warmest expressions of affection and sympathy by her own people, it was a sad and disconsolate woman that one saw, as she went from place to place. The ruin and wreck that met her eyes throughout the country increased her gloom. Unhappy, anxious and at sea, it was inevitable that she would at times offend someone that had been connected with the Confederate government. It was a time when none could move along any course without censure. Both she and her husband suffered much from criticism in the South along with that of the North. Any day the newspapers were liable to carry garbled statements about her husband or herself. These were misleading and at times mischievous. When they related to herself she suffered intensely since she dreaded, she says, for her husband to see any unfavorable criticism of her efforts to secure his release. He was the one person above all others that she would not have think she made mistakes.

Some person sent him a paper in which there was a statement that she, while in Georgia, had written angry and offensive letters to President Johnson. The fact that no such letters could be produced on demand, was proof enough that they had not been written. Johnson himself later added his own denial to the statement. So far she had written but one letter to him and that had been entrusted to Francis P. Blair, an old and valued friend.[1] That Varina had written him fully of her disapproval of the manner in which her husband was being treated may be seen in the style in which she wrote to Horace Greeley and others. Johnson, however, was not versed in letter writing; was at first somewhat self-inflated, and perhaps Varina's incisive sentences that scorched a little even in her letters to Greeley, offended him. On second perusal he found that no offense was offered. However it may have been, Varina was greatly perturbed about the matter. There was a time, when her position had been more secure, that she would have resented at being misrepresented, but too much was now at stake. She was even growing cautious enough in matters relating to her husband to write a friend that "Nothing is more insane than to crush out the sympathy of the North." That she would regain her old spirit of diplomacy is evident. Still she was wounded at the misrepresentation of her efforts, and not even her husband's assurance that he gave no credit whatever to the statement, could quite overcome her mortification.

But she was not to be deterred in her efforts by the gossip floating over the country. A fearlessness began to show in her persistent efforts that finally won her Johnson's admiration. Besides he, himself, now suspicioned that he had

[1] "Memoirs," vol. II.

been led astray by Holt and Stanton. He, too, was opposing with many vetoes the revengeful policy of the Republicans along all lines affecting the South. Welles says that Seward was now attending Cabinet meetings regularly and his influence over the President was daily increasing. But Stanton and other radicals were telling President Johnson that no clemency would be shown Jefferson Davis and the Confederate States. Still Varina persisted.

From Vicksburg she went to Canada by way of New York, to join, she says, "my strong-hearted, old mother and my children." Messages reached her constantly that Jefferson Davis was slowly dying from the restraints and rigors of prison life. Then the news came that he was not expected to live. Varina hesitated no longer and another effort with the President brought her permission to visit her husband. That much was gained by her unremitting efforts. She was now playing her part well despite criticism from those who had not the remotest idea of the difficulties that surrounded every concession that was granted her. The discussions in the Federal Cabinet touching the punishment of Jefferson Davis give an idea of the difficulties she had to contend with. It was a strong woman and one with a single purpose that now confronted the world. To fight inch by inch the tremendous forces arrayed against her until she beat them down, was a task that she had set herself.

It was May 10th, 1866, when she, with little Winnie, reached Fortress Monroe. She found him worn and wasted with an almost unearthly pallor on his thin emaciated face. But with his wife and the child near him and eager for the release that would give him back his freedom, he seemed, for a while, to improve. Each day as he played with the baby Winnie, they talked of his trial and of the many forces that had been set at work in his behalf. And not sometimes, but often, she berated the powers that continued to extend his confinement. Though she now had a strong legal counsel aiding her, she was conscious always of his impaired health and failing strength. Her letters to prominent people reveal her constant, untiring efforts in his behalf. Welles gives a harsh picture of Seward's part in the accusations brought against Jefferson Davis; but he affirms that you could never discover Seward's real purpose in any position he took. The position first taken by him at the time of Jefferson Davis' incarceration when the Republicans were clamoring for his execution was that the whole matter should be deferred. His attitude towards Jefferson Davis appears hostile and vindictive, but it may have been subtle like all that he did. Welles says that while voting that he should be tried for treason he knew that a military court that he contended for had no authority in the matter. He voted with the entire Cabinet for him to be tried for treason and then refused to vote for the court that alone could try him. Though always seeking to outwit the harsh policy of his party, Seward knew that he must not appear so far out of line with it as to lose all control of it. With all the ability and genius for real statesmanship he lacked a certain convincing power and employed scheming to obtain his ends. But his motives were always in the interest of good government. The war had estranged and embittered them and neither Varina nor her husband ever considered him in any of their efforts to secure a trial.

May and June passed without bringing Varina any nearer her goal. From Fortress Monroe, on July 19th, 1866, she wrote to Mr. Reverdy Johnson, a warm friend of her family:

"My dear Mr. Johnson,

"You will acknowledge that I have not been importunate about Mr. Davis' liberties. I have been supinely looking on at his steady decline and hoping against hope, but now even the surgeon here sees that he is rapidly failing. In more than the spiritual sense it can be said that man cannot live by bread alone. Still he has been weakened by disturbed sleep—less disturbed than it formerly was but he is weaker and more nervous—Now his fevers return daily, and he is so patient, so uncomplaining, so entirely quiescent in 'this death in life.' It breaks my heart. Could the President be induced to parole him until his trial? If not will you follow up my letter to him with entreaties that Mr. Davis may be given the entire parole of the Fort to which he may be removed, and that he be removed immediately to some of the Forts in New York Harbor where he can see his counsel. My dear Mr. Johnson I may say to you, who know I am not one who cares to display sacred feelings to effect an object, that when I look upon the husband of my youth, now beatified by such holy resignation, slowly dying away from his little ones to whom I could offer no brighter example, or better guide, that I feel it is a bitter cup, and doubt if my Father wills that we should drink it. I would not trouble the President with another perplexity if Death would wait upon expediency, but I fell assured that a month, perhaps less, delay will be fatal. I came here in health, have been prudent and previously had been exposed to every variety of miasmatic influence, yet for fifteen years I have not suffered a chill until now, and I have had two, and am still confined to my room. How then can a man reduced to a shadow with a predisposition to malarial influences resist them here?

"With a hope founded upon the President's courage and kindness and your efforts assisted by Mr. McCullough I shall wait, not as one who has lost all, until I hear from you.

"Affectionately your friend,

"VARINA DAVIS."

By October, nothing of clemency having been extended, Varina began to fear the unfavorable action of Congress. Again in extremity she wrote from Fortress Monroe, on October 16th, 1866, to Mr. Reverdy Johnson, marking her letter strictly private.

"My dear Friend,

"Mr. Johnson's published correspondence with Mr. Stranbery upon Mr. Davis' case leaves me almost without a hope for our future. It seems to me to mean that he is to be given over to the jury of a Radical Congress and that his life if not terminated in prison will be so by their act. What can be done, can anything? It seems to me that if my husband's friends are to do anything for him now is the accepted time. The circuit court meeting on the third Monday in Nov., the Chief Justice would not be able to try the case before the meeting of the Supreme Court would require his presence. This postpones action upon Mr. Davis' case until next June, when Congress will so legislate as to render his destruction certain. It seems to me that his life hangs upon his being released before the meeting of Congress. Can you not enlist some of the Republicans in his cause. President Johnson asserted to my niece Mrs. Broadhead that it was the wish of Mr. Davis' friends that he should remain as he is. If these friends (?) have so advised, having assisted to jeopardize his life, should they not undo it as far as in their power? Can you not bring influences to bear upon them which will awake them to this fact?

"My dear Mr. Johnson, I am very miserable, scarcely knowing what I write. Do write to me at length. There is no danger in doing so, or better still *do come to see Mr. Davis.* Will you not do this for old friendship's sake?

"As ever sincerely your friend,

"VARINA DAVIS."

CHAPTER XLII

DURING the spring of 1867, Varina found her husband daily growing weaker. He had now been in prison nearly two years and another summer within the damp prison walls, where her own health had failed, she felt would result in his death. One morning when she found that not even the baby Winnie attracted his attention she determined that she would go herself to see the President. He could not refuse to, at least, change the conditions that surrounded the prisoner. General Miles had been removed and what might she not now accomplish for her husband in the way of more freedom if not a speedy trial. His condition urged her to hasty action. The hot weather must not find him within the dark casemate dungeon. With her own hands she had kept it clean, but she could not keep it wholesome. She must act. Congress might force on the sorely beset President some fresh action against the Confederate leader. The tide had not yet turned in his favor.

Varina had not been slow to see that Johnson was now fighting the powers in behalf of the Lincoln-Seward policy towards the Southern States. Though they were beginning to defend Lincoln's war measures, which they had greatly influenced, Republicans deliberately ignored his policy in the restoration of the conquered states. She had to learn further to what shame and degradation that President Johnson was being reduced in his attempts to carry out a policy that had its roots in Seward's old one towards the seceding states.

Her visit to Johnson, while it did not bring her assurance of immediate relief, was such as to give her courage to renew her efforts. On her visit, both General Grant and Francis P. Blair, and others of prominence were courteous and sympathetic. Johnson was touched; was very kind. Varina was frank, but friendly. She had wisely obtained a statement from Dr. George E. Cooper, Surgeon of the United States Army, in which he fully agreed with her as to the precarious condition of her husband's health. Her interview with the President brought about a permission for the prisoner to be allowed the parole of the Fort by day; also that friends might be permitted to visit him. Varina was greatly encouraged. Her efforts were bearing fruit at last. To her great joy, numbers of her husband's friends, men of every rank in the army, civilians, ministers and bishops immediately came to see him. The beloved Minnegerode, Gordon, Hampton, Preston, Mason and other distinguished visitors ate dinner with them in the casemate dungeon. Varina made a brave effort to be cheerful but her heart was heavy as she sat among them. The company sat about on candle boxes and any support that could be had and talked over the days of "their honorable past, of their glorious dead, and less happy, living heroes." They were beaten and their land was a prey of political harpies, but there was something in their faces that could never be taken for defeat. Jefferson Davis was weak and his limbs were mere skeletons but his thin form was still erect and his mien and bearing noble. It was a frequent observation among them that he "always looked like a President." With Varina's help he began to take regular exercise, which she says slightly improved him in both health and spirits.

It was but a short while when General Burton received instructions from authorities at Washington that if he deemed it safe, the prisoner should be given the full parole of the fort. This also carried with it permission for him to remove from the casemate dungeon to better quarters. Four rooms at the end of Carroll Hall were fitted up for the use of the family, and here Varina busied herself in making him comfortable. The baby Winnie was beginning to talk and was a source of delight to him. He played with her constantly. Varina's sister Maggie in time came to her and soon the children were brought to them from Canada. It was a great pleasure to them to have their children with them again. They had been kept for some time in school in Canada and Varina wrote that they had grown taller and had improved. Little Jefferson's manly appearance especially pleased her.

With so much gained, Varina recovered her spirits sufficiently to write long chatty letters to her friends, in the relaxed, spicy, almost volatile style to which she was given, when writing to her own sex. In the same humorous vein she speaks of a young woman who had married an elderly man. "I hear that she does not deprecate her impending crysis—is not that a fearful pun?" She tells her friends in her letters, "The Yankees, both male and female, are very civil to us and indeed some of them are quite pleasant." A reference to a friend living in Washington may strike some as pertinent at the present. "I think Washington develops whatever there is in a woman both of good and evil." And again one finds the pretty little story about the baby Winnie written with such tender motherly pride—

"Our little girl is lovely—she is so bright and good tempered and amuses us all day long with her quaint notions. She has a little story book in which there is an account of David and now she calls herself little David and says, if you do not mind I will put a stone in my flunger and fling at you, meaning the sling."

Although conditions were greatly improved Varina was far from satisfied as matters stood concerning her husband, and continued her efforts in behalf of his release. In more comfortable surroundings he had gained strength, though he continued weak and listless. The four rooms in Carroll Hall had been converted into something of a home, she says, with a home-like atmosphere that was grateful to his feelings after so many dark months of imprisonment. His one great blessing while there, she says, had been the society of his physician, the kindly and humane Dr. Craven who later wrote his prison life. How long he would have lived had this been denied him, one cannot say; but it is certain that he would have not survived his imprisonment. Public opinion, however, was changing. The harsh attitude of Miles that in the past went unrebuked, was now condemned in high places. In New York especially, prominent families like the Vanderbilts were open in condemnation of the Republican policy towards the distinguished prisoner. Still there were enough to object to any clemency for him, to call for swift censure from such men as Horace Greeley. The *Tribune* carried weekly editorials that stirred the public mind to a sense of justice. Jefferson Davis did not read these with more pleasure than Varina.

With many of the ablest public men in the nation enlisted, she now had strong hopes that he would be acquitted and exonerated. Too, in all the clamor that had been kept up for years regarding his imprisonment, there began to be doubts of the legality of the whole matter. The indictment lost merit, and it leaked out that Chase and others did not believe that Jefferson Davis was subject to trial under the provisions of the Constitution. The time was ripe for more action and Varina began to think of his final release. Always shrewd in her judgment about whom to enlist in her husband's behalf, she now applied to J. W. Garrett, President. of the Baltimore and Ohio Railroad. She had discovered that he had great influence with Stanton, Secretary of War, and had won some distinction during the war. She had met him often and he had expressed deep interest in her husband. She would take the risk. Dressing herself in her worn black silk, every fray of which was carefully mended, she set out with the baby Winnie on her mission. It may have been a shrewd whim of hers that the young child would help to arouse sympathy, one cannot say; even good women resort to various expediencies where their hearts are concerned. Anyway she carried her baby constantly with her. The child was very attractive and was noticed by many. It had pleased Jefferson Davis when one of the officers told him that he had seen and played with her when Varina was bringing her to Fortress Monroe.

Varina obtained the coveted interview with J. W. Garrett to win the whole-hearted sympathy of the influential official. But when he went to Washington to consult with Hugh Mc-Culloch, Secretary of the Treasury in Johnson's Cabinet, he found him dubious of the attempt. Who could melt Stanton? Varina had herself talked with McCulloch of the anticipated effort but he had given her little hope that he could do anything with Stanton. She still urged the interview with the implacable Secretary of War. He had boasted that he had removed the magnificent portrait of Jefferson Davis from the walls of his official apartments and so much hate had grown up in his heart for the South that it did seem, as McCulloch intimated, a fool's errand. But with the powerful president of the Baltimore and Ohio the war was over, and it was time he reasoned that the people should begin to have friendly relations with each other. Others even more powerful were of the same opinion. O'Conor and Greeley and numerous strong men had drawn about them influences that reached into the very vitals of the Republican party. Pressed by Varina, Garrett and McCulloch determined to make the effort. They found the Secretary of War sick, himself worn out with all the strife still existing between the two sections. Beset on all sides, in a moment of exhausted will power he threw up his hands and exclaimed that he had no objection to the attorney-general arranging for the release if it could be done. There was Sumner reversing himself and now old "Andy Johnson" considering a pardon. The vindictive Secretary of War was baffled. The *Tribune* continued to expose the whole matter as a piece of maliciousness or else of gross ignorance. Varina had won. On May 4th, 1867, after Jefferson Davis had been held a prisoner without trial for two years, he was released on bail in Richmond, Virginia. His bond was signed by Horace Greeley, Cornelius Vanderbilt and other distinguished Northerners.

If the North thought that the Capital of the Southern Confederacy had for an instant forgot its past, it had yet to learn more about the South. The world might move on what axis it might, but her history was secure. Jefferson Davis, whom his accusers had that very day proclaimed

the very "head and front of the Rebellion," was never more
of a hero during the four years he strove in her behalf
than on the day he walked slowly in and out of the court
room. The city put aside its widow's weeds and burst into
a celebration that had hardly been equalled, even when it
made war. Burton Harrison was there, his fine face
wreathed in smiles, to record the scene for the eyes of all
mankind. Others, too, were to tell how the Virginians announced to the world their love and reverence for the man
who had suffered every pain and indignity for having defended her Constitutional rights.

Varina wrote proudly of it in after days—"A concourse
of people"—"a sea of heads"—"men of every age, rank and
station joining in the great ovation."

But it was not the light-hearted woman they had once
known in Virginia who accompanied her husband to and
from its capital. Still she would give no outward sign of
what the revolution had cost her. There was a time when
she would have keenly regretted the rusty black silk, the
worn kid gloves, the faded hat and limp veil; but her pride
now, though it had been trampled, as it were, under the feet
of men, was stronger and of a finer quality than it had ever
been. Some said that she was prouder and haughtier than
ever. Not even Pollard, before whose thrusts she had paled
so often in the past, could now make her flinch. She was
stripped of all distracting interests. She, who had been a
stickler in the past for all the conceits of public opinion, had
learned to value them at their true worth. But Varina,
though she had learned much, was not through with life.
With the return of happier circumstances, she would still
remember, in certain moods, that the London *Times* had
carried a charming report of her, and that people had called

her "Queen Varina." It might be an old woman's memories, but with an old woman's vanity she would often recall them. At present she asked little of the world. She
had her husband and children, and there seemed nothing
more that she wanted.

From Richmond she went with her husband to Montreal,
Canada, where a reunion of her family took place. "One
by one," she says, "my brothers and sisters joined us, and
our mother rejoiced to have her children with her once
more." Not only these but many throughout the Confederacy had left the South and were scattered in every country
and city of the world. Liverpool and Paris, it is said, had
the largest colonies. However, when passion cooled and the
reconstruction of the Southern States had relaxed, they in
nearly every instance returned. Still, some descendants of
these self-imposed exiles may be found in other countries!
A family has been located in Brazil. It was the same way
with the royalists during the American Revolution, and the
English Cavaliers who followed the fortune of Charles I.
It is the tribute men pay to conviction.

Nothing came of the action against Jefferson Davis by
the United States court, and Varina with her family settled
in Montreal, was hopefully looking forward to the future.
In the autumn, Judge O'Conor and numerous other prominent citizens made a determined and successful effort to
bring his case up for final settlement. During the winter
Jefferson Davis came down from Canada to Richmond,
when the case was disposed of, bringing to an end a base political scheme that had been instituted in conflict with the
Constitution of the United States. Varina later wrote satirically of the matter which at the time had been so painful
to her. "It was a somewhat inglorious sequel to the threats

of the United States Government to make 'treason odious.' His deeds were not done in a corner. He had openly avowed his principles before leaving the United States Senate. If he were the arch conspirator, who inspired and compelled the act of treason, why was he not arrested then and there, before he had accomplished the ruin of the Southern States and cost them and the United States millions of money and thousands of valuable and innocent lives? If, on the contrary, he were unwillingly borne to the position of Chief Executive of eight millions of people of the South, who knew their rights and thought it incumbent upon them to maintain them, why was he, who was one of the last to yield to the dread necessity of strife, held more accountable than those whom he had tried to restrain?"

Varina's thorough sympathy with her husband's political convictions is seen in the following criticism of his persecutors:

"Might prevailed, but could not wrest from us the right of secession, or lawfully punish its assertion." Fond of the use of her Latin, of which a biographer has said that she had a remarkable knowledge, she added, *"Dormitur aliquando jus moritur nunquam."* [1]

[1] "Wives," by Gamaliel Bradford.

CHAPTER XLIII

WANDERERS

VARINA grew restless—"uprooted and floating," she wrote her friends during these years. While they lived in Montreal, her mother, who had been a great comfort to both herself and husband, died in a friend's home in Bennington, Vermont, where she was visiting. Varina left her family in Canada and was with her in her last illness. Her death, she says, deepened their gloom. She was a Virginian by birth, but made no claim to it that one finds. In old age, she grew fanatical upon the subject of religion and was intensely patriotic. Of the goodness and purity of her mother's life, Varina speaks with great tenderness and admiration in her "Memoir." She always referred to her as my "stout hearted old mother" and says in the soft, loose style in which she sometimes wrote, "And with her passed as much of goodness as could die."

On returning to Canada she found Jefferson Davis ill. He continued pale and emaciated. Friends came and went and prominent Confederates who had settled at Niagara and other places visited them. While in Canada, he suffered greatly from a fall he received while carrying little Winnie downstairs in his arms. To save the child, he was compelled to expose his own body to the blow. Again Varina nursed him through a long illness, and of his own patience and fortitude under the trying circumstances, she wrote beautifully. In their misfortunes, they drew close to each other. The world seemed a strange place to them, and the woman was trying to help the man see his way. For a time she seemed to lose confidence in herself. "Long restrictions," she said, "had stiffened and impaired my power. I could not think clearly or act promptly, difficulties seemed mountain high. The trees sheltered, and flowers bloomed for others, I knew they were fair, but they were not for me or mine."

Both Varina and her husband longed for action of some kind. It was too early, she says, for him to think of writing a history of the Confederacy. He tried it, but abandoned the task as one too painful for the present. Placing their children in school at Lenoxville, they began a series of long and tiresome journeys that took them to Havana, hoping somewhere to find a spot that held some prospect for the future. One thing they found to their sorrow—there was no place in the South for them. It would endanger both themselves and the country, which was now a wreck of its former self and in possession of the military authorities of the Federal government. Their names were anathemas to the authorities then in possession of the blighted land. Among the painful sights that met their eyes was their Briarfield home that had been confiscated. That some of their negroes were permitted to still occupy the land, eased their hearts in a measure. But they looked in vain for the roses, the Glory of France that grew by the gate, that had become so famous in history.

Though perplexed and baffled, beneath their frustration was a purpose the strength of which they were not conscious at the time. It was at this period that they determined to go abroad. They were again in Canada, and with their four children sailed from Quebec with a large party of English

friends who were returning home. They were in strait-
ened circumstances, but many gifts of money and boxes of
clothing containing everything they needed for themselves
and the children were constantly sent to them from Virginia and the other states. Varina now had all the new
black silks she could wear. One Virginia woman sent her a
box valued at five hundred dollars. While both she and
her husband shrank from becoming a burden on their
friends and had declined several large gifts that included
houses and tracts of land, they were deeply touched by the
generosity of the people. "Everything I or my children
needed were always provided and everywhere homes
offered us," she wrote in grateful remembrance after the
war.

But they felt that they should do something for themselves and continued restless. Jefferson Davis, she says in
her private letters to friends, longed for some occupation
that would enable him to care for and educate his children.
Their education had begun to greatly concern them. They
could but be aware that they still had much to live for.
Their four children were very attractive and wherever
the family appeared it drew admiration. Both Jefferson
Davis and Varina possessed an air of distinction, which they
had retained, and it has been said that the woman was far
more aware of the fact than the man. She now looked
forward with new hope to a long and peaceful rest from all
the tragic circumstances that had darkened their lives for so
many years. Her high position in the Confederacy had
brought her much happiness and social distinction, but the
flame had soon turned to ashes. She was now to reshape
her life along new lines. There were days on the ship when
she grew resigned and even expectant. Her first thoughts

were of her husband and a tinge of the old pride came back as she noticed that the people around them were deferential and solicitous of his every comfort. His health improved and he began to take interest in the people about him and to enjoy his children. The thought often came to Varina that while she had suffered, it was in a small degree when compared with what he had endured. For his sake, as much as from personal vanity, she threw off her gloom and despondency, wore the handsome dresses that had been sent her and took her place in the charming circles around them. She found it easier than she thought. She had become interested again in life; temperament asserted itself. When the voyage came to an end both had been greatly benefited by it.[1]

To say that she or her husband loved the Government they had left behind, one still with its foot upon the neck of their people, would not be true history. There was now little love in Jefferson Davis' heart for his foes, and certainly none in Varina's at that time. She admitted that on their arrival in Liverpool, when their feet touched English shores, the land did not look strange to them. "Perhaps," she wrote, "atavism of memories was unconsciously felt and the welcoming cheers of the people on the docks gave my husband a comfortable sense of Anglo-Saxon sympathy." It has been said that Varina sometimes arranged for the crowd in Wales and other places to cheer him, some announcement in advance to set off a spark that always burst into a flame on sight of any one connected with heroic exploits. Exactly how she arranged this is not clearly seen; but Varina was full of ingenuity. Anyway the English were lavish in social attention to the distinguished party.

[1] "Memoir," vol. II.

Jefferson Davis was to them a great man, had headed one of the most tremendous revolutions of the age, and by far the haughtiest; its rumblings had been heard on both continents. Whether he had been successful or not did not detract from his prominence in their eyes. There had been several such spirits in their own history.

But the bustle and stir were too much for Jefferson Davis; nor had Varina's nerves recovered from the heavy strain of the past. In Ireland they found at the castle of Lord Lovells the calm and quiet both so much needed. As they moved from place to place they were at times in a hopeful mood. But even here the unfortunate wanderers were pursued. Bitter, vulgar, sharp-tongued women and gruff, raucous-voiced men from the Northern states were traveling everywhere. Poor Varina, who treasured this brief hour of respite from the past, found herself and husband and often her children in hotels and on railways objects of their contemptuous smiles and covert derision. In after years, not all the good will that had grown up in her heart for the reunited country could keep her from indicting witticisms against them. These might be applied to some tourists from the "land of the free" today who are either too self-confident or else not enough so at times, in both instances to appear at a disadvantage. In many of the great houses in England, Scotland and Wales, Jefferson Davis and his family were cordially received and "paid every delicate attention of hospitality." It has been claimed that some of his best writing was lost when the manuscript of his travels was misplaced.

Aside from the illness of their youngest son Willie, who contracted typhoid fever at Waterloo, out from Liverpool, Varina's trip abroad was filled with many pleasant experiences, the recital of which make some of the most charming pages of her "Memoir."

Her children were highstrung and spirited and wherever they stopped Varina insisted that they should have the discipline of the school room. It was while he was at school at Waterloo that young Jefferson met young Teddie Roosevelt, who was visiting a cousin. That there was an altercation of some kind between them is seen in the latter's juvenile diary in which he says that he had "a nice time but met Jeff Davis' son and some sharp words ensued." It should not concern good Americans so much as to which came off best in the encounter as it should as to how both conducted themselves.

It was during her first trip abroad that Varina wrote to Mrs. Howell Cobb on the death of her husband the following letter that has attracted the attention of historians as a deep insight into her nature.

"Waterloo [England], Oct. 22nd, 1868.
"My dear afflicted friend,

"A telegraphic item from the U. S. bears the woful news to us of your deep bereavement, and has filled me with a longing akin to heart sickness to be with you in this greatest grief of your checkered life. May God give you strength and patience to wait for your reunion with the love of your life, your greatest earthly stay. Mr. Davis and I feel deeply our loss in him, and know full well that we have no friend left so judicious and wise in counsel, so brave and strong hearted, so tender and true to his friends. If we cannot become reconciled to his loss, how are we to speak comfort to you, to whose life his was a constant glow of warmth and sunshine? My memory conjures a thousand tender rec-

ollections of him as I write, and I can only pray that you
may be able to say, 'not my will but thine, O Lord, be
done'; and that 'He with is own hand' may wipe the tears
off your face and enable you by faith to see that blissful
reunion which has been promised to those who patiently
watch and pray. If you can only write a few words *do, do*
try to write them to me. If it is a great effort remember
how dearly I love you and how truly I am a fellow mourner
with you and with his children. Tell me of them all and
where they are, where you are, how you are. If you cannot
write to me then pray ask my dear little Mary Anne to do
so. Words do seem so poor when a heart is so full of love
and sorrow as mine, that I will not try to express even a
part of what you know I feel. Our poor country is not the
least one of the sufferers to be pitied when we realize our
great loss. Where will she find so staunch and wise a leader
in her hour of peril. It is a poor consolation, yet it is one
to know that a whole country mourns with you and that
your children will be ever dear to our people for the sake
of their great father. The good he has done truly 'lives
after him.' " She closes her letter with the following tender
farewell. "Dear, dear heart, 'heaviness endureth for a
night, but joy cometh in the morning.' May God give you
hope and peace equal to your faith."

In their wanderings abroad, seeking a cheap place in
which to live and educate their children Varina was at times
greatly depressed. The future was dark and there were
scarcely enough funds left them to eke out a scanty living.
Jefferson Davis, though broken in health, was anxious to see
his children educated. This weighed upon his mind. Al-

though she would not willingly have thrust another care upon him, she still looked to him to extricate her from the difficulties they found themselves in. "I am filled with terror," she wrote a friend, "whenever he leaves me." It would be best, she says, that she should go first. Her depression, however, was to pass with any return of good fortune. The resiliency of her nature was such as would last throughout life.

CHAPTER XLIV

LIFE IN MEMPHIS

AFTER their return from Europe, Jefferson Davis settled with his family in Memphis, Tennessee. He had accepted the presidency of the Carolina Life Insurance Company and had invested all his available means in the company. For a few brief years, the company, which was not strong at the time of his acceptance, struggled along to finally fail in 1874. He then turned his attention to his private affairs. General Lee's death, which had occurred in October of 1870, affected him deeply and in November he went to Virginia to pay honor to his memory. His voice, they said, had its old ring of vindication of the South.

During Varina's life in Memphis there was much at times to tempt her to pick up its broken threads. They were now receiving some aid from his plantation and were living, though in modest style, in comparative ease and surrounded by numerous friends. Jefferson Davis was in better health after his trip abroad and Varina herself had regained something of her old spirit. Old letters describe the family as happy, in a measure, with Varina once more in the enjoyment of home-making for which she had marked talent. Margaret had grown to womanhood and bore a strong resemblance to Varina, with the same good bearing, large dark eyes and smooth comely face. It was while her parents lived in Memphis that she was married to Mr. J. Addison Hayes, a gentleman of culture and position. It was the first event in Varina's life after the war that did not in some way relate to the Confederacy. It gave an entirely new aspect to her life. It is said that she took much delight in the marriage and wore for the occasion a gorgeous white silk. People in the city made a great social occasion of the wedding, and it was an event of special interest throughout the South. New York papers carried a full account of the marriage, and, in fact, though the masses could not at first be sensible of the fact, the war spirit had slowly begun to die out of the hearts of the people. The bitterest hate that arises between people is found in civil strife, but when it does die, it leaves not even a spark. The solidarity again asserts itself, a thing that cannot happen where the people were never one.

It was while Varina lived in Memphis that the death of her second son, William Burr, born in Richmond during the war, occurred. She tells us how the quiet little boy would sit for hours and watch his father at work in his study. This shrouded her again in sorrow. She turned her thought and time to church work, to find in it relief, in a measure, from her grief. It was during her stay in Memphis that she began the famous quilt that became the wonder and admiration of so many of her friends. No mention of it is made in her "Memoir" nor letters, and since this volume contains nothing that does not have a record to sustain it, excerpts from a letter of A. Dudley Mann to her, which gives a history of the quilt, is reproduced. What became of the embroidered silken memento of the Confederacy is a mystery still unsolved. The letter, however, gives one the impression that it might have been purchased by the author. The letter, written in the style common to the day, also gives news of many unreconciled Southerners who took refuge in the French capital to escape the evils of the military rule, then in full sway throughout the South.

"51 Rue de Luxembourg,
"Paris, June 20, 1873.

"My dear Mrs. Davis:—

"Mrs. Allen and her daughter promptly, after their arrival, sent me your letter. I called upon them immediately after its reception and had a delightful interview. They are, indeed, estimable ladies, and I cherish their acquaintance all the more because they are so cordially attached to yourself. They were preceded a fortnight by Mrs. Bayliss whose husband brought me an introduction from the Ex-President who carried me, by an interesting account of each member of your family, into the midst of your dear little circle. Her description was as minute as it was touchingly beautiful. She spoke of the bereavement,—so blighting to your hopes—so crushing to your joys; of its excessive suddenness, its utter unexpectedness; of the rare qualities of heart and head of the darling departed. But pardon me if in the short recital I have inflamed the wound, which I would so gladly heal, from which you have suffered as much as mortal woman can well bear. Accumulated years, with their attendant experience, have made me a philosopher. *Earth's life*—its cares and sorrows, its ever occurring ups-and-downs—has satisfied me that it was designed as a test to our fitness for *Immortality*. If there were nothing else in the character of our Saviour to admire there is enough in his *resignation* to commend the adoration of every virtuous human heart. . . .

"Mrs. Bayliss informed me that Miss Maggie thought somewhat of accompanying her to Europe, but that it was feared her health was scarcely equal to the long travel. I should have hailed her coming with joy and would have been a father to her during her sojourn here however long. I trust that her health will quickly be re-established.—Mrs. B., as also Mrs. Allen, tells me that your son Jefferson has grown up to early manhood and that you have every reason to be proud of him, and that the little darling is wonderfully intelligent, and generally sensible for her age—as full of promise mentally and physically as you could desire.[1]

"The ladies each in their turn and manner have given me a description of a wonderful *Quilt* upon which you are engaged with your own fingers. That in design and execution it is of matchless beauty and rare perfection: And that it is eloquently commemorative of the glorious, overpowered, Southern cause. The conception and the consummation are worthy of your eminent ability. They reflect credit upon your sex and shed luster, in his retirement, upon the noble Chief, whose joys you have shared and whose sorrows you divide.

"This splendid picture, the ladies tell me, is to be disposed of for the benefit of the Church to which you belong. Sacred idea, sainted purpose! But I am not quite satisfied of the propriety of the *Raffle* of *such a gem* in *such a cause*. The subject is too grand—the object too benign—for Dice to determine the destiny as respects future ownership. In this connection I might largely moralize but I will refrain from so doing in view of the laudable end by which you are inspired.

"Were I in affluent, or indeed easy, pecuniary circumstances I would send herewith an order to draw upon me, at sight, for the sum total of all the [word vague] intended

[1] Winnie.

to be sold. I beg you to frankly write me how large an amount is expected to be realized from the *Raffle* (I abominate the word). If it be within the scope of my capacity to compass I will joyously close with the chance. . . . There is not sufficient field for it, with all deference to your adopted home, in Memphis, nor indeed anywhere in the patched up rickety Union. I told a good friend, Mrs. Wood (dear lady, she has been distressfully unwell) all that I had been informed about it, yesterday. She observed: 'I readily believe that there is no exaggeration in the statement. Mrs. Davis is a woman of the most extraordinary genius that I ever knew.'

"I have no intelligence of special interest, as concerns the Parisian world, to communicate to you. It is swarming, beehive-like, with Americans. They come not singly and slowly but swiftly and in battalions. Memphis is most creditably represented.

"The Perkins's have been here since October. For more than three years I have had no intercourse with them, but I hear that they are *extremely* fashionable. Miss Evelyn is among the *distinguished* favorites of the hour—with many offers and, of course, as many crushed hearts at her feet.— Of so classed Southerners the Hitzes are by far the most magnificent display. It is given out to the fashionable ear that they have an income of 125,000 a year from an interest in a Gun Invention! This may or may not be so. I never chose to know him beyond the strictest reserve of formality, for although a peculiar favorite of Mr. Benjamin he was not in the slightest to my liking.

"Mrs. Pendleton, your old acquaintance, has a splendid establishment, and is much taken, *on dit,* with Parisian ways. Her husband and son, having tired out, wended their way homeward. She is well on with the Washburns and easily finds her way into such circles as they penetrate. —Miss Emily Mason is at the head, nominally, of a female institution, of her own creation, which is prospering; and from the profits of which she is laying up a little for her old age,—when it comes.

"You remarked, in the Letter brought me by Mrs. Allen, —'I long to have an old fashioned Letter from you once more.' I will be but too happy if this will gratify the wish, yet I have doubts of such a result. Much love to your beloved husband and to each of your darling children.

"I wrote a few weeks ago to the President.

"Ever affectionately your friend,

"A. DUDLEY MANN." [1]

Soon after Margaret's marriage, Jefferson Davis and Varina again went abroad. They took Winnie with them with the intention of placing her in school in Germany.

The South was still under military rule. Law and order had not yet been restored and it was from this that Varina wished her husband to escape. There was some frustration of purpose for them both during these years. But the travel was diverting and served to give them a new outlook on life. "The hedgerows of old England were pranked out," Varina wrote, "in their May garments of pink and looked very lovely to us after our long absence." Still it had been hard for Jefferson Davis to lead a life of inaction. It was on this trip to Europe that he made several business propositions to foreign companies, thinking he could restore the South to prosperity by a more intimate intercourse with foreign markets. The economic depression, however, was too

---

[1] A. Dudley Mann of Virginia, consul to Liverpool and special agent of the Confederate government.

great in the devastated Confederate States for foreigners to become interested.   But it was intellectual stimulus that Jefferson Davis craved, and a long cherished desire to write the history of the Confederacy again possessed him.

While the South was still in the clutch of military despotism, signs were appearing that presaged an overthrow of the rapacious hordes that vulture-like were feasting upon it.   In this connection it might interest historians to find that Jefferson Davis was the only public man at the close of the war who foresaw the tragic period of reconstruction that awaited the Southern States.   See his letter on page 408, in which he laments "the long night of oppression which will follow the return of our people to the Union."

CHAPTER XLV

DURING their last visit to England Varina's health had not been good and she was unable to take the trip, then a long and trying one, when Jefferson Davis returned to America to collect the material for his history. Leaving her daughter Winnie still at school in Carlsruhe, Germany, Varina joined him the following April on the Mississippi Gulf Coast. He had purchased the Beauvoir place near Biloxi, from Mrs. Sarah A. Dorsey, an intensely patriotic and intellectual woman who a year later died with cancer. On her death it was found that she had willed him the property, upon which he had already made several payments. A number of homes had been offered him by Southern friends, but he had always been averse to accepting gifts from the people. Small gifts, however, poured into the family from many sources and at times even Varina, who had not been as averse to receiving assistance as her husband, felt sensitive about such donations. It is not generally, if at all, known that they owned a tract of uncultivated land on the Mississippi Coast which had been purchased before the war. It seems to have been an investment of Varina's since a letter from her father, William Burr Howell, in 1853, congratulated her upon the purchase of the land, adding that it would in all probability increase in value. It was this tract of land that doubtless led him to think of the Coast as a place for a future home.

When Varina joined her husband, she found him busily collecting data for his history of the Confederacy and eagerly began to assist him in the work. Here at last was a definite purpose; here at last the thorny bush might bear a rose. At many periods in the past she had acted as his amanuensis. The labor on the book while it was exacting renewed their interest in life as nothing else had done. Varina was in a measure happy. For a little while it seemed that life might hold for them the peace and calm they craved and so much needed. But it was not to last. While she was busy assisting him on his history news came to her that her young son Jefferson was dying of yellow fever in Memphis. It was one of Varina's greatest sorrows. She was overcome with grief and determined to go to him, but finally yielded to Jefferson Davis' better judgment. Memphis was in the throes of the epidemic that scourged the South in 1878. Some of the most beautiful letters found in her correspondence were written in connection with her young son's death. The death of her two sons and that of her brother, Jefferson Davis Howell, who lost his life at sea while saving some of the crew in a shipwreck, saddened her life. But she always found relief in action and began feverishly to assist her husband. His society, she says, meant much to her at this time. He had grown more self-contained in his literary labors and Varina found comfort in his calmer outlook.

Jefferson Davis' historical undertaking that resulted in the preparation of "The Rise and Fall of the Confederate Government" in two volumes, did not meet his expectations. The history was welcomed in the South but the North was chary in accepting Southern history relating to the Confederacy. Publishers had even cautioned their agents not to stress Southern matter.[1] However, on account of Jefferson Davis' prominence publishers still sought him and his family.

Soon after the publication of the history Jefferson Davis and Varina again went abroad to bring Winnie home. Varina was now attracting some unfavorable attention in the South for going abroad so often. A letter from Mrs. Clement Clay to Jefferson Davis twits her a little for these frequent trips to Europe while she herself had never had one. But this was Varina's last.

She was now back at Beauvoir. The place had many attractions with its broad expanse of gulf waters and old historic setting. Both the husband and wife toiled eagerly to make the gardens and orchards thrive. It was more like the old Briarfield days than any that they had known for long weary years. There were vines to prune and possibly roses to grow. Jefferson Davis, though much past middle age, was still erect and graceful and his face had lost much of its stern bitterness. He spent long hours in his gardens and vineyards. With the exception of a triumphal tour, beginning at Montgomery, with the Old South again in review, the world and its affairs largely went by. Still the public sought him, perhaps at times more than he cared for.

They tell an amusing little story of Varina, about this time, that the author would like to withhold, but since it is the only instance in which anything of the nature has ever been brought against her, it is hoped that it will not do her any great harm and some may at least smile at the frank sincerity. Jefferson Davis during these years received much

[1] The Belford Company.

attention from the ladies at local fêtes and other celebrations,
and the story runs that in the presentation of a fancy walking cane on one occasion, a rather frisky old lady ignored
Varina's presence completely in her lavish attentions to him.
It is said that Varina slyly poked the cane under a bench
where it was later found, and some declare that it was
actually broken in two pieces.

In the autumn of 1889, Varina and Jefferson Davis were
at the Beauvoir house alone. Winnie, who had been with
them since her return from Europe, was now in Paris with
her friend, Mrs. Pulitzer, wife of Joseph Pulitzer, editor
of the New York *World*. Margaret was living in Colorado
Springs where her husband had removed for his health.
Winnie had gone abroad, at her father's suggestion, after
a breakdown caused, gossip said, by an unhappy termina-
tion of a love affair with Mr. Alfred Wilkinson of
New York City. Some were certain that there had been an
engagement and many romantic stories found their way
into print relative to the circumstance. All Southern
sources reveal a pathetic story of self-effacement on the part
of the young daughter. She was an exquisite type of the
womanhood of the aristocratic South, and in her unhappy
love affair bore herself in a manner becoming the traditions,
customs and ideals of her class. That these laid a heavy
restraint upon the aristocracy of the old South is well known
to students of history. In Winnie's instance the requirement had been doubled on account of a sentimental idea
that since she had been born in the White House of the
Confederacy, she should be set apart as a kind of shrine at
which none but those below the Mason and Dixon line
should worship. The Southern people at this particular
period were a highly sensitive people, quick to feel criticism

and as quick to find fault with everything outside of their own concept of life and how it should be lived. Winnie's story of loyalty to the Confederacy in her love affair was just as they wanted it to appear in history, and none dared put any other construction upon the circumstance. Gossip had it that Varina was greatly worried over the turn that fortune had taken in her young daughter's affairs; that she made some "very nice, ladylike efforts" to cultivate several of the eligible young Southerners whom they frequently met in New Orleans and other cities of the South. But the romance stood, nor would work out any other way. Suitors came and went; but Winnie remained true to her Northern lover and found ease for her heartbreak in much fine literary work which the publishers were always eager to print.

One gathers that Varina's love for this daughter was much like the passionate devotion that she gave Jefferson Davis; and in a matter that concerned her so vitally, she would have risked any satire as a "matchmaking mother" to see her happy. Those who were near them most said that mother and daughter were very congenial and found great pleasure in each other's society; nor is it found that Varina, though the dominant spirit, ever sought to restrain or shape the daughter's self-expression. Both had a decided taste for literature and had been of great assistance to Jefferson Davis in much of his writings. With the years, Varina grew more jealous of his fame and reputation, and took a kind of defiant pleasure in placing him above others, one to whom the world would do well to make daily offerings. She had taught her children this from infancy; but Jefferson Davis seems to have withstood it. She records that he lived for his family and denied himself that "they should have

comforts and some of the luxuries." If there were any
new clothes, the family got them. He wore the well-brushed
old ones. Life could not be barren in such an atmosphere.
There is too much beauty and strength in such relationships
for atrophy of any nature to take place. Their reverence
and devotion touched him deeply, but his pride in it did not
come of any selfish egotism, but of a sympathetic comprehension and understanding of their loyalty to him in
adversity.

He was now interested in his private affairs, and had it
been possible would have lost sight of the world. Varina's
interest in public matters, however, continued as strong as
ever. She was still eager and emotional, while he in old
age had grown more serene. The circumstances of their
lives had driven her to take this attitude. As the master
alone of Briarfield she might still have been somewhat
tenacious in any matter concerning him; but now that
circumstance had in a manner crucified him for the convictions and rights of a great body of people, and he had
upheld and suffered for these with the fortitude of the
martyr, she would move heaven and earth to see that justice
should be done him. She was obsessed with the idea of
his superiority, but if it was a weakness she got a warmth
and glister out of it that come to few. This propensity has
already been referred to, but if one finds the person one
writes about thinking the same thoughts day after day, the
fact must be more than once recorded.

With Winnie in Paris, life at Beauvoir for Varina would
have moved along quietly and humdrum enough but for
the constant disputation and explanations going on in the
newspapers and magazines concerning the faults, errors and
general wrong-doing of Jefferson Davis, while President of

the *ci-de-vant* Confederacy. Historians, editors and writers of all classes could not, it seemed, write about anything but the war. Scarcely a week passed that Varina did not have a tempestuous outburst over some false statement or gross misrepresentation in matters relating to her husband. These accumulated daily, and in some instances came from his own people. For all their isolation they were the objects of an intense curiosity from the outside world. It sought them in various guises, both innocently and ulteriorly. People sent them clippings from publications that often demanded an explanation of a lengthy nature. Varina enjoyed the public's attention when it brought her husband praise and homage, but openly resented it when it contained censure. She continued combative upon certain subjects, but could easily return to the ease and good humor for which she had been so noted in the past.

Jefferson Davis, after his several pertinent efforts at vindication, with the passing years had grown more contained, at least in outward appearance. One can but surmise what lay beneath the placid exterior. But at least the wounds were not bleeding. The world was beginning to marvel at his dignity and self-restraint, and what today they laud as poise. Distinguished authors from the North, like Bigelow, visited him to be captivated by the rare personalities of both husband and wife. Scarcely a month passed that an article did not appear in the papers written by some distinguished writers relative to the Beauvoir household.

As the autumn passed Varina noticed that his step had less ring; his spry, trim figure was less elastic. It alarmed her sometimes when she noted how thin and emaciated his body was becoming. He had improved in weight at times but now he was a mere skeleton. She was writing to friends that she must conserve her strength that she might live to care for him in his old age.   There was a time when left alone with her little children that she shrank from the thought of him dying first; but now that he was old, her mothering sense of protection grew stronger. In the matter of his health she had always made a great to-do.

But Jefferson Davis kept his clarity of thought longer than most men.   Although near the age of eighty-one, he still attended to the business of his Briarfield plantation.   It was now December, sometimes a dreary month even for the latitude of Briarfield where flowers usually bloomed throughout the winter, but the time had come to make the fall collection of rents.   He had a strong affection both for the place and its tenants, since the occupants were in many instances his former slaves.   The old house was always made ready for his return.   Varina usually accompanied him on his visits to the plantation but guests kept her at home on the present occasion.   She had feared for him to go alone to the plantation.   It was a rough trip with few accommodations en route.   She was alarmed a few days later by a message from one of the Briarfield tenants that he was very sick and suffering from the effects of a severe cold. Hastening to him through the chill December weather, she says that she met him on the river returning home.   On finding that he had high fever, they changed their plans and went directly to New Orleans, and were immediately invited to the home of Judge Charles E. Fenner, an intimate and valued friend.

CHAPTER XLVI

IT WAS in the home of Judge Charles E. Fenner that Varina, to her great joy, found that Mr. J. U. Payne, another close friend, lived. Jefferson Davis was in a serious condition, and the first physicians of the city were immediately summoned to his bedside. Varina had him to herself in his sickness and he had preferred it so. His love for his daughters was deep and tender, and he dreaded to shock them with the news of his illness; besides, this was a time for the two who had trod the long, hard road together to be alone with each other. "Let our darlings be happy as long as possible," he told her. She was all he now needed. Every one in the stately old home and in the city as well were at their service; but among the countless news items relative to his illness, one continually finds comment like the following: "His constant attendant has been his wife, who has never left his bedside since his illness. Clad in a simple gray and black wrapper, she is always at her invalid's side. If she leaves him for a moment he asks for her and is fretted and uneasy until she returns."

Among the long and innumerable editorials and reporters' articles, one reads again: "On Wednesday afternoon a reporter of the *Picayune* was fortunate enough to have a few moments' conversation with Mrs. Jefferson Davis. She was worn and wearied with service at the sick bed, but would

not allow any other to take her place, and her step was lag-
ging as she came into the room."

Though no longer young and increased weight had made
her figure look somewhat pudgy and stocky, she was still
striking in appearance. Her soft, dark eyes were still beautiful and magnetic and held a charm for the young reporters
who sought her daily with hopes of an interview. It was
her destiny to always occupy a place where the fierce light of
publicity shone upon her. Once more she was called from
seclusion to take a part in world affairs, and it was a world
affair indeed that now engaged her. When one reads of the
tremendous stir that the sickness, death and funeral of Jefferson Davis created in the old French city that knew so
well how to respond to the emotional, it fills one with a wonder tinged with awe. Nothing perhaps as colorful and heroic
could have taken place anywhere in America save in the old
Southern center of romance and sentiment, so given to the
spirit of pageantry. It was with the passing of Jefferson
Davis that the people were now concerned. The papers had
been full of his sickness, and later of his death, every small
detail of which was minutely described—his heroic cheerful-
ness during his illness which none but he himself seemed to
realize would prove fatal; his getting worse day by day; his
eating nothing; his being allowed to see no one because of his
courtesy that led to an effort to be gracious, and his growing weaker hour by hour, all were minutely reported. Then
came the ominously curious rally which took place before
his death when he had seemed better than he had been at
any time during his illness, though he had taken but little
nourishment for days. This had renewed their hopes, but
the slight animation was soon followed by a sudden and
rapid sinking.

The Fenner home, the papers of the day reported, was the one point of interest in the city that held its whole attention. Physicians, nurses, newspaper reporters and messengers were constantly going and coming, and hundreds daily gathered and waited outside to hear the last reports from the sick bed. The reader of today in perusing the memorials, is reminded of the excitement and commotion in England over the illness of King George.

As the days passed, Jefferson Davis grew weaker, taking but little nourishment, to finally take one. Nor could Varina press medicine upon him. He had at first been anxious to get well, but was now weary of the effort and begged her to excuse him from the last prescription. He lay now with only one physical desire left in the feeble frame—to have her near him. As the end drew near, eager watchers stood about his bed, with hearts wrung with anguish. Something out of the far past gripped their hearts, something belonging to him and themselves alike, a faith which they had shared in common. They saw again the legions of Jefferson Davis in a fierce, impotent struggle for victory. The whole story of it was there in the straight, shriveled frame before them. He had been ill twenty days when it was forced upon them that the end had come. It was far into the night when they noticed that an unearthly pallor had settled upon the calm, thin face and they knew that death had come to him. A few minutes after one o'clock on the morning of December 6th, the news flashed through the city and flew over the wires and cables throughout the world, that Jefferson Davis, ex-President of the Southern Confederacy, was dead in the city of New Orleans.

Newspapers in the city told the story in column after column of vivid phrases, and once again the Southern Confederacy and its only President became themes for the world's discussion.[1] Not a dry eye had watched his passing. Love had had its way with the last earthly hours of Jefferson Davis. And now stiff and stark, his body lay before them upon the low Victorian bed in the beautiful high-walled room, scented with a thousand roses which they had heaped about him in his last illness. There was a certain calm dignity upon the face, they said, that it always wore in life's great climaxes. The papers throughout the city claimed that his passing was like the death scene of a monarch. Stripped of all its significance, it was in reality only the parting of two old people who, notwithstanding adversity, had found happiness in their relationship and hated to be separated. Varina could not be consoled. Breaking down in the first collapse since his illness, she gave vent to her grief in a bitter cry that reached the streets. People living near the Fenner home could hear her weeping and friends wondered how, as his constant nurse, she had physically stood the shock of his illness and death. Nothing, she said later, but the thought that she should bear herself as his wife, kept her from running out into the streets and screaming aloud. She had lost much that was dearer to her than her own life—"My precious boys, my brothers, my parents," she records in her "Memoir"—and now that the main object for which she had lived was removed, life felt like an empty husk. But her physicians were right when they said that she would pass safely through the trying ordeal.

Without the comfort of her two daughters she bore her-

[1] Six volumes have been collected from American and foreign papers concerning Jefferson Davis, and await the study of some impartial historian.

self heroically throughout his illness and the many ceremonials connected with his death, all which were filled with countless situations that required good judgment as well as patience in dealing with them. In all the funeral arrangements she was consulted and deferred to, with a tender, solicitous regard that pleased her. Had it been otherwise, it is certain that she would have felt it deeply and perhaps would have secretly resented it. She was always quick to exact whatever was her due, and the disposition had increased with the years.

As soon as the news of Jefferson Davis' death was announced, the city immediately began a ceremonial that lasted many days. There was an impetuous rush of the civic and military authorities to do honor to the illustrious dead. The hurried appointment of committees, the official announcement of the sad tidings to the governors and other prominent officials of the Southern States, the telegraphic replies announcing their immediate departure for New Orleans, all created a commotion and stir that reached every street and byway of the city. Tributes like the following from New Orleans papers immediately began to appear in the newspapers of the South, and in some publications in the North: "The greatness of Jefferson Davis stands confessed, as we now write, in a people's tears. Tenacious of principle, the slave of conscience, resolute, yet filled with inspiration that comes from unyielding belief, the giant figure of the ex-President of the Confederacy stalked across the nineteenth century as some majestic spirit that strong in the consciousness of its own right doings scorned the plaudits of the world; and lived only that in himself duty might be deified. Such was Jefferson Davis, and such will history declare him to be."

From the Fenner home the body was removed to the city hall where it lay in state amid a mass of flowers, crossed swords and faded and tattered ensigns of the Confederacy, with here and there the flag of the Union waving above all. In all the demonstration there was no word of bitterness spoken; only the spirit of the old South revived to do homage to the representative of all for which it had waged battle in the past. Thousands poured into the city to view for the last time the calm face, the lines of which were resolute even in death. Mingling together during the funeral were great bishops of the church, surpliced clergy, priest and rabbi, and noted citizens from every state in the South. The funeral was both military and civic. The peal of church bells mingled with the hoarse roar of cannon. People on horseback, in carriages and afoot lined the streets so thickly that it was difficult to pass through the dense throngs. After the funeral ceremonies, the body was removed from the city hall for temporary interment in the tomb of the Army of Northern Virginia to remain until its final resting place in the South should be selected. It was followed to the sacred tomb by a monster parade that included military organizations from every state in the Confederacy, their brilliant uniforms and white shakos lining the streets for many miles.

The great funerals of Lincoln and Grant still lacked a certain glamor and spontaneity that marked that of Jefferson Davis. One who for a moment doubts this statement has only to turn to the records of that day to find that language is inadequate to, in any new form and color, picture the six days' scenes that were hourly presented to the public. Little in history presents a more profoundly stirring and, one might say, dazzling spectacle. Few burials of royalty have been attended with a more gorgeous display and spontaneous demonstration by the people. The ceremony was not more brilliant and elaborate when the French brought Napoleon's body back to rest in the soil of France. But it was not with any thought of reviving and opening up old issues now dead that inspired it; memories of what had been were stirred. That the South could be itself again was an evidence of its returning vitality.

In viewing the panoply of that distant day, one wonders if the time has not arrived when representatives of the two great armies should in the spirit of Hanover and Stuart, stack their colors together in some great museum of the country. There were tendencies in that direction even at that day among the strong editorial writers of the North; but not yet among American historians are there any Macaulays and Carlyles. Though the country was a reunited one these continued, and do so today, to write *we* and *they* in narratives of the civil strife. With such a spirit animating certain of the country's authors and speakers, it was no wonder that the Grand Army of the Republic beheld, with anxiety and resentment, this dazzling spectacle of the Southern Confederacy once more on parade. And it did seem to the casual eye that there was some cause for anxiety, for, though the spirit flared up of its own initiative in the city, it instantly was in full blaze throughout the South. Its ideals and honor had all to do with Jefferson Davis.

Beneath her tears, Varina's heart throbbed with pride. One gathers the impression from her "Memoir" that her joy at the reverence paid Jefferson Davis in his illness and death was something akin to ecstasy. And in the gorgeous pageantry and outflow of affection, she had her place. Though facing difficulties she rarely became confused, and whenever she did, it proved more of an asset than a disadvantage, drawing the people to her in deeper sympathy. She had a frank sincerity even in her mistakes that appealed to people. Her loss was the greatest she had ever sustained; but as painful as the realization of it was, she found herself in a glow of gratitude that he was being given the burial befitting the rulers of great nations.

But even this early she was beset with difficulties. Each state had already begun asking that his body should rest in its soil. So insistent were some of these that she decided to postpone the whole matter. In this as in other instances she exhibited a disposition not unlike Queen Elizabeth's, to temporize with a difficult situation. She was nervous and ill from all the strain and excitement of the occasion—she was grateful but could not now decide the matter—these and other excuses she made with skill and tact. Still she read eagerly the announcement that Virginia had united in asking that Richmond should receive and care for the body of Jefferson Davis. Varina instinctively knew the right thing to do in the matter—she knew that the capital of the Southern Confederacy was the place where the body of Jefferson Davis should rest; that like Hampden he belonged to history. Still she let the matter rest.

CHAPTER XLVII

THE "MEMOIR"

VARINA remained with friends in New Orleans a few days after the death of her husband. The great funeral had passed and the city was quiet once more. Margaret had gone to Beauvoir with her children where Varina would join her as soon as she felt able to make the change.[1] People around her continued to talk of Jefferson Davis' peaceful life after the war. Possibly Varina had a different conception of what was meant by a peaceful old age; may have felt that a load heavier than flesh had been cast aside by the limp form that they had placed in the Tomb of the Army of Northern Virginia; that beneath the calm, smooth exterior the long pent-up bitterness that came of misrepresentation had found relief in death. What had it cost him all these years to maintain the calm, contained outlook that marked his latter days? What anguish and weariness of spirit had he got rid of with the flesh? She knew, ah she knew! But she would let the world's interpretation stand, and so well had he performed his part none gainsaid it.

Although his death hurt her at times she says, until it seemed her very flesh suffered, there was no moment that she was not aware of a burning desire to see the world acknowledge his greatness and worth. Like Empress Eugenia she had brooded; but unlike Eugenia, she had never for a moment lost faith. There had been between Jefferson Davis and herself conflict of opinion, fierce enough, perhaps,

[1] "Memoir," vol. II.

at times; but she believed that he possessed in full measure all the essential requirements of greatness.

One thing that aided her in recovering her keen interest in life for which she became so noted in after years, was that the instant the breath left the body of Jefferson Davis, and noticeably while the great ceremonies were going forward, the Southern people began to see in her the lonely and picturesque representative of its Lost Cause. They immediately began lavishing upon her the regard and solicitude that it had bestowed upon the dead President of the Confederacy. One has only to read the tributes and eulogies of that time to know this.[1]

But along with their consideration went the weight of their exactions, and these at times would have been heavy had Varina been pliant. This fervid outburst of interest to an extent cooled; but it continued as lively as ever on the part of some and was a source of great pride and happiness to her. But the widespread public demonstration in behalf of herself and family remained at white heat long enough to influence her life, and invest it with the definite purpose to give to the world what she knew of those four years of her husband's life as President of the Southern Confederacy. This new homage paid her may have increased her self-importance. The waning of it in some quarters, however, was met with a smile half humorous, half sarcastic, but with no loss of purpose and the inward reverence of self-respect.

Irrespective of praise or criticism, the thought took a permanent hold that she must stand as the defender and representative of the President of the once renowned Confederacy. The name of Mrs. Jefferson Davis piqued an in-

[1] Memorial volume compiled by J. William Jones.

terest that few feminine names in America aroused, and Varina knew it. With life, it seemed, at a standstill, one finds her, even before she went back to Beauvoir, sitting with bandaged brow to ease the pain in her head, cutting out and filing with meticulous care every editorial and reporter's article that in any way referred to her husband at the time of his death.[1] Among all the tributes and estimates, and there were thousands, for the moment, she seemed to be more elated over those in the English papers than any other. Commendatory editorials in the London papers, all of which "had leaders on Jefferson Davis," fixed her eyes on the paper in a kind of transport. She could never forget, even though she had become reconciled to failure, that Gladstone had regarded Jefferson Davis in his triumphant organization of the Confederacy much in the light of another Washington, and that many in England, even Victoria herself, had looked on his struggle with a sympathy more than once confessed.

But it would not be just to Varina to stop here. Sensations almost of love for his enemies found place in her heart, warming its cold places, as she read the tributes to her husband from a number of Northern papers. Her hands fluttered and trembled as she read the following from the New York *Sun:*

"From him came no accent of self-exculpation or self-reproach. Failure had brought sorrow, but no compunction. Amid irreparable disaster Jefferson Davis was sustained by a serene consciousness that he had done a man's work according to his lights, and that while unable to command success he had striven to deserve it. Even among those who looked upon him with least sympathy it was felt that this

[1] Letters and newspapers filed among the Davis collections.

man bore defeat and humiliation in the high Roman fashion, and that of him in his loyalty to a lost cause it might be said, as of another majestic soul at Utica, that

" 'Victrix causa deis placuit, sed victa Catoni.' "

Again, from the New York *Times,* she eagerly read:

"The funeral of Jefferson Davis and the observances that attended it throughout the South were very noteworthy for the spirit manifested in them. . . . The South loves his memory as it should love it and as the people of every patriotic country should and ever will respect it. Were the people of the South to forget him, or fail to honor the man who endured so patiently for their sake, they in turn would deserve none of respect or place in the minds of men who have manhood.

"Jefferson Davis will live longer in history and better than will any who have ever spoken against him."

Far into the night, when they thought her sleeping, she searched the great Northern dailies for every shred of comment.[1] Then after pride had been gratified, and for the moment she had felt that the world at last had done him justice—they had kept from her the bitter sayings of some Northern papers—she clasped in her hands the tributes that had been paid him by his own people. It was hours before she ceased weeping. From that day she began hoarding up all records that in any way related to him or the Confederacy. As the days passed her purpose began taking a more definite shape. She would write the story of it all in a memoir of its leader's life. How well she did it is seen in the two colossal volumes that she gave to the world, volumes unusually accurate and well written, considering the vastness of the subject and the very short time she spent on them.

[1] Conversations and old letters.

One who reads her "Memoir" can but be conscious of its lack of vindictiveness or any sort of malice. The deep-sighted student of character, Gamaliel Bradford, has noted its entire absence of malignancy as remarkable in view of the fact that she had great cause to take revenge upon her enemies.

In connection with the death of Jefferson Davis the New York *Times* gave out that in view of this total absence of any hostility on the part of the Southern people there was no fear that any vindictive political action would hence-forth be taken against the South. This was a rather frank admission of all that had been put upon the South. How-ever, it is to the great editors of the day that we are most indebted for the return of good will between the sections; certainly not to the historians.

From the great funeral of her husband in New Orleans, Varina came home to Beauvoir, overcome for a time with the sense of her loss, but burning with the desire to keep his memory alive in the hearts of others. The Empress Eugenia in her downfall lived a life of repression, of sup-pression, but Varina was voluble. Like Victoria, she would talk; even more, she would write.

It was, nevertheless, a sad-faced old woman others saw at the Beauvoir house during the first days of her bereave-ment. She had aged in appearance, and people said, his-torians also, that life was for all purposes over for her. But they mistook the woman. She seized upon her new task; her fingers fumbled among old records and papers in nervous anxiety to begin. It suited her eager, energetic nature; one that always had been somewhat given to contro-versy. While Jefferson Davis lived, she was contented for him to defend the cause for which both in the eyes of the

world had suffered failure and humiliation. None she believed could do it as well. But now that he was dead she
seemed to feel that some responsibility in the matter had
been transferred to her. She loved intensely her two daughters, Margaret and Winnie, and in her sorrow over the loss
of her sons had centered much of her thought on them. But
even with this to fill her life, she must go on caring for her
husband's fame. Too little was known of the man's life during the years he had headed the great Southern revolution,
the man who many were still saying had instigated it. The
world must have her added proof of his association with it.

Varina began to live for her task, to saturate herself
with her "Memoir." She changed her name to V. Jefferson Davis, and began to write many letters in which she
both sought and gave information, and in all of which her
husband and the Confederacy were the central theme.

Her daughter Margaret, who had remained with her for
some time, had returned with her children to Colorado.
Varina was fond of her grandchildren and with Margaret
took much pride in having the eldest son's name changed by
legislative act from Jefferson Davis Hayes to Jefferson
Hayes Davis. They made quite a ceremony of it, and
Varina had lost none of her zest for public display. In
time, her daughter Winnie joined her at Beauvoir. With
her coming Varina brightened and at times entered with
much interest in the life around her. More than with any
of the children there had been an intimacy between them.
As a child, Winnie had been closely associated with all
her bitter past—her "Glory of France"—her "Little Pie,"
who had rarely left her arms throughout the terrible years
when she demanded of a harsh and unbelieving world the
release of her husband from Fortress Monroe.

Her pride in her children grew even more noticeable after Jefferson Davis' death. Margaret was very handsome, and it is said that Varina was intensely proud of the appearance that she and her children made in public. Some said, for Varina still had her critics, that she was a selfish, haughty, vain old woman, who sought only the aggrandizement and glorification of herself and family, but her daughter Winnie knew better. Both were now pinching and saving and putting up a brave face to the world though life for them was hard and difficult, and there were many to misinterpret their motives.

In the midst of their sorrow and plans for the future came constant calls, somewhat authoritative, for Varina to remove the body of her husband to the soil of Mississippi. She had not believed it her right to decide the matter and at first gave no response to the insistent demand. Though emotional and impulsive in her sympathies, she rarely lost her head in grave matters of judgment. Again she began to temporize, to delay before she would act; she had to hear from the other states of the South, to all of which she believed Jefferson Davis belonged. Nothing pleased her more than to think that each State regarded him in that light. But he had upheld and contended for a constitutional principle of government in a manner that had caused the whole world to hold its breath, and fitted into a larger scheme.

Life at the secluded seaside home became one of passionate devotion to one object—that of writing the great "Memoir." When Jefferson Davis lived she enjoyed working with him in the vineyards and gardens of Beauvoir where it was said they often worked with their own hands.

A zest for planting seeds and setting out trees had never left them and it did seem that here close to nature they found at least a partial antidote for human pain. But the gardens interested her no longer. The "Memoir" was all that occupied her thought. New York publishers encouraged her and made many enticing offers. She had already begun to write articles and reviews for the *World*. Its editor, Joseph Pulitzer, was very kind. His wife was in some degree related to Jefferson Davis, a circumstance that must have worked greatly in Varina's favor. The "Memoir" was a prodigious undertaking, but she had always been used to heavy tasks, and to this greatest of all she brought the thrifty energy and mental power with which she had been so liberally endowed by nature. Days of arduous toil, endless research and devotion to her task, all went into its preparation. In addition to Winnie's assistance, the company had sent down the scholarly James Redpath who had often been with Jefferson Davis in the preparation of his histories. The Appletons had published her husband's "Rise and Fall of the Confederate Government." The Belford Company, publishers of *Belford's Magazine,* had arranged to take her "Memoir." They were already bringing out the "Short History of the Confederacy," that Jefferson Davis, just before his death, had prepared for schood purposes. This volume grew into voluminous proportions like so many hurriedly prepared histories of the war. The Company wrote to Mr. Redpath at Beauvoir complaining of its size and giving their opinion that it was out of all proportion, was as "big as a dictionary" and "looked like he devil." It should have gone into two volumes" and other worried comment.

Like her husband, Varina knew the history of the four

years of the Confederacy better, perhaps, than most of its participants. But here was no task for memory; every fact had to be verified from records, every word chosen with serious dignity. She had studied his life closely and though she was his wife, she must write the truth. Let men call it eulogy if they chose, she would tell the world in her famous "Memoir" all she knew about him.

Historians have sought to find in her phrase, "out of a preponderance of these virtues he failed," some explanation why he had not succeeded with the Confederacy. The same in a different phrasing has been said of Lincoln by a eulogist who had no thought of impressing the world with any idea of his failure. It does not here refer to any particular failure, but to conditions that the moral soul must sometimes encounter when eschewing a Machiavellian policy. One suspects that Varina was trying to pay her husband a tremendous compliment in some literary form. She has been accused of striving in her "Memoir" to deify Jefferson Davis as so many historians have so ardently striven to do for Abraham Lincoln. That she is every whit as partial to her hero as James Ford Rhodes and Nicolay and Hay are to theirs must be admitted.

Varina was eager, at times somewhat fussy, about her "Memoir"; at least the Belford correspondents leave one to infer as much; but it is evident that while they complained, they stood somewhat in awe of her. They assured her that everything should be just as she wanted it. She fretted at times over what she supposed to be their carelessness. They misplaced certain pages of the manuscript, left words out that meant so much to her; she would write them; Mr. Redpath must caution them. All the correspondence, however, shows that Varina personally prepared her own manuscript. Original copy is found in her hand-writing. She was now imitating her husband's handwriting with some success. She also developed much skill in run-ning down false statements regarding his official acts; not one or two but dozens, to prove that there was not a bare pretense of truth in them.

Varina enjoyed the preparation of her "Memoir." She worked on it all through the day and far into the night. It added greatly to her prestige. Her correspondence in search of information was heavy; people wrote to her on all sorts of subjects and matters concerning her husband, all of which brought her before the public.

As the "Memoir" progressed her assistants, Mr. Redpath and Winnie, especially the latter, saw that she was break-ing down under the strain of constant work. When the two large, unwieldy volumes were finished, she was suffer-ing from her first attack of heart failure. Winnie was shocked one day to find her lying unconscious upon the floor of their study. She soon rallied from the attack, and the entire manuscript was immediately placed in the hands of the publishers. With feverish anxiety she looked for-ward to its publication. Her vanity was still strong, and the thought that she would become distinguished as an author was very gratifying. Winnie, too, was beginning to write poems and short articles for the New Orleans papers and aspiring to a novel. Though the remuneration was small that came from their labors at this time, they kept con-stantly at it. One had to live, and people flocked to the Beauvoir House—friends, acquaintances, sightseers, many of whom shared the five o'clock tea in the library or on the large open veranda overlooking the sea. It was observed, however, that Varina never arranged the tea table with the zest that she had in the past when Jefferson Davis sat there, and people said that they sometimes found her sitting alone on the back porch weeping bitterly. But she did arrange it, numerous writers inform us, and gave a gracious welcome to all who came. And none went who did not seek and finally get a glimpse of Mrs. Jefferson Davis. The Coast had not become the great Mississippi Riviera that it is now, and to see Beauvoir was principally for what they went. To say that she had been invited to a tea at "Beauvoir House" raised the social status of any snob who had ferreted her way into society.

Still Varina liked to have them come; liked to have a crowd about her even if some were not altogether to the manor born, and enjoyed being the object of its attention. But it took means to keep up an establishment and she hardly knew at times how to meet expenses. The Briarfield plantation was not as remunerative as it once had been. The river had eaten away many of its fair acres. Besides, there was a mortgage on the place which called for much of the yearly income as interest on the debt. Occasionally royalties were paid her from her husband's books and sometimes a check for a contribution of her own to some publication came. Although she was becoming sensitive on the point occasional gifts of money from special friends and her church were also received. But on the whole there was no great amount of income coming from anywhere. There had been some talk of a pension but Varina had been too proud to give any intimation of a desire for it. However, as things grew worse with her finances she admitted to a friend that she would have accepted it.

Both mother and daughter had now started upon a literary career and were anxious to be nearer their publishers. It

was at this time, while Varina was engaged with the
galley proofs of her "Memoir," that the editors of the
World offered her a position on the paper. She decided
to accept it, little dreaming that it would create a furor
not only in her own state but in many places in the South.
She still was attached to Beauvoir, but she had never looked
upon it as a permanent home after the death of her husband; had never cared for it as a home as she had during
his life and now regarded it more in the light of sentiment.
People, however, felt that in a sense she belonged to the
South and should have remained in it—something like a
living monument to remind them of the past.

People began to talk and even friends and relatives agreed
that Varina was headstrong and had become indifferent to
the South. The writer herself has heard one woman say,
"No, I don't love her—she went up North to live with the
Yankees." That Varina heard some of the criticism is
certain but in the seclusion of Beauvoir much of it escaped
her. Since coming to Beauvoir, she had rarely been in
Jackson, the capital of the state, though she sometimes
visited Natchez and Vicksburg where she had many personal friends. But now that the manuscript of the "Memoir" was in the hands of the publishers she accepted an
invitation from the people of Jackson to be present at a
reception in her honor. We find among her papers a letter
about this time saying that she would leave for Jackson to
be the guest of Judge and Mrs. Wiley P. Harris. She had
recovered from the strain of her heavy work upon her
"Memoir," and a lady who was present at the reception
afterwards told a niece that she had never seen a hand-
somer woman. It was during the month of February and
someone had put a heap of early golden jonquils in her

arms. Another lady who was present said that Varina was "still doing all the talking."

After her visit to the State Capital, her plan to remove to New York City became more definite. Now was the opportunity to carry it out. The page-proof sheets of her book were returning to her. She would go to New York for the last reading and to be with her printers. Winnie would remain at Beauvoir and join her later. She, too, would get on with her literary work better than at Beauvoir. For both Varina and her daughter, it was a successful venture. In the instance of the former, it added more color to the latter days of a life that had always been splashed with color, a life that had refused to become drab and commonplace. Both mother and daughter welcomed the change and never expressed as much delight in it as they really felt for fear of being misunderstood in the South. In New York they secured apartments at the Marlborough, then one of the fashionable hotels in the city. Varina was determined to present her young daughter in the proper surroundings. As for herself, the fact that she was Mrs. Jefferson Davis was all that was necessary. With this mantle drawn about her she took her place among the conspicuous people of the nation.

It was after Varina had been living in New York for some three years that Virginia made final arrangements to remove the body of Jefferson Davis from New Orleans to Richmond. The demonstrations connected with the reinterment later filled many columns in the daily papers, but the cementation of the country had begun, and there was less critical comment in the North. The younger generation was marrying across the Mason and Dixon line and the strife was confining itself to the writers, politicians and historians.

But it would not be fair to history to drop the curtain this early upon the scene. The woman seated nearby in a carriage under the trees, shrouded in black and convulsed with grief that shook her large, heavy frame, would doubtless have preferred to have been alone with her dead. Still she wanted Jefferson Davis honored and would not have been satisfied with a less demonstration. She was not to be disappointed. The momentous occasion had brought together the Old South again.

Of the removal of his body from New Orleans to Richmond, the *Times Democrat* of May 27th, 1893, said: "Today will begin the ceremonies attendant upon the removal of the body of Jefferson Davis to the Capital of the Confederacy. For three years and a half the body of the great Southerner has rested in Metairie Cemetery in the Tomb of the Army of Northern Virginia. The people of New Orleans would gladly have had it remain here forever, and would have raised over it a monument worthy of the great man who lay buried there; but when Mrs. Davis thought Richmond was the better place of burial, they, of course, yielded. Her decision in the matter was final. Fortunately ceremonies like these have lost all political significance, and the sensible people of the North see nothing to criticize in our showing respect, devotion and admiration for our heroes. But even were it different, and a display of the kind excited Northern animosity and brought down denunciation upon us, it would make no difference. The South would still pay every honor and respect it could to the man who most truly represented the Southern cause, and who was made the chief victim of its failure."

A New York paper of May 26th announced the removal to Richmond: "Arrangements for the removal of the body of Jefferson Davis, ex-President of the Southern Confederacy, from its grave in Metairie Cemetery, New Orleans, and its reinterment in Hollywood Cemetery, Richmond, Virginia, were completed in this city yesterday at the Marlborough Hotel, where J. Taylor Ellyson, mayor of Richmond, held a long conference with Mrs. Jefferson Davis."

The reinterment took place in Richmond on May 31st. The papers were filled with editorials of the following nature: "The United Confederate Veterans and the entire South today paid a tribute of love to Jefferson Davis with imposing ceremonies. From the appearance of the streets one who was unacquainted with what was going on might have supposed that preparations were being made for war. Crowds of soldiery surged along the streets on their way to join their commands. Cannon and caissons drawn by chargers dashed along the roads, and scarred veterans were seen everywhere upon the streets. Hotels were crowded, and those who wanted rooms on their arrival in the city had to engage them in advance by wire. The lobbies of every hotel were overflowing with people. Business was suspended entirely. It was impossible even to buy a cigar. Private residences and mercantile houses were draped in mourning. Many of the private carriages were drawn by horses with funeral trappings. So great was the throng in the city that carriages were at an added premium, and furniture wagons and even carts were pressed into service to bear persons to and from Hollywood Cemetery."

The body lay in state in the rotunda of the Capital throughout the day surrounded by a guard of honor. A vast concourse of people viewed it, and every school child brought a flower, to claim in after years that they were at the burial of Jefferson Davis. At five o'clock in the afternoon the body was borne by six gleaming white horses to Hollywood Cemetery and interred upon a high mound overlooking the James River. It was heaped with roses. And roses, as a charming writer has said, had been much in the life of Jefferson Davis—roses and white horses and "innumerable thorns." The light was gilding river and spire with the mellow glow that precedes the sunset, when a sharp volley of cannon boomed across the hills. The leader of the Lost Cause was again within Virginia's gates. Far out around the Capital of the Southern Confederacy, imperishable as the Eonian hills that encircled it, ran the battle lines that he had planned in defense of the constitutional rights of men.

The event passed into history. The South once more resumed its difficult work of rehabilitation, and nothing subdues the emotions so soon as toil and effort. Southern women, however, had written "Lest we forget" in their recessionals and not even a "New South" would ever be able to efface it. When Varina went back to New York City, comment broke out afresh that she was fast becoming "Northernized." It annoyed her greatly and Winnie sometimes found her in tears. There is some very salty correspondence in existence in which she gives her reasons for living in the North. In the matter of forgetting, however, none perhaps remembered so well as Varina.

CHAPTER XLVIII

ALONE

VARINA had been living in New York City for about seven years when her young daughter Winnie died September 18th, 1898, of pneumonia at Narragansett Pier. It was a heavy blow, one from which it was difficult for her to recover. She had begun unconsciously to lean upon the younger woman and at first she showed signs of frustration. After Winnie's death, though alone and heart-broken and beginning to feel her age, with a masterful will that nothing could break she decided to remain in New York City.[1] She had made a circle of warm friends in the Southern Colony in whose society she found much pleasure. They were the friends of her daughter as well, and it was a great comfort to her to be near them. She had also connected herself in the city with several benevolent societies in which she was deeply interested. She impressed people favorably. On the street people turned to look at her and were often heard to ask, "Who is the distinguished looking old lady?"

She had been spending much of her time in literary work of a varied nature and there was scarcely a public matter of general interest about which the editors did not seek her views. After the death of her daughter, she gradually resumed her writing. In addition to the pleasure she derived from it, the prestige it gave her appealed to her. She was in no financial strain at this time. The Beauvoir property

[1] Research, Miss M. Alston Buckley of New York City.

535

that had belonged to Winnie had been willed to her, and
it had been her purpose for some time to sell the place, provided she could do so with a provision that it should be kept
as a memorial to her husband.   Thinking that she could
accomplish this by disposing of it to the State of Mississippi,
she came to Jackson, the Capital, in the winter of 1902, during the session of the Legislature.   That body took no action
in the matter; in fact many did not, it has been said, know
that it had been suggested, and Varina was too proud and
sensitive to press it.   There is some gossip still to be heard
which runs that she did not like what she took to be
indifference to her proposition.   She had not forgotten the
grandiloquent promise of the people to make an appropriation for her old age.   "Buncombe," she would sometimes
exclaim aside to friends.   She was still capable of a keen,
sarcastic humor from which she derived enjoyment rather
than bitterness.   Varina's charm increased with old age.
Her voice and manner lost the slight stridency that as a
younger woman some detected in them.   Notwithstanding
her failure to sell the Beauvoir property to the state, she
was fêted extensively by the prominent people of the city.
She held a large reception in the Representative Hall of the
State Capital, and later at the Executive Mansion where
she was the guest of Governor and Mrs. A. H. Longino.
She was still fond of a social stir in her honor and was
greatly pleased at the demonstration.

On this last visit to the South, she found that many of her
former friends had died.   It was a new generation, she records in letters, that greeted her.   And Varina herself!   It
was a large, stout, white-haired old woman who filled one
with a reverence not unmixed with awe, that one resident
remembers.   Others recall that while she bore herself with

grace and dignity, there was a deep melancholy in the large, dark eyes, and in attempting to reply to the greeting of the Governor and other state officials, her voice trembled and broke down. But her vitality and mental powers were remarkable. Though now stripped of everything, husband, sons and the beloved daughter Winnie, with only one of her children left to her lonely old age, and having undergone many tragic experiences, she still stood up among men and women, the commanding figure in any crowd about her. There was a great stir wherever she went. At Vicksburg, Natchez and other places, receptions were held in her honor, and little girls named their finest dolls "Mrs. Jefferson Davis." It was a name that thrilled the ear wherever it was spoken and Jefferson Davis himself had not borne it with more grace and dignity. It was on this visit that a story is told of her so characteristic that it would be a loss not to preserve it. While at Beauvoir it seems that some public honor was intended for her and it came to her that several citizens had said that in view of Northern investments it would be best to keep silent about Jefferson Davis. Varina instantly sent them the following caustic message, "If you must keep silent about Jefferson Davis *you will not toast me.*" [1]

Varina's journey South and back brought her through the length of the once teeming land. She had not been unobservant on this last visit. She studied it as never before; the change dismayed her. Her dark, shrewd old eyes peered about with a close inquiring scrutiny. While living on the seacoast, she had rarely been in the interior since the war and saw the country largely only as it was reflected in the people of the principal cities and in the appearance of the

[1] Dr. William Walker, a member of the Sons of Confederate Veterans.

visitors who came to the Beauvoir house. These were generally of the better class. It was the South generally that she was now scrutinizing—the open country with its immense country seats and small hillside farms. Of a land that had reflected a well ordered life, nothing remained as she had remembered it before the war, except as faint ridges of snow survive a heavy rainful. Neglected fields; shaggy plow horses and mules; unsightly cabins; unpainted country houses with sagging colonnades; weather-beaten churches with broken windows; hordes of dirty, idle negroes walking the streets and crowding about the small dusty wooden stations, mingling with swarms of lean, lank, undernourished, poor whites, peering curiously up at the car windows—this was the picture that met her gaze. Here and there grim-faced, white-haired, old men sat on dilapidated front galleries besides frail, quiet old women who had never taken off black. How could she believe her eyes, and this a half century after the war!

And even more, she saw—shrewd, upstart politicians and public officials haranguing the people with demagogic promises, vulgar, pushing women—they were at her own receptions—joining all sorts of organizations and determined to make the "rise" in the new order of things. "The grace of a day that is dead," she kept murmuring, always given to quotations. Would it ever be revived? Never in its original form, she was certain; that was lost forever like the better part of the Parthenon. It was as if a *sèvres* cup, luminous as light, had been broken in pieces and mended together with rough cement that bulged in knotted clots from every seam; or as if a well ordered, remembered grainfield had suddenly grown a crop of surly weeds. It had life; one could see that—life that was once more beginning to spring from the ashes of war and reconstruction, but ugh, what manner of life! From Maryland and war-torn old Virginia down to the gulf tier it had shared the same fate. But well for any land that has a printed page. Here and there, too, the soft voice lingered in old mansions, and would long be heard above the raucous noises of rank democracy and industrialism, foes that were yet to bite deep into the land. But Varina saw only what the Yankees had done to the South. Although she got along famously with them in New York City, and was beginning to like them, there was a sly, foxy look in her dark old eyes when she sometimes quoted the self-condemnatory order of Sherman's "Forage liberally on the land."

Forgetting that she was old, she went back to New York with a new energy and purpose to renew her efforts to aid her people. But even in this she must be circumspect. The old slaveholding aristocracy resented in a high and haughty manner any proposed charitable educational assistance for the South on the part of Northern organizations. Bread became bitter and sodden no sooner than the Yankee offered it. It had to be carefully explained that the movement was principally in the hands of Southerners living in the North and that it was intended for the benefit of out-of-way districts inhabited by the nonslaveholding class. These were forging out of obscurity and had to be made fit and worthy to hold the high places they were now seeking in both social and official circles. With the ten thousand dollars later paid her in cash for Beauvoir by the Sons of Confederate Veterans clutched tightly in her trembling, old hands, she went about spending it mainly for the purpose that lay close to her heart. Her love for the South was so pronounced that by common consent, Northern friends and newspapers were calling it *her* South.

Varina in old age was a proud, self-contained old woman. A sketch of her by Randall Blackshaw in *Putnam's Monthly Magazine* in 1904, just two years before her death, refers more than once to her remarkable mental alertness and conversational charm.[1]

It was of her place in the public eye that Mary C. Francis in the *New Voice,* a New York publication, wrote:

"It is superfluous to say that Mrs. Jefferson Davis represents the spirit of the South as no other woman could. Alone in the world, living amid the garnered memories of a life ripe with surprising experiences and vicissitudes, Mrs. Davis is a notable figure in the history of the country."

There had been much in Varina's life to make her believe that she was worth while. She had had a long life, the experiences of which had been highly-colored and often tragic; but life for her had been full of incentives and purposes. She had had a large share of both good and evil and by some rare psychic insight, or some harmonious mental process, had found a way to convert the evil into good. Though shrewd and practical and thrifty when it became necessary to further some purpose that was dear to her, she possessed rare idealism. This she sometimes gratified to her material hurt. It has been authoritatively stated that she refused an offer of $90,000 for the Beauvoir estate on the Mississippi Coast made by a Northern hotel syndicate. But when the United Sons of Confederate Veterans moved towards the purchase of Beauvoir to establish a home for indigent Confederate Veterans, she was entirely ready to sell for $10,000, provided the house should be a monument

[1] Research, M. Alston Buckley of New York City.

to her husband and maintained in his memory. A long correspondence with the leaders of the organization contains strict requirements to this effect in the sale.

Memorial windows seem to have been something of a craze with her. These she placed in memory of her husband and her daughter Winnie in the church at Biloxi; and not content with erecting such memorials in the South, she placed another to her entire family in the church which she attended in New York. But scarcely any of her undertakings for pure fancifulness and imagination compete with her attempt to embroider the story of the Confederacy upon a silk cloth to be sold for some church purpose. It would be difficult to believe this were it not a matter of record, which has already been noted in this volume.

Varina grew more interested in national affairs as the years went by; still she continued to be wrapped up in the history of the Confederacy. She welcomed any opportunity of discussing it with Northern people whenever and wherever she could find one with an open mind. This devotion to the subject increased and sometimes brought covert little smiles to the faces of her Northern listeners; but so sincere and earnest were her efforts to defend the Southern position that these confessed that she won their admiration. Always fearless, she grew haughtily so at any intended reflection upon the South and its institutions and customs. After she had been bereft of nearly all her family and was alone in the world, there continued two burning purposes throughout; one to impress the world with the nobility of her husband, the other the righteousness, if not practicability, of the cause that he had defended. One who knew her in New York City wrote of her, "Mrs. Davis felt that the fact that she was Jefferson Davis' wife invested her with a certain dignity and that she was in some way helping to maintain the honor of the Confederacy." [1]   This preyed upon her as touches of senility appeared, and she began to have obsessions that she and her husband stood for the Confederacy.   It requires a strong personality and ability, amounting to genius, to uphold an unpopular cause in a community, especially one that had created so much bitterness, and at the same time retain its respect and admiration; yet this old woman, dressed immaculately in dull black silk with the inevitable black crêpe veil shrouding her soft dark eyes, large, waddling a little, but never ungraceful, went her way alone in the most conspicuous city of America with a dignity and charm that compelled every eye.

One of Varina's proud boasts during her life in New York was that she was a staff correspondent of the *World*. With a natural flair for writing she wrote on all sorts of subjects.   Through the courtesy and at the suggestion of Mr. Claude Bowers who knows so well the value of such materials in writing, the author secured a large collection of illustrated photostat copies of Mrs. Davis' contributions to the *World*.   Many of her articles bear directly upon the history of the Confederacy, but all portray her Southern culture and all bear the Victorian impress; for Varina, with all her individualism and ridicule of the merely affected in Southern women, remained a Victorian to the end.   An instinctive appropriateness seemed to have been an art with her that extended even to the matter of dress.   A friend wrote that during these years she dressed simply, but in good taste and always in black.   "When she went out she continued to wear her widow's bonnet and veil and apparently had little tolerance for elderly women who appeared

[1] Research, M. Alston Buckley.

in flashy clothing." [1] Varina's criticism of any weakness of her sex was never without humor and her power of mimicry continued down to old age. She was companionable with both old and young and many stories are told of her humorous descriptions of persons and things.

As restricted and drab as she sometimes thought her life in New York City, it was not without color. Between the city in winter and Narragansett Pier and other resorts in summer, she managed to see much of life. Numerous old letters recount many meetings with celebrities, all of which reveal the admiration and affection with which she was regarded by people both of the South and North. She did not like to dwell on it on account of the misunderstanding that had arisen relative to her motive for removing to the North, but she enjoyed life in New York City. Too constantly had Varina lived in the great world centers— Washington, Richmond, London, Paris and like places to content herself with the narrow routine of small towns. "I am rusting out, and I'd rather wear out than rust out," she is quoted as sometimes saying with much impatience when at Beauvoir. Contrary as it appears, she was intensely fond, for brief periods, of isolated country life, and often recalled the open country with a vivid poetic imagination. Though living, as she claimed, quietly in hotels, and suffering at times from ill health, she was still perhaps, more than any other woman of the city, in the public eye. No Southerner of any social importance ever visited the city who did not seek her out to offer some courtesy. Frequently a proud-faced majestic old woman could be seen driving in Central Park in one of the best equipages the city stables

[1] Mrs. C. Phelan Beale.

afforded, seated beside some distinguished Southerner. Judge Charles B. Howry of Washington City once told the writer that one of the heartiest laughs he had ever had was when he was taking one of these drives with her. While speaking of the greatness of Jefferson Davis and L. Q. C. Lamar, he was surprised and for a few moments greatly disconcerted on hearing her reply quickly with the *naïveté* and frankness of a child, "But neither one had a grain of common sense." Just what she meant by this, he could not quite make out until she added presently, with a shrewd little smile, "Money-making sense like George Washington had."

Though possessing and maintaining an aristocratic bearing, Varina had always been a good mixer and never lost her taste for a crowd. At summer resorts she attracted much favorable attention. She was extremely fortunate in her manner of meeting Northern celebrities. In 1893, she met Mrs. U. S. Grant at West Point, a place of which Varina was very fond on account of its association with the early life of her husband. The two old women, both of whom had suffered much, became warm friends and exchanged many confidences. It is said that Mrs. Davis and Mrs. Grant met on one occasion at General Grant's Tomb and the latter said, "I will soon be laid beside my husband in this solemn place. Please visit it sometimes and think of me." [1] A short time after she passed away. Down to extreme old age, Varina was fond of cards and gossip said that she was at a card party when Mrs. Grant died. On hearing this, she flew into a passion and exclaimed, "Nobody but Shakespeare could picture the slanderer as he is?"

[1] Beale.

Though tenacious of maintaining all the rights that she thought due the South, Varina lost much of her bitterness and aggressiveness relative to the war as the years passed. She grew sociable with any of the North who recognized in her husband a worthy foe. She numbered many friends among the prominent men and women of the Northern cities. General James G. Wilson, a distinguished officer of the Union Army, was one of her most interested visitors. Friends often met him in her drawing-room that she laughingly called her "salon." [1] It is said, however, by those close to her during her last years that she never forgave General Miles for placing her husband in irons while he was in prison at Fortress Monroe.[2]

In these last days she was not as able as she had been to parry the disagreeable. There was one subject about which she always grew angry and hysterical, that of the statement continued to be made by some Northern critic that her husband was in disguise when he was captured. At such times, with her large fat hands pressed tightly over her heart, she would excitedly tell the whole story over. She warmly asserted that she did "throw her shawl around him." "And what wife" she would excitedly ask, "would not have done so, even more, to save him from the fate that awaited him?" Varina rarely failed to ask if that was any more of a disguise than the large cap that Lincoln wore pulled down over his face on his night ride into the Capital City to his inaugural. "And locked up in a box car!" exclaimed a Southern woman who was present. But Varina did not tell the story that way, although something like it is found in the Chesnut Diary. She always claimed that she had had to deal

[1] Beale. [2] *Putnam's Monthly.*

with too many falsehoods to accept anything about another,
that could not be verified.

It was at this time that she wrote for the *World* her
famous letter in explanation of her husband's speech relative to the country's future in which, after fully explaining
his own position, he said to the young men of his
state: "Let me beseech you to lay aside all rancor, all
bitter sectional feeling and take your places in the ranks of
those who will bring about a consumation devoutly to be
wished—a reunited country." Up to her last days, her
correspondence relative to historical subjects shows that she
still possessed an accurate memory; but this, she claimed,
she "never trusted without verification." "The oldest inhabitants you know," she often laughed and said, "are always the biggest liars, and one reciting past glories is prone
to exaggerate." [1]

In old age she continued to be a great reader and friends
coming to her room sometimes found her reading as light
literature as "fairy tales," which she said always amused
her. Varina must have made a good impression upon her
Northern friends during these years since one very ex-
travagantly recorded of her that "Her faculties were clear,
her wit keen, and she

   " 'Wore the marks of years well spent,
   Of Virtue, truth and wise experience.' "

Her energy never flagged in old age. From early
morning until far into the evening, she kept busy writing,
receiving calls, reading or else engaged on some kind of
fancy work. Many days, though not well enough to be out
of bed, propped up in it, she would go through her regular
routine. She had her breakfast at the same hour each day,

[1] Beale.

MRS. JEFFERSON DAVIS AT THE AGE OF EIGHTY.

after which she would read her morning mail, which consisted sometimes of as many as fifteen or twenty letters. These came from all parts of the world and on all imaginable subjects. Historians sought her opinion or decision on debatable points of history relating to the Confederacy; people solicited contributions for charitable purposes; requests came for letters of recommendation or of introduction, to all of which she gave prompt attention. To this was added a large correspondence with friends and relatives.

In her work, it is claimed, she had no secretary.[1] This would seem impossible were it not for the fact that she generally wrote her letters in a voluble easy style that, while it is not always precise, is wonderfully good for a first copy. Her drives through the park were one of her chief diversions. When not invited to drive with friends, she used an old-fashioned carriage that became known throughout the city. Her acceptance of new methods was highly Victorian, but she consented to use the automobile in 1906 during her stay at the Grammatan Inn. A social courtesy in which she took much pleasure was a five o'clock tea served in her drawing-room to callers. A circle of friends and admirers could always be found with her at this hour. Writers, both of the North and South, came to her to read certain pages of their work. Often actors would ask the privilege of performing in her presence merely for the pleasure of entertaining her. It became a fad for musicians and artists to pay her some special attention. Her rooms, it is said, were very attractive, not expensively furnished, but in such taste that one could feel their charm. She had brought very little with her from the

[1] Beale.

South and after Winnie's death gave almost everything she possessed to the various Southern museums.

Varina wrote occasionally for the New York *World* up until a few weeks of her death. She was now spending her income principally for charitable, patriotic and educational purposes. It is said that at this period she was giving away almost her entire income. She herself received many gifts, and her apartments were constantly filled with flowers from friends in the city and elsewhere. Her birthdays were particularly remembered by organizations throughout the South. The Southern Colony which was becoming a part of the social life of the city regarded her with the deepest veneration and affection. People reading the Sunday edition of the *World* of that period, often saw her described as "Our Southern Queen." It was at about this time that Jennie DeLoney Rice made an oil painting of her.[1] The artist, it is said, took the privilege of adding the white bands at her wrists, but Varina stoutly refused to wear anything but black, except on occasions of family weddings.

One of her great pleasures during the winter was the series of morning musicales known as the Bagley Morning Concerts that were held in the old Waldorf Astoria. The conductor always sent her complimentary tickets and reserved, for her use, a special, high-backed chair. After the concerts were over, she invariably held a reception, and Northerners as well as Southerners came forward to greet her.

Much in this manner Varina spent the last eight years of her life after the death of her daughter, Winnie. It was at this time of her life that an accident occurred that morti-

[1] Research.

fied her deeply. She attended church regularly when her health permitted. Like all Southern women of her day, she could not conceive of life apart from the church. On one occasion, when taking the communion at St. Timothy's, on returning from the altar she dropped her stick and fell full length on the floor. Various explanations of the probable cause of the fall in the church have been given. One is that it disconcerted her when she suddenly discovered a large black negro man at her side. Varina had thought nothing of worshiping in the same church with her own slaves before the war and the faithful colored maid she kept at this time always knelt in prayer with her; but this new phase of an old social custom had something sinister in it for the Southerners. The incident was always an unpleasant one. Laughing on one occasion about it, she said, "It is no disgrace to fall down in company, but even an accident smacks of a *faux pas* and is nevertheless a mortification." [1]

During the last summer spent at the Gramatan Inn, old letters and newspaper articles describe her as a distinguished, charming, lovable old lady, to whom every one paid marked attention. Asked how Mrs. Jefferson Davis at this period of her life impressed her, Mrs. Livingston Rowe Schuyler, past president of the Southern organization of United Daughters of the Confederacy, said that when she met her, she felt that she was "in the presence of some one not only distinguished but great."

[1] Beale.

CHAPTER XLIX

LAST DAYS AND DEATH

VARINA had now passed her eightieth year. Her initiative was declining and she was more dependent upon others. Her conversation largely grew reminiscent. During the autumn evenings of 1906, she talked frequently to her friends of her husband and the Confederacy, also of her daughter Winnie, whose portrait in oil hung on the wall of her reception room. It was made of the daughter as the Queen, on one occasion, of the Mardi Gras celebration in New Orleans. Some have claimed that the dress for historical purposes is not in good taste and have suggested portraits of her made in the customary evening dress of the period. Varina's grief at the death of her young daughter must have continued through the eight years she survived her, since one finds in several sketches in the New York *World* of that period the statement that "Mrs. Jefferson Davis' last years were infinitely saddened by the death of her daughter, Winnie." [1]

And now the lonely old woman was herself getting ready to die. Her papers were all sent out to Colorado to her daughter Margaret. These were later presented to the Confederate Memorial Hall in Richmond, though it has been stated that many were destroyed, and at Varina's own request. Gossip said that she and her daughter Margaret were not as congenial as she and Winnie had been; that

[1] The *World*, October 16th, 1906.

550

they argued whenever they met and the least opposition would start Varina off. Those who best understood the situation have said that while Varina was accused of being "arbitrary and dogmatic" with her daughter, she "loved her dearly and was exceedingly proud of her"; that Margaret was devoted to her mother, but had become "Western in her tastes." [1] Varina had never relinquished the Southern ideal. But there were other reasons for their differences of opinion; Margaret, while not as brilliant and gifted, was, both in temperament and appearance, much like her mother—large, handsome, dark-eyed, suave and gracious, and equally individualistic and self-assertive, though hardly as indomitable. A description of Margaret at the time would easily pass for one of Varina at a more youthful period of life.[2]

During the last months of Varina's life, a deep nostalgia at times seized her and she often told her friends that she wanted to go South again—to Montgomery to see the first White House of the Confederacy "where so much began that filled my life." Here would follow a minute description of the gorgeous white silk she wore at one of her first receptions. Her thoughts turned constantly to Richmond. "I want to see my graves," she often repeated with tears in her eyes. The desire grew stronger each day and she was at times very restless. She was more given to tears in her last days, and at any mention of Richmond wept bitterly. She was now getting too feeble to take a long trip or even to leave the hotel to attend functions of any kind. She began to walk with difficulty and had to use a cane.

One of the last public meetings she attended was an en-

[1] Beale.
[2] Publications of the Southern Historical Society.

tertainment of the Woman's Educational Board for educat-
ing the poor whites of the South. The effort exhausted
her very much, but she was voluble and happy over the
honors paid her at the meeting.[1] She was present at the
wedding of a grandniece on the 22d of February, 1906.
For the occasion, she laid aside her black and wore a gorgeous white silk trimmed with rare old lace. The same
dress, it is said, became her burial robe.[2] Margaret had
been with her from November to the latter part of December, 1905. She came again in May of 1906, and remained
until the middle of July, returning to Colorado at Varina's
request, to be with her husband, whose health was failing.

By the 27th of September, 1906, after a summer at the
Gramatan Inn, at the advice of her friends, Varina decided to remove from the old Girard Hotel, where such
celebrities as Admiral Schley had made their home. Varina
had liked the place, but it was, they told her, losing its
reputation for exclusiveness. Her Southern friends placed
great emphasis upon the fact. But she herself had grown
more indifferent in old age to Southern caste and had
many friends among all classes. This was noticeable on
her last trip to the South, when the poor people about
Beauvoir flocked to see her. When she lived there her old
top-buggy, drawn by an "Old Dobbin" of a white horse,
was frequently seen at the gates of the poor people living
near Beauvoir. She was often heard to say that, "One
should not be afraid to be seen with anybody if they can
be of any help to the person." [3]

Her friends, however, induced her to remove to the

---

[1] Research, Miss M. Alston Buckley.
[2] Beale.
[3] Letters.

Majestic Hotel. Though past eighty, she was still particular about her personal appearance and insisted that her faithful maid should carefully dress her for every occasion. "I don't want my friends to think that I am a thousand, even if I am past eighty." [1] Unable to mingle with the public, she still relished the tidbits of news that came her way. The times that always seem out of joint to the elders of any generation, were putting some of Varina's friends' teeth on edge. New York clergymen were already denouncing divorce and other social evils. The general wrongdoing cited in the Sunday sermons all reached Varina, and people said that they were surprised at nothing much today. But Varina held out that there were always new surprises. It had seemed so at least to the now soft and resigned old woman. In her last conversations with her friends she seemed to realize that she could not live much longer. "The world is very beautiful," she said to those about her, "but we must meet death with the same courage and fortitude that we met the various experiences of life." She seemed at times depressed, but at any favorable turn in the conversation she grew bright and cheerful, and at times shook with laughter.

While removing to the Majestic Hotel she contracted a cold and on Sunday, October 7th, was seized with a severe chill and rapidly developed pneumonia. [2] Margaret was informed of her condition and arrived on Tuesday, the 11th, with her entire family. Varina was very ill but conscious when Margaret reached her bedside. Those about her claim that she displayed great strength and fortitude in her last illness, and that there was a serenity on her face

[1] Beale.
[2] The *World*. Research by M. Alston Buckley.

during her last days that made it beautiful. After an illness
of ten days, she died on October 16th, 1906. Once, arousing from unconsciousness, during her illness, she said to
Margaret, "My darling child, I am going to die this time but
I'll try to be brave about it. Don't you wear black. It is
bad for your health, and will depress your husband." [1]
Varina carried the religion that had sustained her through
life to the grave, and in death they heard her whisper, "O
Lord, in thee have I trusted, let me not be confounded."

A brief funeral service was held in her apartment at the
Majestic Hotel on Friday evening of the 19th. It was con-
ducted by the Rector of her church assisted by the New
York Camp of United Confederate Veterans. Only the
relatives and a few intimate friends attended this service.
Among them were Miss Mary Custis Lee, daughter of
General Robert E. Lee, Mrs. Joseph Pulitzer and Mrs.
Phelan Beale. [2]

Arrangements were immediately made by a committee
sent from the state of Virginia to take the body to the station where it was placed on a special train for Richmond. [3]
An escort of mounted police was furnished by the Mayor as
a tribute from the city of New York, and a military band
marched before the hearse playing a dirge and at times a
familiar hymn. These were followed by a company of
United States regular troups, as a guard of honor, making
the funeral march to the train a solemn and impressive sight.
According to official reports it was the first time in the history of the Republic that the obsequies of any woman had
been honored in such manner. Under orders from General

[1] Beale.
[2] The *World*, October 18, 1906.
[3] Research, M. Alston Buckley.

Frederick D. Grant, commander of the Department of the East, a company of artillery from Governors Island accompanied by a guard of honor from the New York Camp of United Confederate Veterans, under command of Major Owen, formed a part of the funeral procession. The casket was draped with a large Confederate flag. Gorgeous floral offerings of lilies and roses covered it and filled the vans and carriages. Handsome designs came from Governor and Mrs. Theodore Roosevelt, the Vanderbilt family and other prominent citizens of New York City. Beautiful designs were also sent by the governors of all Southern States, state divisions of United Daughters of the Confederacy and other organizations throughout the South. The New York papers, especially the *World,* had daily announcements of her illness, and photostat copies of several obituaries have been secured from old files of that paper. The New York *Herald* carried the following graceful notice of her death: "As a noble victor might pay tribute to a worthy adversary, the United States Government yesterday accorded a signal honor to the memory of Mrs. Jefferson Davis, widow of the President of the Confederacy, by sending an escort of Federal troops to her funeral, and side by side they marched with the Veterans of the Lost Cause of her own South."

Among the many other tributes that filled the papers, the following from a Minneapolis paper reveals the spirit of the reunited country: "The years of care, sorrow, disappointment and regret; the anxious nights, and the long weary days which came to the lot of this American wife and mother, were a test of endurance such as few are called upon to withstand. Yet she endured all, and lived to a ripe old age, a triumphant example and honor to her sex. Every true American, North and South, will honor the memory of the brave woman who has gone to her reward.   She was an American by birth and lineage; her great-grandfather, Governor Richard Howell of New Jersey, was the intimate friend of Washington."

Both editors and reporters left their desks to view the unusual funeral procession, and numerous articles of the following sentiment appeared in the leading papers of the city: "The vanguard of the Confederacy marched to the front, flags flying and bands playing the strains of 'the Bonny Blue Flag,' 'Dixie' and 'My Maryland.' It made a brave and martial show and stirred the hearts of men. The rear guard of the 'Lost Cause' marched behind to the solemn dirge of funeral music; it bears to its last resting place the remains of the wife of its President, an American woman, ennobled by suffering, sacred by reason of sorrows triumphantly endured.   The last scene of the sad pageant is more glorious, more inspiring and more beautiful than the first, and the Nation does well to bare its revered head in honor of it."

It was all as Varina in life would have liked.   She had made peace with her adversaries without any loss of self-respect, nor forfeiture of principle, and had won a nation's admiration.   The funeral train banked with flowers arrived in Richmond on Saturday morning, October 20th. Followed by a great concourse of people, the body of the heroic, invincible old woman was borne to St. Paul's Church, where the funeral took place at three o'clock in the afternoon, after which it was reverently laid beside that of Jefferson Davis in Hollywood Cemetery, only a pleasant walk from the White House of the Confederacy.   The day was stormy but nothing longer mattered.

INDEX

A

Abbeville, S. C., 403, 404, 418.
Abolitionists, consternation of over England's recognition of the Confederacy, 120.
fan the war spirit, 212.
Adams, Charles Francis, 225, 279, 303.
Alabama, the, 124, 279.
Alabama, withdraws from the Union, 4.
Alabama-Kearsarge naval battle, 376.
Alexandria, clash at, 116.
Amelia Court House, 392, 393.
Anderson, Major, 47-49, 53, 54; defense and surrender of Fort Sumter, 55-69.
Antietam, 289.
battle of, 278, 324.
Appleton, D. & Co., 526.
Appomattox, 116, 366, 392.
Aquia Creek, skirmish at, 115.
Arkansas joins the Confederacy, 77.
Ashby, Gen. Turner, 115, 272.
Atkinson, Edward, 211.
Atlanta, 370.
Augusta, Ga., 444.

B

Baker's Creek, battle of, 331.
Ball's Bluff, engagement, 224.
Baltimore, 163.
activity of the sympathizers of the South, 106, 107.
mêlée between 6th Mass. Regt. and city crowds, 103.

riot a torch to fire passions of North and South, 109.
R. W. Davis, citizen, mortally wounded, 104.
Bancroft, Frederic, 6.
George, 295.
Banks, Gen. N. P., 272.
Bartow, Colonel, at Montgomery Convention, 8.
death of, 183.
Beale, C. Phelan, 543, 554.
Beauregard, Gen. P. G. T., 41, 53, 55, 78, 88, 108, 111, 136, 137, 162-164, 171, 177, 182, 214, 273, 288, 307, 366, 399, 407.
Beauvoir, 505, 506, 508, 519, 528, 530-531, 535-536, 543.
bought by Sons of Confederate Veterans, 539, 540.
estate bought by Jefferson Davis, 503.
Varina Davis returns to, 523.
Bee, Colonel, 183.
Beecher, Henry Ward, 160.
Belford Company, publishers, 526.
Belford's Magazine, 526.
Benet, Stephen Vincent, 455.
Benjamin, Judah P., 121, 218, 222, 304, 342.
had he been made ambassador to England, 125.
Big Bethel, engagement at, 116, 137.
Big Black River, battle of, 332.
Biloxi, Miss., 503; memorial window in church presented by Mrs. Davis, 541.

Howry, Judge Charles B., 544.
Huger, General, 136.
Humanitarianism characterizes
  both North and South, 286.

I

Indiana troops, 138.
"Irrepressible conflict," origin of
  the phrase, 4.
Irving, Washington, 66.
Island No. 10, 266.

J

Jackson, Andrew, 116, 136, 326, 379.
  killed defending flag at Alexandria, 116.
  Gen. "Stonewall," 169, 177, 219,
    272, 274, 283, 303, 324, 325,
    327.
Jackson, Miss., 331, 530, 536.
James River, 114, 116, 136, 137,
  144, 268, 274, 366.
Jefferson Davis Volunteers, the,
  145.
Jefferson, Joseph, 239.
  Margaret, 386.
  Thomas, 131.
Jetersville, Va., 393.
Johns, Bishop John, 244, 271.
John Brown raid, the, 115.
Johnson, President Andrew, 438,
  451, 473, 479, 484.
  Reverdy, 471; letter to, from
    Varina Davis, 476, 477.
Johnston, Gen. Albert S., 125, 215,
  265, 364, 435.
  Gen. Joseph E., 108, 111, 125,
    150, 158, 164, 171, 177, 182,
    214, 219, 229, 267, 272, 277,
    307, 315, 330-333, 370, 406-
    408, 480.
  controversy over rank with
    Gen. Lee, 215-217.
  piqued by promotion of Gen.
    Lee, 135.

Shenandoah Valley defence,
  136, 137.
  wounded at Fair Oaks, 273.
  Mrs. Joseph E., 146, 148, 151,
    182, 206, 314, 315, 399.
  Col. William P., 399, 431, 432,
    435, 436.
  sent to Fort Delaware, 447.
Jones, J. William, 520.

K

Kearsarge-Alabama naval battle,
  376.
Keitt, of South Carolina, 10, 150.
Kentucky, opposition to Federal
  troops, 108.

L

Lady Harriette Lane, the, 51, 63.
Lamar, L. Q. C., 153, 210, 544.
Lanier Hotel at Macon, captives at,
  439.
Lee, Mary Custin, 554.
  Gen. Robert E., 119, 125, 135,
    144, 151, 167, 198, 214, 215,
    229, 273, 278, 283, 303, 307,
    315, 324, 325, 327, 328, 329,
    339, 340, 353, 358, 359, 360,
    364, 365, 366, 370, 371, 374,
    384, 391, 392.
  arrangement of Confederate
    forces, 136.
  assumes command of Army of
    Northern Virginia, 274.
  death of, 496.
  his opinion of the Southern
    secession, 349.
  letter to R. S. McCulloh, 350.
  long friendship with Jefferson
    Davis, 348.
  offers to resign, 342.
  satirical criticism of, 220.
  Mrs. Robert E., 298, 338.
  Stephen D., 54.
Lee's retreat from Richmond, 392-
  394.